LONDON REVIEW OF B

A 25TH ANNIVERSARY

ANTHOLOGY

London Review of Books

A 25TH ANNIVERSARY

ANTHOLOGY

Edited by Vanessa Coode

PROFILE BOOKS

First published in Great Britain in 2004 by
PROFILE BOOKS LTD
58A Hatton Garden
London ECIN 8LX
www.profilebooks.co.uk

London Review of Books
28 Little Russell Street
London WC1A 2HN

1 3 5 7 9 10 8 6 4 2

Designed by Peter Campbell
Typeset by MacGuru Ltd
info@macguru.org.uk

Printed and bound in Great Britain by
Clays, Bungay, Suffolk

A CIP catalogue record for this book is available
from the British Library.

ISBN 1 86197 613 5

The contributions that reappear here were published in the *London Review* over the eight years that have passed since our last collection.

Contents

INTRODUCTION

Frank Kermode

TWENTY-FIVE YEARS IS, by convention, a generation, and those who were in at the birth of the LRB who still have hair will have noticed silver threads among their gold. It was a strange event. The *Times* and its satellites, most relevantly the TLS, had disappeared months beforehand – might, for all we knew, have ceased to exist – but time went by and nobody perceived its absence as an opportunity to replace it. Some 16 years earlier the *New York Review of Books* had come into existence when the *New York Times* had similarly ceased publication *sine die*. It had been strong enough to survive the return of its huge rival, and by 1979 was indisputably a success. So many of its contributors were British that it was sometimes known as the 'London Review of Books', which might have been read as another reason to do something over here. In the end, and probably just in time, these hints were taken. The notion that a new journal might occupy the gap left by the TLS finally took hold.

There were several suddenly enthusiastic contenders, and many urgent telephone calls from prospective editors demanding to know what 'our' plans were, sometimes proposing mergers on the specious ground that the more new periodicals of this kind hit the stands the smaller was the chance of any of them surviving. As far as I know, none of these overtures was seriously considered. The LRB went on alone, at first not very securely, once the basic financial and editorial arrangements were agreed. The NYRB withdrew its early support, the *Times* went back to work, and for some time the prospects of the new paper looked wintry.

These birth-pangs were the principal topic of a 'thin-skinned' introduction by Karl Miller, the first editor, to the first LRB anthology, published in 1981. Miller lamented the studied neglect of the new journal by newspapers and the BBC, and commended the fidelity of the few who had endured with him the 'rough ride' of those early years – Mary-Kay Wilmers, Susannah Clapp and Peter Campbell. He also declared, as editorial policy, an intention to arrange that articles should be 'tuned to one another on the page' – an important element in the establishing of the distinctive tone or, to borrow Perry Anderson's gratifying expression, the 'mysterious elegance' of the journal's discursive habit.

Anderson's obliging phrase occurs in his substantial introduction to a florilegium which appeared in 1996. By now Miller had left the paper in the hands of

Mary-Kay Wilmers. Its appearance had changed considerably; for example, Peter Campbell, who had been the designer from the outset, had begun his long and continuing series of elegant watercolour covers. In a criticism of the journal's performance in its early years Miller had lamented its 'failure to sustain a political discussion', and clearly there had been an effort to put that right. This later anthology contained articles by Edward Said on Palestine, Christopher Hitchens on Clinton, Linda Colley on the Reagans, Paul Foot on the Gulf War, and R.W. Johnson on the nouveaux riches of South Africa. Perry Anderson, in the piece already mentioned, commented on the journal's 'overt political profile'. Lacking, and probably not wanting, the more direct connections of the NYRB to the centres of political power, the LRB, after a brief show of interest in the SDP, adopted a more radical stance, varying unpredictably according to the sentiments of the contributors but fundamentally consistent in many respects, notably in its detestation of Thatcherism.

Yet Anderson, in 1996, correctly predicted that the LRB would never become an ornament of the New Labour regime then confidently and correctly expected to take over government. The editors have rarely published pieces by politicians. The present prime minister is said to have contributed during his nonage, and there have been articles on that inexhaustible subject, how to get a settlement in Northern Ireland, by the sometime Taoiseach, Garret FitzGerald. But the LRB was never to be a platform for any party. Anderson's praise was muted, but not on what may well be the most important of its qualities, the superior quality of its prose, for which the editors, who choose the contributors and then seriously edit them, may claim the credit.

Change, in the life of such a journal, is inevitable and necessary, but anybody who has read it from the beginning will know there is evidence also of continuity. So it is agreeable that a few of the earliest contributors are still to be found in this new collection, and from 1996 there are naturally more survivors. Edward Said, who in 1993 wrote with such clarity and withering force about the Oslo Accord and the accompanying antics at the White House, is here represented by an equally devastating essay, written almost at the end of his life, on the Road Map. To read these articles is to realise once more how incalculable is the loss of this author, whether one is thinking rather selfishly of the LRB or of all the events, treacheries, cynicisms and betrayals that will happen and remain unilluminated by Said.

Jeremy Harding's grim piece about Kosovo further testifies to an urgent concern with the state of the world. More extraordinary, and of course without precedent in the history of the paper, was the round-up of instant opinion on the atrocities of 11 September. This enterprise may well have been unexpected, and the publication of these hot commentaries caused a considerable stir. They provoked many letters to the editor, expressing approval or indignation, mostly the latter. Some, though not all, were based on hasty and imperfect reading of the offending material; but even the least temperate, even the subscription-cancellers, were sustaining political discussion.

All these manifestations are firmly attached to their historical moment, yet rereading them at this distance, rapidly written and assembled as they were, it seems to me that some of them were remarkably just and prescient. It can hardly be denied that if sustained political discussion was what was required, they provided it.

The LRB could afford to take such leaps into novelty because of its secure radical base, because it understands that to be lively one need not forfeit trust and truthfulness, even on occasion sobriety, because readers are comfortable with its tone, even when it seems, for good reasons, to violate that discursive composure. In fact that tone is a quality not easy to describe except by negatives: never portentous, yet never exactly flippant; a little knowing at times, yet willing to be instructed (which is why it has found a readership afflicted or endowed in just those ways). Probably it owes a debt to Alan Bennett, who not only has a sympathetic eye for the droller accidents of his and other lives but can, on occasion, deploy a startling because unexpected ferocity of expression, much as those comments on 9/11 burst into an issue that was normally and instructively concerned with quite other matters.

Above all, however, the success of a journal that has now come to seem indispensable probably depends less on its political coups than on its having identified a readership that looks forward fortnightly to serious but unobtrusively elegant and often unexpected essays on all manner of subjects. Mary Beard destroys our Bulwer-Lyttonesque notions of what happened at Pompeii, James Davidson clears our mind on the Homeric tradition, Hilary Mantel tells us things we didn't know, or expect to know, about Robespierre, John Lanchester blows the gaff on Bill Gates. Andrew O'Hagan, an *echt* LRB writer, displays all the best qualities of this kind of journalism: while writing about Scottish nationalism he has a go at a senior contributor, Neal Ascherson, along the way. In the same spirit Stefan Collini takes a disparaging glance at Christopher Hitchens, a former contributor well known for his repertory of disparaging glances. No hard feelings, one hopes.

Somehow or other, in listing the virtues of the paper, one also needs to mention such professional reports as Peter Campbell's on painting as well as on the details of the metropolitan scene, John Upton's account of his defence of a violent convicted burglar in a magistrates court, Hal Foster's essay on Frank Gehry, and Wynne Godley's extraordinarily candid account of a perverse psychoanalyst who came close to destroying his life – incidentally an example of an article that continues to have repercussions in the debates and disciplinary arrangements of the psychoanalytical profession. And of course one could go on naming and praising, dutifully performing the prescribed tasks of one who introduces a collection of this kind, but there is no need: the following pages will speak better than I can of the virtues of the indispensable *London Review of Books*. It may be added that it would not be difficult to make many more anthologies of comparable merit without unduly depleting the files. The best thing about this book, in fact, is the assurance it offers that there will be a new issue of the paper, exhibiting that same mysterious grace, that same radical openness to discussion, that same variety of interest, every couple of weeks.

21 April 2004

LIKE A METEORITE

James Davidson on Homer

TWO THOUSAND SEVEN HUNDRED and thirty years ago, somewhere on the west coast of Turkey, not far perhaps from Izmir, you are attending a feast. Although some of your neighbours are still noisily tucking in, the entertainment is due to begin. You have been looking forward to this. Your host claims to have secured the talents of the best singer in the world. Your cousin heard him in Chios three years ago and has been talking of nothing else ever since. The word is that for tonight, and the next few nights, he will be telling the tale of Troy. To fill so many evenings he will have to start right at the beginning, with another banquet, the nuptial feast of Peleus and Thetis. He will give lavish descriptions of all the wedding presents sent by the gods, a flattering or ironic commentary on the current festivities, but at some point in his song, a golden apple will appear on one of the tables, delivered by an uninvited guest. Athena will fight for it with Hera and Aphrodite, and before too long Paris, their adjudicator, will be seducing Helen and Agamemnon will be sacrificing his daughter to secure a favourable wind for Troy. There will follow long accounts of battles and heroic deeds, perhaps something on the untimely death of Thetis' son, Achilles, Odysseus' victory in the dispute over his arms, and the madness and suicide of Telamonian Ajax, the embittered loser. The bard will doubtless finish in the middle of next week, with the Wooden Horse and graphic descriptions of pillage and mayhem when the proud city fills. You are especially looking forward to the bit where Cassandra gets raped by the lesser Ajax at the altar of Athena and the other bit where Pyrrhus, son of Thetis' son, flings little Astyanax, scion of Hector's house, like a gammadion from the top of the city walls.

When the poet begins, however, the action is already in full swing. It seems we are only to be given a short episode. His sole subject, he says, will be the wrath of Achilles, and he starts on about some priest of Apollo you have never heard of and some squalid dispute over rights to a female prisoner of war. At this rate you will be down at the beach tomorrow morning looking for a boat home. You catch the eye of your host; he is looking rather anxious. There must have been some argument over Homer's fees.

Reading Homer for the first time is like watching Athena crack out of Zeus' skull fully armed or like opening the caves at Lascaux and discovering the Sistine Chapel ceiling inside. He arrives on the field of literature like a meteorite out of a cloudless sky, our very own qibla, our inscrutable Black Stone. That the first surviving Western poetry, born within a generation or two of the alphabet, should also be so well-achieved is astonishing. There is nothing tentative about the opening books of the *Iliad* or the *Odyssey*, no indication that these are literature's first faltering steps; and there is no sense as we travel through the length of his narrative that there is anything more for poetry to achieve. When we have stopped marvelling, however, we are left with an aporia. If it is the ordinary function of a classic to obliterate local frames of reference and smooth away points of critical purchase, how much more difficult is it to place Homer, the first classic, who materialises out of nowhere, without juvenilia or antecedents, or any kind of poetic hinterland to help comprehend his project. Later traditions about Homer are quite unreliable. What we definitely know about him amounts to nothing at all. He might belong to the mainland or to Italy, to Cyprus or Syria even, rather than Anatolia. He might have lived two hundred years later than we imagine, or five hundred years before. We don't even know if he is a him, and not a she or a they.

It is true that we have many material artefacts from his approximate time, but the funeral art of the well-named Geometric period, with its matchstick mourners and its matchstick horses and hearses, is the very opposite of forthcoming and might prepare us, if we didn't know better, for a literature similarly abstract and monochrome, some kind of epic Beckett or a haiku, perhaps, rather than anything so vivid and humane. The severity of eighth-century painting, such a contrast to Homer's description of Achilles' lifelike shield, has been enough in itself for some to down-date the epics, securing a more figurative environment for them seventy years later. Indeed, when the classical Greeks discovered Geometric graves and tombs they not only failed to connect them with their greatest poet, but denied they were Greek at all. The more we find out about Homer's period, the more his poetry comes as a surprise.

With so little information coming from elsewhere, our only certain recourse is to the poems themselves, and for well over two thousand years critics and academics have focused minutely on the texts in an attempt to read past them into the origins of epic and to flesh out Homer's world. Plato noticed that the heroes of the *Iliad* did not eat fish, although they were encamped by the Hellespont. Others working at the great library of Alexandria noticed that fish were eaten in the *Odyssey* and concluded that the two epics must have had different authors. This started a long tradition of multiplying Homers. Running a close eye over the fabric for signs of patches, mismatches and seams, scholars discovered numerous episodes and whole books which seemed to be later interpolations. In the 18th and 19th centuries, the age of Ossian and the *Kalevala*, Homer was claimed for folk literature and German scholars managed to separate the poems into discrete, manageable mini-ballads, stitched together only at a later date by mere editors, ancient equivalents of Lönnrot or the Brothers Grimm. The bards glimpsed performing in the *Odyssey* for entertainment at feasts provided a useful model for their own composer. Other scholars, delving deeper into the origins of the epics, thought they could detect earlier, more primitive stories woven clumsily and incompletely into the final version, even supplying their own more coherent and logical versions of the prototype fairy tales.

Much of the impetus for dividing Homer came from the realisation that he was an 'oral poet', a conclusion derived both from his apparently idiosyncratic style and from the lack of any evidence for writing at the presumed date of composition. It was the first-century Jewish writer Josephus, taking a pot-shot at Greek self-esteem, who first suggested Homer had been illiterate, but it was not until the 1920s that the Californian Milman Parry set out to prove Josephus right. He dressed up in traditional Serbian costume and went looking for Homer in the highlands of Yugoslavia. There he found a number of bards still working and was impressed by how much they could produce. The quality was not great, but they used formulas and repetitions which seemed to cast light on Homer's own mode of composition. The crucial point was that the poets did not need to memorise their poems, they could improvise them around a well-practised scheme. What this meant was that there was no longer any need to divide the poems into more manageable parts. Thanks to the formulas, which some of Parry's over-zealous followers calculated to be as much as 90 per cent of the work, each epic could easily have been composed by one man, but really it was, as Vico had suggested, the work of a whole people, who had been rehearsing it for generations, with hundreds of years to get it right. The Black Stone had not come from nowhere. Homer was a mere pinnacle projecting above the surface, part of the long and ancient chain of the oral tradition. If this meant that his reputation as a creative poet was diminished somewhat, he could be revered instead as a hexametrical technician, a masterful choreographer of the material he had inherited.

In Oxford in the 1980s, the technicalities of oral composition still loomed large in Homer classes, and critical studies full of word-counts, Serbians and statistics dominated student bibliographies; but in the lecture-halls there were signs of a reaction. Jasper Griffin and Oliver Taplin in particular drew attention to the imaginative world of the poet, emphasising unity, humanity and narrative complexity. This seemed a much more rewarding approach to those for whom the most remarkable feature of the epics had always been not repetition but variety, a particularly noticeable achievement of the *Iliad*, where so much of the material is the same: fighting, killing and maiming. Meanwhile, the evidence for writing kept getting earlier and earlier, reaching back well before the presumed date of composition. There was now a possibility that the epics were not the improvisations of some jazz poet, but careful written compositions, perhaps never even performed in Homer's lifetime, but stored in a late Geometric garret and discovered after his death, like Webern's late cantatas or Bach's *Art of Fugue*. Curiously, although T.E. Lawrence had found Homer 'bookish' and 'house-bred', this line of thinking was never explored, but the question of orality began to focus more on performance and narrative technique than on the difficulties of composition.

One of the most tantalising aspects of these new approaches has been a revived interest in Homer's relationship to the rest of the epic tradition. It had always seemed quite improbable that he had made the whole thing up from scratch, inventing Achilles, Odysseus and Troy out of his own imagination. From an early date, images appeared of scenes which belonged outside the *Iliad*. One of the earliest is a bizarre storage jar from the island of Mykonos showing the Wooden Horse. One of the most poignant shows Ajax preparing to fall on his sword. Another popular subject shows heroes playing board-games to while away the vast stretches of empty time. Moreover, by the fourth century at the latest, the *Iliad* and the *Odyssey* had been slotted into a great cycle, which told the complete story of the Trojan heroes, from the wedding of Peleus and Thetis to the later adventures of Odysseus: Telegonus, his son by Circe, comes to Ithaca and accidentally kills him with an arrow made from the sting of a sting-ray, Penelope marries Telegonus, Telemachus marries Circe and they all live happily ever after. These poems seem to have been composed later, in response to the success of the Homeric epics, to fill in the gaps that Homer had left, and some of it – the *Telegonia* seems an obvious candidate – is probably itself pure invention, based on no long-standing tradition, an inferior sequel, perhaps, *Odyssey II*. Much of the rest, however, seems to derive from a whole collection of myths about the Trojan heroes that must have provided the background to Homer's own enterprise and present us with the possibility of illuminating the audience's expectations, even throwing light on the poet's originality.

The starting-point, again, needs to be Homer himself and, as it happens, both epics are dotted with occasional references to events of the Trojan War that the *Iliad* does not cover. Some of these are straightforward. The marriage feast that started it all is remembered in the magical talking horses lent in vain to Patroclus, one of the wedding gifts presented to Achilles' father by the gods. The Judgment of Paris is never mentioned, but it seems always to be assumed, with Hera and Athena the most zealous partisans of the Greek side and Aphrodite, revealing a kind of complicity with Helen, trying ineffectually to help the other side. There are several occasions when the death of Achilles or the fall of Troy is foreshadowed, and Telamonian Ajax won't talk to Odysseus when they meet again in Hades, still resentful about the dispute over dead Achilles' arms. Again, it is just possible that these allusions have been placed there by the author as a kind of trompe l'oeil, to create the illusion of a world outside his narrative or to tantalise the audience with the promise of future instalments or regret for past appearances they had missed; but here we begin to sound like creationists arguing that fossils were planted by God.

Other references are more oblique and therefore more controversial. Why does Athena hate the lesser Ajax unless she is thinking of the future rape of Cassandra in front of her image? How much more poignant is the famous scene on the battlements between Hector, Andromache and their son, if we know that it is from here that the child will be thrown when Troy meets its fate? How much more futile does all the fighting seem, if we are mindful that the city will finally succumb only to a ruse? The extent of Homer's subtlety in the *Iliad* will always be debated, but it seems certain that he assumed his audience already knew the tale of Troy and that he plays against this background, using their assumptions to create effects of irony, suspense, pathos and surprise. What he did was not so different, after all, from what the great tragedians did, or what Ovid did, or Apollonius of Rhodes, putting a new spin on ancient tales.

Building on this assumption, we can begin to approach the question of Homer's originality. From what we know of the other epics, they covered much longer periods and many more fantastic events in many fewer lines. The bards who entertain the court in the palace of the Phaeacians and the suitors of Penelope in Odysseus' home also manage to get more action into a shorter space of time. Almost the whole of the immense *Iliad*, by contrast, covers only a few days in the ten-year saga of the Trojan War and it tells of only one episode out of many, the wrath of Achilles. It is a small detail from the big picture, blown up to monumental size. It should have been a short interlude, perhaps, a little entertainment between courses. The surprise that greets modern readers, therefore, when they discover that the *Iliad* does not in fact begin at the beginning and contains no mention of the Judgment of Paris or the fatal Horse, may well have been the reaction of Homer's original audience. Instead of adding on other episodes, Homer brings a magnifying glass to the tale and fills the time by deepening his characters, by realising more fully their imagined world, by broadening the narrative, rather than simply extending it. The other storytellers in the epics are not models for Homer's project, but designed to point up a contrast with his own more detailed, more lifelike work. He thus sets himself off against the balladeers, self-consciously highlighting his own originality.

The *Odyssey* seems to take innovation even further. Odysseus is a prominent figure in the *Iliad* and features in several Trojan tales that lie outside it. One story tells how he tried to avoid serving on the expedition by feigning madness and ploughing a field, until someone places baby Telemachus in his path, arresting his lunatic progress and exposing his folly as a sham. There is little sign, however, of a non-Homeric tradition of his return. Troy is a famous story and its fame resonates throughout the *Odyssey*. But when Homer begins the tale of Odysseus' return he seems to have little idea of where the story is going, as if his audience have never heard it before. The earliest painted scenes, moreover, look like precise illustrations of Homer's text, leaving the impression that he has a monopoly on the subject. Even the fabulous Phaeacians seem to crop up nowhere else. There must, therefore, be a distinct possibility that the story of the *Odyssey* is largely Homer's own. With all their twists and turns and feints and illusions, both the plot and the voyage look like projections of the hero's multivalent Iliadic personality (or inventions of his subtle imagination), his homecoming an extrapolation from his reluctance to leave his wife and son. There were traditions, to be sure, about other voyages. Homer already knows of the Argo, and both Hercules and Perseus were sent to the ends of the earth in search of exotic quarry. The *Odyssey* seems to have used some of this material. The witch Circe, in particular, looks like she is in the wrong saga. She really belongs to Aia (Colchis) rather than the island of Aiaia, being Aeëtes' sister and Medea's maiden aunt. Read against these other myths, the *Odyssey* looks not like another version but an inversion of the fantastic voyage. Odysseus' journey is always being deconstructed. A favourable wind from Aeolus takes him in sight of Ithaca, but then he gets blown back off course. He visits and revisits Aeolus, Circe, Scylla and Charybdis and ends up on Calypso's aimlessly floating isle. His journey keeps unravelling itself teasingly like Penelope's famous loom. His odyssey is not a linear journey to more and more peculiar realms; it is a quest without a quarry that spirals dispiritingly into time. Far from searching for a Golden Fleece or the Head of Medusa or the Golden Apples of the Hesperides, Odysseus turns down the prize offered him of immortality. He just wants to go home.

The voyage itself, moreover, is related not by the poet's voice but out of Odysseus' own mouth as a guest of the Phaeacians, as if Homer was marking his distance from the more fantastic elements of his tale from the *mythodes*, from oral history. It has to be like this, of course, because Odysseus alone survives. No one else knows what he has been up to these past ten years. His cannot be a famous story because he has disappeared from the heroic tradition, out of sight of men and the earshot of bards. He has disappeared from fame. When we see him clinging to the pieces of his broken craft, close to extinction, the fate of the poem itself is in the balance.

He alone carries with him the account of his exiguous history. Without Odysseus, the *Odyssey* is sunk. The contrast with the *Iliad* and the *Argonautica* could not be more profound. The *Odyssey* is presented as a new and terrifying venture in literature, a story that has never been told. If the *Iliad* is the first example of great literature built up out of old stories, the *Odyssey*, perhaps, inaugurates the bizarre tradition of making things up.

The cloud of unknowing that has always made it difficult for Homer's readers to put him in perspective presents particular problems for translators. Here we come up against another facet of the miracle of Homer beyond his excellence and his primacy: his enduring popularity. E.V. Rieu's translation of the *Odyssey* for Penguin Classics has been one of that publisher's most successful products and there seems an insatiable market for new versions, especially in English. According to George Steiner,* in his introduction to *Homer in English*, this particular 'translation act . . . surpasses in frequency that of any other act of transfer into any other Western tongue and literature', including versions of the Bible. But how do you begin to put Homer into another language when you have little way of knowing at any particular point if his language is highfalutin or contemporary, low-key, bathetic or grand? Is Homer's readability an illusion created by two and a half millennia of scholarly exegesis or was he equally limpid when he was first performed? Did his audience greet each other with long-winded epithets like MPs or flatterers at the court of Zaire, or did they consider such addresses a touch of archaic colouring now thankfully obsolete? And what was the significance of composing in hexameters when there was no possibility of a literature in prose?

As Steiner's selection shows, translators have offered very different solutions to these questions. There have been lots of grand Homers, lots of Biblical Homers, but also plenty of plain-speaking Homers. There have been primitive, bloodthirsty Homers in the style of Conan the Barbarian, and also elegant Augustan dandies. There have been in-yer-face performative translations and withdrawn scholarly Homers sheltering behind pages of notes. Above all, there has been a running debate over whether he fits better into poetry or prose. The only Homer who is not well represented in this vast array is the difficult, obscure and artificial Homer, although there is some evidence that this in fact is how he must have been received.

Along with the difficulties of gauging the tone, translators have been harried by vigilante groups of scholarly theorists trying to pass on their own obsessions. Matthew Arnold set the agenda for modern versions when he insisted Homer

---

*George Steiner (ed.), *Homer in English* (Penguin, 1996).

should be pacy, noble and plain. Since then, the Oralists have insisted the text should also somehow reflect the 'orality' of the poems, which often comes down to a more urgent encouragement of the same thing. The last two of Arnold's requirements have often proved the most difficult to resolve, representing the Scylla and Charybdis of the translator's journey, threatened with bathos and pedestrianism on the one side and bombast on the other. Stanley Lombardo's new Iliad* has a photograph of a D-Day landing on the cover and makes a reckless dash for the idiomatic. It is generally a fine and enjoyable version, but its colloquialism sometimes lapses jarringly, occasionally amusingly, into cliché. Robert Fagles's new version of the Odyssey,† on the other hand, is a classic modern Homer: elegant, natural and smooth. His solutions to the difficulties of rendition are always so neat that it is easy to forget there has been any effort made. Such easiness is a great achievement and he manages to avoid any hint of bathos, but he is so keen on plain-speaking that the whole effect is sometimes rather bald, even colourless, especially in comparison with Robert Fitzgerald's 1961 version, which is itself hardly extravagant in its language. Both Lombardo and Fagles have produced translations to be read aloud, and Fagles's Odyssey is issued with 18 hours of cassettes, performed at a brisk pace by Ian McKellen, but I can't help thinking that the academic insistence on the 'orality' of the text – a rather oxymoronic idea, which should give Derrida something to chew over – has become a distraction. Most ancient literature was oral inasmuch as it was performed, but it could also be difficult, like Aeschylus, and complex, like Gorgias. Greek, in particular, is also very rich in dialects (Homer uses both Ionic and Aeolic), registers and tones. English is one of the very few languages that can match it for vocabulary and range. It seems a shame if English translators, working under the dogma of accessibility, do not make some effort to use that opportunity. Passed through the sausage-machine of modern English, writers as different as Homer, Euripides and Theocritus emerge sounding much the same. Everything begins to seem as if it had been rewritten by Lucian: simple, transparent and plain.

Perhaps it is inevitable that translators from Greek, so anxious to open doors, will always over-translate, modernising old-fashioned vocabulary, shortening sentences, homogenising dialects and unravelling difficult knots, but Homer's English readers need not despair. Homer's achievement may or may not have depended on six hundred years of oral tradition, but we have four centuries of English versions with which to pin him down. To get the gist of it you could read Fagles or Rieu. For

---

*Stanley Lombardo (trans.), Homer's 'Iliad' (Hackett, 1996).
†Robert Fagles (trans.), Homer's 'Odyssey' (Viking, 1996).

some idea of how he must have sounded to his audiences or to the classical Greeks, we have our own archaic Chapman. To get a taste of his originality, try James Joyce, or Derek Walcott. For drama and pathos try Christopher Logue, and for sheer poetic artistry try Fitzgerald or Alexander Pope. And if, after this, you feel in need of some orality, have some friends round for dinner, put on some music and read it aloud.

31 July 1997

SNOOP DOGGY DOGG
FOR LAUREATE

Ian Hamilton

WHEN CECIL DAY LEWIS was appointed Poet Laureate in 1968, he got – within days of the good news – a letter from his bank manager. 'The whole Midland,' it said, 'rejoices with you.' And this, it might be felt, comes close to summing up what's wrong with being Poet Laureate. Since banks began, poets have received many letters from bank managers but few have been at all like Cecil's. To send the Midland into raptures of this kind, a fellow would surely need to have done something rather seriously unpoetic.

Day Lewis, though, was thrilled to have so thrilled his money-minders. And he was thrilled, too, by the antiquated perks that went with his new job: the 'butt of sack' and all the rest of it. At the same time, he knew that his butt would have to be worked for. His first poem as Laureate, called 'Now and Then', appeared on the front page of the *Daily Mail* and was promoted as part of that paper's 'I'm Backing Britain' campaign. Of 'Now and Then', Bernard Levin rather tastelessly observed, years later, that it 'made many regret their impulsive rejoicing at the death of his predecessor'. Even Day Lewis's admiring editor and close friend, Ian Parsons, when he was putting together a *Collected Poems*, shrank from reprinting the poet's Laureate offerings. He called these works 'banal when they were not embarrassingly disingenuous'.

And this, over the centuries, has been the way of things with Laureates. So far, there have been about twenty of them, and – although there is still pleasure to be had from quiz questions like 'what do Henry Pye and Laurence Eusden have in common?' – the whole thing is now generally agreed to be a joke. Or is it? Sometimes I am not so sure. The other day, for instance, I was contacted by a highly serious poet friend who was, he said, thinking of starting up some kind of campaign to head off PL challenges from light versifiers and streetwise demi-minstrels. He seemed to think that the choice of Laureate would send out important signals to do with the prestige of the contemporary poet, and of poetry in general. Maybe he was joking. I think not, though. When I replied that, for all I cared, they could give the thing to Snoop Doggy Dogg, or even to Snoop's dogg, should he possess one, my friend was not wholly amused.

It seems significant, too, that none of the poets touted in the papers as possibles to fill the current vacancy has said that he or she won't take the post, should it be offered. Evidently the Laureateship is still thought of by some poets as a plum. One recalls, with condescension, the anguish of Tennyson in 1843 when he was passed over for the job. He needed the money, it was said – the publicity, the extra sales. But he also had a dark hunger for the prize itself. Nowadays the money benefits are unlikely to add up to much, and the prestige is pretty much in tatters. The dark hunger, though, seems to persist. But why, oh why? Maybe poets want to be Laureates because they secretly fear that they've already made the most of whatever gifts they started out with. Since nobody expects a PL to be any good, why not accept the job and let it take the blame for your next book?

Cecil Day Lewis's predecessor as Laureate was John Masefield, who held the post for nearly forty years without seeming to know, or greatly care, what was required of him. Masefield was in place for so long that, by the time he died, most people had forgotten that we had a Poet Laureate. Every so often, he used to remind us by sending off some resolutely dreadful verses to the *Times*. He was always careful, though, to enclose a stamped, addressed envelope, just in case. Some of his submissions, the story went, were sent back by return of post, with a rejection slip.

Day Lewis, it was predicted at the time of his appointment, would be much more on the ball. After all, had he not been limbering up for this honour for some years, with his clubs and his committees and his suave, actorly 'recitals' of gems from our poetic heritage? At my school in the 1950s, a regular item on the assembly song-sheet was a turgidly patriotic hymn with words, I was confused to note, by C. Day Lewis: a poet who, according to my English teacher, was actually the rear end of MacSpaunday, and the only one of 'that lot' who'd been an authentically red Red. By 1968, Day Lewis was a cleaned-up act, entirely tame, and more than qualified to seize those laurels. Indeed, it would have been a callous decision, I recall thinking at the time, not to have chosen him.

The appointment of Ted Hughes in 1984 was rather different. For one thing, he took over from cuddly John Betjeman, a poet who – with all his charm – was not too strong on Laureate-style gravitas. With Betjeman, we felt and hoped, there was always the possibility of mischief. Also, Hughes was known to be the sovereign's second choice, a useful consideration to be kept in mind should things go wrong. Philip Larkin had already given the honour a (possibly reluctant) thumbs-down: he was very ill. If there were question marks about Ted Hughes, they would have been to do with his reputation as a rebarbative cave-dwelling type, and as a connoisseur of bestial unpleasantness. All in all, it was hard to imagine him getting worked up about a fleet of corgis. And there was perhaps discussion also of his long-ago marriage to an unstable American (although by 1984, Hughes had weathered the worst attacks on him by feminist Plathologists). On the plus side: Hughes did write books for children and one of his best-known poems was about a fox, so – who could tell? – he might turn out to be another Masefield.

For my part, I was mildly surprised at first that Hughes had accepted the position. Although I knew him to be somewhat more literary-worldly than he liked to seem, the drift of his self-presentation had always been to stand craggily aloof from metropolitan book-circuses. Also his most recent *Moortown* poems had impressively traversed the dead-end he seemed to have run into with the blood-drenched *Crow*. He appeared to have found a new line for his work, part narrative, part diary-entry, and to have discovered, too, a more coherent speaking voice, a human voice. (Looking back, we can easily surmise that several of the poems in *Birthday Letters* were composed around this time: Hughes had just finished editing Plath's journals, in which she gave her version of certain key episodes in their courtship and marriage.)

It soon became clear, though, why Hughes wanted to be Poet Laureate. As he perceived them, the Royals were not the Royals as rendered by *Spitting Image* and the *Sun*; not for him your Fergies and your Di's. In his sub-Shakespearean scheme of things, ancient notions of kingship were still coursing in the nation's veins, or should be. Disregarding tabloid debunkery, he would make it his business to assimilate a conceptualised monarch into his personal blueprint for tribal renovation. In short, he would poeticise the Windsors.

It was easy enough to smile at such an enterprise but it was also hard not to be touched by Hughes's perception of what a true Laureate might be: a kind of patriotic bard magician whose task was to reconnect the English to their primal selves. Why shouldn't the Royals – even unto the Fergies and the Di's – be similarly reconnected? By the sheer force of his impassioned deference, a genuine Laureate might restore the land's rulers to – well, to the land. And by the land Hughes did not mean Sandringham and Balmoral, although we understand that he liked visiting such places. He had in mind certain remote areas of South Devon and North Yorkshire, where the land is always freezing and rainswept and where the sun, should it appear, is 'like a torn-out eye'.

In Hughes's worldview, so far as we can piece it together from his prose, Nature is always credited with deep health-giving powers: it's good for the instincts, good for the imagination and good for our animal self-knowledge, should we want that too. In his most effective verses, though, Nature is mostly seen as hostile. It may be good for us but it wants nothing from us in return, beyond our trembling capitulation. Caught in Nature's war-zones, even the most elemental humans – even the poet Hughes himself – come across as wimpishly inept, riddled with feebleness and hesitation. And this, the poet seems to think, is how it should be, how it really is. One of the instincts we have lost over the centuries is our fear of the barbaric, a fear that used to shade into the reverential. Regenerate the fear and you will regenerate the reverence. Ted Hughes poems, it often seemed, were intended to re-frighten us.

And so they did, and do, from time to time – especially the early ones, in which Hughes flaunted his descriptive powers as if to betoken some rare truce that he had managed to negotiate with the forces of unreason. His descriptions were actually inscriptions. No pig you'd ever seen looked quite as scary as a Ted Hughes pig. And this applied also to his sheep and cows. Rereading *Moortown* – his best book, I would say, since *Lupercal* – I was drawn to wonder how (in farmer's terms) Hughes rated as a farmer. Silly question, I suppose, but hard to shake off once you've thought of it. And what did he get up to when he wasn't contending with the elements? There has been talk about black magic, or some such. Do we believe it? Do we care? Or, to get back to those Royals, did Hughes really go on fishing trips with the Queen Mother? And if so, what did they catch: a tiddler or a pike?

There is a great deal about Hughes that we don't know. His obituaries, though gushingly fulsome on the verse and on his shamanish 'persona', were actually quite thin on factual background. On the whole, they repeated what little Hughes had himself vouchsafed and then added a few scrawny anecdotes. He was of course a fierce opponent of biography. I remember a review he wrote of a biography of Dylan Thomas: who else, I wondered, could write about Thomas and scarcely mention drink and money? You had to admire it in a way but it was also pretty annoying: who do these incantators think they are?

But then Hughes did have his special reasons for despising the dogs and hyenas, as he called them, of life-writing. Curiosity about Hughes has been inseparable from curiosity about his marriage to Sylvia Plath. He knew this and, at times, it must have hurt. Did he find it at all depressing that his most successful book of verse turned out to be the one in which he finally 'spoke out' about his love affair with Plath? There are some fine things in *Birthday Letters*, but few can deny that the chief impact of the book was biographical – and not biographical re Hughes.

Altogether, though, one rather shudders at the prospect of a Ted Hughes Life. When Philip Larkin died, there was a period of seeming desolation but it was soon followed by an enthusiastic surge of reappraisal when it turned out, from the Life and the Letters, that this most delicately sorrowing of poets had in his drab daily life been a near-champion of coarseness. Can Hughes avoid some similar comeuppance? It seems unlikely. Indeed, with him perhaps the demystification will be extra-gleeful. Larkin, after all, never pretended to be touched with any purifying flame. Nor, to be fair, did Hughes pretend to be a 'god of granite who could shatter stones with plain words', which is what the *Independent* called him a couple of days after he died.

7 January 1999

THAT WOODEN LEG

Michael Wood on Buñuel

'STUDIO VINGT-HUIT – high up a winding street of Montmartre, in the full blasphemy of a freezing Sunday; taxis arriving, friends greeting each other, an excitable afternoon audience'. The description is Cyril Connolly's, the occasion a showing of Luis Buñuel's first film, *Un Chien andalou*. The audience seemed baffled at the end, and some of its members were angry, unprepared no doubt for what Connolly called the 'destructive reverence' of the film. 'With the impression of having witnessed some infinitely ancient horror, Saturn swallowing his sons, we made our way out into the cold of February 1929, that unique and dazzling cold.'

Connolly's sense of the horror of the work, and of its romance ('*Un Chien andalou* brought out the grandeur of the conflict inherent in romantic love, the truth that the heart is made to be broken, and after it has mended, to be broken again'), led him to ignore its farcical aspects, its echoes of Buster Keaton and its complementary truth that romantic love is as often as not a matter of violent grabs and dashes, a pantomime of lust wagging its human puppets. But his experience anticipated that of thousands of others. The first film we see by any major director usually makes a mark, but we don't always feel we have seen Saturn swallowing his sons.

The first Buñuel film seen by most people of my generation who were not film-club addicts was probably *Viridiana* (1961). After two Surrealist films made in France (*Un Chien andalou* and *L'Age d'or*, 1930), and an astonishing documentary made in Spain (*Las Hurdes*, 1932), Buñuel's career was interrupted by the Spanish Civil War. He spent some time in the United States, then in 1946 settled in Mexico, where he made 18 films, of which only *Los Olvidados* (1950) got any real notice. *Viridiana* was made in Spain under Franco, and caused a tremendous scandal. After that Buñuel made one more film in Spain (*Tristana*, 1970), two more films in Mexico (*The Exterminating Angel*, 1962, *Simon of the Desert*, 1965), and six films in France (*Diary of a Chambermaid*, 1964, *Belle de Jour*, 1966, *The Milky Way*, 1969, *The Discreet Charm of the Bourgeoisie*, 1972, *The Phantom of Liberty*, 1974, *That Obscure Object of Desire*, 1977).

Viridiana has a number of startling and now famous images – a small crucifix flicks open to become a menacing knife; riotous, feasting beggars compose themselves into a parody of Leonardo's *Last Supper*, a snatch of Handel's 'Hallelujah Chorus' blaring in the soundtrack – and a ferocious implied argument about charity. All charity which is less than infinite leaves the world unchanged, and what charity is not less than infinite? Yet the most memorable feature of *Viridiana*, I think, is not its imagery or its argument but the harsh, reckless intelligence behind it, its manifest intention to disturb us beyond repair. Buñuel used to say in lectures and interviews that his films are designed to show us that we don't live in the best of worlds. They certainly do that, but the formulation is not strong enough. Whatever we think about the world we live in, Buñuel wants to send us home from the cinema feeling rattled and uncomfortable. This feeling, mysteriously, is not incompatible with being highly amused, but then the very idea of amusement seems troubling. '*Viridiana*, at heart, is a humorous film,' Buñuel says in a typescript published in *An Unspeakable Betrayal*,* but immediately adds that the humour is 'corrosive'.

A few months after seeing *Viridiana* for the first time, I was in Spain, and met a charming man, a doctor, who claimed to know Buñuel intimately, and to have helped him recruit the beggars for that film. I can't remember whether I believed him or not. Probably I did. Buñuel for me was as distant as Cervantes or Saint Teresa, and I didn't even know where he lived. Then I forgot about the encounter, except for thinking kindly of the doctor and Madrid whenever I saw *Viridiana* again, or when my mind turned to Spain. And with time I certainly ceased to believe in the story. The doctor was entitled to his fantasy, after all; Buñuel was the kind of figure who attracted legends and anecdotes. Then some 13 years later I saw *The Phantom of Liberty*.

Right at the beginning of the film a group of Spanish prisoners is led out to be shot by Napoleon's soldiers. They include Buñuel himself, as a monk; Serge Silberman, Buñuel's producer; and the writer José Bergamín, an old friend of Buñuel's. They also include the uncannily familiar figure of my old acquaintance the doctor, Buñuel's pal José-Luis Barros. It took me a while to place the recognised face, and of course I didn't fill in all the details even then. A few years later I met Buñuel in Mexico. He was delighted when I told him the story – he loved coincidences – and thought it would have been even better if Barros and I had turned out to be long-lost twins, perhaps identified by a birthmark. I hang onto that moment in the cinema because when I saw the film and found the face I realised I had caught a piece of lost time. Not only Madrid and Dr Barros and an earlier self, but *Viridiana* as it felt when I first saw it: blasphemous, brilliant, ragged, indifferent to the preoccupations of unity and coherence which most aesthetics demand – Saturn swallowing a daughter.

---

*Luis Buñuel (trans. Garrett White), *An Unspeakable Betrayal: Selected Writings* (California University Press, 2000).

If I had been less devoted to the notion of the death of the author I might have got more out of my encounters with Buñuel himself. But I'm not sure. He was so courtly and entertaining, so willing to treat me as a new-found friend rather than a nosy writer, that I had real difficulty in thinking about our conversations as material. Material for what? For the book about his films I was trying to write, or the biography I had no intention of writing? The anecdotes he told were the ones he usually told, often ones I'd already read somewhere: his stock of stories. He was a 78-year-old famous man, he had his best memories organised, he had shaped them into tales, and he was soon to put them in a book called *My Last Breath* (1982), which he wrote in collaboration with his scriptwriter Jean-Claude Carrière. Didn't I gather rich insights into the films? Some, but not as many as you might think. This was manifestly the Buñuel who made Buñuel's films, there were plenty of continuities between the mind I'd met in the work and the mind I was meeting over drinks. The author was fully alive in that sense, and discussing his films with Buñuel was a delight. But I didn't understand the films a whole lot better for talking to him, and any language I might find for writing about the films was going to be quite different from the language in which I could describe him, if I was even going to try to describe him. A person is not a film, and films have all kinds of adventures once the director has finished editing them. 'I don't believe one's life can be confused with one's work,' Buñuel says in the book I've just mentioned.

What I did get from meeting Buñuel, apart from much pleasure and laughter, was a feeling for the kind of artist he was, the peculiar mixture of austerity and mischief he brought to the cinema. You can see this in the films as well, of course, but there is so much else in them, so much obsession and yearning, so much appetite for pain, so much unappeased theology. All this must have been in the person somewhere, certainly, but it wasn't in the person you met. He had trained himself, I believe, to save his nightmares for his movies. What was left in daily life was a curious mind and an imagination always playing with possibility, but above all his craft and his career, the sense of film as an art and a discipline, a kind of experiment in which even the wildest jokes took on a certain aspect of rigour or purity.

I met Buñuel in July 1978, through an old friend, Santiago Genovés, a Mexican anthropologist. Santiago, born in Spain, always called Buñuel Don Luis, and after a bit of practice, so did I. I saw him a number of times in company over the next three years, and I had many conversations with him in the late afternoons. The last time I saw him was in June 1981. I didn't go back to Mexico for a while after that, and he died in July 1983.

First impressions. He is old, bent, has rather crooked teeth, large intelligent eyes behind heavy glasses. An amiable, mischievous grin resides almost constantly on his face. He is very deaf, but can hear if you speak loud and clear, although communication is always a little uncertain, apt to misfire or lose its sequence. A small terrier called Tristana trots in and sits on the sofa. Don Luis, the scourge of actors and actresses, can't get her to move or leave. 'I am a monk,' he says, 'I don't go out.' It's largely true. The world comes to him, insofar as he allows it to. But it doesn't come much or often. He says he feels old, that he was 'formidable' between 40 and 60, and felt fine in his sixties. Now he can't remember the name of the pills he's supposed to take for his diabetes, he starts to do a sum and can't remember what he has just multiplied by what. He feels dizzy at times. He says all this with genuine impatience and distaste, but also with an energy which comes out as a kind of unshakable gaiety.

Buñuel likes some contemporary directors, but not many. American films, he says. Woody Allen. Stanley Kubrick. 'That film with those shots of the man's eye.' 'A Clockwork Orange?' 'That's the one.' Nice thought, coming from the man whose film career began with the image of an eye slashed by a razor. Buñuel tells me a Hitchcock story, which he tells again in *My Last Breath*. There is a dinner in Buñuel's honour at George Cukor's house in Hollywood in 1972. Fifteen famous directors are there, including John Ford, Rouben Mamoulian, Robert Mulligan, George Stevens, Robert Wise, William Wyler, Billy Wilder. Hitchcock sits next to Buñuel, says very little, then at one point puts an arm round his companion's shoulder and says with deep admiration: 'Buñuel, that wooden leg in *Tristana*. That wooden leg.'

Buñuel and his wife Jeanne lived in a small and tidy house in the southern central part of Mexico City, the place Buñuel called 'this metropolis without end'. Both had become Mexican citizens in 1949. The street was a quiet cul-de-sac off a busy thoroughfare; the house had a small enclosed garden. 'Come and see me when you like,' Buñuel would say, 'but telephone first to set up a time.' I would telephone, talk to Jeanne, and ask if I could see Don Luis. She would consult him, and he would invariably say: 'How about tomorrow around five?' So I learned not to call if I couldn't go the next day.

Generally I would watch a film of his at the Mexican Cineteca and then drive over to his house. I would say, 'I saw *El* today, or *Robinson Crusoe*,' or whatever I had seen, and he would say: 'Terrible film, the director should be shot.' I would murmur in polite disagreement, and ask him a question about the work. One day I said I had very much liked a French film he had made in Corsica, *Cela s'appelle l'Aurore* (1955). 'Yes,' he said. 'I liked it when I made it.' He didn't care for technical queries, and I discovered that general questions, critics' questions, didn't interest him, that he didn't want to discuss ideas or meanings. But he would talk about all kinds of things, if you could get him started on the right sort of detail – the ostrich in close-up at the end of *The Phantom of Liberty*, say, the garrulous duel between Jansenist and Jesuit in *The Milky Way*. He even loved ideas. He just didn't like the idea of them.

One day I didn't offer my polite disagreement. I had been to see his *A Woman without Love* (1951), a version of Maupassant's novel *Pierre et Jean*, a truly terrible film by any standards, without a single redeeming or even interesting moment, as far as I could see. In *My Last Breath*, Buñuel was to say this was 'no doubt my worst film', but I didn't then know that he thought that. A number of Buñuel's Mexican works are jagged and uneven, but virtually all of them have luminous features, touches that reveal the quirky or reckless hand of the master. Not this one. I said I didn't think the director should be shot but the film was awful, and asked what happened. Buñuel nodded, remembering. Finally he said: 'I couldn't think of anything' – 'No se me occurió nada,' literally 'nothing occurred to me.' He couldn't think of anything? Yes, he knew the film was boring from the start but assumed something would occur to him while he was shooting, some gag or angle or twist that would liven it up. That was how he worked, and almost always something occurred to him. There is a little fable about art here. You plan carefully, and you leave room for inspiration, in fact you rely on its arrival. But then inspiration, always an uncertain dancing partner, fails to show up, and you just keep going and finish the job. Then you make another plan.

I was then rather keen on the idea of Buñuel as a permanent Surrealist, of Surrealism as a continuing state of mind, and so was slightly shocked to hear him place the movement so firmly in the past. 'When I was a Surrealist', he said, and 'in the days of the Surrealists' – as if the group was a club or a team you could join or leave. He was right, of course, Surrealism was always a thinner, more privileged form of revolt than it liked to imagine it was – or than I liked to imagine it was. The bourgeoisie revolting against the bourgeoisie, Buñuel said in *My Last Breath*. But there is a continuing mentality, too, which has to do not with shock or rebellion but with resistance to settled or predictable meanings: resistance to interpretation itself, if by 'interpretation' we mean not just trying to make sense of things but succeeding in doing it. Early in our first conversation we spoke about *That Obscure Object of Desire*, then a recent film, which was to be Buñuel's last. This work, notoriously, has two actresses playing a single role, that of the taunting, endlessly desired Conchita, the role played by Marlene Dietrich (on her own) when Sternberg made *The Devil Is a Woman*, his film based on the same novel. There is a single fictional character, with a name and a mother and a place in the plot, and indeed a single voice on the soundtrack, that of Carole Bouquet. On the screen, though, we see Carole Bouquet alternating with Angela Molina. They look quite different, although audience reactions to this trick have varied immensely: some people haven't noticed it, and some haven't been able to take their minds off it, and many have had reactions situated somewhere in between. The point, for most viewers, is to make meaning out of the alternation. The point for Buñuel was to defeat meaning. There was to be nothing psychological about the switches, he said to me, no Jekyll and Hyde story, only random alternation.

Buñuel's films are full of touches like this, there to scramble old meanings, not to provide new ones, and they could have been fuller of them. Buñuel himself was proud of the idea of the two actresses but was ready to agree that it was crazy. He had started shooting, in Paris and Madrid, with one actress, Maria Schneider, and when he fired her thought the production was over – but Serge Silberman, his producer, took to the suggestion instantly. Unlike Oscar Dancigers, the producer of Los Olvidados, who had persuaded Buñuel to take a series of similar moves out of the film: a full symphony orchestra playing in a building under construction, a glossy top hat briefly glimpsed on a stove in a Mexico City hovel. Most viewers would miss these moments, Buñuel thought, and those who saw them would wonder what they had seen, just as we wonder, in That Obscure Object of Desire, whether we have really seen two actresses or weirdly misremembered just one. Dancigers's view, which Buñuel accepted in practice without agreeing to the principle, was that the director was ruining the film. 'I don't care if I ruin films,' Buñuel said. This could be a motto for him: when he is lucky, his films are the ruins of films he didn't want to make.

My wife and I celebrated our wedding anniversary at the Buñuels' house in 1978. There were a number of guests, much festivity, champagne, many Spanish jokes. Everyone had a good time, and I had a small illumination. This orderly, good-humoured house, these kindly people: isn't there something odd here? Only what Buñuel has taught us to find odd. We are the people who managed to have a meal together, unlike the characters in The Discreet Charm of the Bourgeoisie. When the meal is over, we shall be able to leave (we were able to leave), unlike the characters in The Exterminating Angel. Buñuel himself is not outside the world he criticises, he is part of it, and so are his friends and family. Social arrangements are foolish and apparently fragile, because they are so arbitrary and groundless. Everything about them could be different, and is different in other times and places. 'Everyone is a barbarian for someone,' as a character says in The Phantom of Liberty: 'On est toujours le barbare de quelqu'un.' And yet it is because these arrangements are arbitrary and groundless that we have so little purchase on them, and they seem so strangely unchangeable. The radical instability of things in Buñuel's films is a wish, an act of fictional defiance, the expression of a political and moral need. Their durability in reality is their discreet and remorseless excess of charm. Buñuel's great subject is the intimate failure of the bourgeoisie to revolt against the bourgeoisie.

Hence Buñuel's fondness for heretics, and stories about heretics. Heretics are not atheists, outsiders, they are believers who believe something different, they are with us and not with us. That's why we have to persecute them, or why, if we are the heretics, we get persecuted. *The Milky Way*, Buñuel said, could have been made about any form of heresy, artistic, scientific, sociological. He chose religious heresies because he happened to know something about them – because of his Jesuit education, he said. Buñuel attended a school in Zaragoza that sounds at all points identical with the school Stephen Dedalus attends in Dublin in *A Portrait of the Artist as a Young Man*. There is something disingenuous, even mischievous, about this claim, since Buñuel's religious preoccupations are clearly more firmly anchored than the remark suggests, more like a trauma than an option. But the intellectual reach of the idea is interesting, and says something about the intimacy of failed revolt in Buñuel's works, from *L'Age d'or* through *Los Olvidados*, *Nazarín*, *Viridiana*, *Tristana* and *The Phantom of Liberty*. Heretics often suffer dreadfully because they are so close to the doctrine they dissent from. But then they are close to it. Even their dissent can be seen as a form of complicity, a failure to get outside the engulfing system. This is a revolt which can't escape its family of thought, which will always have been the secret friend of its worst enemy.

Buñuel was born in Calanda, near Teruel, in Spain, just over a hundred years ago (22 February 1900), but he insisted that the place itself plunged him into an older time. 'My infancy slipped by in an almost medieval atmosphere'; 'I had the good fortune of spending my childhood in the Middle Ages.' One effect of this ancientness was that his films, after a certain point, stopped ageing, since they so fluently mingled contemporary violence, drugs, high-tech killers, up-to-date political jokes with much older customs. When a car hits a tree in *The Milky Way*, a voice comes out of the car radio preaching a sermon on the pains of hell. The text is from a work by Fray Luis de Granada, a medieval mystic. The voice is Buñuel's. Although Buñuel thought that film, as a medium, was peculiarly the 'victim of time', he managed if not to refute time at least to confuse it. When the Argentinian writer Julio Cortázar uses the word 'Buñuel' as an adjective he means skipping without warning 'from Actium to the Anschluss' – or as happens in *L'Age d'or*, from an imagined foundation of Rome to a troubled 1930.

This is not quite the impression we get from the rather miscellaneous collection of materials in *An Unspeakable Betrayal*. Time's hand is all over this work, pushing everything remorselessly towards the past. The book is an English-language version of a French book published in 1995, which in turn contained work assembled in

Spanish in 1982. Some of the material was even gathered in Francisco Aranda's biography of Buñuel, published in Spanish in 1969, and available in English in 1975.

The book opens with a selection of whimsical prose pieces Buñuel published between 1922 and 1927. Some are Surrealist avant la lettre – Buñuel says in *My Last Breath* that he wasn't much interested in Surrealism until well after he moved from Madrid, where he had studied, to Paris in 1925 – and some are literally Surrealist. The cymbals in an orchestra are said to be 'light shattered into fragments'; a personified wind, 'howling with delight', uproots trees, spins houses round and turns 'three priests sneaking down the street into as many inverted umbrellas'. A piece of roasted meat takes a walk, has all kinds of adventures. The least dated of these self-consciously artful pieces is perhaps 'La Sancta Misa Vaticanae', which describes a competition held in Rome to see who can say mass fastest:

> At the word 'go', the priests begin to say mass as fast as they can. Turning toward the faithful to say the Dominus vobiscum, making the sign of the cross etc, they reach incredible speeds, while the altar boy goes back and forth with the missal and the other ritual objects. A few fall down exhausted, like boxers. Finally, Mosén Rendueles, of Huesca, is declared the winner, having said the entire mass in a record 1 minute and 45 seconds. As a prize he receives a monstrance and a large Aragonian wicker basket.

An Unspeakable Betrayal also has the texts of a brief pre-Surrealist play called 'Hamlet', which Buñuel put on with his friends in the cellar of the Café Select in Montparnasse ('At the end of each act, the peasants will be foreshadowed'; 'Marquises artificially bleed to death along the nauseating walls'), and of a rather learned lecture on the puppet theatre. The rest of the book offers a selection from Buñuel's film criticism, a handful of more theoretical pronouncements on the cinema, some notes on three of his own films (*L'Age d'or*, *Las Hurdes* and *Viridiana*), some screenplays and/or synopses, including the version of *Un Chien andalou* which Buñuel published in *La Révolution surréaliste* in 1929, and some autobiographical jottings.

Already in the late 1920s Buñuel liked American films, especially the comic shorts of Ben Turpin, Harry Langdon and above all Buster Keaton. 'The finest poems that cinema has produced', he said of American two-reelers, 'far more Surrealist than the films of Man Ray'. 'Keaton's films,' Buñuel wrote, 'give lessons to reality itself.' He loved Dreyer's *Passion of Joan of Arc* ('the humanity in these faces floods the screen and fills the room'), and was very funny about Adolphe Menjou's moustache ('a page of Proust brought to life on the upper lip'). What Buñuel has to say about film as a medium, about découpage and close-ups and the rest, is rather disappointing, since it seems like watered-down Eisenstein – but then we have the films. Among the later work in the volume is a set of film ideas which Buñuel noted down some time in the 1940s (probably), and called 'Gags'. This one anticipates a moment in *The Exterminating Angel*:

> The owners of the castle and their guests, some six or seven people in all, climb the staircase of the main hall to go to bed. In the corridor on the second floor, where various doors lead to their rooms, they bid one another good night and retire. A short while later, one of the guests cautiously leaves his room on a mysterious expedition. As he approaches the staircase he hears the nearby voices of people coming up the stairs. They are exactly the same people as before, who again say good night and retire to their rooms.

And this one has several echoes in Buñuel's last films, especially *The Phantom of Liberty*: 'In a room, with four candles placed around it, is a coffin in which lies a very beautiful woman who might be the bride. As the protagonist draws near her, the corpse opens its eyes and says: "Would you mind leaving me in peace?"'

There is also an unlikely treatment, written in English in 1937 for Paramount, for a film about Goya and the Duchess of Alba, which is so terrible that Buñuel must have had the time of his life writing it. Goya is 'a large man, warm, passionate, yet retaining the peasant's virtues of simplicity and sincerity'. He saves the Duchess from a street escapade, but she doesn't yet know who he is. 'He leads her into the atelier where the walls are covered with paintings that are famous all through Spain. The Duchess regards them in amazement. "You are Goya!" she exclaims. He nods.'

Buñuel said of *Un Chien andalou* that it was 'nothing other than a desperate, impassioned call for murder', although his misguided audiences ('this imbecilic crowd') kept finding it 'beautiful' or 'poetic'. Buñuel's sons Juan Luis and Rafael rather ungratefully repeat the charge in a brief afterword to this book. 'That's what his films and writing were all about. To provoke, to shock, to destroy a society that he found corrupt and idiotic, to ridicule a religion that had oppressed millions of people and continues to do so . . . Now many of his books and belongings have been put into museums.' Or even reprinted in works published by university presses. We might rather say, as I think Buñuel himself would later have said, that if an audience can mistake a call for murder for a beautiful poem, there is something wrong with the work as well as the audience. Or something wrong with the description of the work. What Buñuel learned magnificently to do as a film-maker was to make it impossible for us to settle for beauty and poetry, however much we liked the works. The desperate call for murder was more than a metaphor but less than a programme, a response to the pain of a world which not even the most extreme violence could alter.

The last time I saw Buñuel we had an extended talk about chance. I had said how much I liked the moments in *Tristana* where the main character forces herself or her companions to make choices between two virtually identical things, to prefer one over the other: the chickpeas on her plate, the pillars of a colonnade in a court-yard, two narrow streets in Toledo. Buñuel said that the things are not different but you can make them different. You look at any two identical things, two copies of the same book, two objects of the same colour, and they begin to seem differ-ent. 'This red is more red.' Then you act on this invented difference and your life changes – or it doesn't. This way of thinking is about as far from determinism as it could be, but it doesn't seem to afford much human freedom. Our acts would have scarcely any antecedents, we could literally go either way with the chickpeas or the streets or the books or the colours: chance masquerading as choice. But then these same acts are heavy with consequences, just as they would be if we had made fully considered choices between radically different alternatives. We create a moment of meaningless freedom and then we squander it. Or perhaps we create the momen-tary flicker of freedom because we know the larger options are not available to us. When Tristana chooses between two chickpeas or two pillars, she insists on the real but slight difference between the candidates: 'There's always a little something that makes me like one of them more.' The despairing corollary to this view would be that differences as slight as this convert every choice into a self-deluding game. On the other hand, when Tristana takes the street to the right rather than to the left, she meets the man who is to become her lover. Would she otherwise have missed him? What we call causes, Buñuel says in *My Last Breath*, are really a limitless pro-fusion of chances. 'Chance is the great master of all things. Necessity arrives only afterwards.' Did Buñuel believe this? Not exclusively or always, but it was one of his favourite stories about human behaviour, and I suddenly remember that at one time he was planning to make a film of Gide's *Les Caves du Vatican*, a novel predicated on the notion of the *acte gratuit*. The acts in *Tristana* are gratuitous in their making, but a mere phantom of liberty in their effect.

7 September 2000

'WHAT A MAN THIS IS, WITH HIS CROWD OF WOMEN AROUND HIM!'

Hilary Mantel on Robespierre

F OR A TIME, early last year, there was no trace of Robespierre to be found on the street where he lived in the days of his fame. The restaurant called Le Robespierre had closed its doors, and after a while its portrait sign was removed from above the entrance of the house on the rue Saint-Honoré. Once again, the plaque on the wall had been smashed. The marble was shattered, the letters gouged away by a vindictive chisel. Just before the Bastille celebration, on a day of misty heat, a new plaque appeared. In the interim, only the staff of the new patisserie were able to confirm that it was true: Robespierre lived here.

The house on the site has been rebuilt, and so the room he occupied is, as his biographer J.M. Thompson has said, a metaphysical space. You go down a passage between shops; it widens a little, into a high-walled enclosure. It doesn't look like a place where a tragedy would occur, but if we had a diagnostic for such places we would always cross the road and stay away. In 1791 the gateway opened into a yard, with sheds where wood was stored; Maurice Duplay, who owned the house, was a master-carpenter. In this courtyard, Paul Barras saw two generals of the Republic picking over the salad herbs for dinner, under the eye of Madame Duplay. Robespierre lived on the first floor, in a low-ceilinged room with the plainest of furnishings.

The historian François Furet tells us: 'The revolution speaks through him its most tragic and purest discourse.' It does not matter where he lived or what he was like, or that he walked through this gate the day before his horrible death. His temperament is of no consequence, nor the will that drove his punitively controlled body through the all-night sittings. But this abstract Robespierre is not the one that interests you, as you stand inside the passage, sheltered from the street. After all, you keep his portrait on your wall; if Furet's formulation convinced you, you would not feel so desolate, and almost panic-stricken. The passage itself is confined and dark. Your throat constricts a little, and you remember what Michelet said: 'Robespierre strangles and stifles.' There are closed doors on your left. You glance up to the first floor. The windows are dirty. You say: 'it is only a metaphysical space.' Metaphysical wild horses would not drag you into Robespierre's room or any space that might have been occupied by it. You lean against the wall, expecting something to happen.

When the restaurant was still trading, the management used to hand out a photocopy with a brief life on it. Someone thought its tone lacked warmth, and had scribbled in the margin what follows: 'These walls still resound to the speeches, *ardent and flawless*, of Maximilien Robespierre.' The phrase delights you, but you would feel exposed if you had written it. Objectivity is such a god, and your brain, such as it is, interests itself in subjective trivia. He was a man of spectacular absent-mindedness. He liked flowers. Sometimes he laughed till he cried. He caught Madame Tussaud when she slipped and fell downstairs on her sightseeing-trip to the Bastille. Discern a subject, not an object, and feelings creep in. You throw up ramparts and dig trenches to defend yourself against them; one day, perhaps, you will notice that the house you are defending is empty and nobody has been at home for years. Meanwhile you are here in the half-dark with the *patriote isolé*. 'Millions of French people were brought up in the worship of Robespierre,' says François Crouzet in an essay here.* How is it that none of them come by? Sometimes you think of leaving flowers in the passage. But you never do it, or let us say, you have never done it yet.

To write about Robespierre you have to find the courage to allow yourself to be mistaken. Otherwise every sentence will be freighted with conditionals and quali-fiers, and every quotation prefaced by 'alleged to have said'. You will contradict yourself, because he contradicts himself. If you want to know why he excites such extremes of adoration and loathing, you have to study not just the biographies but the life stories of the people who wrote them. His 19th-century biographer Ernest Hamel worshipped him, the socialist historians Mathiez and Lefebvre championed him, George Sand called him 'the greatest man not only of the Revolution but of all known history'. Lord Acton described him as 'the most hateful character in the forefront of human history since Machiavelli reduced to a code the wickedness of public men'. In 1941 the historian Marc Bloch tried to call time: 'Robespierrists, anti-Robespierrists, we've had enough. We say, for pity's sake, simply tell us what Robespierre was really like.'

But it's not so easy. It's not only novelists who perpetrate fiction, and it seems that whatever you say about him, you say about yourself. 'The whole corpus of Robes-pierre studies is a hall of mirrors,' Mark Cumming says in his piece in this volume. Intending only to look at Robespierre, we see ourselves with our own startled eyes, starved or gross, inflated or diminished. Carlyle's 'thin lean Puritan and Precision' scuttles forever through the English imagination. But would he have been recog-nised by the man who met the Incorruptible strolling in the Bois de Boulogne, wearing a waistcoat embroidered with roses?

---

*Colin Haydon and William Doyle (eds.), *Robespierre* (Cambridge University Press, 2002).

The present book contains 16 essays about what Robespierre thought, what he did, and how he has been perceived and interpreted, not only by historians but by playwrights and novelists. There are chapters on his ideology and vision, on his political role, and on how he has been represented to posterity in the 19th and 20th centuries. The authors are the leading scholars in their field and each essay is presented with impressive clarity of thought and expression. They have avoided the kind of history that asks, in George Rudé's words, 'whether he would have been an agreeable dinner companion or a suitable match for my daughter'; though contemporaries did ask these things, of course. The tone is judicious, though an outburst of ritual name-calling from David Jordan belies the subtlety of his longer study, The Revolutionary Career of Maximilien Robespierre. For him, Robespierre is 'unworldly, resentful, vain, egotistical, susceptible to flattery, contemptuous of or indifferent to all the social pleasures except conversation . . . inflexible, unforgiving . . . secretive . . . obsessively self-regarding'. It's as well to have it over in the first paragraph. As Baudrillard puts it, 'there are those who let the dead bury the dead, and there are those who are forever digging them up to finish them off.'

The editors' introduction highlights the problem of evidence. When Robespierre was dead, outlawed and guillotined in July 1794, his papers were sorted by Courtois, a relative of Danton's, and Courtois did his job dishonestly, selecting and destroying. Those closest to Robespierre died with him, and few of his former colleagues were interested in putting the record straight. As the editors tell us, the victors of Thermidor 'not only blackened his memory but possibly also exaggerated his importance for posterity'. Once dead, he could be blamed for the 'excesses' of the Terror, but the blame would only stick if he could be shown to have been a powerful, singular figure. There were men who were far more bloody, in intention and in deed: Fouché, Collot, Carrier. He had acted as a check on their ferocity. But he was the best-known of the members of the Committee of Public Safety, their ideologist and spokesman. He is remembered as the theoretician of the Terror. It is he who bears the blame, when blame is handed out.

Robespierre went to live with the Duplays in 1791, in the summer of the backlash against the 'patriots', when the radical papers were closed down, presses were smashed, and the left were on the run. Marat disappeared from view, Danton crossed the Channel, but Robespierre simply moved house. He had already gained a Christ-like reputation, but Maurice Duplay was not much like the carpenter of Galilee. A member of the Jacobin Club, he owned other houses besides the one on the rue Saint-Honoré, and had a good business. The Duplays were a plain-living, high-minded family, all of them politically committed. One daughter was married and away, three daughters were still at home. Eléonore, the eldest girl, was an art student. Danton called her Cornélia Copeau: little Miss Woodchip, the carpenter's daughter. Elisabeth, who was in her mid-teens, talked many years later to the dramatist Sardou. 'He was so good!' she said of Robespierre. He listened to all her troubles. He was patient and kind. We used to go for walks and take his dog to swim in the river; in season, we picked cherries and cornflowers. Interpreted by Elisabeth, the Duplay household takes on the bourgeois calm of a painting by Chardin, its inhabitants entranced and absorbed among everyday objects, blocks of colour and light overlaid with a sober, reverential geometry. Sardou was horrified. 'Which Robespierre had she known?' He proceeded to demolish her memories. Silly woman! Sentiment was blocking her access to her own history.

It is possible – if fiction is your business – to feel some disturbance about the Maison Duplay. Once behind the gate, Robespierre left only briefly, when his sister Charlotte turned up in Paris and demanded her sisterly right to keep house for him. He would only agree to move a street away, and then at once became ill – he was subject to every kind of psychosomatic attack. Within days he was back in his room over the woodyard. He and Eléonore were seen to walk hand in hand. 'Eléonore thought she was loved,' said a fellow-student, 'but really she only scared him.' Many people assumed that she was Robespierre's mistress. It is interesting, if he was the judgmental prig of legend, that he didn't seem to care what people thought.

Robespierre was 36 when he died and we know almost nothing about the first 30 years of his life. There is a persistent legend that the Robespierres were of Irish origin, but both J.M. Thompson and the painstaking French novelist Marianne Becker have traced the family back to Northern France in the 15th century. Maximilien was born in Arras in 1758, four months after his parents' marriage: so he was by way of an accident. His father François was a lawyer, and his mother was the daughter of a master-brewer. When he was six, she died in giving birth to her fifth child. After her death, François ran up debts, started disappearing for long periods and finally went for good. The children were parcelled out among the family. Maximilien was a quiet child who liked to keep small birds, though later, of course, people would decide that it was for the purpose of cutting off their heads with a toy guillotine which he had – with uncanny prescience – invented for the purpose.

When Maximilien was 12 he was awarded a scholarship to the Collège Louis-le-Grand in Paris. He was poor to a humiliating degree, but formidably diligent and clever. In his early twenties he returned to Arras, having qualified as a lawyer. He began to pay off his father's debts. He had a reasonable success and was appointed to a minor judicial position. Sometimes he drove into the country with friends; sometimes he wrote light verse. But he soon managed to alienate sections of the local establishment. He did not want what the old regime could give him, and within a few years he would make himself a person with nothing to lose. He identified with victims, and would use the language of victimhood like an offensive weapon. He constantly declared that people were trying to 'oppress' him; if you disagreed with him, he would declare himself 'oppressed'. He began to refer, in his writing, to the 'laborious life' and early death he foresaw. He had an unspecific but powerful intimation of disaster and glory. Montesquieu informed his intellect and Rousseau informed his emotions. Later he described himself as 'timid as a child' and said that he shook with nerves when he had to make a speech. He was not constituted for confrontation. His voice, people said, was not strong; so it was up to him to create, in those halls of the Revolution with their disastrous acoustics, a climate in which he would command a hushed assent.

In 1789 he was elected to the Estates General and went to Versailles. In the National Assembly which evolved from the Estates, he was part of a tiny radical minority, but this did not bother him because he did not count in the ordinary way. He was always part of a greater majority: the People and Maximilien, Maximilien and the People. He quickly suspected that the heroes of '89, when in power, were merely old regime politicians with a different vocabulary. They spoke the language of the Declaration of the Rights of Man, while furthering their sectional interests. He tried to shame them into following the logic of their proclaimed principles; mostly, he failed. In the two years following the taking of the Bastille, he pursued an impeccably liberal and far-sighted agenda. He spoke for manhood suffrage and against a property qualification for voters: against slavery, in support of civil rights for Jews, against capital punishment, and against censorship.

The two latter principles, notoriously, would buckle under pressure. In the early years of the Revolution he let the radical press establish his credentials. From the spring of 1792 to the early summer of the following year he made a low-key venture into journalism, publishing a weekly paper, of comment rather than news. His distributor was in the cour du Commerce, on Marat's doorstep. It is hard to imagine him in that territory of inky little hacks, trading sneers and insults over each others' misprints. He had been, as Hugh Gough's essay says, 'consistent and tenacious' in defence of press freedom and had refused to take legal action over the many libels published against him, believing that public opinion would vindicate him. After the fall of the monarchy, the anti-censorship case had to give way; only a community of saints would have allowed the royalist press the opportunity to campaign for a restoration. In the spring of 1794, his childhood friend Camille Desmoulins would tell him that it was not *vertu* but freedom of thought that was the basis of a republic; but the offending issue of the *Vieux Cordelier* would not make it into print and the childhood friend would go to the scaffold. In this affair you can convict him of timidity, or of coldness of heart, rather than hypocrisy. It is unhelpful to read a man backwards. Robespierre's early commitment to press freedom was genuine, but did not extend to a press which, as he saw it, had been systematically corrupted. As Gough shows, the Committee of Public Safety, when Robespierre was a member, did not reintroduce the repressive censorship of the old regime nor anticipate that of the Directory; though perhaps it was want of capacity, rather than lack of will. By late 1793, Robespierre profoundly feared the press. A syllable, he felt, could sabotage his policy. For example, he had said: 'the republic, one and indivisible'. The press reported that he had said 'one and universal'; thus aligning him with distrusted cosmopolitan radicals. He did not think this was a mishearing, but a plot to trap him.

His personal history gave him no reason to believe that the world would let him have his say. He was, it is reported, frequently shouted down and silenced early in his parliamentary career. He had no presence, there were no crowd-pleasing mannerisms or orator's flourishes. Historians usually report that his speeches are arid. It is interesting, then, to read his speech against capital punishment, which is as fresh as if it had been made today. It is perfectly constructed, a brilliant fusion of logic and emotion: as much a work of art as a building or a piece of music could be. You can believe that, as Desmoulins reported, he could bring 800 men to their feet in a single moment. You could quibble over the head-count, but the power seemed to be real. It extended to the women of Paris, who attended the public galleries of the Jacobin Club. This worried his contemporaries. They thought he was taking some sneaky advantage. 'What a man this is, with his crowd of women around him!' said Rabaud Saint-Etienne. Condorcet, the champion of women's rights, sulked because he had got their attention.

The status which Robespierre achieved in the Revolution cannot be explained in traditional political terms. For most of his career he fought shy of office, and most of the parliamentary measures he proposed were rejected as too progressive. When he joined the Committee of Public Safety he did so in the quietest manner possible, simply replacing a member who had fallen ill. Soon after he joined the Committee, it began to accrete executive power, till it was the effective government of France. Its proceedings were generally not minuted, so his role is often unclear. Is he speaking for himself, or for the government? Whatever the source of his authority, he was undeniably effective. David Jordan's essay describes him as 'that rare being, an ideologue with exquisite political reflexes'. Part of the secret of his success, no doubt, was that initially he was underrated. He was cautious, and could bury himself in detail; these traits were thought the hallmarks of mediocrity. But he had a canny sense of timing and the kind of persistence that wore his opponents down; the weary Danton, at his trial, described him as 'above all, tenacious'. The Robespierre of 1793 is the patron saint of the formerly overlooked, one of the meek who are to inherit the earth. His moral authority held together under pressure of circumstance, and his reputation for probity often seemed the one constant when coalitions were fragile and the reading of events uncertain. He was an idealist who did not believe in losing. As Coleridge put it, 'Robespierre . . . possessed a glowing ardour that still remembered the *end*, and a cool ferocity that never either overlooked or scrupled the means.'

In May 1793 he told the Convention: 'To fulfil your mission, you must do exactly the contrary of what existed before you.' Alan Forrest's essay on his part in war organisation shows him confronting the generals with unblinking radicalism. He had opposed a declaration of war by the French, which made him temporarily unpopular. But he knew that, in times of war, public liberty never increases. He was suspicious of soldiers in general, their outlook; they were oppressors by nature, he thought. He was sceptical of the notion that the French army would spread freedom through Europe: 'Who loves armed missionaries?' He suspected that the war was unwinnable, and that once it began it could not be limited. Victories might be more lethal than defeats; he saw a military dictatorship as the end of it, and of course he was right. But as Forrest shows, he became 'a war leader in spite of himself', his imagination and his willingness to tear up the rule book contributing to the high morale of the volunteers and helping to win the republic's battles. Ideology reinforced strategy. The ambit of heroism was not narrowly defined; a woman who sent her son to the front was also a hero. The soldier was not a brute, but a citizen: not cannon-fodder but a free man whose intelligence must be addressed.

But it's not enough to win; you have to be right. The Revolution, he believed, must be justified at every step, and every Revolutionary action must be an expression of virtue. No cynic ever learns anything about Robespierre; unable to come to grips with 'virtue', he retires, baffled. There is a problem with the English word 'virtue'. It sounds pallid and Catholic. But *vertu* is not smugness or piety. It is strength, integrity and purity of intent. It assumes the benevolence of human nature towards itself. It is an active force that puts the public good before private interest. Its meaning is explored in Patrice Higonnet's *Goodness beyond Virtue* (1998), which is an extraordinary manual of practical Jacobinism. Higonnet has not much time for Robespierre, who, he says, 'probably died a virgin' (not that historians ever gossip, of course). But his book shows the day-to-day vitality, during the Revolution, of ideas which had a venerable pedigree, but which had been presumed to be entirely theoretical. Robespierre thought that, if you could imagine a better society, you could create it. He needed a corps of moral giants at his back, but found himself leading a gang of squabbling moral pygmies.

This is how Virtue led to Terror. Virtue and Terror became inseparable, a single Janus-faced god who guarded the gate to a better world. Was the violence of 1793-94 just the product of circumstances, forced on an unwilling government panicked by war, civil war and sabotage? Or was it somehow the logical outcome of everything that had gone before? By late 1793 there was a rotten substructure to the Revolution, a web of crooked army contracts, stockmarket frauds and forgeries, and a capital full of spies and foreign persons of, as Robespierre saw it, dubious worth and allegiance; all information which came to the government was suspect at source. Also, it was clear that the Sovereign People did not always act in its own best interests. It seemed, from the actions of looters and strikers, that it was given to short-term thinking. Robespierre tried to forge an inner consistency, clinging to the idea of a virtuous people misled by corrupt and factious politicians, by enemies who were masked and veiled. If the Revolution didn't have moral force behind it, it was merely a series of self-serving crimes. Danton had laughed at the idea of virtue; he was therefore not fit to govern. After the courtroom battle with the Dantonists, Robespierre began to fear that the trial process was itself anti-patriotic, criminal, dangerous: the existing law bred crime, if it protected the enemies of the people. Four years of polemics had failed to save the *patrie*, which was a spiritual, rather than a temporal space; the battle for territory was less important than the battle for the imagination. From now on, there were to be no trials, in the old meaning of the word. The enemy could be judged by his actions, not by a hypocritical form of words he might wield in his defence. There were to be no more arguments, only justice, as swift as death on the field. It was Hérault de Séchelles who, before falling victim to the guillotine, had described it as 'a sabre cut'.

It is monstrous, of course. But – in practice – the monstrosity did not belong to Robespierre alone. What he embraced as principle, others embraced for aggrandisement. His religion, which some Jacobins mocked as a private hobby of his, was a creed for toughened spirits, for the habitually unconsoled, and in discovering it he had consulted intuition, not reason. For him, and for Saint-Just no doubt, terror was a means of discovery and self-discovery. In public, one might say that the triumph of good was inevitable. In private, there were spiritual doubts. 'Vice and virtue forge the destiny of this earth; these two opposing spirits fight each other for it.' In Robespierre's mind, the Year II was a battleground, the stage stripped for apocalypse.

Now I will ask you, look at the portraits. Ask what they can tell us. He was so much drawn and painted, as if every amateur artist reached for his pencil, in wonder at what he knew to be a transitory phenomenon. So there is plenty to look at; it is our fault if we can't see. An Englishman called John Carr, travelling in Paris in 1802, was surprised by a bust 'taken of him, a short period before he fell'. He noted:

> History, enraged at the review of the insatiable crimes of Robespierre, has already bestowed on him a fanciful physiognomy, which she has composed of features which rather correspond with the ferocity of his soul, rather than with his real countenance. From the appearance of this bust, which is an authentic resemblance of him, his face must have been rather handsome. His features were small, and his countenance must have strongly expressed animation, penetration and subtlety.

There is a salon portrait of 1791, attributed to Mme Adelaïde Labille-Guiard. Two years into the Revolution, she has painted a boy with a face of conspicuous sweet-ness, gentle and shy: a black coat, white cuffs falling over those exquisite, boneless, long-fingered hands that only portrait painters have ever seen. In the posed por-traits, he is always smiling: faintly, perhaps; impatiently, perhaps. Then there is a sketch taken from life, 1793, in the National Convention. He is not smiling. He has pushed his spectacles into his hair. His eyes have moved sideways, in suspicion or a kind of dread. Under the sketch the artist Gérard has scribbled: 'eyes green, com-plexion pale: coat of green stripe, gilet blue on white, cravat red on white'. A man, as Belloc put it, for colour rather than ornament. The face is still very young; the expression is closed, guarded, as if he had seen something move in the shadows. By Thermidor, it appears he has aged ten years. The final sketch, taken again from life, shows features pared to bone, jaw muscles rigid, every line drawn taut and fine. A day or two after it, Mme Tussaud took his death mask.

The Revolution represented a ruinous physical struggle for its front-line person-nel. You didn't need to be a soldier to be wrecked by it; the home front shattered constitutions, with its unrelenting schedules, its emergencies and exigencies as punishing to the mind as to the body. 'I confess an immense fatigue,' Robespierre said, in his last speech to the Convention. In the weeks before it, he had preserved a silence which worked on the nerves of his colleagues. His face became unreadable. But the narrative behind it is always old and always new.

Danton thought he had the story straight: 'He can't fuck, and he's afraid of money.' Broad-brush portrayal is as far as many historians ever get, because Robes-pierre is judged in a way that is visceral as much as intellectual. He is a monstrous archetype of the grand inquisitor and mystic, and both historians and imaginative writers have been happy to set up archetypes around him; chiefly Danton himself with his 'prodigious *tout ensemble*'. Imagination creates a false opposition between the two men; for most of the Revolution, there was little difference of policy between them, and Robespierre – on the principle that it is better to win even the battles you have not chosen to fight – abandoned Danton when he could do nothing more for him. But as Norman Hampson says elsewhere, the Danton of legend is hard to resist, especially since he imposed himself on contemporaries as well as posterity. After his death this well-read, greedy, secretive lawyer became a sort of roaring boy, a great-hearted, common-touch, chicken-in-every-pot man. As the 19th century progressed, Robespierre acquired a set of nervous twitches and shudders, and a hideous yellow complexion highlighted by green veins. The 18th-century inch being a variable measure, he shrunk physically, while Danton expanded. As Mark Cumming's essay describes, Robespierre is accused of 'physical impotence, cowardice and effeminacy'. Of course, most people who have written about Robespierre are men, and wish themselves to be, *au fond*, masculine, beneath their academic gowns or tweed jackets. They like to believe that if it came to it they could knock their opponents down: more like Danton than like Robespierre, after all.

Two essays in this collection concentrate on Robespierre in drama and in French fiction. The most famous play about the Revolution is Büchner's *Danton's Death*. Astonishing in form rather than content, it embellishes the legend of the world-weary philosopher done to death by a Robespierre-machine. Anouilh's *Poor Bitos*, tricksy in form and hollow at the centre, tells us more about postwar France than about the France of 1793, just as Andrzej Wajda's film *Danton* tells us about Poland in the 1980s. If we suspect that Danton is both flattered and denigrated by Gérard Depardieu's mesmeric performance, we are still repelled by the film's sick, neurotic, elderly Robespierre. Romain Rolland complained that 'the greatest figure of the Revolution still has no stature in France' and proceeded to commemorate him in an unperformable play with a 300-page text and a notional playing time of six hours. Henry Irving played Robespierre in a Sardou melodrama of 1899, in which the Great Terrorist was forced to compromise his principles to save his long-lost illegitimate son. But William Howarth's essay shows that Robespierre has not been entirely ill-wished by the theatre. An 1888 play by Combet has a memorable stage direction: 'Then Robespierre appears, borne on clouds. At his entry, the heavenly choir bursts into song.'

Howarth's piece on Robespierre in drama has little to say about Stanislawa Przybyszewska, on whose work Wajda based his Danton script. She was the maddest of all female Robespierrists (and in this matter I yield to few). Born in 1901, daughter of a Polish writer, she was an artist of starvation and frost, who dated her letters by the Revolutionary calendar, and died at 34, in Danzig, where she had been living in a sort of outhouse, unheated through the winters, painting her food with lysol to preserve it, while thinking intensively and extensively about 'this handsome petty lawyer who at the age of 35 single-handedly ruled France'. Tuberculosis, morphine and malnutrition were adduced as the causes of death, but she could more truthfully be diagnosed as the woman who died of Robespierre.

If you try to write either drama or novels about the Revolution, you have to consider your likely audience and the state of their prejudices. For historians, creative writers provide a kind of pornography. They break the rules and admit the thing that is imagined, but is not licensed to be imagined. It's no use insisting that you have applied for your licence, either; you may as well brace yourself for attempts to run you off the territory. The editors of this volume are generous about the possible role of fiction in reimagining the past, but Mark Cumming warns about 'the perilous delights of picturesque history'. We are likely to succumb to them, until history is written by machines; there are not two kinds of history, one sceptical and rational, and the other imaginative and erratic. Cumming makes the uncontentious observation that 'the historical image is two-faced, pointing outwards to the historical subject and inwards to the author's psyche.' This is as much true of academics as of accredited fictionalisers. But it is Carlyle who is the subject of this essay, Carlyle who made it so difficult (for the English-speaking reader, anyway) to look at the Revolution except through the highly-coloured filters which gave us 'the sea-green incorruptible'. A real heroine of the Revolution is the housemaid who lit the fire with his first draft. Dickens borrowed from Carlyle his best effects, and as Orwell pointed out, A Tale of Two Cities is largely responsible for the English reader's notion of the Revolution as 'a frenzied massacre lasting for years . . . whereas in reality the whole of the Terror, so far as the number of deaths goes, was a joke compared to one of Napoleon's battles . . . To this day, to the average Englishman, the French Revolution means no more than a pyramid of severed heads.'

The general view has not changed much since Orwell's day. In the non-Francophone world, the bicentennial was dominated by Simon Schama's Citizens, which does not challenge comfortable preconceptions. Schama uses his narrative skill and his wealth of illustration to confirm people in the belief they already hold, which is that the Revolution was a bloody and nonsensical waste of time. For the French, of course, Schama is irrelevant, because he is telling them nothing they have not heard from their own revisionist historians.

In the present book, Malcolm Cook's chapter on Robespierre as seen by French novelists serves to show their general timidity, their failure to break with stereotype. But the scope of his enquiry is not wide. Has he not read Dominique Jamet's 1988 novel Antoine et Maximilien ou la Terreur sans la vertu, with its refreshing portrait of Robespierre as a paedophile and child-murderer? Worth five minutes of anyone's time, it leads a novelist to examine the ethics of the trade. Imagination must be free, the dead have no remedy in law; all they can do is haunt you.

Which, in effect, is what Robespierre does. He takes a grip on the imagination and does not easily let you go. Michelet, ambivalent about the Incorruptible, always crossing and recrossing the line of his own argument, accused Louis Blanc, Hamel and others of a corrupting partiality: 'You have a friend in the city, and this friend is Robespierre.' But in her 1997 book *Mourning Glory*, Marie-Hélène Huet quotes a passage in which Michelet, having completed his great history of the French Revolution, speaks of what Robespierre had come to mean to him:

> In this entire history, which was my life and my inner world for ten years, I formed, on the road, many deep bonds of friendship . . . The greatest void I felt at this whitewood table, from which my book now departs, and where I remain alone, was the departure of my pale companion, the most faithful of them all, who had not left me from '89 to Thermidor; the man of great will, hard-working like me, poor like me, with whom I had, each morning, so many fierce discussions.

Michelet's book is finished; the argument still smoulders in the air.

In his last weeks, Robespierre stayed out of the public eye. He went for walks in the woods or shut himself up at the rue Honoré. No one supposed he was a spent force, but after the death of the Dantonists he had seemed to lose his sureness of touch. He could not survive if he trusted nobody, and could not work out whom to trust. The truth about the motives of his fellow-Revolutionaries seemed to be beyond mortal reach. In his 1978 biography of Danton, Norman Hampson pointed out that 'the truth was whatever corresponded to anything that Robespierre wanted to believe at any particular time.' But there is a difficulty here: in what words can the truth be told, when the secret enemies of the Revolution have stolen its language? He had always warned that the devil had the best tunes. All that is left for him is the word which is guaranteed because it is spoken by a dying man. 'What objection can be made to a man who wishes to speak the truth and agrees to die for it?'

The Revolution, as a creative enterprise, died with him. There is a formulation in which his death is a kind of blessed release for the nation; but after it, the Terror continued, and what lay ahead was a new tyranny and 20 years of war. In his last speech to the Convention, he said: 'My reason, not my heart, is beginning to doubt this republic of virtue which I have set myself to establish.' The heart leaves its faint trace: Michelet alone at the whitewood table, Stanislawa obsessively rewinding her typewriter ribbon. Otherwise, not much is left except a battered document case in the Musée Carnavalet, placed in proximity to Danton's large monogrammed knives and forks. The leather is stamped with Robespierre's name, but it has almost faded away. As Lamartine says, 'he was the last word of the Revolution, but nobody could read it.'

On the final document his signature is unfinished. He had written just two letters of his name, before a pistol shot shattered his jaw; whether he fired the shot himself, no one really knows. Lying in his own blood in an anteroom of the Committee of Public Safety, he gestured that he wished to write, but no one would give him a pen. I would have given him a pen, Barras said later, uneasy at the cruelty and the lack of a possible disclosure. He was half-dead when he was taken to the scaffold, and his decapitated remains were buried near the Parc Monceau. Eléonore survived, and was known as 'the widow Robespierre'. Maurice Duplay was imprisoned and driven out of business. His wife was found dead in her cell. Fear sealed the lips of witnesses, papers were burned, memories were reformulated. After the revolution of 1830, a group of admirers tried to locate the body. But though they dug and dug, no one was there.

30 March 2000

THE SOUND OF VOICES
INTONING NAMES

Thomas Laqueur on French Children of the Holocaust

I N A HAPPIER AGE, Immanuel Kant identified one of the problems of
understanding any of the genocides which come all too easily to mind. It is
the problem of the mathematical sublime. The arithmetician has no more
difficulty in principle comprehending one murder than 600,000 – the number
murdered in the Armenian atrocities of 1916-17 or by Nazi Einsatzgruppen on the
Eastern Front in 1941 before the death camps were fully geared up – or five to six
million, the best estimates we have of the number of Jews murdered in the camps.
At a purely cognitive level any number can be understood by adding, unit by unit,
to the unit that comes before. But for Kant, the ability to take in great magnitudes
– to feel their sublime terror – is ultimately an aesthetic act and one which depends
on gaining the right distance from the subject. His example comes from a French
general's account of a visit to the Pyramids and his anxiety about how to feel the
emotional effect of their sheer magnitude. Too close and we see only stone by stone
without taking in the full sweep from base to peak; too far away and we lose the
sublime wonder predicated on the sense that something so massive was made
discrete block by discrete block.

Writing about the Holocaust has faced a similar dilemma. One strategy has been
historical business as usual. However enormous, monstrous and disproportion-
ate the disaster seems, it can be comprehended by the ordinary strategies of historical writing: appropriate distance, clear reason, fitting narrative. Critics of this
approach have argued that it fails to recognise both the peculiar moral rupture of
the events in question and their subjective terrors. Only recourse to the memoir and
the power of memory itself – i.e. to individual experience – or to a pornography of
brutality which forces the past upon us viscerally could be true to this constellation of horrors. But recourse to the particular ends up as a claim for the transcend-
ental and has led both postmodern theorists and some historians of the period to
conclude that the Holocaust is simply 'un-representable'.

The brilliance of Serge Klarsfeld's book* is that it maintains in shimmer-
ing tension the claims of history – to give an objective account of the past – with

---

*Serge Klarsfeld, French Children of the Holocaust: A Memorial (New York University Press, 1996).

those of memory: the subjective, the discrete, the momentary brought to life in the present. Whether by intention or inspired inadvertence, he has produced a form in which documents of many sorts speak both to historical distance and to the immediacy of memory. He has succeeded in representing the Holocaust simultaneously as sublime and particular. And he has produced a book which makes a moral claim of enormous importance today. Memory is a means of making loss survivable, and thus of allowing the past to have closure.

More specifically, this is an attempt at 'a new reference work in the domain of memory and feeling', 'a full memorial book to the Jewish children deported from France'. Born of 'an obsession to be sure that these children are not forgotten', it is compiled by a man whose father fought for France in defence of what he believed to be its commitment to civic equality and, after the German victory, literally sacrificed himself to the SS so that his family, huddled behind a false wall, would escape discovery. The eight-year-old Serge survived the rest of the war in hiding in the Upper Loire, where, he says, 'the Gestapo had no antennae.'

The greater part of *French Children of the Holocaust* consists of an album of pictures of the deported children themselves, at least 2500 of whom are identified by name and by such details of their lives and arrests as hard-won evidence provides. It follows, and is deeply indebted to, Klarsfeld's *Mémorial de la déportation des Juifs de France* (1978), which gives the name, date of birth, nationality and convoy number of all 75,721 Jews deported from France between 27 March 1942 and 22 August 1944: Convoy One, Drancy, the main transit camp on the north-east outskirts of Paris, to Auschwitz, 1112 men, mostly French nationals, none chosen for immediate gassing, 22 survivors in 1945; through Convoy 46, 9 February 1943, 1000 deportees, of whom 816 were gassed on arrival and 22 survived (15 men, seven women); to the last ill-organised departures – No. 79, 17 August 1944, carrying 51 'special Jews' whom Eichmann's man on the spot, SS Hauptsturmführer Alois Brünner, managed to transport by trading some pigs for three cars that belonged to an aircraft battery; and No. 82 from Clermont-Ferrand, 22 August 1944, about which little is known except that it arrived at Auschwitz on 8 September, that it contained three adolescent girls and that 39 men were selected for work. (Convoy numbers, like names, are printed in bold face as if to enlist typography in the affirmation of their adamantine reality.)

French Children of the Holocaust follows also Klarsfeld's *Calendrier de la prosécution des Juifs de France* (1993), which provides the scaffolding for this book with its detailed chronicle – week by week, month by month, sometimes day by day – of the legislation, the meetings and negotiations, the round-ups and arrests, internments, loadings, unloadings and shipments East, the precise how, where and when of

73,157 murders (i.e. 75,721 deportations less 2564 survivors) arranged on French soil with active French assistance.

The murders themselves are left largely implicit in the chronicle and in the book as a whole. The death camps are there as the telos of its thousands of micro-histories; readers will not miss the fact that the overwhelming majority of those deported did not return and would mostly have been swallowed up in the historical oblivion of aggregate loss, had Klarsfeld and his associates not accounted for them one by one. The defence of criminals like Klaus Barbie, the SS chief in Lyon, and many others – that they did not know what awaited the human freight of the rail convoys – is exposed in detail for the mendacity that it is. But there are only a handful of reports from the East, dispersed as captions to the pictures or as supplementary material in the chronology section. Denise Holstein, 17, who was deported – Convoy 77 – to Auschwitz with nine younger children, for whom she cared in a Jewish refuge, reports that she alone survived because, in the glare of searchlights that illuminated the darkness in front of the selection ramps, she was warned by an experienced inmate to drop the child she was comforting so that she would be allowed to move to the left. All children and all women with children were sent to the right, to a truck that took them to the gas chambers.

The story of Ida Fensterszab is set out in two pages, between the picture of a plump, well-dressed girl of ten or 11, barely pubescent, standing with her well-dressed, stolidly bourgeois parents in 1939 or 1940, and that of the more knowing 15-year-old, wan but not emaciated, with large beautiful eyes and hair beginning to grow back, who has survived Auschwitz. Her parents had hidden her, the caption to the first picture tells us, with a French family in June 1940; the mother was deported on Convoy 11, 27 July 1942, from Drancy to Auschwitz (13 out of 1000 survived). Ida writes after the Liberation that two gendarmes came to get her at midnight on 30 January 1944. Various neighbours tried to dissuade them; the family's resistance was broken by the threat that if she was not produced, the man of the house would be taken in her stead. On the train she was befriended by an old grey-haired woman. Dreams of seeing her mother again were shattered by the stench of overflowing buckets of excrement. At the unloading ramp she ran, as commanded by the SS guards; her elderly new friend called, 'Ida, wait for me,' but she did not respond. Ida believes that her hairstyle saved her at the first selection: the last time she had seen her mother, she insisted that Ida wear a comb to make her look more 'like a young woman'. On the Auschwitz ramp, she speculates, it made her look old enough for a work-detail. There are a few more such testimonies. But the Shoah is by and large represented here neither in first-person accounts of the camps nor in pictures of its worst atrocities. Instead we are offered a complex interweaving of sources and artefacts that document the individual lives lost. Each has its particular resonance.

The list: 75,721 names from the master-list of all deportees, winnowed to a more limited category, 11,400 boys and girls under 18. To the information on the longer list Klarsfeld and his co-workers have laboriously added, where possible, the addresses of the places from which the children were taken so that the full route to the gas chambers can be traced: Daniel Brunschwig, aged three or four, shown in two pictures, standing in a garden next to his seated mother in the first, his father in the second, was taken from 28 rue du Titien, Cannes, and from there to an assembly point in Nice, and from there to Drancy, and from there to Auschwitz on Convoy 61.

The chronology: the master chronology is supplemented by the more limited chronologies that accompany individual pictures and by the interpolation of events pertaining especially to children – the week-to-week negotiations in June and July 1942 in which the French authorities induced the Germans, who at first wanted only adult slave labour, to accept thousands of bereft children, caught in the round-ups, into the trains bound for Auschwitz; negotiations as to when to arrest children in various refuges or which children to spare for the time being, until the Germans were in full murder mode. Historical information and interpretation, based largely on Michael Marrus and Robert Paxton's *Vichy France and the Jews*, have also been added.

The 2503 photographs themselves: these have been reproduced from identity cards and gravestones, from formal studio portraits and intimate snapshots, from school, camp and playground groups, from newspaper clippings and postwar missing-persons posters. Some are beautiful, some charming, some pleasingly conventional, some technically incompetent. In some the children look happy and fetching, in others tolerant of the occasion. In short, what one would expect from any collection of pictures, except for the jarring and very public Star of David which feels eerily as if it had invaded the private space of the pictures without its bearers having noticed. There were 1536 such pictures in the first, 1994 French edition; 1834 in the 1995 edition; another 497 in a January 1996 supplement; and a further 172 added to this, the first English edition, amounting to a total of 2503. The evolving, unfinished nature of the project of memorialisation is evident in the ordering of its visual artefacts: the strictly alphabetical arrangement of the first series ends on page 1414, with Elisa Zytaner, of whom we know only her date of birth, that she was arrested in the Toulouse area and deported on Convoy 77. It is not clear why Georges Lyon, shown sitting on a satin-covered box and looking as if he would rather not be having his picture taken in what must be a 1928 or 1929 photographer's studio, is next. But on page 1416 a new alphabet begins with Robert

Bergman, in short woollen trousers, knee-length socks and sweater, holding a sand pail, posed in front of a studio backdrop of a rural road. He has the chubby, still slightly babyish body of a three-year-old; his head is covered with long curls of the sort boys wore in another age. He lived at 24 rue Jessaint and was a month short of his seventh birthday when deported on Convoy 24. (Many of the children were either deported or gassed on their birthdays, not surprising when one considers the odds.) This series ends with Paul Zubrichas, looking impishly at the camera, and yet another new portfolio starts at B with the Bloch twins and their brother Jean-Pierre. From here to the end, alphabetical order breaks down.

Additional faces and bodies of children without names appear in these pictures, not to speak of the hundreds, perhaps thousands of adults: mothers and fathers, grandparents, nurses, older brothers and sisters. Fortunée Tordjman, for example, sits behind another woman so that her body is mostly hidden; both women are smiling. Tordjman's daughter Louise, seven, peeks out from behind her five-year-old brother, Jacques, who looks resolutely into the camera – that is to say, at us. All the Tordjmans were captured at a UGIF (Union Générale des Israélites de France) home in the South of France on 20 October 1943 and deported to Auschwitz on 28 October. But who is the round-faced woman sitting in front of Madame Tordjman, or the three children sitting on the grass in front of them, or the cheery, dark-haired and charming ten or 11-year-old girl with her hand almost on her hip and a self-satisfied sort of look on her face? There are images throughout the book of bodies in shadows and of faces blocked. Photographs are torn or cut up. There are Christian schoolmates in class portraits whose fate is beyond the scope of this book. Only one of seven faces in a Jewish Boy Scout troop photographed in 1941 is identified: Maurice Wasserman, 14 in the picture, living at 6 rue Sevran in Grenoble with his parents and brother Georges, deported 7 March 1944 on Convoy 69. On page 1043 is a snapshot of two Jewish boys boxing at a sports club at the Saint-Martin-de-Vésubie station in the Alpes-Maritimes; nine other boys crowd around. Only one, Isaac More, bare-chested and wearing short trousers, is identified. (He is shown in a colourful tunic on the tomb picture above the snapshot.) But who are the other nine, the littlest boy whose face is almost blocked by the body of one of the boxers, the next littlest in a black bathing-suit, whose face is identifiable but so hidden in shadows that I missed him on my first three or four scans of the snapshot? Their fate? Eight young women each dangling a baby in the grounds of the Rothschild Hospital, spring 1943. Suzanne was interned until she gave birth to her baby, so that both she and the infant Jacqueline could be deported, on Convoy 57, 18 July 1943. And the others? All were deported with their babies. Like the graves of soldiers 'Known but to God', all these ciphers have a haunting quality which is different from that of the identified images, or of historical photograph albums in which no one is identified or in which identity is not so central a theme.

The rhetorical force of the book arises from the subtle interplay of the memorial and the mundanely historical within and between its main elements: the list, the chronology, the photograph. It belies the view that the Altagsgeschichte, the 'history of the everyday', renders the Holocaust banal, for its victims, or indeed for its perpetrators. For Klarsfeld, God resides in the quotidian detail.

The List

Any list is a work of extreme artifice. Names, dates, things are not arranged thus in nature. However natural a list might seem, it incorporates an enormous amount of work and judgment and makes enormous claims on those who confront it. It is as much a work of art as any stone monument. It is both an agent itself and an object of regard. Klarsfeld's list of deportations delimits a domain of what or whom precisely is to be remembered. The Nazis hoped to forget the whole murderous thing. Himmler told his generals in 1942 that their work in ridding Europe of Jews was particularly glorious not only because of their discipline in the face of the discouraging popular view that there might actually be a 'good Jew' but because the story of their glorious deeds would go untold. No accounts were kept of those gassed on arrival at Auschwitz nor, incidentally, of the more than half a million or so who were murdered, more or less face to face, on the Eastern Front in 1941. Klarsfeld's list thus makes manifest to our regard one sub-group of those whom the Nazis would have had us forget – and whose oblivion the passage of time threatens to achieve.

The list also orders and delimits the domain of the dead in a very particular way: as Jews. This is no small matter in France, where there had been a tendency to conflate racial deportees with the 100,000 French men and women, including Jews, who died as political deportees – mostly Communists – or as forced labour in Germany, or with the roughly comparable number who were killed in the Resistance, executed, or victims of Nazi atrocities. (The national monument on the Ile de la Cité behind Notre Dame is 'to the deported' without further specification.) In other words, Klarsfeld's work demands that a sort of universalist memory of the 'deported' be refined; when first published it had, as he puts it, 'a profound impact' on both Jews and non-Jews, neither of whom had come to grips with the defining quality of this Nazi crime.

At the same time, his efforts show, perhaps inadvertently, how difficult it is to fashion a list which signifies precisely as intended. He includes among the photographs of deported children pictures of young Jewish men killed in the Resistance – 'mort pour la France' rather than 'dead because they were Jewish', by one of the ever-shifting bureaucratic definitions of what 'Jew' meant. Reprinted letters show that some of these dead thought of themselves, in the particular circumstances of their deaths, not primarily as Jews but as French. And even if it is admitted, as it manifestly must be, that Jews were deported qua Jews, the French defence has been that the Vichy regime cunningly saved the second highest percentage of Jews in Occupied Europe – Denmark came first – by making what it claimed to be the necessary, if unfortunate, sacrifice of the foreign-born to save citizens.

Klarsfeld does not enter into this debate directly but his list, with its many sub-lists, does constitute a community of the dead whose defining characteristic is their 'race'. (There are also lists of the saved, the not dead: 252 Jewish children from OSE homes who were sent to the United States in 1941-42 – OSE was the Oeuvre de Secours aux Enfants, the Jewish Children's Welfare Agency.) Even without anything being said about the negotiations in which French officials co-operated with the Germans in ridding France of its Jews, or any reference being made to the extraordinary cosmopolitan quality of the French Jewish community evident in the deportation lists, other sub-lists speak to the point. There were 42 children bound for arrest and Auschwitz on Klaus Barbie's manifest of those arrested at the children's refuge in the village of Izieu; one, who turned out to be Christian, was taken off and released to the custody of an aunt. A quick scan of the list of children in Convoy 36, for example, to ascertain their birthplaces reveals the following: Paris, Luneville, Paris, Paris, Strasbourg, Strasbourg, Angers, Paris, Tours, Paris, Strasbourg, Metz . . . Not counting the first – listed only as 'un enfant' with no surname or other particulars – we are 15 children down the list before we encounter a foreign birthplace; and eight more before the next.

Once named, the members of this reconstituted community of the dead can be commemorated and memorialised as well as historicised as a community of another kind. The children of this community are present to our memory in this book; the community as a whole is reconstituted in the larger book from which the children's list is derived and on the walls of a monument at Roglit in Israel, the largest assemblage of names on any memorial in the world. Names can be read and the duration of the reading measured as a sign of the magnitude of loss. The practice of reading names from monuments is, of course, not limited to the Holocaust. The names from the Vietnam Memorial, for example, are read once a year and the exact time taken is reported in the press. At 32 names per minute – the rate at which I pronounced the names of the children deported from France – it would take five hours and 56 minutes to read them all aloud. In short, the mathematical sublime can be imagined as space, as a wall filled with letters, or as time filled with the sound of voices intoning names.

The list in this particular case also bears a set of complex metonymic relationships to the thing being commemorated. It is disconcerting that the form of commemoration is to a large extent determined by the fact that Klarsfeld's categories are perforce Nazi categories, since his sources are the lists of various sorts which they used to identify, classify, locate, arrest, deport, and ultimately kill Jews. Klarsfeld's memorial practice follows the paper trail of criminals. Paper was murderous. In the first place there are lists of who is to be arrested; there were adjustments to these lists. Klarsfeld reproduces two registration cards from the Drancy camp. René Lévy, born in France on 27 May 1934, arrested as part of the 'Allg. Massnahmen gegen Juden' ('general measures against Jews') is released despite both his grandparents being Jewish, because his mother was an Aryan. His card is marked, in pencil, 'Libéré'. Ten-month-old Arlette Chabbat's card, on the other hand, is marked 'Evakuiert, 20 Mai 1944'. She, too, had two Jewish grandparents but her mother was Jewish. She got onto another list – that for Convoy 74, Drancy to Auschwitz. There were 16 sub-lists for Convoy 36 and it is a testimony to the energy, labour and intelligence of Klarsfeld and his co-workers that they were able to reconstruct so much of the bureaucratic skein of lists upon lists: four names from Besançon; 53 from Clairvaux without date of birth or nationality; 135 names sent from the camp of Lalande to Drancy, many children without parents. There are 51 last-minute additions on a sub-list to Convoy 26, mostly people wanting to leave with members of their families but also one child listed as 'a boy of three' and another as 'a little girl wearing placard #36'. No effort is spared to make these lists monuments to the actual victims. Bernard Dziubas, pictured in a dark woollen jump suit and wearing knee socks, a great mess of dark locks surrounding his face, was known to have been deported at the age of five but Klarsfeld was not able to find his convoy number. By imagining a phonetic version of his name as a five-year-old might pronounce it – Jubes, Bernard – he was able to determine that Dziubas, Bernard left for Auschwitz on Convoy 49, 2 March 1943.

Klarsfeld's lists also make it possible to imagine the micro-geographies of mass murder. I am reminded here of the French conceptual artist Christian Boltanski's Berlin installation, *The Missing House*. On the walls bearing the outlines of floors and rooms either side of the gap between two buildings where a third had been bombed out and not replaced, he erected plaques marking the names, occupations and dates of death of the former occupants of these ghostly spaces. A group of students discovered that 20 of these former inhabitants were Jews murdered by the Nazis; the material they unearthed was displayed in glass cases in an open-air museum that occupied the grounds of a bombed-out museum. The documentation is also in a book, *La Maison manquante*. Klarsfeld's list suggests a similar gesture, although to call it conceptual art would be untrue to its creator, if not to its effect. In window after window in the Marais and other heavily Jewish sections of Paris, one sees, in the weeks either side of 16-17 July, hand-lettered signs letting passers-by know that in 1942, at some very early hour in the morning, this or that Jewish family – father, mother, young children – were taken by French police from this precise address, across this bit of pavement on which the passer-by stands, to the Vel d'Hiv, the winter bicycle stadium, and from there deported.

Klarsfeld offers the means to imagine, with stairway-by-stairway, convoy-by-convoy, car-by-car precision, the spaces in and through which the Jews of France were destroyed. In Stairway Nine at the transit camp at Drancy were 64 people, all adolescents and young children, whose names we know, slated for Convoy 27 which left for Auschwitz on 2 September 1942; Car Seven of Convoy 24 held one man and 33 children; Car Eight, 40 children and seven adults including Ita Epelbaum, aged 31, and her seven children, aged 11, nine, seven, six-year-old twins, Henri, five, and Arlette, three. Many of the children in this convoy had already been through various other camps en route to this, their final, French stop before their departure on 26 August 1942 to Auschwitz (937/1002 gassed on arrival).

The Chronology

Klarsfeld's chronologies, too, memorialise in the manner of the lists, by delimiting the community of the dead whom we remember and representing their fate. The 'Children of the Holocaust' are thus revealed as a special object of memory not only because of their innocence – they are of course innocent, but no more or less innocent than their parents or grandparents – but because they were singled out. Klarsfeld forces us to recognise that children were murdered on the basis of their being children and precisely, meeting by meeting and census by census, how this was accomplished – and that they constituted a bureaucratic category which caused particular bureaucratic difficulties and offered particular bureaucratic opportunities. The French were dismayed by the indifference of the Germans to the 4115 children caught in the big 16-17 July round-up and wanted to avoid having to deal with the special problems children, especially the very young ones, presented: who was to take care of them; once separated from their parents, how would it look to have to deport them on their own later on? Moreover, they wanted the Germans to count children towards the deportation quota so as to postpone another big round-up on the heels of the first, which had yielded disappointing numbers. (Neither Pierre Laval nor his police chief, René Bousquet, had a record of anti-semitism; Bousquet told the imprisoned former prime minister Edouard Daladier that he and Laval hoped that by appearing keen on deporting Jewish children, the French would gain some advantage in future negotiations with the Germans on other matters, even if their new masters were at first reluctant to take them.)

The Photographs

Old photographs almost demand that we see them as memorials; by their nature they bear witness to their subject's irrefutable existence in the past, to the death of an instant – a second or two in the 19th century, 1/100th of a second or less by the 1930s – which is frozen through the chemistry of light on some sort of emulsion and preserved on glass, metal or paper. Then suddenly this thing of the past is brought into the present, like the image of a star whose light, we know, has travelled for years to reach us. Living as we have for so long with a superabundance of photographic images, the terrible magic of the art is not as apparent as it was. It is nevertheless magic. Nadar, the great mid-19th-century French pioneer of photography, looking back in 1900, thought that it was far more disturbing, far more astonishing than the other momentous discoveries of his century – the steam engine, electric light, the telephone. In its sheer 'peculiarity' the photograph surpassed these and more wonders. It 'endowed man', he thought, 'with the divine power of creation: the power to give physical form to the insubstantial image that vanishes as soon as it is perceived'. It captures 'the ripple on the surface of the water', the moments that in their succession make up a life. Maurice-Mandrel Mildiner will always look out at us, on his bar mitzvah day, wrapped in his talis. He was deported to his death nine months later on Convoy 24.

Perhaps all photographs – but certainly these ones – subsist in the present perfect conditional. History on whatever scale is written in the past tense or the historical present. Liki Bornsztajn was born on 27 August 1927 in Nancy, had taken refuge in the département of Vienne in Central France, lived in a Jewish social services home for children in rue Vauquelin, and was arrested there and deported on Convoy 77, which carried her and 326 other children to Auschwitz on 31 July 1944; 726 out of the 1300 men, women and children on this particular convoy were gassed on arrival at Auschwitz. All this is in the past indicative. On 16-17 July 1942: 'The Vel d'Hiv round-up begins as planned before dawn, at 4 a.m.' Historical present.

But Liki's picture exists in another tense: she 'would soon have been 17', the caption tells us. Her half-brother Wolf, born on 21 October 1933, also in Nancy, is shown as a two-year-old, very much the child of another age; his shoes could be hand-me-downs; his tunic dates from the 1920s. He would be three, and four, five and so on in the present conditional until 31 July 1944, when he would have been 11 on his next birthday. The Wolf we see is of course not the Wolf who was deported and, indeed, the world he came into was not the world which would destroy him.

The baby girl Myriam Piper, whom we see in 1928 or 1929, stark naked, her face peering just a bit to her right in this, the only surviving picture of her, is not the 15-year-old who was deported with her mother on 19 August 1942. Hitler was not in power; France still welcomed immigrants. This mixing up of time, this invitation to project what we know will happen, is irresistible. Michael André Bernstein in his *Foregone Conclusions: Against Apocalyptic History* (1994) warns convincingly against backshadowing, against the tendency to narrate the Shoah as if it were a tragedy in which the protagonist's fate were sealed by his very nature. The Nazi murders are not immanent in all Jewish history and it would be wrong both morally and as a matter of historical practice to rob this past of its contingency. The Jews of Europe lived, as we do, without foreknowledge.

Klarsfeld is careful not to read what he knows into the past; his narratives emphasise historical contingency at every level, from that of officials who might have acted differently to the small happenstances that permitted some people to escape near-certain arrest and deportation. He does not pretend that these pictures were made to preserve a world which was soon to be lost or even that they are collected here to resurrect that world. They were made for every conceivable reason that one might make a photograph; they give a sort of spectral flesh to the specific name. This memorial thus has none of the mood of claustrophobic elegy which suffuses Roman Vishniac's *A Vanished World*. That collection of stunningly beautiful photographs of traditional Eastern European Jewish life can only be seen now in the terms set by the photographer. He tells us that, living in Germany in the 1930s, he knew 'Hitler had made it his mission to exterminate all Jews,' and that being unable to save his people, he set out to save their memory. Using a hidden camera – most Orthodox Jews thought that photography violated the Second Commandment – he took 16,000 pictures. All but 2000 were confiscated. Here Klarsfeld's and Vishniac's projects converge: the latter's father 'remained in hiding in Clermont-Ferrand . . . during the entire war in order to save my precious negatives'. Vishniac's is a world preserved against great adversity. Klarsfeld's remembering, however, is not merely elegiac; it has the redemptive force of history as well. By assuaging the anxiety of forgetting, it makes history possible.

However much the historian in me resists the temptation to read Klarsfeld's images proleptically, I succumb, particularly when the baby pictures are not part of an age that would be fading anyhow – pictures that look historical – but ones which might be from my infancy. I begin to measure their subjects against my own life and their death becomes more immediate. Liki's half-brother, Wolf, looks like a baby from my parents' generation, although he was born in 1933, twenty years after my father. Gilbert Glück, born Paris, 19 January 1935, and deported 21 August

1942, Convoy 22 (1000 people, among whom there were 293 boys and 318 girls; 817 of the passengers were gassed on arrival; no females and seven men survived), is pictured holding a large hoop and stick. It is a toy out of a Bruegel painting, the toy my father holds in the picture I have of him at roughly the same age, the timeless sign of the European boy.

The very last photograph in the book is different from these. It shows ten children, all perhaps two years old, the back row standing, the front row sitting on the grass. They are wearing the sort of baggy shorts that served as nappy covers but could also be worn on their own. I recognise them from my baby pictures. The boys all have haircuts of the sort I had. These are my sort of kids, potential school chums, just as many of the older children in the book could well have been Klars-feld's mates. They would now be three years older than I am. In fact, 'I' might have been that old. A few years before my mother died she told me that, despite the fact that she was then 37 and anxious to have a child, she had had an abortion three years before I was born because a German invasion of Turkey, to which my parents had fled, still seemed possible and she did not feel safe having a child in such cir-cumstances. I was conceived in early January 1945, just about the time the news of the failure of Hitler's desperate counter-offensive in the Ardennes would have reached Istanbul. As it turned out, however, the children in the last picture who look like I looked are not three years older than I am. The SS arrested them and their nurses at a UGIF children's refuge in Neuilly and sent them, along with 230 other very young children from similar refuges, to Auschwitz on 31 July 1944 – Convoy 77, the last regular full shipment – where all of them were immediately gassed.

This dialectic between memory and history drives Klarsfeld's book. On the one hand, it is exactly what it says: 'A Memorial'. On the other, it is a vertiginous *mise en abyme* of memory. Among the photographs hundreds are pictures of pictures on tombstones. Some are not unlike those that abound in Mediterranean cemeteries, although the sort of family groupings one finds here – a father in a fine business suit fills the frame of the studio portrait with his children, both deported, in the lower right third – are relatively rare. Some are reproductions of broken images – Albert Szpidbaum's face is almost completely gone, unlike the luminous face of his younger sister Monique, which is intact; both deported on Convoy 67, 3 February 1944 – as if to announce some eternal truth about the transience of all things, including memory.

Many close-up reproductions have the vitreous overlay of tomb pictures that produces a ghostly haze through which the faces seem to shine. Cracks in the surface give these extreme close-ups the quality of old masters. Scores of pictures are embedded in what look like photographic albums covering what we know to be an empty grave in a cemetery. Suzanne Kappe, born in Paris in 1931 and deported with her older sister and mother on Convoy 24, 23 August 1942, looks out at us from the oval cut-out with slightly embossed borders that determined the placements of pictures. Her mother and sister fill the other slots. The album is in white marble and it sits on a black polished slab on which we can just see, at the very bottom of the image, four stones, two black and two white, which are put on Jewish graves by visitors. The legend in black reads: 'Mortes en déportation'. Each page threatens to sweep the reader into the abyss. Henri Flamenbaum, not quite five, dressed in a double-breasted suit, arm on pedestal, hand in jacket pocket – the pose of the 19th-century statesman – looking out at us and the camera with the apprehensive smile of a little boy who wants to please in unfamiliar circumstances. (We know his age because a legend in cursive hand across the top of the picture identifies it as taken on 24.1.42 and the caption gives his date of birth.) This rectangular photograph of a photograph is positioned on the page to cut at a right angle into a stone representation of an Edwardian photo album, one in which some paper-lace work – a rose in this case – pops out as the book is opened. Here the head from the lower portrait appears again – picture upon picture upon picture – in a framed oval below others which contain images of the faces of his two sisters, almost grown-up, and their mother. On the right of the book a note in French reads: 'To my dear wife and children whose death broke my heart which ever bleeds and weeps and which will never forget their woe. Died during the deportation to Auschwitz.' (They were on Convoy 20, Drancy to Auschwitz, 17 August 1942, 878 of whose 1000 deportees were gassed on arrival. No women survived.) Behind this album we can just glimpse another that lies open on the same black slab; the word 'Déportés' is just visible; the name P . . . OFF is obscured by the rose.

   In the final analysis it is the pain which some small detail of each photograph elicits – what Barthes called its 'punctum', its barb, its capacity to pierce – that makes this book 'memorial'. Images of the dead wound the hearts of the living. The abyss – the superabundance of particularities is endless, each disturbing in its fashion: the boys and girls holding toys, sometimes absorbed in them like seven-year-old Jeanine Gotteiner who carries a stiff creature almost her own size and plays with the ribbon around its neck; sometimes bearing them less personally as signs of child-hood that bridge the unnatural milieu of the studio and the world of the nursery; the twins Claude and Guy Gotteiner absorbed as naked infants in the rug whose soft hairs are visible against the shadows of their bodies; the fingers of Stella Radomysler's hand peeping from between her father's thumb and index finger as they walk down the street, two years before their deportation to Auschwitz, he in a three-piece suit, she in a white dress trimmed with fur and a hat with pompoms;

the shaving-brush wielded on the smiling, lathered face of his father by a laughing three-year-old Jean-Pierre Guckenheimer; two five-pointed stars cut in the wooden doors of a garage – meaningless decoration – that contrast so poignantly with the six-pointed badge worn by a resolute-looking man sitting for this picture with his wife and three daughters (Andrée Marie, aged 14, survived from this group: the hour on the watch pinned to her dress, 1.20). There are stereotypically happy pictures of the age, scores of girls in Shirley Temple poses; stereotypically serious poses – boys and girls with violins or books whose titles are just visible (*Contes de . . .*). There are pictures that pierce in other ways: a little girl with a bare chest, a heart-locket around her neck; a bracelet barely visible on her wrist; she is looking straight at the camera – at us – her arms folded below her exposed nipples; long blonde hair. On the facing page she is dressed in a smock and standing next to her naked doll, which lies on the table. The first of these pictures was used for a poster advertising an exhibition about the Loiret Internment Camp. Innocence protests too much, as if the innocence of every man, woman and child in this book were not as great.

In the end we are rescued by history. The power, beauty and moral authority of the book derive from its being anchored by Klarsfeld's two monumental earlier works, by the array of micro-histories which inform every page and by the historicity of the photographs themselves. It is history modelled on legal processes, forensic history: someone did something to someone at this or that place with this or that intention and caused this or that harm. It is a history of tight causal connections, a history which keeps careful track of each piece of evidence, history as detection. Klarsfeld, of course, is a prosecutor, among other roles. In 1987 he acted on behalf of the Association of Sons and Daughters of Jews deported from France, as the 'avocat de parties civiles', one of the private prosecutors for the civil plaintiffs, against Klaus Barbie for the murder of 41 Jewish children taken at his orders from a farmhouse in the village of Izieu on 6 April 1944. (The plaintiffs were relatives of these children.) He does not spend much energy on questions that have exercised Holocaust historiography: whether it is 'representable', whether the destruction of European Jews is inherent in the history of Western anti-semitism or that of a particularly vehement German anti-semitism, whether it was a largely opportunistic response to the possibility of factually murdering large numbers of Jews or a fully planned and organised conspiracy with deep roots in the past, as the Nuremberg prosecutors argued. He and his wife Beate are involved in a similar process to that of the truth commissions which have recorded the crimes of the regimes of Argentina, Chile and apartheid South Africa: one of making certain what happened so that it can be allowed to become history; remembered, to be sure, but past. A leaf is turned as the truth is established.

The photographs at the heart of this memorial book are also crucial to it as a piece of history. As remains, they are, in the first place, evidence of murder. At Beate Klarsfeld's urging, and with her help, Fortunée Massaouda sat with an enlargement of the only picture she had of her three children – Jacques, 13, Richard, six, Jean-Claude, five – in front of the office of the German prosecutor bearing a sign which read: 'I am on a hunger strike as long as the investigation of Klaus Barbie who murdered my children remains closed.' This story of political action is not in the book under review. Here we have only the picture of the three boys, all with dark, deep-set eyes, delicate lips. The oldest boy whose last Mother's Day letter to Fortunée is reprinted, rests his hand on his little brother's shoulders (Fortunée survived Auschwitz). Jacques wears short trousers held in place with a belt and lace-up shoes. Richard's shorts are held high by cloth suspenders; he wears androgynous shoes with buckles. The youngest brother is in a knitted shirt and toddler pants. They stand in front of a ludicrously picturesque studio background. Victims of murder.

They are also clues to the narrative form in which to write the history – tragic irony – although Klarsfeld does not make this explicit. The hundreds of identity cards with JUIF stamped across them signal the betrayal of the Revolutionary tradition to which the Jews of France were so passionately committed. In 1860 a group of French Jews issued a manifesto to the Jews of more benighted lands, an invitation to subscribe to the universalist principles they believed so fervently that France embodied, and urging them to join the Universal Israelite Alliance in spreading the French language and French values to Jews everywhere. As it happened, the identity card which was created during the Revolution as a certificate of membership in the new political community, a sign of friend against foe, became after 1940 an instrument of exclusion and ultimately murder. Klarsfeld restores it to its original purpose and reincorporates its Jewish bearers into the community which had rejected them.

If the photographs and names are signs of the dead, the list and the chronology explain how they came to be that way. Consider the Izieu raid. We know that the OSE at the end of 1943 and early in 1944 had already dispersed children in other homes to safe havens throughout rural southern France. Izieu was uniquely vulnerable. We also know that the Vichy authorities had by the time of the anti-Jewish raids in Bordeaux on 10 January 1944 given up any pretence of protecting French Jews – foreign ones had long since been written off. It had already happened elsewhere. Laval had sanctioned the raids, over the initial objections of his regional prefect. The stage was thus set. On page 87 we have a copy of the telex in which Barbie announces to his bosses in Paris what he has achieved. (Every shipment was accompanied by a telex announcing that such and such a number of Jews were en route from A to B.) I translate from the German retaining as much as possible its telegraphic style:

6.4.44 2010 Subject: Jewish Children's Home in Izieu. In today's morning hours the 'Jewish Children's Home', 'Children's colony' was cleaned out. [The verb is *ausheben* and perhaps the better translation is 'robbed', as of eggs from a nest.] A total of 41 children aged three to 13 years were taken into custody. Further success in securing the entire Jewish staff consisting of ten heads, of which five are women. Cash and other valuables could not be secured.

Klarsfeld juxtaposes this with another micro-history of the same event. Many of the children had already been arrested with their parents and been freed into the custody of the OSE. We know from other sources that they were having a breakfast of hot chocolate and bread when the SS came and threw them 'like parcels' into the trucks. He reprints letters from some of the children to their parents as captions to their pictures. Henri Goldberg, aged 14, to his mother: 'I'm going to study hard to make you happy . . . and the headmistress and our teachers happy, and myself too, so that after the war you'll find us intelligent and not consider us [him and his brother Joseph] dunces.' The picture shows him, his brother, three unidentified children and an adult – perhaps the farmer for whom he worked occasionally – looking at a sketchpad.

Klarsfeld tells us precisely and in mundane detail what happened at each small step of the French Holocaust. On 9 February police acquire lists of children in the Rothschild Foundation; at 6.30 in the morning on 10 February five inspectors break into a dormitory, wake 12 children and take them away; at one in the morning on 11 February they come to take away four girls aged 15 and 16. But the coolness of this account modulates when we turn the page and see a picture of 19 children with pillow-cases containing belongings on their backs leaving an orphanage in secret on their way to refuge with non-Jewish families. Klarsfeld's point in this juxtaposition is not to redeem one history, or way of recounting a history, with another, happier one. The picture of the children saved and the snippet of a chronology of murder are both aides-mémoire. But the brilliance of this memorial doesn't have to do with the effort to erect a barrier against amnesia or denial – nor is the book a plea for justice, despite the role Klarsfeld has played in bringing war criminals before the law – but with its insistence that private memories and a nearly bottomless record of evil become part of the public record. It is precisely by remembering in public that the past can become past – and that memory becomes survivable by entering history.

5 *June 1997*

AT THE NATIONAL GALLERY

Peter Campbell

THREE MASTERS – Carel Fabritius, Pieter de Hooch and Johannes Vermeer – dominate the exhibition *Vermeer and the Delft School*, at the National Gallery until 16 September. It shows painting done in the town during the first 75 years of the 17th century. Of the three masters Fabritius is the least Delft-like. His subject-matter is not domestic, predictable or repetitious – and that of most of the Delft painters, even the very good ones, is one or all of those things. He matured quickly – we wouldn't be able to rate him so highly if he had not, for he died at the age of 32 when the city gunpowder magazine blew up. (The ruins are recorded in a very neat painting by van der Poel.)

A substantial proportion of the dozen or so pictures safely attributed to Fabritius are on show here: two self-portraits, *The Goldfinch* from the Mauritshuis, a sleeping sentry and the National Gallery's own perspective peepshow. The finish of his pictures (also unlike Delft) is painterly, not smooth. In the goldfinch you can count the strokes – one for each wing feather, one for the patch of red around the beak and so on. They achieve a lively verisimilitude with wonderful directness and economy. You have a strong feeling that Fabritius was clever, curious and interested in experiments – he was the best of Rembrandt's pupils, and the one who was most clearly emerging from his master's shadow. Literally so, for seen alongside Rembrandt's portraits, his, with their pale backgrounds, suggest that a window has been opened somewhere. Light is the thing that links him with de Hooch and Vermeer and with other Delft painters who seem intellectually much less ambitious. He seems to look outward; they look inward. Yet looking inward can also be a strength, as it is in the calm, fastidious, self-abnegating intensity of the two kinds of inwardness which characterise de Hooch and Vermeer. The simple, physical looking-in at still interiors, little courtyards and small houses, at bare rooms and their self-possessed inhabitants, is the vehicle for another kind of inwardness, a quietness mirrored in these unemphatic accounts of things as they are. The character of this double quietness – quietness of subject and of style – is more mysterious in the case of Vermeer. De Hooch, like the greatest still-life painters, shows in his domestic interiors that the simpler the raw materials are (one hare, not a pile of game, three plums, not a cornucopia spilling fruit), the more likely it is that you will get a sense of the solemn actuality of the physical world. But in his case little clumsinesses of drawing and perspective and variations in finish from one part of the picture to another allow us to track the struggle of imperfect human abilities in their attempt to find a match for the look of things. His tonal judgment is wonderful. There are passages, in particular those which show transitions from one kind of light to another (for example, from a brighter to a dimmer room, or from the light in a courtyard in, it seems, late afternoon, to a patch of pale sky above a wall where the day fades), which are more ambitious and poignant than the uncomplicated perfection of the light in Vermeer's cool interiors.

In Vermeer you find none of de Hooch's provincial infelicities of drawing. But both began by making pictures of something different. De Hooch did low lifes (albeit rather polite ones) – soldiers drinking and chatting up servant girls – and Vermeer religious and historical subjects. In the earliest picture by Vermeer in the exhibition, *Christ in the House of Mary and Martha*, his assurance is already formidable. In *The Procuress* you begin to see the anonymity of surface, the determinedly uncalligraphic brush strokes, the dispassionate attention which gives every part of the canvas the same look. One effect of this is to make those parts the eye scans first – faces and hands in particular – seem a little out of focus: you expect more detail. In the later pictures the surface is so uninflected and the composition so still that they seem – even when you look back to *Christ in the House of Mary and Martha*, not a roistering picture in any sense – to be evidence of an abnegation of invention (no more complicatedly overlapping bodies, no kneeling and turning) and of pleasure in paint (no more expressive brush marks like those shaping the drapery). The change has a quasi-moral force – as though impressing your personality on the stuff you use to represent the world were sacrilegious.

But the change may in fact have been due to Vermeer starting to use an optical device – a camera obscura perhaps. To my eye a picture like *The Art of Painting* is as good evidence that he did so as anything short of documentary proof could be. The spread-out points of brightness are like unfocused highlights on a camera's ground-glass screen, and the perfectly controlled perspectives seem to be observed, as they would be in a projected image, rather than calculated. Optical transcription of a more or less mechanical sort would also explain the pervading calmness.

In some of de Hooch's pictures, awkwardness subtracts from the enveloping calm. Vermeer's figures cause no tremor of that kind – for good or for ill. You sense that the pose needs no interpretation or apology and makes no positive demands on your kinetic imagination either. But the physical ease in these images is not just a matter of optical precision. Vermeer's pictures have an extreme abstract formality which brings to mind the intervals in a composition by Mondrian – except things are more complicated in Vermeer because the space in which they operate is extended, by chequered floors and the edges of pieces of furniture, into the third dimension. You see why people trace vanishing points and construct little models to prove that they are indeed perfect representations of possible spaces. They suggest the possibility of a kind of order which is both human and in the real world, and, at the same time, almost mathematical or musical in the way it resolves complexity.

The picture by Vermeer which is least quiet here – and thus least pleasing to modern taste – is *Allegory of the Faith*. His contemporaries seem to have valued it highly, but now the figure of Faith, hand on heart and eyes on heaven, sitting in front of an image of the crucifixion, is too much a piece of play-acting – and one made slightly absurd by the solid presence of the surrounding room and props. The picture we are most fortunate to see, *The Art of Painting* from Vienna, causes no such embarrassment. The girl dressed up as Clio is clearly an artist's model, and the fancy-dress worn by the painter just a game. This is a painting about painting. We are in tune with that now – perhaps to the exclusion of too much else.

How far did Delft itself influence the work its painters produced? An essay by Walter Liedtke in the catalogue characterises the town and its life in ways which seem significant. Its population fluctuated, but did not increase dramatically, as Amsterdam's did. It was close to other towns where pictures might be seen. There were fairs every year where paintings could be bought, but the local artists' guild protected the rights of native producers.

And there are the buildings themselves. Delft had no Saenredam to make transcendent perspectives of ecclesiastical architecture, but the church interiors here by Gerard Houckgeest, Hendrick van Vliet and Emanuel de Witte are splendid, if sometimes flashy, exercises in painted perspective. Where Vermeer and de Hooch make ordinary rooms solemn, the church painters made ecclesiastical ones lively with dogs, children drawing on the floor or the columns, and figures who, even when they are listening to a sermon, have none of the gravitas Vermeer could give a milkmaid.

All the pictures here are commodities, shaped by markets and fashion. It might seem that compared with the opportunity to make whole walls alive with religious stories, or to give form to dynastic power in portraits, supplying portable wall decorations and collectibles of this sort was a limiting task. In fact it appears to have made possible, almost accidentally, an art of pure painting. While Vermeer may have been read by his contemporaries as a moralist (what we think of as a sleeping woman was seen as a warning against drunkenness, while the woman with the scales may have been thought of as an admonition to live a balanced life), we turn to them – rightly or wrongly – for the more abstract virtue which resides not in the thing shown but in the decorum and precision of the act of representation.

5 July 2001

THE PUSH FOR WAR

Anatol Lieven

THE MOST SURPRISING THING about the Bush administration's plan to invade Iraq is not that it is destructive of international order; or wicked, when we consider the role the US (and Britain) have played, and continue to play, in the Middle East; or opposed by the great majority of the international community; or seemingly contrary to some of the basic needs of the war against terrorism. It is all of these things, but they are of no great concern to the hardline nationalists in the administration. This group has suffered at least a temporary check as a result of the British insistence on UN involvement, and Saddam Hussein's agreement to weapons inspections. They are, however, still determined on war – and their power within the administration and in the US security policy world means that they are very likely to get their way. Even the *Washington Post* has joined the radical rightist media in supporting war.

The most surprising thing about the push for war is that it is so profoundly reckless. If I had to put money on it, I'd say that the odds on quick success in destroying the Iraqi regime may be as high as 5/1 or more, given US military superiority, the vile nature of Saddam Hussein's rule, the unreliability of Baghdad's missiles, and the deep divisions in the Arab world. But at first sight, the longer-term gains for the US look pretty limited, whereas the consequences of failure would be catastrophic. A general Middle Eastern conflagration and the collapse of more pro-Western Arab states would lose us the war against terrorism, doom untold thousands of Western civilians to death in coming decades, and plunge the world economy into depression.

These risks are not only to American (and British) lives and interests, but to the political future of the administration. If the war goes badly wrong, it will be more generally excoriated than any within living memory, and its members will be finished politically – finished for good. If no other fear moved these people, you'd have thought this one would.

This war plan is not like the intervention in Vietnam, which at the start was supported by a consensus of both political parties, the Pentagon, the security establishment and the media. It is true that today – for reasons to which I shall return – the Democrats are mostly sitting on the fence; but a large part of the old Republican security establishment has denounced the idea and the Pentagon has made its deep unhappiness very clear.

The administration has therefore been warned of the dangers. And while a new attack by al-Qaida during the war would help consolidate anti-Muslim American nationalism, the administration would also be widely accused of having neglected the hunt for the perpetrators of 11 September in order to pursue an irrelevant vendetta. As far as the Israeli lobby is concerned, a disaster in the Middle East might be the one thing that would at last bring a discussion of its calamitous role into the open in the US.

With the exception of Donald Rumsfeld, who conveniently did his military service in the gap between the Korean and Vietnam Wars, neither Bush nor any of the other prime movers of this war served in the military. Of course, General Colin Powell served in Vietnam, but he is well known to be extremely dubious about attacking Iraq. All the others did everything possible to avoid service. If the war goes wrong, the 'chicken hawk' charge will be used against them with devastating political effect.

Vietnam veterans, both Democrat and Republican, have already started to raise this issue, stirred up in part by the insulting language used by Richard Perle and his school about the caution of the professional military. As a recent letter to the *Washington Post* put it, 'the men described as chicken hawks avoided military service during the Vietnam War while supporting that war politically. They are not accused of lacking experience and judgment compared to military men. They are accused of hypocrisy and cowardice.' Given the political risks of failure – to themselves, above all – why are they doing this? And, more broadly, what has bred this reckless spirit?

To understand the administration's motivation, it is necessary to appreciate the breathtaking scope of the domestic and global ambitions which the dominant neo-conservative nationalists hope to further by means of war, and which go way beyond their publicly stated goals. There are of course different groups within this camp: some are more favourable to Israel, others less hostile to China; not all would support the most radical aspects of the programme. However, the basic and generally agreed plan is unilateral world domination through absolute military superiority, and this has been consistently advocated and worked on by the group of intellectuals close to Dick Cheney and Richard Perle since the collapse of the Soviet Union in the early 1990s.

This basic goal is shared by Colin Powell and the rest of the security establishment. It was, after all, Powell who, as chairman of the Joint Chiefs of Staff, declared in 1992 that the US requires sufficient power 'to deter any challenger from ever dreaming of challenging us on the world stage'. However, the idea of pre-emptive defence, now official doctrine, takes this a leap further, much further than Powell would wish to go. In principle, it can be used to justify the destruction of any other state if it even seems that that state might in future be able to challenge the US. When these ideas were first aired by Paul Wolfowitz and others after the end of the Cold War, they met with general criticism, even from conservatives. Today, thanks to the ascendancy of the radical nationalists in the administration and the effect of the 11 September attacks on the American psyche, they have a major influence on US policy.

To understand the genesis of this extraordinary ambition, it is also necessary to grasp the moral, cultural and intellectual world of American nationalism in which it has taken shape. This nationalism existed long before last September, but it has been inflamed by those attacks and, equally dangerously, it has become even more entwined with the nationalism of the Israeli Right.

To take the geopolitical goals first. As with National Missile Defense, the publicly expressed motive for war with Iraq functions mainly as a tool to gain the necessary public support for an operation the real goals of which are far wider. The indifference of the US public to serious discussion of foreign or security affairs, and the negligence and ideological rigidity of the US media and policy community, make searching debate on such issues extremely difficult, and allow such manipulation to succeed.

The immediate goal is indeed to eliminate Iraq's weapons of mass destruction. There is little real fear, however, that Saddam Hussein will give those weapons to terrorists to use against the United States – though a more genuine fear that he might conceivably do so in the case of Israel. Nor is there any serious prospect that he would use them himself in an unprovoked attack on the US or Israel, because immediate annihilation would follow. The banal propaganda portrayal of Saddam as a crazed and suicidal dictator plays well on the American street, but I don't believe that it is a view shared by the administration. Rather, their intention is partly to retain an absolute certainty of being able to defend the Gulf against an Iraqi attack, but, more important, to retain for the US and Israel a free hand for intervention in the Middle East as a whole.

From the point of view of Israel, the Israeli lobby and their representatives in the administration, the apparent benefits of such a free hand are clear enough. For the group around Cheney, the single most important consideration is guaranteed and unrestricted access to cheap oil, controlled as far as possible at its source. To destroy and occupy the existing Iraqi state and dominate the region militarily would remove even the present limited threat from Opec, greatly reduce the chance of a new oil shock, and eliminate the need to woo and invest in Russia as an alternative source of energy.

It would also critically undermine the steps already taken towards the development of alternative sources of energy. So far, these have been pitifully few. All the same, 11 September brought new strength to the security arguments for reducing dependence on imported oil, and as alternative technologies develop, they could become a real threat to the oil lobby – which, like the Israeli lobby, is deeply intertwined with the Bush administration. War with Iraq can therefore be seen as a satisfactory outcome for both lobbies. Much more important for the future of mankind, it is also part of what is in essence a strategy to use American military force to permit the continued offloading onto the rest of the world of the ecological costs of the existing US economy – without the need for any short-term sacrifices on the part of US capitalism, the US political elite or US voters.

The same goes for the war against al-Qaida and its allies: the plan for the destruction of the existing Iraqi regime is related to this struggle, but not as it has been presented publicly. Links between Baghdad and al-Qaida are unproven and inherently improbable: what the administration hopes is that by crushing another middle-sized state at minimal military cost, all the other states in the Muslim world will be terrified into full co-operation in tracking down and handing over suspected terrorists, and into forsaking the Palestinian cause. Iran for its part can either be frightened into abandoning both its nuclear programme and its support for the Palestinians, or see its nuclear facilities destroyed by bombardment.

The idea, in other words, is to scare these states not only into helping with the hunt for al-Qaida, but into capitulating to the US and, more important, Israeli agendas in the Middle East. This was brought out in the notorious paper on Saudi Arabia presented by Laurent Murawiec of the Rand Corporation to Richard Perle's Defense Policy Board. Murawiec advocated sending the Saudis an ultimatum demanding not only that their police force co-operate fully with US authorities, but also the suppression of public criticism of the US and Israel within Saudi Arabia – something that would be impossible for any Arab state. Despite this, the demand for the suppression of anti-Israeli publications, broadcasts and activities has been widely echoed in the US media.

'The road to Middle East peace lies through Baghdad' is a line that's peddled by the Bush administration and the Israeli lobby. It is just possible that some members of the administration really believe that by destroying Israel's most powerful remaining enemy they will gain such credit with Israelis and the Israeli lobby that they will be able to press compromises on Israel.

But this is certainly not what public statements by members of the administration – let alone those of its Likud allies in Israel – suggest. Rumsfeld recently described the Jewish settlements as legitimate products of Israeli military victory;

the Republican majority leader in the House, Dick Armey (a sceptic as regards war with Iraq), has advocated the ethnic cleansing ('transfer') of the Palestinians across the Jordan; and in 1996 Richard Perle and Douglas Feith (now a senior official at the Pentagon) advised Binyamin Netanyahu to abandon the Oslo Peace Process and return to military repression of the Palestinians.

It's far more probable, therefore, that most members of the Bush and Sharon administrations hope that the crushing of Iraq will so demoralise the Palestinians, and so reduce wider Arab support for them, that it will be possible to force them to accept a Bantustan settlement bearing no resemblance to independent statehood and bringing with it no possibility of economic growth and prosperity.

How intelligent men can believe that this will work, given the history of the past fifty years, is astonishing. After all, the Israelis have defeated Arab states five times with no diminution of Palestinian nationalism or Arab sympathy for it. But the dominant groups in the present administrations in both Washington and Jerusalem are 'realists' to the core, which, as so often, means that they take an extremely unreal view of the rest of the world, and are insensitive to the point of autism when it comes to the character and motivations of others. They are obsessed by power, by the division of the world into friends and enemies (and often, into their own country and the rest of the world) and by the belief that any demonstration of 'weakness' immediately leads to more radical approaches by the 'enemy'.

Sharon and his supporters don't doubt that it was the Israeli withdrawal from Lebanon – rather than the Israeli occupation of the Palestinian territories – which led to the latest intifada. The 'offensive realists' in Washington are convinced that it was Reagan's harsh stance and acceleration of the arms race against the Soviet Union which brought about that state's collapse. And both are convinced that the continued existence of Saddam Hussein's regime of itself suggests dangerous US weakness and cowardice, thus emboldening enemies of the US and Israel across the Middle East and beyond.

From the point of view of the Arab-Israeli conflict, war with Iraq also has some of the character of a *Flucht nach vorn* – an 'escape forwards' – on the part of the US administration. On the one hand, it has become clear that the conflict is integrally linked to everything else that happens in the Middle East, and therefore cannot simply be ignored, as the Bush administration tried to do during its first year in office. On the other hand, even those members of the American political elite who have some understanding of the situation and a concern for justice are terrified of confronting Israel and the Israeli lobby in the ways which would be necessary to bring any chance of peace.

When the US demands 'democracy' in the Palestinian territories before it will re-engage in the peace process it is in part, and fairly cynically, trying to get out of this trap. However, when it comes to the new rhetoric of 'democratising' the Arab world as a whole, the agenda is much broader and more worrying; and because the rhetoric is attractive to many liberals we must examine this agenda very carefully.

Belief in the spread of democracy through American power isn't usually consciously insincere. On the contrary, it is inseparable from American national messianism and the wider 'American creed'. However, this same messianism has also proved immensely useful in destroying or crippling rivals of the United States, the Soviet Union being the outstanding example.

The planned war against Iraq is not after all intended only to remove Saddam Hussein, but to destroy the structure of the Sunni-dominated Arab nationalist Iraqi state as it has existed since that country's inception. The 'democracy' which replaces it will presumably resemble that of Afghanistan – a ramshackle coalition of ethnic groups and warlords, utterly dependent on US military power and utterly subservient to US (and Israeli) wishes.

Similarly, if after Saddam's regime is destroyed, Saudi Arabia fails to bow to US wishes and is attacked in its turn, then – to judge by the thoughts circulating in Washington think-tanks – the goal would be not just to remove the Saudi regime and eliminate Wahabism as a state ideology: it would be to destroy and partition the Saudi state. The Gulf oilfields would be put under US military occupation, and the region run by some client emir; Mecca and the Hejaz might well be returned to the Hashemite dynasty of Jordan, its rulers before the conquest by Ibn Saud in 1924; or, to put it differently, the British imperial programme of 1919 would be resurrected (though, if the Hashemites have any sense, they would reject what would without question be a long-term death sentence).

Beyond lies China. When the Bush administration came to power, its major security focus was not the Middle East. There, its initial policy was benign neglect ('benign' at any rate in the case of Israel). The greatest fears of right-wing nationalist gurus such as Robert Kagan concerned the future emergence of China as a superpower rival – fears lent a certain credibility by China's sheer size and the growth of its economy. As declared in the famous strategy document drawn up by Paul Wolfowitz in the last year of the first Bush administration – and effectively proclaimed official policy by Bush Jr in his West Point speech in June – the guiding purpose of US strategy after the end of the Cold War should be to prevent the emergence of any 'peer competitor' anywhere in the world.

What radical US nationalists have in mind is either to 'contain' China by overwhelming military force and the creation of a ring of American allies; or, in the case of the real radicals, to destroy the Chinese Communist state as the Soviet Union was destroyed. As with the Soviet Union, this would presumably involve breaking up China by 'liberating' Tibet and other areas, and under the guise of 'democracy', crippling the central Chinese administration and its capacity to develop either its economy or its army.

To judge by the right-wing nationalist media in the US, this hostility to China has survived 11 September, although in a mitigated form. If the US can demonstrate overwhelming military superiority in the Middle East, there will certainly be groups in the Republican Party who will be emboldened to push for a much tougher line on China. Above all, of course, they support formal independence for Taiwan.

Another US military victory will certainly help to persuade these groups that for the moment the US has nothing to fear from the Chinese navy or air force, and that in the event of a Taiwanese declaration of independence, the island can be defended with relative impunity. Meanwhile, a drastic humiliation of China over Taiwan might well be seen as a key stepping-stone to the overthrow of Communism and the crippling of the Chinese state system.

At present these are only long-term ambitions – or dreams. They are certainly not shared even by a majority of the administration, and are unlikely to be implemented in any systematic way. On the other hand, it's worth bearing in mind that the dominant groups in this administration have now openly abandoned the underlying strategy and philosophy of the Clinton administration, which was to integrate the other major states of the world in a rule-based liberal capitalist order, thereby reducing the threat of rivalry between them.

This tendency is not dead. In fact, it is strongly represented by Colin Powell, and by lesser figures such as Richard Haass. But their more powerful nationalist rivals are in the meantime publicly committed to preventing by every possible means the emergence of any serious rival or combination of rivals to the US, anywhere in the world, and to opposing not just any rival would-be world hegemon, but even the ability of other states to play the role of great power within their own regions.

Under the guise of National Missile Defense, the administration – or elements within it – even dreams of extending US military hegemony beyond the bounds of the Earth itself (an ambition clearly indicated in the official paper on *Defense Planning Guidance for the 2004-09 Fiscal Years*, issued this year by Rumsfeld's office). And while this web of ambition is megalomaniac, it is not simply fantasy. Given America's overwhelming superiority, it might well work for decades until a mixture of terrorism and the unbearable social, political and environmental costs of US economic domination put paid to the present order of the world.

As things stand, the American people would never knowingly support such a programme – nor for that matter would the US military. Even after 11 September, this is not by historical standards a militarist country; and whatever the increasingly open imperialism of the nationalist think-tank class, neither the military nor the mass of the population wishes to see itself as imperialist. The fear of casualties and of long-term overseas military entanglements remains intense. And all opinion polls suggest that the majority of the American public, insofar as it considers these issues at all, is far more interested than this administration in co-operation with allies.

Besides, if the US economy continues to stagnate or falls sharply, the Republicans will most probably not even be in power after 2004. As more companies collapse, the administration's links to corrupt business oligarchies will become more and more controversial. Further economic decline combined with bloated military spending would sooner or later bring on the full consequences of the stripping of the public finances caused by this administration's military spending and its tax cuts for the rich. At that point, the financial basis of Social Security would come into question, and the Republican vote among the 'middle classes' could shatter.

It is only to a minimal degree within the power of any US administration to stimulate economic growth. And even if growth resumes, the transformation of the economy is almost certain to continue. This will mean the incomes of the 'middle classes' (which in American terminology includes the working proletariat) will continue to decline and the gap between them and the plutocracy will continue to increase. High military spending can correct this trend to some extent, but because of the changed nature of weaponry, to a much lesser extent than was the case in the 19th and most of the 20th centuries. All other things being equal, this should result in a considerable shift of the electorate to the left.

But all other things are not equal. Two strategies in particular would give the Republicans the chance not only of winning in 2004, but of repeating Roosevelt's success for the Democrats in the 1930s and becoming the natural party of government for the foreseeable future. The first is the classic modern strategy of an endangered right-wing oligarchy, which is to divert mass discontent into nationalism. The second, which is specifically American, is to take the Jewish vote away from its traditional home in the Democratic Party, by demonstrating categorical Republican commitment not just to Israel's defence but to its regional ambitions.

This is connected both to the rightward shift in Israel, and to the increasingly close links between the Republicans and Likud, through figures like Perle and Feith. It marks a radical change from the old Republican Party of Eisenhower, Nixon and Bush père, which was far more independent of Israel than the Democrats. Of key importance here has been the growing alliance between the Christian

Right – closely linked to the old White South – and the Israeli lobby, or at least its hardline Likud elements.

When this alliance began to take shape some years back, it seemed a most improbable combination. After all, the Christian Right and the White South were once havens of anti-semitic conspiracy theories. On the other hand, the Old Testament aspects of fundamentalist Christianity had created certain sympathies for Judaism and Israel from as far back as the US's 17th-century origins.

For Christian fundamentalists today the influence of millenarian thought is equally important in shaping support for Israel: the existence of the Israeli state is seen as a necessary prelude to the arrival of the Antichrist, the Apocalypse and the rule of Christ and His Saints. But above all, perhaps, this coming together of the fundamentalist Right and hardline Zionism is natural, because they share many hatreds. The Christian Right has always hated the United Nations, partly on straight nationalist grounds, but also because of bizarre fears of world government by the Antichrist. They have hated Europeans on religious grounds as decadent atheists, on class grounds as associates of the hated 'East Coast elites', and on nationalist grounds as critics of unconstrained American power. Both sides share an instinctive love of military force. Both see themselves as historical victims. This may seem strange in the case of the American Rightists, but it isn't if one considers both the White South's history of defeat, and the Christian Right's sense since the 1960s of defeat and embattlement by the forces of irreligion and cultural change.

Finally, and most dangerously, both are conditioned to see themselves as defenders of 'civilisation' against 'savages' – a distinction always perceived on the Christian Right as in the main racially defined. It is no longer possible in America to speak openly in these terms of American blacks, Asians and Latinos – but since 11 September at least, it has been entirely possible to do so about Arabs and Muslims.

Even in the 2000 elections, the Republicans were able to take a large part of the white working-class vote away from Gore by appealing to cultural populism – and especially to those opposed to gun control and environmental protection. Despite the real class identity and cultural interests of the Republican elite, they seem able to convince many workers that they are natural allies against the culturally alien and supercilious 'East Coast elites' represented as supporting Gore.

These populist values are closely linked to the traditional values of hardline nationalism. They are what the historian Walter Russell Mead and others have called 'Jacksonian' values, after President Andrew Jackson's populist nationalism of the 1830s. As Mead has indicated, 11 September has immensely increased the value of this line to Republicans.

If on top of this the Republicans can permanently woo the Jewish vote away from the Democrats – a process which purely class interests would suggest and which has been progressing slowly but steadily since Reagan's day – there is a good chance of their crippling the Democrats for a generation or more. Deprived of much of their financial support and their intellectual backbone, the Democrats could be reduced to a coalition of the declining unionised white working class, blacks and Latinos. And not only do these groups on the whole dislike and distrust each other, but the more the Democrats are seen as minority dominated, the more whites will tend to flee to the Republicans.

Already, the anti-semitism of some black leaders in the Democratic Party has contributed to driving many Jews towards the Republicans; and thanks to their allegiance to Israel, the liberal Jewish intelligentsia have moved a long way from their previous internationalism. This shift is highly visible in previously liberal and relatively internationalist journals such as the New Republic and Atlantic Monthly, and maybe even in the New Yorker. Indeed, it is no exaggeration to say that as a result the internationalist position in the Democratic Party and the US as a whole has been eviscerated.

The Democrats are well aware of this threat to their electorate. The Party as a whole has always been strongly committed to Israel. On Iraq and the war against terrorism, its approach seems to be to avoid at all costs seeming 'unpatriotic'. If they can avoid being hammered by the Republicans on the charge of 'weakness' and lack of patriotism, then they can still hope to win the 2004 elections on the basis of economic discontent. The consequence, however, is that the party has become largely invisible in the debate about Iraq; the Democrats are merely increasing their reputation for passionless feebleness; whereas the Republican nationalists are full of passionate intensity – the passion which in November 2000 helped them pressure the courts over the Florida vote and in effect steal the election.

It is this passion which gives the nationalist Right so much of its strength; and in setting out the hopes and plans of the groupings which dominate the Bush administration, I don't want to give the impression that everything is simply a matter of conscious and cynical manipulation in their own narrow interests. Schematic approaches of this kind have bedevilled all too much of the reporting of nationalism and national conflict. This is odd and depressing, because in recent decades the historiography of pre-1914 German nationalism – to take only one example – has seen an approach based on ideas of class manipulation give way to an infinitely more subtle analysis which emphasises the role of socio-economic and cultural change, unconscious identifications, and interpenetrating political influences from above and below.

To understand the radical nationalist Right in the US, and the dominant forces in the Bush administration, it is necessary first of all to understand their absolute and absolutely sincere identification of themselves with the United States, to the point where the presence of any other group in government is seen as a usurpation, as profoundly and inherently illegitimate and 'un-American'. As far as the hardline elements of the US security establishment and military industrial complex are concerned, they are the product of the Cold War, and were shaped by that struggle and the paranoia and fanaticism it bred. In typical fashion for security elites, they also became conditioned over the decades to see themselves not just as tougher, braver, wiser and more knowledgable than their ignorant, innocent compatriots, but as the only force standing between their country and destruction.

The Cold War led to the creation of governmental, economic and intellectual structures in the US which require for their survival a belief in the existence of powerful national enemies – not just terrorists, but enemy states. As a result, in their analyses and propaganda they instinctively generate the necessary image of an enemy. Once again, however, it would be unwise to see this as a conscious process. For the Cold War also continued, fostered and legitimised a very old discourse of nationalist hatred in the US, ostensibly directed against the Communists and their allies but usually with a very strong colouring of ethnic chauvinism.

On the other hand, the roots of the hysteria of the Right go far beyond nationalism and national security. Their pathological hatred for the Clinton administration cannot adequately be explained in terms of national security or even in rational political or economic terms, for after a very brief period of semi-radicalism (almost entirely limited to the failed attempt at health reform), Clinton devoted himself in a Blairite way to adopting large parts of the Republican socio-economic agenda. Rather, Clinton, his wife, his personal style, his personal background and some of his closest followers were all seen as culturally and therefore nationally alien, mainly because associated with the counter-culture of the 1960s and 1970s.

The modern incarnation of this spirit can indeed be seen above all as a reaction to the double defeat of the Right in the Vietnam War – a defeat which, they may hope, victory in Iraq and a new wave of conservative nationalism at home could cancel out once and for all. In Vietnam, unprecedented military defeat coincided with the appearance of a modern culture which traditionalist Americans found alien, immoral and hateful beyond description. As was widely remarked at the time of Newt Gingrich's attempted 'Republican Revolution' of the mid-1990s, one way of looking at the hardline Republicans – especially from the Religious Right – is to see them as motivated by a classical nationalist desire for a return to a Golden Age, in their case the pre-Vietnam days of the 1950s.

None of these fantasies is characteristic of the American people as a whole. But the intense solipsism of that people, its general ignorance of the world beyond

America's shores, coupled with the effects of 11 September, have left tremendous political spaces in which groups possessed by the fantasies and ambitions sketched out here can seek their objectives. Or to put it another way: the great majority of the American people are not nearly as militarist, imperialist or aggressive as their German equivalents in 1914; but most German people in 1914 would at least have been able to find France on a map.

The younger intelligentsia meanwhile has also been stripped of any real knowledge of the outside world by academic neglect of history and regional studies in favour of disciplines which are often no more than a crass projection of American assumptions and prejudices (Rational Choice Theory is the worst example). This has reduced still further their capacity for serious analysis of their own country and its actions. Together with the defection of its strongest internationalist elements, this leaves the intelligentsia vulnerable to the appeal of nationalist messianism dressed up in the supposedly benevolent clothing of 'democratisation'.

Twice now in the past decade, the overwhelming military and economic dominance of the US has given it the chance to lead the rest of the world by example and consensus. It could have adopted (and to a very limited degree under Clinton did adopt) a strategy in which this dominance would be softened and legitimised by economic and ecological generosity and responsibility, by geopolitical restraint, and by 'a decent respect to the opinion of mankind', as the US Declaration of Independence has it. The first occasion was the collapse of the Soviet superpower enemy and of Communism as an ideology. The second was the threat displayed by al-Qaida. Both chances have been lost – the first in part, the second it seems conclusively. What we see now is the tragedy of a great country, with noble impulses, successful institutions, magnificent historical achievements and immense energies, which has become a menace to itself and to mankind.

3 October 2002

REFLECTIONS ON 9/11

On 16 September 2001 we sent the following note to some thirty or forty of our contributors. Almost all of them responded. Some of their reflections are republished here. 'For the last few days we've followed the coverage of events in New York, and their international repercussions, with a sense that the intensity of the shock and the extent of journalistic spectacle have left little scope for reflection of the kind we try to muster in this paper. We were wondering what our contributors inside and outside the UK thought and if they'd like to say something about what has happened and why.'

MANHATTAN THAT MORNING WAS a diagram, a blue bar-chart with columns which were tall or not so tall. A silver cursor passed across the screen and clicked silently on the tallest column, which turned red and black and presently vanished. This is how we delete you. The cursor returned and clicked on the second column. Presently a thing like a solid grey-white cauliflower rose until it was a mountain covering all south Manhattan. This is how we bury you.

It was the most open atrocity of all time, a simple demonstration written on the sky which everyone in the world was invited to watch. This is how much we hate you.

Six thousand lives: men and women and some children, Americans and foreigners, Christians and Jews and Taoists and Muslims and all those who asked a god to save them in the last minutes. Five thousand was a heavy task for the SS backshift at Auschwitz-Birkenau, in the summer of 1944. Two or possibly three trainloads. But they could process that in an afternoon and evening, if they tried. The difference was that their killing was a secret. People living a few miles away could see tall towers which every few hours gushed flame-red and black. But they were not meant to know why. Once there was a time when the most evil people on earth were ashamed to write their crime across the heavens.

Now, too late, leaders are writing 'Retribution' on the clouds. Nothing good will come of that, and a choking fog of speeches and bulletins will fall between the dead and those who swear they will remember them. Auden wrote once of powers that direct us. He meant blind chance, but the poem also works for powers who wear suits and mount platforms:

It is their tomorrow hangs over the earth of the living.

And all that we wish for our friends; but existence is believing.
We know for whom we mourn and who is grieving.

Neal Ascherson
London

I N A T E L E P H O N E poll last week, readers of the *Cambridge Evening News* voted decisively against any military action aimed at those responsible for the attacks on the USA. A readership better known for its implacable hatred of joyriders on the A14 ('flogging would be too good for them') was having no truck with the cowboy president's plans for battle; still less with Prime Minister Blair's idea of dispatching our few remaining gunboats and jump-jets to cheer him on. This was just one of the domestic surprises that came in the wake of 11 September. Another was Peter Mandelson's strangely off-key suggestion that the secret services should be recruiting in Bradford rather than St James's (apparently on the grounds that immigrants would find it easier than Old Etonians to disguise themselves as Islamic extremists). But almost the oddest response has been our terrified certainty that there remains a plentiful supply of suicide pilots and bombers. Anyone who has scratched the surface of early Christianity will realise that full-blown martyrs are a rare commodity, much more numerous in the imagination than on the ground.

The horror of the tragedy was enormously intensified by the ringside seats we were offered through telephone answering machines and text-messages. But when the shock had faded, more hard-headed reaction set in. This wasn't just the feeling that, however tactfully you dress it up, the United States had it coming. That is, of course, what many people openly or privately think. World bullies, even if their heart is in the right place, will in the end pay the price.

But there is also the feeling that all the 'civilised world' (a phrase which Western leaders seem able to use without a trace of irony) is paying the price for its glib definitions of 'terrorism' and its refusal to listen to what the 'terrorists' have to say. There are very few people on the planet who devise carnage for the sheer hell of it. They do what they do for a cause; because they are at war. We might not like their cause; but using the word 'terrorism' as an alibi for thinking what drives it will get us nowhere in stopping the violence. Similarly, 'fanaticism', a term regularly applied to extraordinary acts of bravery when we abhor their ends and means. The silliest description of the onslaught on the World Trade Center was the often repeated slogan that it was a 'cowardly' attack.

Mary Beard
Cambridge

L AST TUESDAY MORNING, 11 September, I was planning on finishing up an LRB review I was writing – of a book called *The Devil's Cloth: A History of Stripes and Striped Fabric*, by the medievalist Michel Pastoureau. Now, as I stagger numbly round my house in San Francisco, hardly able to read or eat or think, I don't know when I'll get back to it. Too bad, because, in any normal time, the book would be one worth mulling over. Pastoureau argues that over the centuries stripes have gone from being 'bad' to 'good'. In the Middle Ages Western Europeans considered striped fabrics to be diabolical – mainly because they were associated with the infidel Saracens and Turks. When the Carmelites came back from a Crusade in 1254 wearing brown and white striped robes – a funky new fashion picked up in the Ottoman East – they were made to renounce them by papal edict. Medieval laws often required that social outcasts – thieves, traitors, prostitutes, lepers, madmen, hangmen – wear garish striped garments; in illuminated books, Biblical malefactors such as Judas and Cain were regularly depicted in striped robes and breeches. Stripes were for people who were crazy and mean and ugly – people in cahoots with the devil.

But things changed, Pastoureau says, in the 18th century. During the American and French Revolutions – as newly invented national flags like the Stars and Stripes and the Tricolour suggest – stripes came to be associated with life and liberty and the era's emerging egalitarian ideals. Stripes started getting happy and breezy. In the 19th century, with the growth of huge oppressive cities and the spread of industrialism, stripes came to symbolise – even more broadly – cleanliness, nature, physical activity and the open air. By 1900 the devil seemed to have been forgotten: stripes made people feel healthy, free and safe. Today, Pastoureau suggests, we continue to wear 'good' stripes to protect us from bad and frightening things:

> We still wear striped shirts and underwear; we use striped bath and hand towels; we sleep under striped sheets. The canvas on our mattresses has remained striped. Is it going too far to think that those pastel stripes that touch our bodies not only respond to our worries about keeping clean but also play the role of protecting us? Protecting the body against dirt and pollution, against external attacks, but protecting it also from our own desires, from our irresistible appetite for impurity?

Yeah yeah, as they say in New York. It's a week later now and I still can't make up my mind if any of it matters – or will matter for very long. There are stripes everywhere, of course: Old Glory and bunting all over the streets, big sad flags draping down from windows, little bristly plastic ones sticking up from people's car antennas. I live in a gay neighbourhood (near the Castro) and the dykes and queers turn out to be pretty patriotic. (We're all proud of Mark Bingham, the gay rugby player from San Francisco who helped crash Flight 93 into the ground.) Every few hours I talk to my lover Blakey in Chicago. She lives in a big high-rise off Lake Shore Drive – we don't know when we'll see each other again. At night I crawl into bed with my little dog Charlemagne, rescued from the pound just last month, and he burrows down under the sheets to my feet. I feel like an effigy. Sirens go off outside; a lonely plane goes by. I've been wearing my usual old striped T-shirt to sleep in, but it feels pretty fucking useless.

Terry Castle
San Francisco

I NDIA IS NO STRANGER to terrorism. But the terrorism that India has had to face for some decades can by no means be connected only to Islam; and in almost every case the ruling government has played a part in causing and even nurturing the phenomenon. If we look at the story of Sikh extremism in the 1980s in Punjab, we find it has an eerie resonance with the events that took place in Washington and New York.

For Mrs Gandhi, the Congress Party – a euphemism for herself and her family – represented democracy, stability and secularism; and, in order to perpetuate Congress rule, she used every undemocratic means at her disposal. She tampered with India's federal structure, and made destabilising non-Congress state governments something of a bad habit; the damaging effects this has had on Indian democracy are evident today. Her deadliest intervention was the sponsoring of a Sikh fundamentalist in Punjab, Jarnail Singh Bhindranwale. The Akali Dal, a regional party with a strong Sikh identity, was posing a threat to the Congress. Mrs Gandhi's son Sanjay decided the best way to counter this was by cynically promoting Bhindranwale – a figure who was violently assertive in his religious and regional identity. Unfortunately, Bhindranwale turned against Mrs Gandhi to preside over a militant secessionist movement. The consequences are well known: the military attack on the Golden Temple, where Bhindranwale was hiding, the death of Bhindranwale, the killing later, in retaliation, of Mrs Gandhi by her Sikh bodyguards, and, in the aftermath, the murder in Delhi of innocent Sikhs by Congress-led hoodlums.

Like Mrs Gandhi in India, America has been a great, self-appointed proponent of democracy in the modern world, while, in actuality, it has treated it as a nuisance and an obstruction when it gets in the way of its self-interest. It now justifies war by speaking of the 'will of the people', but the will of the people in Palestine has, for decades, meant little more than the rubble of Palestine. In order to root out Communism from Afghanistan, it armed a religious extremist group; and created, in effect, a Bhindranwale. For years, America's foreign policy, like Mrs Gandhi's domestic policy, has been concerned solely with extending its own sphere of influence, whatever the cost. Only the American public can put pressure on, and change, that aberrant policy: but the American public's main source of information about its country's foreign policy is Hollywood with its images of terror and frightening rhetoric of 'good' and 'evil'.

Amit Chaudhuri
Calcutta

I T IS ONE THING to believe without knowing, quite another to know without believing. Never have world-shattering events been so relentlessly documented, the evidence of testimony converging with the hideous evidence of things. Yet I still cannot at some level believe what I have seen and heard about the events of 11 September. One of the incongruities at which my slow-moving mind balks is the combination of two forms of life that Max Weber taught us were immiscible: the symbolic-religious and the calculating-rational. Obviously, those who carried out the attacks on 11 September practised both, and simultaneously. It took painstaking planning, meshed co-ordination of people and objects, and a strategic eye for opportunities. This is means-end rationality with a vengeance. It also took a steely commitment to an ideal powerful enough to motivate suicide and mass murder. We don't yet know which ideal was here so bloodily served, and whether it was strictly religious. People have been known to blow up themselves and innocent bystanders in the cause of anarchism or nationalism. But all powerful ideals, religious or secular, hold followers in thrall through symbols and values. If the symbolic had not been trump, the pilots of the hijacked planes would have aimed straight for a nuclear power plant, with which they could have wreaked still more horror. So the terrorists also inhabited the realm of what Weber called the rationality of values, and not in the compartmentalised way the rest of us balance these two ways of ordering our lives. During World War Two, the intellectual challenge went out to physicists and chemists, mathematicians and engineers to solve technical problems of enormous complexity. If there really is to be something like a war on terrorism, then the new challenge seems to be addressed to anthropologists and historians, sociologists and theologians, students of the symbolic rather than the technical.

Lorraine Daston
Berlin

B ECAUSE I LIVE TEN blocks from the site of the World Trade Center, my response to the events of 11 September is intensely localised; but because I was a thousand miles away in a foreign country when the events occurred, my experience of those events was – like most people's – mediated by the television screen.

For me, the terrorist attack precipitated a series of time-consuming missions: it took me eight hours to reach my wife on the telephone, I had to wait forty-odd hours for the US-Canadian border to open, and then spent 18 hours on a train back to New York which was delayed not only by a lengthy police search but by the ninety or so bomb threats that plagued Manhattan all day Thursday. I arrived at Penn Station sometime after 2 a.m. on Friday morning in the middle of a thunderstorm. The weather was a comfort. I took a taxi-cab to 14th Street, the site of the first police barricade, and – showing my ID whenever necessary – walked two miles downtown in the rain past floodlit checkpoints and army convoys. I wish I could have kept that intensity of purpose for the rest of my life but since then I have been completely distracted. My neighbourhood was empty but my block was eerily untouched. There was no sense of catastrophe until you walked to the corner and saw the smouldering mountain of rubble used by CNN for updating its rescue reports. By Saturday afternoon, the street had become a tourist site.

It seems incredible to me that the period between the fall of the Berlin Wall and the collapse of the World Trade towers will be perceived as some sort of golden age – albeit one characterised by the production of disaster movies ranging from the Gulf War to *Pearl Harbor*. After several days of uncertainty, the US president found his role as a front man; he has been making many appearances and talking like a cowboy. My reaction, however, is still intensely localised: it seems almost inevitable to me that the very traits for which New York was the paradigmatic 20th-century metropolis – its spectacular verticality, density, heterogeneity and mediacentricity – will now make it an irresistible theatre for the shadow war of the 21st century that has long been anticipated but never really expected.

J. Hoberman
New York

S UICIDAL MILITANTS WHO HATE us and want to kill us obviously cannot be deterred by threats. But can recasting US policy – say, withdrawing our troops from Saudi Arabia or putting pressure on Israel to retreat within its 1967 borders – blunt Arab and Islamic anti-Americanism soon enough to deflect the harm already flying our way? We will upgrade airport and airplane security, no doubt. We will invest millions in foreign language training for our intelligence operatives. We might conceivably launch a super Marshall Plan for distressed Islamic economies. But will such efforts bear fruit in time?

Those who committed this savage act against generic Americans see the United States as a giant who walks unthinkingly across the earth, barely noticing the small peoples it crushes. In response, they burrowed under our skin, flew into our body and blew themselves up inside us. At long last, we have noticed their existence. Some of the 'sleepers' will be tracked down. But how many will remain at large? Apparently well trained in counter-intelligence, the group of zealots involved in the recent events knew how to blend into the landscape, working in modular 'cells' able to continue operations when contact is broken with a controlling hand abroad. What has thrust the US foreign policy establishment into a panic is the possibility that such stealth fanatics, bruised by real and imaginary humiliations and intoxi- cated by self-certainty, will eventually master the delivery of those frighteningly destructive weapons that Western science has bequeathed to all mankind.

Any action we take, especially if it inflicts Muslim civilian casualties, will recruit more foot-soldiers to the jihad. So what is to be done? Talk of punishing states that 'harbour' terrorists is simplistic and misleading. It is more accurate to say that failed states incubate terrorism. Therefore, bullying these states, ignoring the need of weak governments for domestic political support, will be devastatingly counter- productive. Precipitating a coup in Pakistan, above all, is too high a price to pay for the small gain of eliminating Osama bin Laden. That Americans now see their own destiny at risk in such distant goings-on is a direct result of that unforgettable, unforgivable, life-shattering Tuesday morning.

Stephen Holmes
New York

I SLAM WAS A MEDIEVAL religion that had managed to stumble on into the 20th century. This was the view held in the 1950s by academic pundits in the West, such as Alfred Guillaume and Wilfred Cantwell Smith, who wrote general guides to Islam. The final chapters in such books invariably pontificated about how, if Islam was going to thrive in the future, it was going to have to adapt to Western ways and accommodate its outdated theology and law to modern science and democracy. The Islam the experts concentrated on was Sunni Islam, for they perceived Shi'ism to be even more medieval and irrelevant. As for a popular image of Islam, it existed as a ragbag of visual icons: flowing robes, camels, dancing girls, minarets, scimitars, tarbushes and weirdly squiggly writing. It was seen as primarily a religion of Arabs who galloped around the desert invoking the beard of the Prophet and dutifully submitting themselves to the decrees of destiny. 'The glory that was Islam' had happened centuries ago and its chief legacy was some rather splendid buildings, among them the Alhambra and Topkapi palaces and the Taj Mahal.

The political and social programmes of such leading figures of the 1950s and 1960s as Nasser, Bourguiba and the Shah of Iran suggested a Middle East in which the role of Islam and of traditional institutions would be much diminished. Western pundits went on to write books about the future of Arabia without the sultans and about an Iran in which the autocracy of the Shah should have been replaced by a modernising left-wing democracy. Things changed. Nasserism was seen to have been a military and economic failure. Pious, traditional-minded peasants migrated to Cairo, Istanbul, Tehran and Kabul, and urban congregations became seedbeds of revived, rigorist Islamic movements. Khomeini's triumph provided inspiration and hope for fundamentalist movements. There was nothing very medieval about the new Islamic revivalism and many of its leaders had studied such subjects as engineering, aeronautics or computer science in America or Europe. They knew what Western culture was and they did not like it. The Rushdie affair made people in Britain and elsewhere realise that Islam was far from moribund (some thought that its vitality was really rather sinister).

Western observers of Islam had to revise their views and, in doing so, went into overdrive. In the 1990s, once Communism had collapsed, it was possible to present Islam as the last great adversary. This was a good splashy topic for grand cultural seminars. Samuel Huntington in *The Clash of Civilisations* (1996) wrote at length about the West's confrontation with Islam, 'a different civilisation whose people are convinced of the superiority of their culture and obsessed by the inferiority of their power'. Today some of his readers must be hailing Huntington as a latter-day Nostradamus (and so much more lucid than his Renaissance precursor). However, I am confident that the alignments in the coming conflicts will demonstrate the precise opposite of the Huntington thesis. There are many versions of Islam and many, probably most, Muslim regimes will side with the United States. On the other hand, quite a few thoroughly secular-minded organisations will be found to have been giving aid and comfort to the Islamists' struggle against the global hegemony of the United States.

Robert Irwin
London

I HAVE BEEN RELUCTANT to comment on the recent 'events' because the event in question, as history, is incomplete and one can even say that it has not yet fully happened.

Obviously there are immediate comments one can make, in particular on the nauseating media reception, whose cheap pathos seemed unconsciously dictated by a White House intent on smothering the situation in sentiment in order to demonstrate the undemonstrable: namely, that 'Americans are united as never before since Pearl Harbor.' I suppose this means that they are united by the fear of saying anything that contradicts this completely spurious media consensus.

Historical events, however, are not punctual, but extend in a before and after of time which only gradually reveal themselves. It has, to be sure, been pointed out that the Americans created bin Laden during the Cold War (and in particular during the Soviet war in Afghanistan), and that this is therefore a textbook example of dialectical reversal. But the seeds of the event are buried deeper than that. They are to be found in the wholesale massacres of the Left systematically encouraged and directed by the Americans in an even earlier period. The physical extermination of the Iraqi and the Indonesian Communist Parties, although now historically repressed and forgotten, were crimes as abominable as any contemporary genocide. It is, however, only now that the results are working their way out into actuality, for the resultant absence of any Left alternative means that popular revolt and resistance in the Third World have nowhere to go but into religious and 'fundamentalist' forms.

As for the future, no one (presumably including our own government) has any idea what the promised and threatened 'war on terrorism' might look like. But until we know that, we can have no satisfactory picture of the 'events' we imagine to have taken place on a single day in September. Despite this uncertainty, however, it is permitted to feel that the future holds nothing good for either side.

Fredric Jameson
North Carolina

T HE THOUSANDS WHO DIED in New York, Washington and Pennsylvania were people of all races, faiths, classes, nationalities. We in Israel have mourned them; many of us have mourned for NYC as part of our real life, unlike Khartoum or Baghdad. Indeed, 'Israeliness' had its best week for some time. The street leading from the Defence Ministry into the heart of Tel Aviv has been renamed Pentagon Street (for a month only). Ariel Sharon, known for his delicacy, phoned President Bush explaining that 'Everyone's got his own bin Laden.' To sum up, the public discourse was kind of 'Hey, America, look at us. We are mourning more than anyone else, and wishing you a happy new war.'

Who is not sickened by the idea that these crimes have something to do with 'liberation'? But Western nihilism, too, knows no limits; it switches, almost whimsically, its definitions of 'freedom' and 'terror', 'moderates' and 'extremists', and everything solid melts into air. Bush says: 'The world has never seen such a crime.' It all comes down to visibility and invisibility: the crimes we never see, the crimes we'll see for ever, again and again, 'live' and relived. Terror now can involve massive killing, almost like an American air-raid on Basra, or Baghdad. Is it not that very fact that our Hebrew media have been celebrating? At last Israel's victim status can be properly understood – no need to mention the Holocaust – while as perpetrators, we are unseen again. And the Arabs? They are criminals: no more chance for them to be seen as victims. We are in, they are out. We, the Jews, belong with you, dear Old West. Dear sponsors, we – like you – are victims.

In the week after the atrocities in New York and Washington, the IDF killed about twenty Palestinians. Nobody even noticed, said one of our ministers with satisfaction. Then came holy night, the beginning of the Jewish New Year. I wandered in my flat, between my little son's bed and the TV set with its nerve-racking news. I called a friend in Ramallah, to find out if the invasion (for that night) was over, how many dead, and if the children were safe, or 'just' terrified, and all those silly questions put by the privileged having nothing to offer but sympathy. 'And thou shalt show thy son.' Jews are supposed to tell their children what they were told by their fathers. Your grandfather, my son, like my grandfather, was born and grew up when being a Jew was much like what it is today to be an Arab. But we – you and me – are saved. 'Dad, they say the next American war is good for us. Is it?' Who are 'us'? The living in Kabul, New York, Tel Aviv? Ramallah? Who are 'they'? The dead in New York? In Baghdad? In Gaza? In Jerusalem?

Yitzhak Laor
Tel Aviv

'I NFINITE JUSTICE' – the provisional, perhaps already discarded name for the coming US military operation – could have meant recognising that justice is not the property of any one man, nation, or even religion. Knowing that the just course in dangerous times requires slowing down historical time, making 'time for time' to cite a Jewish proverb; pausing, not as a gesture before the real action begins, but pausing for thought. Acknowledging that those who behave unjustly, you could say 'inexcusably', may even so, in terms of the distribution of the globe's resources, also have justice on their side. The victims of injustice – last week, unequivocally, the US – are not always, automatically, just. The state of Israel, for example, was founded on the back of a horror perpetrated against the Jewish people which was for some the worst, for others the culmination of the injustices carried out against the Jewish people over centuries. This has not made the state of Israel just towards the Palestinians. We should be wary, above all, of the language of righteousness. As we watch our prime minister binding us once again to the United States, not as bellicose in his rhetoric as Bush, but unswerving in his belief, we might choose to remember that less than a week before 11 September, in Durban, Britain was involved in blocking an attempt by the world's 300 million indigenous peoples – Maoris, Aboriginals and Native Americans – to have their rights protected under international law.

Infinite justice could involve recognising these complexities. We talk of infinite compassion or mercy. But if, instead, infinity has been claimed for our hold over justice, then we are in danger of believing – like the Islam now held accountable for all the ills in the world – that our justice, and our justice alone, is divinely sanctioned and follows the path of God. Then infinite justice is most likely to mean – with dreadful and unpredictable consequences for some of the poorest, most deprived peoples of the world – being struck ad infinitum (the struggle, we are told, will be long), being pounded over and over again.

Jacqueline Rose
London

W ERE THE MURDEROUS ATTACKS of 11 September an *act of war* against the United States? We are being told that they were and that America is now at war and (as I write) preparing to wage war against whoever committed this act of war against us.

Certainly this was *like* war, with destruction on the scale of an air-raid and indiscriminate killing on a massive scale. But 'like war' – the metaphor (war on poverty, war on drugs) – is not enough. We are told it was *literally* an act of war – a formulation difficult to decipher in the US, where 'literally' works as an intensifier. Many compared 11 September to Pearl Harbor: both involved massive, unexpected and destructive attacks; and incidentally both were described by their victims (though not by their perpetrators) as utterly unprovoked. That Pearl Harbor was an attack on a military installation, and 11 September mostly not, is a first and obvious disanalogy. And with a second, I think the 'war' description begins to unravel. Notoriously – infamously – Pearl Harbor was not preceded by any declaration of war. But if 11 September was an act of war and if indeed it was bin Laden's organisation that did it, then we have to acknowledge that a declaration of war was issued in February 1998. (That few in America took bin Laden's 'declaration' seriously is neither here nor there.)

How far do we want to go with this characterisation? If the events of 11 September were acts of war, should we judge them by the logic of war? Should the co-ordination, the daring, the self-sacrifice, the sheer audacity of the attacks be admitted to the annals of great feats of arms? As usual we want to have it both ways: it was not crime, it was war; but it is damned with the stigma of criminality and (absurdly) 'cowardice'. When we apprehend the accomplices of the perpetrators, are we to treat them as prisoners of war? (Remember the demands of the IRA hunger strikers.) Is our response to be governed by the laws of war? I hope so, except that the logic (as opposed to the law) of modern warfare is that attacks on civilians are not inappropriate as responses to attacks on civilians. ('We will mete out to the Germans the measure, and more than the measure, they have meted out to us.')

War tends both to unite a people and to dispose them to dispense with the irritations of democracy. But with the temptations we face, we cannot do without things like checks and balances, public hesitations, open and – if necessary – partisan debate, criticism without accusations of disloyalty, caution without attributions of cowardice. Calling 11 September an act of war, and responding to it accordingly, is calculated to deprive us of these necessities.

Jeremy Waldron
New York

THE NOTION OF UNSPEAKABILITY was wheeled in almost straight away, used all over the place. It's true that most people were at a loss, had nothing to say. But to call something 'unspeakable' is quite different from remaining silent, and implies a peculiar disappointment, an assumption that words are supposed to make sense of everything, and have now let us down when we most needed them. This is the gist of many articles written and interviews given since 11 September. 'Language has failed us,' one of them began. But when did words ever make such extravagant, untenable promises?

Once it was clear what was happening, many of us began to concentrate on particular aspects of the disaster, as if we could hide from the whole in one of its parts. We found we could get really interested only in single threads: the rescue operations, the failure of security, the threat of retaliation, the behaviour of politicians, the investigation of the crimes, the future safety of cities and travellers, the fear of violence of Americans against Americans. Children, I gather, often thought about rescue. Non-nationals, like myself, worried about the fall-out of retaliation, and the ease with which people, shocked by the loss of life in New York and Washington, spoke of acceptable collateral damage elsewhere – although, to be fair, many Americans worried about this, too. But of course you can't hide from the whole in any of its parts. You can't hide at all.

Many Americans are concerned about the role American policies have played in the creation of the climate which made the attacks possible, but no one is saying this publicly for fear of seeming to take the attacks out of the realm of gratuitous evil.

The most unforgettable image (among many) was a still photograph which appeared in *Time* magazine and elsewhere. Two-thirds of the picture, from the left, is completely occupied by a section of a tower of the World Trade Center, with neither top nor bottom in view. A small cloud of smoke appears at an edge of the building. The other third of the picture is blue sky, with no ground in view. In the sky and against the building are five tiny figures, people who have thrown themselves from high windows. Everyone has their favourite nightmare, and yours may be getting buried under mountains of rubble. Who could argue with that? But falling from an immense height is the nightmare of many of us, and the thought of choosing this death, of seeing and knowing and refusing a worse death, is surely beyond nightmare.

Michael Wood
Princeton

4 October 2001

'NO BULLSHIT' BULLSHIT

Stefan Collini on Christopher Hitchens

WINNING IS VERY IMPORTANT to Christopher Hitchens. Dr Johnson was said to 'talk for victory', and by all accounts it seems the same might be said of Hitchens. He certainly writes for victory. His preferred genre is the polemic; his favoured tone mixes forensic argument with high-octane contempt. And no one can accuse him of only picking on boys his own size: he is happy to take the ring against tubby, bespectacled former diplomats and little, shrivelled old ladies as well as (special contempt here) relatively fit joggers. His indictments of Henry Kissinger, Mother Teresa and Bill Clinton have been among the glories of the prosecuting counsel's art in recent years. Taking the global village as his courtroom, Hitchens asks us, the jury, to stare with wonder and loathing at these singular specimens of human depravity who are united in being parsimonious with the truth and in being the object of some very good jokes.

From his early Trotskyist days on the *New Statesman*, through extended spells as a columnist for *Vanity Fair* and the *Nation*, and spreading out into contributions to a daunting variety of other weeklies and monthlies, Hitchens has been a prolific journalist, and in addition to his books he has now published four collections of his articles and essays. This is where much of his best writing is found and where he displays the range of his literary tastes as well as the incisiveness of his literary judgments. Hitchens is one of the best contemporary examples of a species we tend to think of as flourishing in the 19th century rather than the 21st, the political journalist as man of letters. He would have been entirely at home with the slash-and-burn style of the early partisan quarterlies, such as the *Edinburgh* or the *Westminster*, disposing of shoddy Romantic poetry and shoddy arguments in favour of the slave trade or the unreformed House of Commons with equal gusto, in a style two parts Hazlitt to one part Cobbett with a dash of Croker's Tory venom.

It's worth considering what kind of cultural authority this type of writing can lay claim to these days. It self-consciously repudiates the credentials of academic scholarship; it disparages the narrow technical expertise of the policy wonk; it cannot rest on the standing of achievement as a politician or novelist. In other words, it has nothing to declare but its talent. Knowing the facts is very important; knowing the people helps (there's a fair bit of anecdotage and I-was-there-ism in Hitchens's journalism). But in the end it stands or falls by the cogency of its case, based on vigorous moral intuitions, honesty and integrity in expressing them, mastery of the relevant sources and a forceful, readable style. Car licence-plates in New Hampshire bear (rather threateningly, it always seems to me, as big SUVs speed by) the state motto 'Live free or die.' In this spirit, the maxim on Hitchens's crest has to be 'Get it right or die.'

In the early part of his writing career, Hitchens's main way of being always right was to be very Left, but he has recently been casting off this identity, at least in its familiar forms. Now it appears that the infallible litmus test of whether one is on the right track is whether most people think the contrary. Comrade Hitchens may still be susceptible to the pull of fraternity when embodied by old buddies from *New Left Review*, but his self-ascribed identity now is as a 'contrarian'. Being 'independent' (of parties, institutions, conventional wisdom, codes of politeness) is the thing. He describes himself in a recent essay as writing in opposition to 'the present complacently "liberal" consensus', when it's pretty clear that what really gets his goat is that it is a consensus and that it's complacent rather than just that it's liberal. In the same piece he introduces a sentence with the nicely self-ironic phrase 'without wishing to seem even-handed', but it's hard to think of anyone for whom this is less of a risk. Irreverence is more highly prized than ever (he's always admired Wilde), and he hates cant, especially pious cant, especially pious radical academic cant. This protects him from any risk of being well thought of by the well-meaning, particularly in the US, and he further insures himself against the danger of being approved of by his conspicuous consumption of fags and booze.

Of course, in choosing to distance oneself from a particular 'consensus', especially a liberal consensus, one inevitably appears to be aligning oneself with its other, more usual opponents. Hitchens's recent high-profile resignation from the *Nation* illustrates the difficulty. His denunciation of his erstwhile colleagues' too predictable criticisms of US foreign policy and their too indulgent perspective on the response of some of those who suffer the impact of that policy in other parts of the world can make him look like a recruit to the ranks of those who would have us all line up against the 'axis of evil'. In such circumstances, too irritable an aversion from one's self-righteously 'radical' associates can lead one into some very unlovely company, and the self-contradictoriness of consistent contrarianism can produce odd outcomes. Surely Hitchens is not going to go the way of Paul Johnson, one of the leading attack-journalists (and *New Statesman* stalwarts) of a previous generation, now reduced to indiscriminate barking at all things 'fashionable', while intoning *pas d'ennemis à droite*?

As it happens, I've been rereading Hitchens's latest collection of essays, *Unacknowledged Legislation* (2001), alongside a couple of other collections that have recently appeared in paperback, Martin Amis's *The War against Cliché* and Frank Kermode's *Pleasing Myself*. That's a tough poker table to ask anyone to sit at, and it's impressive that some of Hitchens's best pieces, or at least some of his best paragraphs, don't seem out of place. It's true that he is quite often doing something different from those two contrasting masters of the literary review-essay, something more argumentative and political, but even when allowance is made for that, this company does in the end make his writing seem a bit blowsy or over-pleased with itself, certainly too prone to go for the cheap shot. Amis is partial to a spot of sitting duck, too, but he pays in full for his day's shooting from his wad of newly minted images, while Kermode mostly contents himself with a saddened shake of the head, a devastating weapon in its way, but one that doesn't leave any mess on the carpet. Hitchens *loves* mess on the carpet.

What Hitchens hasn't previously attempted at any length is the positive tribute, the admiring portrait. It has long been clear, however, that George Orwell is something of a hero of his, as of most political journalists with claims to be both essayists and tellers of unpopular truths, and now, spurred by the appearance four years ago of Peter Davison's marvellously thorough complete edition of Orwell's writings (and no doubt with an eye on Orwell's centenary, which falls this year), he has written a short book entirely devoted to telling us, as the title of the US edition has it, 'Why Orwell Matters'. One therefore turns with interest to see how Hitchens, an acknowledged master of the literary bazooka attack, will acquit himself in the trickier arts of discriminating appreciation.

Orwell's Victory* has both a dedication and an epigraph, not unusual things in themselves, but in this case curious and curiously revealing. The dedication is to Robert Conquest, 'premature anti-fascist, premature anti-Stalinist, poet and mentor, and founder of "the united front against bullshit"'. It seems that Conquest is being saluted here principally for having been against a lot of things; this appears to be an early signal of the connection between being 'anti' and telling it like it is. Hitchens is all for being against things (and one thinks again of the title of that collection by his friend Martin Amis), though here he perhaps risks the mild paradox of 'we contrarians must stick together.' The dedication also seems to suggest that Conquest is being praised for being against certain things before most people were, though the tonal unsteadiness of 'premature', whatever its ironic intent, risks putting Conquest in the company of babies, conclusions, ejaculations. Conquest, it seems, is to be understood in Nietzsche's sense, as an 'untimely man' (contrarians are prone to congratulate themselves on being out of step with their times), or

---

*Christopher Hitchens, *Orwell's Victory* (Allen Lane, 2002).

perhaps, to take up Larkin's more familiar idiom, one of 'the less deceived'. Even though we haven't even got to the contents page, we're starting to catch a whiff of the 'no bullshit' bullshit that is one of Hitchens's trademarks.

The epigraph is from Proust and, being from Proust, is a paragraph long. It is about one kind of genius, genius as 'reflecting power', the kind of genius possessed by those who, though they may not always be those 'whose conversation is the most brilliant' or 'culture the most extensive', can 'transform their personality into a sort of mirror'. The reader is naturally led to hear this as the first touch on the tuning-fork, striking the right note for the ensuing performance about Orwell. Actually, as one reads and rereads this passage, its meaning starts to slip through one's grasp. The 'men who produce works of genius' are those who have the power to 'transform their personality into a sort of mirror, in such a way that their life, however mediocre it may be socially and even, in a sense, intellectually, is reflected by it, genius consisting in reflecting power and not in the intrinsic quality of the scene reflected'. Taken alone, this might serve as a manifesto both for the purest naturalism (the best mirrors are those which reflect most faithfully and in most detail) and for extreme aestheticism (the subject written about is irrelevant, imaginative intensity is all). But what it doesn't seem to be, on fuller reflection (so to speak), is a very apt way to characterise Orwell's strengths, or indeed those of anyone who, like Orwell and like Hitchens himself, writes about what is going on in the public world and about what actually, despite appearances, makes things happen. Although the passage appears at first reading to suggest something about Orwell's self-absenting directness of observation and his much-praised (and self-praised) 'power of facing unpleasant facts', it comes to seem quite the opposite, a celebration of an almost Jamesian capacity for infusing a charged intensity of consciousness into the detail of experience. The passage may also prompt an association with Orwell's endlessly quoted dictum that 'good prose is like a windowpane.' This is a formula whose shortcomings don't need to be dwelled on, but at least it suggests that one looks through the window, at the world outside, whereas the defining quality of the mirror is to bounce vision back at the viewer. As with 'premature' in the dedication, one is left a little uncertain what signal the epigraph is intended to send.

The acknowledgments then begin, with thanks to 'my old English master', who set Hitchens to read *Animal Farm* 'and who allowed me to show him my work, late, as an off-the-subject comparison with *Darkness at Noon*: the first decent essay I ever wrote'. It is often said that Englishmen tend to be fixated on their schooldays, especially when they went to the kind of minor public school that Hitchens went to, and there is certainly an unexpectedly nostalgic tea and crumpets flavour to this, as well as a statue-in-the-marble recognition of early signs of later identity (despite the missed deadline), a kind of coming home. It hints at a more personal answer to the question of 'why Orwell matters'.

And then, as the opening to the introduction, we get a poem (there are a lot of antipasti to this relatively slight meal). The poem is by Conquest himself and is entitled simply 'George Orwell'. It praises Orwell as 'a moral genius': 'honesty', 'truth' and 'truth-seeking' structure the citation, and Orwell is praised for testing words against 'The real person, real event or thing'. Throughout, he is thumpingly commended for directing our attention to 'reality', as in the rather Empsonian line 'Because he taught us what the actual meant'. Orwell figures here as an early (perhaps 'premature') member of 'the united front against bullshit'; or, in other words, as one of Hitchens's predecessors in the 'no bullshit' bullshit.

When we finally get going with Hitchens himself writing about Orwell, the effect is a little anti-climactic. This is partly because one had a pretty good sense in advance of the kind of thing Hitchens would want to say about him. 'The three great subjects of the 20th century were imperialism, Fascism and Stalinism'; Orwell 'was essentially "right"' about these issues; and 'he was enabled to be "right" by a certain insistence on intellectual integrity and independence.' So far, so familiar. (It is interesting to note that Hitchens, loyal to aspects of the Trotskyism he has for the most part abandoned, always says Stalinism where most people would say Communism.) This is very much a political journalist's view of the 'great subjects'; from other perspectives one could make a case for, say, the mechanisation of agriculture, the development of global communications and changed attitudes towards sex – or, indeed, a whole variety of quite different 'subjects', though it's harder to see what being 'right' would mean in such cases.

It is also a rather romantic view of the 'independent' intellectual. Orwell, Hitchens announces, 'faced the competing orthodoxies and despotisms of his day with little more than a battered typewriter and a stubborn personality'. Most versions of 'writers v. Leviathan', to borrow Orwell's own terms, are inclined to hit this over-dramatic, David and Goliath note, including the mandatory weapons-upgrade from slingshot to 'battered typewriter' (it wouldn't do for the typewriter to be newish and in quite good nick). Orwell does seem to have been a brave man when put to the test, but to speak of him 'facing' despotisms from behind his desk ratchets up the register in a rather empty way. The lone protestor in Tiananmen Square, in the unforgettable image, certainly 'faced' the tank in a dramatically uneven contest, but those who write about orthodoxies and despotisms, especially from the distance of another country, don't seem to merit the same verb. Similarly, most writers who address such topics do so with 'little more' than their typewriters and their personalities, battered, stubborn or otherwise. Of course, Hitchens needs to play up Orwell's complete 'independence', partly because he shares with him the animating illusion that to be out of step with a large body of opinion is in itself the most likely indicator of being right.

It is not easy to write a good book about Orwell now. He has been written about so extensively, and sometimes well, that to justify devoting a whole book to him one would really need to have discovered some new material or be able to set him in some new context (not that this will deter publishers eager to cash in on his centenary). The main problem with *Orwell's Victory* is that Hitchens doesn't have enough to say about Orwell to fill a book, so he writes, in effect, as Orwell's minder, briskly seeing off various characters who have in some way or other got him wrong. This is the structuring principle for a series of chapters on 'Orwell and Empire', 'Orwell and the Left', 'Orwell and the Right' and so on. Some of the offenders clearly deserve what they get, but there's something repetitive and relentless about it, as though the duffing-up were more important than dealing with Orwell's own writing. Raymond Williams is taken behind the bike sheds for a particularly nasty going-over; repetition of another kind adds to the problem here, since the substance of this long section was first delivered at the Hay-on-Wye literary festival in 1999 (as the Raymond Williams Memorial Lecture, if you please), then published in *Critical Quarterly* later that year, then republished in *Unacknowledged Legislation*. It's a fair specimen of the Hitchens polemical manner – inveighing against 'the overrated doyen of cultural studies and Cambridge English' and his 'almost deliberate obtuseness', accusing his writing of being 'replete with dishonesty and evasion', and so on – but reading it again is a vaguely dispiriting experience, rather like watching an old video of a one-sided boxing match.

As always with Hitchens's work, one gets the strongest possible sense of how much it matters to prove that one is and always has been right: right about which side to be on, right that there are sides and one has to be on one of them; right about which way the world (in the rather narrow, political journalist's sense of that term) is going, right about which policies will work and which regimes are wicked; right about the accuracy of one's facts and one's stories; and right when so many others, especially well-regarded or well-placed others, are demonstrably wrong. There is a palpably macho tone to all of this, as of alpha males competing for dominance and display.

That one's facts should be right seems desirable from most points of view, but since Hitchens makes so much of others' failings here, one is driven to a spot of murmuring about stones and glasshouses. For example, he describes Friedrich Hayek as succeeding 'Orwell's old foe Laski in the chair at the London School of Economics', but he didn't: Michael Oakeshott did. He quotes from C.P. Snow's

'Two Cultures' lecture, ascribing it to 'the mid-1960s', though it was delivered and published in 1959. Most bizarrely, he even mangles an extremely well-known line of Orwell's, his tirade about 'every fruit-juice drinker, nudist, sandal-wearer' and so on. Hitchens notes, rightly, that Orwell included 'feminist' in this list along, he goes on to say, 'with the fruit-juice drinkers, escaped Quakers, sandal-wearers and other cranks'. 'Quakers', yes, but '*escaped* Quakers'? Escaped from where, exactly?

Trying to characterise for myself a certain tone that seems to be becoming more and more marked in Hitchens's recent writings, I recalled that in Martin Amis's baroquely footnoted *Experience*, there is a relatively brief note on Amis's almost filial relation to Saul Bellow, in which, having clarified that although he was not Bellow's son he was Bellow's ideal reader, Amis added: 'I am not my father's ideal reader, however. His ideal reader, funnily enough, is Christopher Hitchens.' One can see why that could seem odd or unexpected, but the more Hitchens I read the less unexpected it becomes. To be the ideal reader of Kingsley Amis, one would need, among much else, to be responsive to the pleasures of being bloody. Hitchens doesn't actually list 'giving offence' among his hobbies in *Who's Who*, but perhaps that's only because it's not a hobby. It's interesting, too, that Martin Amis can be the ideal reader for Bellow despite the obvious cultural differences; it is unimaginable that Kingsley Amis's ideal reader could be anything other than deeply English.

Of course, 'deeply English' is the accolade that one group of Orwell's admirers are keenest to bestow on Saint George, and Hitchens, though properly suspicious of Tory evocations of deep England, does not dissent from this description or its positive force. At one point he concludes a nice little riff on the resemblances between Orwell and Larkin by acknowledging their front-runner status 'in the undeclared contest for most symbolic Englishman'. What is particularly striking here is the way in which Hitchens, wanting to identify with a kind of Englishness that is at once authentic and radical, free from the taint both of 'heritage' kitsch and of a class-bound nostalgia for social hierarchy, aligns himself with a tradition that goes back to Tom Paine, Milton and the Diggers. This move has structural similarities to the Norman Yoke theory of the 17th century, which claimed that the popular liberties of the Saxons had been (temporarily, for several centuries) suppressed by the alien laws of a conquering aristocracy. And this brings out how much Hitchens, cosmopolitan man of letters and geopolitical analyst though he may be, is also a kind of country-party Whig, quick to sniff corruption at court or abuses of power by over-mighty governments. This affinity almost declares itself when he quotes Orwell endorsing Milton's invocation of 'the known rules of ancient liberty'. This is an 'English tradition' with which he, like Orwell, is proud to identify.

Part of what is attractive and persuasive about Hitchens's take on Orwell is his insistence on the way some of the latter's most admirable positions represent a kind of triumph over himself, as he educated himself into more liberal convictions against the grain of his inherited attitudes and temperamental inclinations (here 'Orwell's victory' can be understood in a more personal, less world-historical sense). One can't help wondering whether there isn't something of this in Hitchens, too, and whether, as with Orwell, we don't sometimes get a glimpse of the attitudes which the son of Commander Eric Hitchens RN might have been in some ways expected to hold (i.e. roughly those of his other son, the *Mail on Sunday* columnist Peter Hitchens). As Christopher Hitchens perceptively, but perhaps also self-revealingly, says of his subject: 'George Orwell was conservative about many things, but not about politics.'

One of the qualities he claims Orwell managed to 'suppress' in himself was his 'anti-intellectualism'. Yikes! If that's how he wrote after having 'suppressed' his anti-intellectualism . . . Perhaps he means 'suppress' in the sense in which he suppresses his own tendencies in this direction, as when he speaks of 'the intellectual rot . . . spread by pseudo-intellectuals'. In the (mercifully short) chapter called, ominously, 'Deconstructing the Postmodernists', he finds the source of contemporary 'intellectual rot' in 'Continental' thinkers and their American disciples. Taking up a comparison between Orwell and Adorno suggested a couple of years ago by James Miller (head of the department at the New School in New York where Hitchens teaches a course), Hitchens reflects that both men might have been surprised that 'only half a century or so after the Hitler-Stalin Pact, every major city in Europe would be able to claim a free press and a free university,' and he goes on to speculate that 'this outcome owes something to both men but more, one suspects, to the Englishman than to the Frankfurt theorist.' I'm not sure either of them would be quite as confident as Hitchens that the press in some of these cities can so readily be described as 'free', but it's hard not to hear a bit of a nativist growl as he awards the palm to 'the Englishman'.

At his best Hitchens is a telling writer, but the occasional appearance of this almost blimpish strain means that he is not always at his best in this book. For example, in referring, with extreme briskness, to the vogue in Britain and the US for certain European philosophers, he speaks of Althusser's doomed project 'to re-create Communism by abstract thought . . . terminating in his own insanity and by what I once rather heartlessly called his application for the Electric Chair of Philosophy at the Ecole Abnormale [*sic*]'. If heartlessness were the quip's main failing the self-quotation could almost amount to an apology: in fact by being still so obviously pleased with his schoolboyish *mot* he condemns himself twice over. But this is just the sort of gag about 'abroad' that Kingsley Amis might have liked, the affinity not serving either of them very well in this instance. It's strange that at the very time when Hitchens is telling audiences in the States that we need to jettison the inherited categories of the 20th century, including those of 'left' and 'right', if we are to make sense of the radically different world of the 21st century, he should also be sounding more and more like *le bloke moyen sensuel* of England in the 1950s.

The sight of Hitchens view-hallooing across the fields in pursuit of some particularly dislikable quarry has been among the most exhilarating experiences of literary journalism during the last two decades. He's courageous, fast, tireless and certainly not squeamish about being in at the kill. But after reading this and some of his other recent writings, I begin to imagine that, encountering him, still glowing and red-faced from the pleasures of the chase, in the tap-room of the local inn afterwards, one might begin to see a resemblance not to Trotsky and other members of the European revolutionary intelligentsia whom he once admired, nor to the sophisticated columnists and political commentators of the East Coast among whom he now practises his trade, but to other red-coated, red-faced riders increasingly comfortable in their prejudices and their Englishness – to Kingsley Amis, pop-eyed, spluttering and splenetic; to Philip Larkin, farcing away at the expense of all bien pensants; to Robert Conquest and a hundred other 'I told you so's. They would be good company, up to a point, but their brand of saloon-bar finality is only a quick sharpener away from philistinism, and I would be sorry to think of one of the essayists I have most enjoyed reading in recent decades turning into a no-two-ways-about-it-let's-face-it bore. I just hope he doesn't go on one hunt too many and find himself, as twilight gathers and the fields fall silent, lying face down in his own bullshit.

23 January 2003

A ROAD MAP TO WHERE?

Edward Said

ARLY IN MAY, on his visit to Israel and the Occupied Territories, Colin Powell met with Mahmoud Abbas, the new Palestinian prime minister, and separately with a small group of civil society activists, including Hanan Ashrawi and Mostapha Barghuti. According to Barghuti, Powell expressed surprise and mild consternation at the computerised maps of the settlements, the eight-metre-high wall, and the dozens of Israeli army checkpoints that have made life so difficult and the future so bleak for Palestinians. Powell's view of Palestinian reality is, to say the least, defective, despite his august position, but he did ask for materials to take away with him and, more important, he reassured the Palestinians that the same effort put in by Bush on Iraq was now going into implementing the 'road map'. Much the same point was made in the last days of May by Bush himself in the course of interviews he gave to the Arab media, although as usual, he stressed generalities rather than anything specific. He met the Palestinian and Israeli leaders in Jordan, after seeing the major Arab rulers, excluding Syria's Bashar al-Assad, of course. All this is part of what now looks like a major American push forward. That Ariel Sharon has accepted the road map (although with enough reservations to undercut this acceptance) seems to augur well for a viable Palestinian state.

Bush's vision (the word strikes a weird dreamy note in what is meant to be a hard-headed, definitive peace plan) is supposed to be realised by the restructuring of the Palestinian Authority, the elimination of all violence and incitement against Israelis, and the installation of a government that meets the requirements of Israel and the so-called Quartet (the US, UN, EU and Russia) responsible for the plan. Israel for its part undertakes to improve the humanitarian situation, by easing restrictions and lifting curfews, though where and when are not specified. Phase One is also supposed to see the dismantling of 60 hilltop settlements (the so-called 'illegal outpost settlements' established since Sharon came to power in March 2001), though nothing is said about removing the others, which account for about 200,000 settlers on the West Bank and Gaza, to say nothing of the 200,000 more in annexed East Jerusalem. Phase Two, described as a transition, is focused rather oddly on the 'option of creating an independent Palestinian state with provisional borders and attributes of sovereignty' – none is specified – and is to culminate in an international conference to approve and then 'create' a Palestinian state, once again with 'provisional borders'. Phase Three is to end the conflict completely, also by way of an international conference whose job will be to settle the thorniest issues of all: refugees, settlements, Jerusalem, borders. Israel's role in all this is to co-operate: the real onus is placed on the Palestinians, who must keep coming up with the goods while the military occupation remains more or less in place, though eased in the main areas invaded during the spring of 2002. No monitoring element is envisioned, and the misleading symmetry of the plan's structure leaves Israel very much in charge of what – if anything – will happen next. As for Palestinian human rights, at present not so much ignored as suppressed, no specific rectification is written into the plan: apparently it is up to Israel whether to continue as before or not.

For once, all the usual commentators say, Bush is offering real hope for a Middle East settlement. Calculated leaks from the White House suggested a list of possible sanctions against Israel if Sharon is too intransigent, but this was quickly denied and soon stopped being mentioned. An emerging media consensus presents the document's contents – many of them familiar from earlier peace plans – as the result of Bush's new-found confidence after his triumph in Iraq. As with most discussions of the Palestinian-Israeli conflict, manipulated clichés and far-fetched suppositions, rather than the realities of power and lived history, shape the flow of discourse. Sceptics and critics are brushed aside as anti-American, while a sizeable portion of the organised Jewish leadership has denounced the road map as requiring far too many Israeli concessions. But the establishment press keeps reminding us that Sharon has spoken of an 'occupation', which he has never conceded until now, and has actually announced his intention to end Israeli rule over 3.5 million Palestinians. But is he even aware of what he proposes to end? The *Haaretz* commentator Gideon Levy wrote on 1 June that, in common with most Israelis, Sharon knows nothing

about life under curfew in communities that have been under siege for years. What does he know about the humiliation of checkpoints, or about people being forced to travel on gravel and mud roads, at risk to their lives, in order to get a woman in labour to a hospital? About life on the brink of starvation? About a demolished home? About children who see their parents beaten and humiliated in the middle of the night?

Another chilling omission from the road map is the gigantic 'separation wall' now being built in the West Bank by Israel: 347 kilometres of concrete running north to south, of which 120 have already been erected. It is eight metres high and two metres thick; its cost is put at $1.6 million per kilometre. The wall does not simply divide Israel from a putative Palestinian state on the basis of the 1967 borders: it actually takes in new tracts of Palestinian land, sometimes five or six kilometres at a stretch. It is surrounded by trenches, electric wire and moats; there are watchtowers at regular intervals. Almost a decade after the end of South African apartheid, this ghastly racist wall is going up with scarcely a peep from the majority of Israelis, or from their American allies who, whether they like it or not, are going to pay for most of it. The 40,000 Palestinian inhabitants of the town of Qalqilya live on one side of the wall, the land they farm and actually live off is on the other. It is estimated that when the wall is finished – presumably as the US, Israel and the Palestinians argue about procedure for months on end – almost 300,000 Palestinians will be separated from their land. The road map is silent about this, as it is about Sharon's recent approval of a wall on the eastern side of the West Bank, which will, if built, reduce the amount of Palestinian territory available for Bush's dream state to roughly 40 per cent of the area. That's what Sharon has had in mind all along.

An unstated premise underlies Israel's heavily modified acceptance of the plan and the US's evident commitment to it: the relative success of Palestinian resistance. This is true whether or not one deplores some of its methods, its exorbitant cost, and the heavy toll it has taken on yet another generation of Palestinians who refused to give up in the face of the overwhelming superiority of Israeli-US power. All sorts of reasons have been given for the appearance of the road map: that 56 per cent of Israelis back it, that Sharon has finally bowed to international reality, that Bush needs Arab-Israeli cover for his military adventures elsewhere, that the Palestinians have finally come to their senses and brought forth Abu Mazen (Abbas's much more familiar nom de guerre, as it were), and so on. Some of this is true, but I still contend that were it not for the Palestinians' stubborn refusal to accept that they are 'a defeated people', as the Israeli chief of staff recently described them, there would be no peace plan. Yet anyone who believes that the road map offers anything resembling a settlement, or that it tackles the basic issues, is wrong. Like so much of the prevailing peace discourse, it places the need for restraint and renunciation and sacrifice squarely on Palestinian shoulders, thus denying the density and sheer gravity of Palestinian history. To read the road map is to confront an unsituated document, oblivious of its time and place.

The road map, in fact, is not a plan for peace so much as a plan for pacification: it is about putting an end to Palestine as a problem. Hence the repetition of the term 'performance' in the document's wooden prose – in other words, the way Palestinians are expected to behave. No violence, no protest, more democracy, better leaders and institutions – all this based on the notion that the underlying problem has been the ferocity of Palestinian resistance, rather than the occupation that has given rise to it. Nothing comparable is expected of Israel except that the small settlements I spoke of earlier, known as 'illegal outposts' (an entirely new classification which suggests that some Israeli implantations on Palestinian land are legal), must be given up and, yes, the major settlements 'frozen', but certainly not removed or dismantled. Not a word is said about what, since 1948, and then again since 1967, Palestinians have endured at the hands of Israel and the US. Nothing about the de-development of the Palestinian economy. The house demolitions, the uprooting of trees, the prisoners (at least 5000 of them), the policy of targeted assassinations, the closures since 1993, the wholesale ruin of the infrastructure, the incredible number of deaths and maimings – all that and more passes without a word.

The truculent aggression and stiff-necked unilateralism of the American and Israeli teams are already well known. The Palestinian team inspires scarcely any confidence, made up as it is of recycled and ageing Arafat cohorts. Indeed, the road map seems to have given Yasir Arafat another lease of life, for all the studied efforts by Powell and his assistants to avoid visiting him. Despite the stupid Israeli policy of trying to humble him by shutting him up in a badly bombed compound, he is still in control of things. He remains Palestine's elected president, he has the Palestinian purse strings in his hands (the purse is far from bulging), and as for his status, none of the present 'reform' team can match the old man for charisma and power.

Take Abu Mazen. I first met him in March 1977 at my first National Council meeting in Cairo. He gave by far the longest speech, in the didactic manner he must have perfected as a secondary school teacher in Qatar, and explained to the assembled Palestinian parliamentarians the differences between Zionism and Zionist dissidents. It was a noteworthy intervention, since most Palestinians in those days had no real notion that Israel was made up not only of fundamentalist Zionists who were anathema to every Arab, but of various kinds of peacenik and activist as well. In retrospect, Abu Mazen's speech launched the PLO's campaign of meetings, most of them secret, between Palestinians and Israelis: these long dialogues in Europe about peace had considerable effect in their respective societies on shaping the constituencies that made Oslo possible.

Nevertheless, no one doubted that Arafat had authorised Abu Mazen's speech and the subsequent campaign, which cost brave men like Issam Sartawi and Said Hammami their lives. And while the Palestinian participants emerged from the centre of Palestinian politics (i.e. Fatah), the Israelis came from a small marginalised group of reviled peace supporters, whose courage was commendable for that very reason. During the PLO's Beirut years between 1971 and 1982, Abu Mazen was stationed in Damascus, but then joined the exiled Arafat and his staff in Tunis for the next decade or so. I saw him there several times and was struck by his well-organised office, his quiet bureaucratic manner and his evident interest in Europe and the United States as arenas where Palestinians could do useful work promoting peace. After the Madrid conference in 1991, he was said to have brought together PLO employees and independent intellectuals in Europe and formed them into teams, to prepare negotiating files on subjects such as water, refugees, demography and boundaries in advance of what were to become the secret Oslo meetings, although to the best of my knowledge, none of the files was used, none of the Palestinian experts was directly involved in the talks, and none of the results of this research influenced the final documents that emerged.

In Oslo, the Israelis fielded an array of experts supported by maps, documents, statistics and at least 17 prior drafts of what the Palestinians would end by signing, while the Palestinians unfortunately restricted their negotiators to three PLO men, not one of whom knew English or had a background in international (or any other kind of) law. Arafat's idea seems to have been that he was fielding a team mainly to keep himself in the process, especially after his exit from Beirut and his disastrous decision to side with Iraq during the 1991 Gulf War. If he had other objectives in mind, then he didn't prepare for them effectively, as has always been his style. In Abu Mazen's memoir, *Through Secret Channels: The Road to Oslo* (1995), and in other anec-dotal accounts of the Oslo discussions, Arafat's subordinate is credited as the 'archi-tect' of the Accords, though he never left Tunis; Abu Mazen goes so far as to say that it took him a year after the Washington ceremonies (where he appeared alongside Arafat, Rabin, Peres and Clinton) to convince Arafat that he hadn't got a state out of Oslo. Yet most accounts of the peace talks stress the fact that Arafat was pulling all the strings. No wonder then that the Oslo negotiations made the overall situa-tion of the Palestinians a good deal worse. (The American team led by Dennis Ross, a former Israeli-lobby employee – a job to which he has now returned – routinely supported the Israeli position which, after a full decade of negotiation, consisted in handing back 18 per cent of the Occupied Territories to the Palestinians on highly unfavourable terms, with the IDF left in charge of security, borders and water. Natu-rally enough, the number of settlements has more than doubled since then.)

Since the PLO's return to the Occupied Territories in 1994, Abu Mazen has remained a second-rank figure, known universally for his 'flexibility' towards Israel, his subservience to Arafat, and his lack of an organised political base, although he is one of Fatah's founders and a longstanding member and secretary general of its Central Committee. So far as I know, he has never been elected to anything, and certainly not to the Palestinian Legislative Council. The PLO and the Palestine Authority under Arafat are anything but transparent. Little is known about the way decisions have been made, or how money gets spent, where it is, and who besides Arafat has any say in the matter. Everyone agrees, however, that Arafat, a fiendish micro-manager and control freak, remains the central figure in every significant way. That is why Abu Mazen's elevation to the status of reforming prime minister, which so pleases the Americans and Israelis, is thought of by most Palestinians as, well, a kind of joke, the old man's way of holding onto power by inventing a new gimmick. Abu Mazen is thought of generally as colourless, moderately corrupt, and without any clear ideas of his own, except that he wants to please the white man.

Like Arafat, Abu Mazen has never lived anywhere except the Gulf, Syria and Lebanon, Tunisia, and now occupied Palestine; he knows no languages other than Arabic, and isn't much of an orator or public presence. By contrast, Mohammed Dahlan – the other much heralded figure in whom the Israelis and Americans place great hope – is younger, cleverer and quite ruthless. During the eight years that he ran one of Arafat's 14 or 15 security organisations, Gaza was known as Dahlanistan. He resigned last year, only to be re-recruited for the job of 'unified security chief' by the Europeans, Americans and Israelis, even though he, too, has always been one of Arafat's men. Now he is expected to crack down on Hamas and Islamic Jihad: one of the reiterated Israeli demands behind which lies the hope that there will be something resembling a Palestinian civil war, a gleam in the eyes of the Israeli military.

In any event, it seems clear to me that, no matter how assiduously and flexibly Abu Mazen 'performs', he is going to be limited by three factors. One of course is Arafat himself, who still controls Fatah. Another is Sharon (who will presumably have the US behind him all the way). In a list of 14 'remarks' about the road map published in *Haaretz* on 27 May, Sharon signalled the very narrow limits to anything that might be construed as flexibility on Israel's part. The third is Bush and his entourage; to judge by their handling of postwar Afghanistan and Iraq, they have neither the stomach nor the competence for nation-building. Already Bush's right-wing Christian base in the South has remonstrated noisily against putting pressure on Israel, and already the high-powered American pro-Israel lobby, with its docile adjunct, the US Congress, has swung into action against any hint of coercion against Israel, even though it will be crucial now that a final phase has begun.

It may seem quixotic for me to say that even if the immediate prospects are grim from a Palestinian perspective, they are not all dark. I return to the stubbornness I mentioned, and the fact that Palestinian society – devastated, nearly ruined, desolate in so many ways – is, like Hardy's thrush in its blast-beruffled plume, still capable of flinging its soul upon the growing gloom. No other Arab society is as rambunctious and healthily unruly, and none is fuller of civic and social initiatives and functioning institutions (including a miraculously vital musical conservatory). Even though they are mostly unorganised and in some cases lead miserable lives of exile and statelessness, diaspora Palestinians are still energetically engaged by the problems of their collective destiny, and all those I know are always trying somehow to advance the cause. Only a minuscule fraction of this energy has ever found its way into the Palestinian Authority, which except for the highly ambivalent figure of Arafat has remained strangely marginal to the common fate. According to recent polls, Fatah and Hamas between them have the support of roughly 45 per cent of the Palestinian electorate, with the remaining 55 per cent evolving quite different, much more hopeful-looking political formations.

One in particular has struck me as significant (and I have attached myself to it) inasmuch as it now provides the only genuine grassroots formation that steers clear both of the religious parties and their fundamentally sectarian politics, and of the traditional nationalism offered up by Arafat's old (rather than young) Fatah activists. It's called the National Political Initiative (NPI) and its leading figure is Mostapha Barghuti, a Moscow-trained doctor, whose main work has been as director of the impressive Village Medical Relief Committee, which has brought healthcare to more than 100,000 rural Palestinians. A former Communist Party stalwart, Barghuti is a quietly spoken organiser who has overcome the hundreds of physical obstacles impeding Palestinian movement or travel abroad to rally nearly every independent individual and organisation of note behind a political programme that promises social reform as well as liberation across doctrinal lines. Barghuti has built an enviably well-run solidarity movement that practises the pluralism and coexistence it preaches. NPI doesn't throw up its hands at the directionless militarisation of the intifada. It offers training programmes for the unemployed and social services for the destitute on the grounds that these answer to present circumstances and Israeli pressure. Above all, NPI, which is about to become a recognised political party, seeks to mobilise Palestinian society at home and in exile for free elections – authentic elections which will represent Palestinian, rather than Israeli or US, interests. This sense of authenticity is what seems so lacking in the path cut out for Abu Mazen.

The vision here isn't a manufactured provisional state on 40 per cent of the land, with the refugees abandoned and Jerusalem kept by Israel, but a sovereign territory liberated from military occupation by mass action involving Arabs and Jews wherever possible. Because NPI is an authentic Palestinian movement, reform and democracy have become part of its everyday practice. Organisational meetings have already been held, with many more planned abroad and in Palestine, despite the terrible travel restrictions. It is some solace to think that, while formal negotiations and discussions go on, a host of informal, unco-opted alternatives exist, of which NPI and a growing international solidarity campaign are now the main components.

19 June 2003

SHORT CUTS

John Sturrock

GIVEN THAT IT'S NOT so far been settled to everyone's satisfaction exactly what the belligerents had in mind when they went to war in 1914, we shouldn't perhaps get too impatient as the junta who ordered up the invasion of Iraq try to settle on a postwar reason for having done so that will make those of us who remain unretractably opposed to it seem to be sulking, or even Saddam-friendly. The happy obliteration of the dictator and his Baathists was, we're asked to accept, a benevolent act and good reason on its own for having a war, trumping the merely provisional reason that is currently being re-aired more and more desperately: the existence of weapons made unduly lethal in the public mind by their invisibility.

Had the deliverance of the Iraqi population been, unequivocally, the declared motive for an invasion of their country before it was launched, support for it nationally here, let alone internationally, would have been very small indeed. The new 'military humanism' may have its rational advocates but they are hugely outnumbered by the sceptics, who refuse to believe that governments commit their armies unilaterally to a war for any such generous purpose. It's not in any case as if we had to wait for American and British soldiers to occupy Iraq and uncover mass Shia graves or torture cells, to be aware that the deposed regime was vile, and the scale and methods of its oppression sickening. They were no more sickening in 2003 than they had been twenty years before, at a time when Donald ('I don't do diplomacy') Rumsfeld was shaking Saddam diplomatically by the hand in Baghdad. To pretend now that the evidence of institutional cruelty is some sort of revelation is outrageous, meant as it clearly is to expunge, as we shudder, memories of how the never less than murderous Saddam was once acceptable as an ally against the perceived danger from a newly ayatollahed Iran.

It's unfortunate that the two parties to the present occupation, members of what must be the most lopsided 'coalition' in history, seem not altogether to agree on how likely they are (they, naturally, not Hans Blix and Co.) to unearth the weapons once assumed to be posing an imminent – and Blair's minatory '45 minutes' sets new standards in imminence – threat to countries such as our own which their owners had no means of reaching. What has tended to go unsaid is that if these weapons did exist, they posed, most obviously, a threat exclusively to the not so distant Israel, in whose interests it certainly was to see Iraq invaded. As Yitzhak Laor has written, for Israeli hawks, the Iraq war came in very handy, since it neutered a serious enemy by proxy, without Israel having to endure any casualties. But a war launched explicitly on behalf of Israel would have stood even less chance than an overtly humanitarian one of being successfully marketed in this country.

You might say that Iraq's mysteriously unused weapons are not going to go away, for as long as they fail to turn up. Our prime minister has continued to assure all and sundry that, give him time, and they will be found, even though his teammate Rumsfeld went earlier on record with the brazenly cynical suggestion that they might no longer be there because the Iraqis destroyed them just before the invasion began: a presumably unique historical instance of a country choosing to disarm itself on the eve of being set upon. And following this contemptuous intervention, the shadowy Paul Wolfowitz went further and described the choice of the weapons issue for an official casus belli as 'bureaucratic', an extraordinary word to use, meaning, one gathered, that it was the only justification – my incredulous fingers originally keyed that in as 'justafiction' – which our side could agree on. In plainer terms: it was the one justification to play fully to American paranoia.

It looks therefore as if Blair may soon be travelling solo up a cul-de-sac in continuing to promise that the anthrax, the nerve gas and all the rest will one day be brought to light. Except that he has recently spoken off the record and in worryingly different terms to a small group of broadsheet journalists. Discounting the weapons issue as pretty much a red herring, he said in this curious private briefing that the real purpose of the war was to serve as a lesson to other potentially dangerous or hostile countries in the Middle East, i.e. Iran and Syria. If this is so, it is disturbing to put it mildly that he has not come out with anything on these lines when addressing Parliament, or the nation, or the servicemen whose lives he put at risk in Iraq.

Assuming that it is so, what are we then to make of the current urge, both here and in the States, to try and pin the blame, should no weapons be found, on the intelligence services, for having offered false assurances of their existence? I for one am loath to believe that intelligence was so very fallible, remembering for how long and how extensively Iraq was overflown and listened-in on. Rather, its assurances, coupled with what was learnt from two generations of UN weapons inspectors, may well have gone in the opposite direction, to the effect that Iraq, heavily defeated 12 years before and further nullified by sanctions, was in a state of ill-armed unreadiness. This proved to be the case and, as a prospect beforehand, it would have had the virtue of making the choice of that country as an exemplary victim a simple one.

19 June 2003

ZOUNDS

Frank Kermode on Blasphemy

BLASPHEMY IS STILL A crime in English law, though I imagine few now think it should be. A quarter-century has passed since anybody was charged with it, but another determined zealot like Mary Whitehouse might still manage a prosecution. The law holds that Christianity, in effect the Church of England with its secular head, is the only religion that can be blasphemed, and one still hears arguments in favour of extending the privilege to other religions. So far they have failed: a cause for rejoicing rather than ethnic envy, for the judges, already notoriously capricious in such matters, would have in each case to decide how the law applied to religions of which they knew little or nothing, and of which it could not be said, as it is of Christianity, that they are inseparably 'part of the law itself'. That was the judgment of a lord chief justice in 1676, since when blasphemy has been an offence in common law; the sanction may be asleep but it is not dead. If tempted to believe that it is, one needs to recall the 1976 prosecution of *Gay News* and the subsequent failure in the House of Lords of an attempt to get rid of it.

I'm not sure whether to believe it, but am told it is even now a criminal offence to own a copy of the poem by James Kirkup that upset Mrs Whitehouse. Would one be guilty of blasphemy? So nobody can say exactly what blasphemy means in our world, only that it is, from case to case, whatever the judges decide. Etymologically the word, of Greek origin, has to do with damaging somebody's reputation, but it came to be used chiefly of trying to damage God's. The standard ruling was Leviticus 24.16, 'he that blasphemeth the name of the Lord shall surely be put to death, and all the congregation shall certainly stone him': incidentally, a passage of which the Greek (Septuagint) translation does not use the Greek word 'blaspheme', perhaps to avoid a range of implication – slander, speaking ill of somebody, not necessarily just of God – that is not present in the Hebrew. Still, in this earliest Judaic form the idea is straightforward: misusing the name of God was blasphemy and the penalty was stoning to death. The prohibition is stated in more general and familiar terms in the Third Commandment (Exodus 20.7).

The idea got more complicated when applied to the more complicated God of Christianity; for instance, it was blasphemy to speak against any Person of the Trinity, or indeed against the Church itself. Inevitably, different versions of the faith held contested views, on all sides cruelly enforced, on the question of what constituted blasphemy. It might well be deemed blasphemous simply to have a divergent but equally pious view of some aspect of doctrine. It could take the form of withholding consent to a political idea that seemed to have religious backing, like the divine right of kings. Indeed the offence became more political than religious, and so less distinguishable from heresy, apostasy, sacrilege, sedition, treason and no doubt other crimes.

Strictly considered, blasphemy, taking the name of the Lord in vain, usually in the form of some casual profanity, was a crime committed with great frequency by quite ordinary people, especially by men who thought that swearing by God's blood or God's death or God's wounds was a commonplace and excusable bit of the everyday conversational rhetoric of male groups – soldiers, for example. Such oaths have now been for the most part ousted by secular substitutes, but they were still giving serious offence in Shakespeare's time and later. Iago is an instance, although he is profane only among soldiers, and is distinguished from other, superior soldiers – such as Cassio and Othello himself – who do not have the habit. A 1606 Act of Parliament to 'restrain the abuses of players' ensured that in the 1623 revised version of the play Iago's blasphemies, very conspicuous in the earlier version, were cut. It is interesting that *Othello* is full of obscenities that would have horrified Mrs Whitehouse, but they were left in; only taking God's name in vain would, under the act, be punished with heavy fines. And this is why Angelo in *Measure for Measure* has to say, 'Heaven in my mouth/As if I could but only chew his name', when, thinking of the Eucharist, he means God, which is probably what Shakespeare, writing before the Act was passed, originally had in mind. There is another curious moment in *Measure for Measure* when Isabella is pleading with Angelo for her brother's life: 'That in the captain's but a choleric word,/Which in the soldier is flat blasphemy.' She is apparently developing a point made earlier, which is that one should not always judge the conduct of others by standards we apply to ourselves, but in doing so she seems to imply that there are different standards for different ranks and classes. Profanity is fine for officers who have a duty to be choleric with the men, but in common soldiers it is simple blasphemy and presumably punishable as such.

Punishments for blasphemy could be dreadfully severe. Stoning went out of fashion, but all manner of tortures, mutilations, floggings, burnings, flourished. It is hardly news in the 21st century that no age or clime has ever suffered a shortage of torturers when they were needed, men who don't even have the excuse of Elizabeth I or Calvin that to diminish the horror of the punishment was somehow to condone or even share in the offence. Sometimes ecclesiastical authorities, in milder mood, asked only for public penance, but up to about 1700 there was a preference for judicial severity, and studies of blasphemy tend to turn into catalogues of torture. Secularisation increasingly made such remedies look excessively theological, at which point blasphemy was to some extent replaced by more expressly political offences that also made it rational and necessary to inflict pain or death.

The present study* is French, and itself suffers from a frightfully tortured translation as well as from a good deal of redundant methodology, though it can hardly be condemned for emphasising French history and experience. It is a supplement to, not a replacement of, Leonard Levy's authoritative *Blasphemy*, from which the author courteously distances himself. Levy is mostly concerned with the history of the offence in England and America, a history in which that judgment of Lord Chief Justice Hale in 1676, later disputed by Jefferson, figures rather largely. Incidentally, the American record is a good deal less repressive and cruel than the English or the French. Levy remarks that the Supreme Court has never had to pronounce on a blasphemy case, partly because of the provisions of the First Amendment and partly because when there is no state religion the possibility of mingling blasphemy with a political charge is much reduced. Although in early colonial America the Leviticus rule was enforced, punishment was humanised, and there were symbolic executions, when the offender simply stood for a while under the gallows with a rope round his neck. By the end of the 18th century, when the British were ruthlessly persecuting political dissidents on blasphemy charges, there were hardly any prosecutions in America.

M. Cabantous is interested in *mentalités* and is the author of works on mutiny and the pillaging of wrecks. Coming now to blasphemy, he seeks to show how that practice, like those of piracy and mutiny, illuminates 'the cultural meanings of communal organisations'. Blasphemy was an intrusion of this-worldliness into the space of the sacred, and the authorities saw it as the breach of a taboo, 'forbidding, enticing and *sacred*'. The notion turns out to be very complex, and among the most interesting arguments is the claim that blasphemy, in spite of its bad record later on, can be thought to have founded Christianity, since Jesus' assertion of his divine nature led to a charge of blasphemy and so to his crucifixion and resurrection. Blasphemy therefore has some claim to be thought holy, and that helps to explain its power, however malign and however hated by authority.

It seems that real subtleties of definition had to wait for the great theologians of the 12th century, when it emerged that blasphemy was the most fearful of sins, worse than murder, because it repudiated God or questioned his goodness or compromised his honour – for instance, by conjoining his name with death or blood. The

---

*Alain Cabantous (trans. Eric Rauth), *Impious Speech in the West from the 17th to the 19th Century* (Columbia University Press, 2002).

dogmatic differences between the main parties at the time of the Reformation were such that one's rivals were bound to be blasphemers, either because they celebrated mass and venerated the Virgin, the saints and the pope – or because they didn't, and worshipped the Bible instead. Both sides thought of the Jews as blasphemy incarnate. In 1553 the Inquisition had the Talmud publicly burned, and Cabantous records no Protestant protest against such acts, though he does mention the more lenient view that since Jews, being born to ignorance of the truth, might blaspheme without intending to do so, they should be spared by human authority, though still guilty before God. (It is worth remembering that the judge at the *Gay News* trial, who happened to be a Jew, held that one could commit blasphemy without intending to – thereby establishing an alarming precedent and strengthening the argument for getting rid of the law altogether.)

Blasphemers were obviously likely to be wicked in other ways, so a strong link existed between blasphemous speech and libertinism generally. Cabantous touches on the excesses of English Restoration libertines like Sir Charles Sedley and on the slightly earlier and more philosophical French examples, notably Théophile de Viau. Atheists were of course blasphemers by definition, and we know from the charges against Christopher Marlowe that, like Théophile, they sometimes larded their tavern conversation with rather juvenile insults to religion – the Virgin was a whore, Christ was a bastard and St John was his bedfellow, and so on. It seems that one somehow needed to publicise the outrageousness of one's heretical opinions by talking in this manner.

And indeed the most curious aspect of blasphemy and profanity in general is this apparent need. What use is blasphemy? It must have some, since one hears every day the modern equivalents of those blasphemous oaths, now severed from any theological context and lacking any literal sense, but still serving as expletives. Unlike those feared by Macbeth, curses may now be loud but not deep, and nobody much minds them. No doubt in the old days informers reported quarrels in the street or the pub that resulted in what is here strangely called 'diarrhoea of the mouth'. And gamblers, though exceptionally stressed, were not alone in needing to curse their luck. There were many apparent inducements to blaspheme; here we are given percentages concerning 17th-century Parisians denounced for blasphemy: 28.9 per cent were violent, 25 per cent constantly drunk, 12.5 per cent libertine or debauched, and so on. Cabantous assiduously supplies evidence of the relevant denunciations, and carefully describes the efforts of the law at deterrence and punishment. All were to suffer royal justice, since the king, as the representative of God, was dishonoured by blasphemy and had the sole right to punish it.

The 17th-century jurist Blackstone is here commended for his sensible distinction between blasphemy and profanity; cursing and swearing are profane but holding the Bible up to ridicule is blasphemy and so more serious. The distinction is between mere vulgarity and philosophical or theological dissent. The latter is obviously more dangerous to the state, and the repressive British governments of the late 18th century used the law against political opponents. The example given here concerns the bookseller Thomas Williams, who was charged with blasphemy for publishing Tom Paine's *Age of Reason*. Although Paine said that the Bible described a devil under the name of God, his real offence was of course his support of the revolutions in America and France. Blake remarked that Paine was a better Christian than the bishop hired by the government to reply to his book, but he understood well enough that the issues were political, and did not publish his offensive remarks on the bishop: 'I have been commanded from Hell not to print this, as it is what our enemies wish.' Doubtless true and also uncharacteristically prudent; the government was in a tough mood.

Yet it isn't difficult to understand why people commit what Blackstone defines as blasphemy, since they are taking the risk of saying what they believe to be very important. The difficulty is to understand why profanity is so common, and was common even when it might be mistaken for blasphemy. Somehow it must have seemed necessary to say 'Sblood' and 'Zounds', and our etiolated modern profanities might still be justified as necessary. Perhaps, as this author suggests, profanity is part of a ritual of male violence; it is probably true that it has always been rarer among women. But the practice seems to have a more obscure social role: it establishes some kind of rapport with one's peers, a clublike atmosphere in which what you do or say can't be wrong because all the other members do and say it, and the community spirit is a pleasant agreement to do as one wills. The social situation might on enquiry turn out to be more complicated than that, and could even include the interdiction of some kinds of behaviour. But that is another subject for the historian of *mentalités*.

As time went by, even in the France of the Ancien Régime there was at least a fitful tendency to be more indulgent to blasphemers, though Cabantous quotes at length an extremely non-indulgent sentence of 1684: the guilty man had to stand in front of Notre Dame wearing only a shirt, having a rope round his neck and carrying a torch. Having begged forgiveness of God, he had his tongue cut out and was despatched to a life sentence of hard labour in the galleys. His possessions were confiscated and he was fined 300 livres. But others got off much more lightly, and blasphemy came to be treated for the most part as less serious and brought up, usually, as an accompaniment of some other misdemeanour.

Considered on its own it came to be thought of primarily as unsocial behaviour and was thus far from being worse than murder. It was even suggested rather boldly that there was no need to punish it – if God felt himself insulted he had remedies in his own hands. But the bloodthirsty still existed. Opposition to the Revolution was blasphemous, but to the opposers the blasphemy was the Revolution itself. Yet as the state progressively distanced itself from religion the pressure was reduced. With the Catholic monarchy extinct it was of course possible to offend other, more enlightened, more modern types of religious authority, but the trend understandably continued towards the point of not worrying too much about it.

Cabantous's final chapter is called 'Blasphemy's Comeback'. After what he or his translator oddly calls 'the slow and dramatic abatement of religious antagonisms' the blasphemer lost his status as 'the Other', except in the thought of the Roman Catholic Church, where it seems it is still held that blasphemers may bring divine punishment on society, just as some American fundamentalists saw the events of 11 September as a punishment for the prevalence of homosexuality and abortion. And even though there's less old-fashioned profanity about, now that we supply the place of wicked oaths with euphemisms, and so less action against it, we are advised not to forget the condemnation of Rushdie and certain contemporary Egyptian writers. And some films, by Scorsese and others, have been banned by Christians. So even if we decide, in accordance with the law of the land, that in this respect Islamic prohibitions and prosecutions are not our primary business and confine our attention to Christianity, we cannot say that blasphemy is absolutely a thing of the past. Cabantous may well be right about this, and in any case we'd be unwise to believe that anything that has so strong an appeal both to the guilty and to their judges, and might also attract the notice of another Whitehouse, another keen custodian of public morals, will ever quite go away.

24 January 2002

WHAT MIGHT HAVE HAPPENED UPSTAIRS

Mary Beard on Pompeii

ONE GOOD THING ABOUT volcanic eruptions is that they rarely come without warning. Days or weeks of insistent rumbling, smoke pouring ever more energetically from the crater, followed by a few light drizzles of ash, are usually enough to ensure that all those with common sense, determination and some means of transport have fled to safety hours before the lava starts to flow or the pumice to rain. That was certainly the case in Pompeii in 79 AD. The ash incinerated the city in an instant, but several days of earth tremors and the appearance of a mushroom cloud above Vesuvius on the morning of the eruption had given a clear signal of what was to come. The notoriously ghoulish Pompeian 'corpses' (in fact, plaster casts of the dead made by the ingenious process of injecting plaster of Paris into the cavity left by the decomposing flesh) represent only a tiny minority of the town's population: the procrastinators; the fatalists; the unlucky; those in the wrong place at the wrong time; the poor with no means to escape; the slaves with no option; the dogs still chained up at the doors. The most famous victim – Pliny the Elder, insufferable polymath and author of a vast encyclopedia of natural history – lost his life in a foolhardy attempt to get a better view of the catastrophe. The rest – and that was the vast majority of the inhabitants – had taken their valuables and left.

Good news for the Pompeians, but disappointing for centuries of archaeologists, tourists, novelists, artists and film-makers, most of whom have longed to cast Pompeii as the *Marie Céleste* of the classical world, with half-eaten boiled eggs still on the table. True, we get occasional vignettes of Pompeian life – and death – that have an immediacy hardly paralleled elsewhere in Greece or Rome: the remains of a man who had climbed a tree to escape the debris but was overwhelmed all the same; the bread just put into the oven by a baker who must obstinately have continued to work right up to the end. Yet overall what survives is emphatically not a frozen moment in the life of a community going about its normal business, but the traces of a city abandoned and already half-stripped. Hence the striking sparsity of household portables and domestic bric-à-brac (which has often given the impression that the prevailing first-century aesthetic was some kind of postmodern minimalism): a lot of it had simply been carted off by its loving owners.

There are other reasons, too, why Pompeii should have given as much disappointment as pleasure to its visitors over the last 250 years; and other factors behind the frustration felt by so many tourists, from Goethe onwards, at its failure to make the Roman world come really alive. ('The mummified city left us with a rather disagreeable impression,' Goethe recalls in *Italian Journey*, though he was much more impressed with the display in the nearby museum.) Looting, for a start. No sooner had the volcanic debris settled than the locals returned to the site and started tunelling down to get anything worth salvaging – from silver cups to bronze statues and marble facings. Almost two millennia later this process merged into what is euphemistically known as the first 'excavation' of the site, when the best of what was left was hacked out and hauled off to the collection of the king of Naples – consigning the 'second-rate' finds to systematic destruction, as unworthy of the royal patron. Looting was a profitable business, no doubt, from the very beginning – but it was dangerous, too. Ironically, a number of the corpses we strive to identify as the tragic victims of the eruption must be those of the far less tragic looters, crushed and suffocated as their treacherous network of tunnels collapsed about them.

Even more to the point, Pompeii was in a state of considerable disrepair long before the volcano erupted. In 62 it had been close to the epicentre of a major earthquake, with maybe a second following a few years later. The worst-case scenario (itself much debated) is that the town was almost devastated and was only very slowly being restored at the time of the eruption. The old moneyed families had left (for their other houses elsewhere, presumably) and their place in the city hierarchy, it is argued, had been taken by the nouveaux riches – who were busy decking out their mansions in the brashest version of the latest style, but giving the restoration of public buildings predictably low priority. By 79 – no less than 17 years after the first earthquake – only one building in the forum had for certain been fully repaired. If this gloomy picture is correct, what we visit in these ruins is not so much the remnant of a town in its prime (albeit looted and half-abandoned), but something more like an ancient building site (with a good deal of squatter occupation). Not an implausible picture; it is just the impression you get when you visit the place today.

Despite all these obstacles, or maybe stimulated by them, there has been an enormous renaissance in Pompeian studies over the last twenty years. The new generation of archaeologists and historians understands the problems of 'decoding' Pompeii all too well, but refuses to accept the absurdity of writing off, as too damaged or atypical to be useful, what must still count as the best preserved Roman town we shall ever have – if you cannot understand Pompeii, what hope is there for Antioch or Alexandria, even the city of Rome itself? They have concentrated on three kinds of project: first, exploring carefully the history of interventions at the site, from looters to diggers, in the two thousand years since the eruption; second, looking beneath the final debris of 79 to the complex earlier history of the town (the site had been occupied for more than seven hundred years by the time of the eruption, and had seen Etruscan, Greek and Italic settlers before it became officially 'Roman'); third and more broadly, attempting to get some better answers out of the ruins, by changing the historical questions put to them.

These approaches have scored some notable successes. Painstaking work in the archaeological archives has made it much easier to determine what the early excavators found and where exactly they found it. For the first time, and for a few select Pompeian houses, we can actually list what artefacts were discovered in which rooms: the essential first step to any discussion of the use of these rooms. In some cases (notably the so-called House of the Menander – named for the portrait of the Greek dramatist found inside) this archival work has been part of a complete re-examination of what survives on the ground, recording and dating the remains more accurately than ever before, disentangling the different phases of occupation and intervention, from origins to final excavation. This should help to reveal, for example, what damage actually occurred in the earthquake of 62 and what kinds of renovation followed – as well as exposing the activities of looters, ancient and modern.

At the broader level, new questions about the social significance of domestic architecture have revolutionised the study of Pompeian (and so, by extension, Roman) housing. By carefully matching up surviving architecture with different styles of wall decoration, by thinking afresh about such simple problems as what you could actually see when you walked through the front door of a house, and by comparing what remains with Vitruvius' first-century handbook *On Architecture*, archaeologists have put 'domestic space' back at the centre of Roman social and political history. The housing of the Roman elite, so this new orthodoxy goes, was not 'private', in the sense of hiding the inmates from public view, but a key extension of the owner's political persona, a stage specifically designed to be a backdrop to his public role as patron and magistrate.

So far so good. But for all these steps forward in our understanding of the city, some of the most basic questions about its history and character remain unanswered, and have become, if anything, even more baffling. You would think that it would be relatively easy to estimate the size of the population. After all, 75 per cent of the area has been excavated fully enough to give reasonably accurate plans of all the houses uncovered; and there are no grounds for supposing that the remaining 25 per cent will spring any major surprises. Nonetheless, estimates vary from as few as 6400 to as many as 30,000 inhabitants. The reason for this discrepancy stems, in part, from a series of very different assumptions about population density. Was Pompeian living an elegantly spacious affair, or were even the rich packed in tight, two or more to a bedroom? And the problem is compounded by the almost total destruction of the upper storeys of the buildings in the town. Many houses still have stairs leading up to a first floor; but what that first floor contained (dormitories for squadrons of slaves, the master bedroom, a nursery, or just attic storage space?) we simply do not know. It is chastening to reflect that none of the new theories of Roman domestic space have made any serious suggestions as to what (might have) happened upstairs.

It is possible of course that the population was considerably depleted in 79 – particularly if the earthquake of 62 was as devastating as some archaeologists have believed, and if all those with property elsewhere had moved out. This earthquake has been at the centre of much recent work: how destructive was it, exactly? How far had the repair programme progressed? What had the effect on the town's population been? Ironically, the more evidence that has been produced, the less clear the answers have become. Take the precise inventories that we now have of the finds made in some houses. Many of these show strikingly little differentiation room by room: in 'dining rooms', hoes and hatchets turned up next to wine jugs and serving dishes; elsewhere, carpentry tools were found next to cosmetic jars, silver spoons next to pruning hooks. This kind of distribution has been seized on as proof of the downgrading of the town in its final decades: that previously elegant houses had been turned over to multiple rented occupation as their owners moved out; that smart rooms, once markers of status and display, were now used to dump the garden tools. But other explanations are equally plausible. The pattern of finds could easily reflect the panic of those final hours before the eruption, as people hurriedly chose (or rejected) the possessions to load onto their carts. Or it might be a normal and characteristically Roman distribution of domestic utensils, earthquake or no earthquake; for one school of thought would reject the neat names and functions we now try to foist onto Roman domestic quarters ('dining room', 'study', 'bedroom'), in favour of a much more 'multi-functional' approach to living space. In the Roman world hoes and hatchets might regularly have lived next to the wine servers.

Paul Zanker's *Pompeii: Public and Private Life** springs from the centre of these debates. Based on three separate essays originally written between 1979 and 1993,

---

*Paul Zanker (trans. Deborah Lucas Schneider), *Pompeii: Public and Private Life*
(Harvard University Press, 1999).

and already published in Italian and German, it inevitably captures the changing world of Pompeian scholarship over that period (Zanker draws attention in his preface, notes and afterwords to all kinds of areas where new work would at least modify the conclusions he draws in the main body of the text). Overall, the book has an agreeably provisional, work-in-progress feel entirely appropriate to its subject.

Zanker, currently the director of the German Archaeological Institute in Rome, is best known for his work on the 'power of images' in the early Roman Empire. Stressing the importance of architecture, sculpture and city planning in the politics of the Roman monarchy (particularly under Augustus), he has had an enormous influence on the practice of ancient history: there have been no serious post-Zanker accounts of the public face of Roman imperial power that have dared to neglect the role of visual images. In the central chapter of *Pompeii*, Zanker turns his attention to a cityscape on a much smaller scale, tracking the changing urban landscape of Pompeii through its last three hundred years or so: from the second century BC (as a prosperous Italian community, with strong links to the Greek world); through its formal incorporation into the Roman sphere in the first century (the grant of Roman citizenship was quickly followed by the forcible settlement of a battalion of Roman veterans in the town); to the final period up to the earthquake and beyond. Predictably, the earthquake damage (and subsequent repairs) prompts some of Zanker's most significant second thoughts: his main text is confident that Pompeii's civic centre had been left almost entirely unrestored, a decaying eyesore, in the years leading up to 79; his afterword trails the possibility that much of it had been renovated – so expensively, in fact, that its brand-new marble was one of the first targets of the post-eruption looters. The other substantial chapter (a version of an essay of 1979) focuses on domestic housing. Again, it puzzles (and re-puzzles in the notes) about quite how far 'late' (i.e. post-62) Pompeii was under the cultural and political sway of the brash *nouveaux riches*, uncomfortably reminiscent of Trimalchio in Petronius' *Satyrica*.

This is an extremely intelligent and observant book (for the most part intelligently translated, though the House of Apollo irritatingly appears throughout as the House of 'Apolline'). For all its self-confessed provisionality, it is by far the best modern account of Pompeii as a historical city: indeed, the best account, more generally, of the visual and architectural impact of Roman power on the face of a medium-sized(?) Italian community in the late Republic and early Empire. Nevertheless, even Zanker occasionally clutches at some implausible historical straws. 'The fields of learning and culture,' he writes, in the course of a discussion of the cultural landscape of first-century AD Rome, 'were politically neutral, and therefore safe' – a statement which is not only demonstrably untrue, but a bizarre claim for

Zanker to make, given that his major work was partly devoted to showing precisely the reverse. Even more extraordinarily, when discussing the large and luxurious houses built in the second century BC, he draws a contrast between the attitudes of Pompeians and those of metropolitan Romans: senators in Rome were caught up in a cultural bind, in which they were attracted by Greek-style luxury but at the same time strongly advocated self-restraint; the population of Pompeii, on the other hand, had no such inconvenient scruples and enjoyed luxury to the limit of their finances. What he really means is that in Rome vast expenditure on building went hand in hand with literary debates which we can still read: with no surviving literature from the hand of a Pompeian, we have no idea what the inhabitants of Pompeii thought, or debated, when they built their vast mansions – but there is no reason to conclude *ex silentio* that their attitudes were any less complex than those of the Romans.

The fact that a scholar of Zanker's experience and distinction can resort to arguments like these raises the question, again, of why the evidence from Pompeii repeatedly proves so intractable. Ancient historians should certainly reflect on why they find it easier to write with confidence about a whole range of Roman cities that they 'know' much less well than Pompeii; and on whether they have become too comfortable with the paucity of evidence that they usually lament. The sheer bulk of what survives from Pompeii is, in some ways, an inconvenient surprise. Ultimately though, the problem comes down to the difficulty of interpreting ancient material remains where there are no literary sources to accompany them. Our longest ancient text that concerns the city is the younger Pliny's highly embroidered account of his uncle's fatal escapade. Apart from that, we have little more than a couple of brief mentions of the earthquake and a few lines on a riot in the Pompeian amphitheatre in 59 AD. The material evidence cannot speak for itself, nor give clear answers to the majority of interpretative questions we want to ask. Even when the artefactual remains are as rich as they are in Pompeii, they cannot speak for the people who once used them nor for their history over time; they can barely hint at the complex processes by which any particular object was finally uncovered by the trowel in any particular part of any particular ancient building. Most of us are less interested in the fact that a hoe was found in a dining-room than in what it was used for (not only hoeing, one would guess), in who put it there and why. And no amount of archaeology on its own, even on Pompeii's lavish scale, can answer those questions.

16 September 1999

TSEEPING

Christopher Tayler on Alain de Botton

IN THE FIFTH CHAPTER of *The Art of Travel*,* Alain de Botton goes on a trip to the Lake District. He takes his girlfriend, 'M', and a paperback copy of *The Prelude*. Applying his talent for summary to the latter, he explains that it prescribes 'regular travel through nature' as 'a necessary antidote to the evils of the city'. Not being the sort to take a poet at his word, de Botton sets out to test Wordsworth's 'suggestion'. With 'M' in tow, he goes for a long walk.

Nature turns out to contain oaks 'of noble bearing' and fields 'so appetising to sheep as to have been eaten down to a perfect lawn'. It even offers some 'suggestions' of its own. Oaks, for example, are 'an image of patience', 'showing no ill-temper in a storm' and 'no desire to wander from their spot'. So it's hardly surprising that 'Wordsworth enjoyed sitting beneath oaks.' Later on, the landscape provokes a more philosophical line of inquiry: 'Why am I me and she she?' 'She', in this case, is a sheep, and further encounters with animals prove Wordsworth triumphantly right: 'If we are pained by the values of the age or of the elite, it can be a source of relief to come upon reminders of the diversity of life on the planet, to hold in mind that, alongside the business of the great people of the land, there are also pipits tseeping in meadows.' True, the palliative effects of tseeping might not last very long, but Wordsworth is on hand with a solution. Wordsworth recommends the gathering of 'spots of time' – and so, as if on cue:

> I too was granted a 'spot of time' . . . M and I were sitting on a bench near Ambleside eating chocolate bars. We had exchanged a few words about the chocolate bars we preferred. M said she liked caramel-filled ones, I expressed a greater interest in dry biscuity ones, then we fell silent and I looked out across a field to a clump of trees by a stream . . . These trees gave off an impression of astonishing health and exuberance. They seemed not to care that the world was old and often sad. I was tempted to bury my face in them so as to be restored by their smell.

Whether the trees were unusually small or his face unusually large, de Botton doesn't explain. Either way, they have the desired effect. Some time later, caught in

---

*Alain de Botton, *The Art of Travel* (Hamish Hamilton, 2002).

traffic and 'oppressed by cares', he returns in thought to the scene (or it returns to him): 'The trees came back to me, pushing aside a raft of meetings and unanswered correspondence . . . and, in a small way that afternoon, contributed a reason to be alive.' As a parting shot, he quotes a few lines from 'Daffodils' and enjoins us to bear them in mind.

So ends Chapter 5 of *The Art of Travel*. There are four more still to come and, by now, the reader might be wondering how de Botton reconciles his gratitude to the trees with the acreage felled to print this stuff. But acreage is the point. In every chapter, de Botton extracts as much verbiage as possible from such 'profound and suggestive' insights as 'it is better to travel hopefully than to arrive' – or, as he puts it, 'the pleasure we derive from journeys is perhaps dependent more on the mindset with which we travel than on the destination we travel to.' What counts is staying power, and this he has in spades. A.P. Herbert, the *Punch* contributor chosen by Ian Hamilton to represent the 'something-about-next-to-nothing school' in the *Penguin Book of 20th-Century Essays*, could just about manage three pages on bathrooms. De Botton sustains his thoughts 'On the Country and the City' for an astonishing 25 – although, to be fair, Herbert doesn't have the advantage of large print.

De Botton achieves this bulk with ruthless application and many ingenious devices. Some of these – like filling a fifth of the book with pictures – may strike purists as cheating. But couching each chapter as a literary essay is definitely a good idea, since quotation, especially of poetry, takes up a lot of space. So do capsule biography and paraphrase: de Botton generates almost four pages by rearranging sentences from Robert Baldick's translation of *A rebours*. And when all else fails, the literary pose gives licence to cod-Proustian long-windedness, replete with 'it is perhaps', 'that which' and the bogus 'precisely'. Here, for example, is his gloss on the notion that things look small from a plane: 'We may know this old lesson in per-spective well enough, but rarely does it seem as true as when we are pressed against a cold plane window, our craft a teacher of profound philosophy – and a faithful disciple of the Baudelairean command: "Carriage, take me with you! Ship, steal me away from here!/Take me far, far away! Here the mud is made of our tears!"'

When he writes about books, though, de Botton's page-count often falls victim to his abilities as a summariser. These have grown steadily more acute. *How Proust Can Change Your Life*, his first big seller, runs to just over 200 pages. *The Consolations of Philosophy*, which deals with Seneca, Socrates, Montaigne, Epicurus, Schopen-hauer and Nietzsche, only stretches to about 250. *The Art of Travel* – 261 pp., includ-ing pictures and acknowledgments – is even more concise, discussing as it does Huysmans, Flaubert, Baudelaire, Xavier de Maistre, Alexander von Humboldt, Ruskin, Burke, Wordsworth, van Gogh, Edward Hopper and the Book of Job. Of course, when de Botton dissects the writings of, say, Schopenhauer, he's only interested in the 'consoling and practical' bits, which obviously means leaving quite a few things out. And since quibbles about 'exactly what Epicurus said' or 'precisely what Keats meant . . . might ultimately be quite dull or mistaken', these can safely be left in the hands of dusty pedants – especially now that 'most letters have been catalogued, most texts deciphered, most lives written up conclusively.' Still, a writer capable of reducing Flaubert's Egyptian travel notes and *Dictionary of Received Ideas* to 'an invitation to deepen and respect our attraction to certain countries' is clearly going to have trouble finding enough material in books alone.

De Botton solves this problem by writing about himself. He does so with studied whimsy, keen to show that even he – the master of thought – is a regular guy. It's true that sometimes he does seem rather grand, the sort of fellow who 'resolves' rather than 'decides' and 'travels' rather than 'goes'; at one point he even alights from a 'craft' which, when you scan the surrounding evidence, turns out to be what others might call a 'car'. But he has a nice line in bathos too, and some of his humorous effects – 'We talked about the colonial system and the curious ineffectiveness of even the most powerful sunblocks' – are almost certainly deliberate. Most of the time, though, de Botton seems largely concerned with conforming to the stereotype of the neurasthenic intellectual. And life, we sense, is hard for this pitiful figure, forever confounded by what he calls 'the distracting woolliness of the present'. He complains of dizziness, sore throats and pressure across the temples; further anxieties accumulate 'like the weather fronts that mass themselves every few days off the western coast of Ireland'. Cleaning staff intimidate him. In Madrid he's too shy to enter a restaurant, and in Barbados he worries about the price of lunch. Leaving a 'gathering' in London he feels 'envious and worried'; he imagines that in summer he might 'feel as much at home in the world as in my own bedroom', but knows that this is probably an illusion.

Most of his problems derive from the pains of love. He seems to have trouble with his girlfriends, perhaps because they're usually called things like 'M'. (Woody Allen: 'Should I marry W? Not if she won't tell me the other letters in her name.') His ideal woman would be 'a reincarnation of Giovanni Bellini's Madonna' with 'a dry sense of humour and spontaneity', with whom he would like to lie in bed 'chatting about existence' and 'occasionally teasing'. Most of the time she seems very far away. In *The Consolations of Philosophy* there's a heartbreaking episode in which he chats up a girl on a train. When she spurns his advances after their only date, our hero, 'beset by melancholy', repairs to Battersea Park with 'a paperback edition of Goethe's *The Sorrows of Young Werther*, first published in Leipzig in 1774'. All seems flat and meaningless. A little girl points at a plane and says: 'Daddy, is

God in there?' Daddy doesn't know. Eventually, de Botton is consoled by thoughts of Schopenhauer. When suffering from impotence, he turns to Montaigne.

Puddings and sweet things in general are his other consolation. In Amsterdam he sees some bricks which remind him of 'halva from a Lebanese delicatessen'; he feels an urge to kiss them. In Barbados some crèmes caramel provoke a serious row with 'M', whom de Botton accuses of stealing the shapelier portion. This arouses 'mutual terrors of incompatibility and infidelity' which even spoil his enjoyment of the beach: 'There was no pleasure for me in such beauty. I had enjoyed nothing aesthetic or material since the struggle over the crèmes caramel several hours before.' Poor Alain! The most important of his confectionery-related insights, however, revolve around chocolate. In *The Consolations of Philosophy*, de Botton revealed that he had the inspiration to write the book while trying to buy 'a glass of a certain variety of American chocolate milk of which I was at that time extremely fond'. In tribute, he inserts a photo of a carton of Nesquik. His meditative trip to a service station in *The Art of Travel* is chocolate-fuelled, as are his walks in Madrid and, of course, his vision of trees in the Lake District. In Provence he wolfs down 'three pains au chocolat in guilty, rapid succession' before launching into a disquisition on van Gogh. He needs the sugar rush – and so, presumably, do the people who buy his books.

Perhaps it's unfair to make fun of de Botton's effusions. They're not meant to be taken that seriously, after all, and a few of his readers might even be tempted to pick up the works of Proust or Xavier de Maistre. Why shoot fish in a barrel when they're not doing anyone any harm? At the same time, though, there's something slightly chilling about the gulf between what de Botton has to say and the way he goes about saying it. Does a sequence of platitudes really need all that padding? This is how de Botton once put the idea that convoluted language doesn't necessarily imply deep thought:

> It is common to assume that we are dealing with a highly intelligent book when we cease to understand it . . . Yet the association between difficulty and profundity might less generously be described as a manifestation in the literary sphere of a perversity familiar from emotional life, where people who are mysterious and elusive can inspire a respect in modest minds that reliable and clear ones do not.

'Such prose masks an absence of content,' he remarks a few pages later, offering 'unparalleled protection against having nothing to say'.

22 August 2002

A MORAL IDIOCY, AN IMBECILITY OF THE WILL, A HAUNTING, AN EMPTINESS, A POSTHUMOUS STATE, A WRITING BLOCK

Susan Eilenberg on Coleridge

He knew not what to do – something, he felt, must be done – he rose, drew his writing-desk before him – sate down, took the pen – & found that he knew not what to do.

FOND READERS WHO DREAM of the poems Keats might have written had he lived past 25 and speculate about what works died with Shelley at 29, humane readers who deplore tuberculosis and drowning (together with rheumatic fever, arsenic and other wasters of Romantic genius), entertain a different and darker regret when they turn their attention to Coleridge, wishing not that he had lived longer, but that he had died sooner. While no one will admit to a wish for any particular form of death – drowning, say, on the way to Malta, or an intestinal catastrophe still more catastrophic than the ones which figured in the psychosomatic melodrama of his life – there is a widespread feeling that it would have been better for all concerned, better even for Coleridge himself, had he simply ceased to exist during the first years of the 19th century.

In certain respects it is as if he had. After the first glorious days of his friendship with Wordsworth, Coleridge set about – or perhaps only resumed – a course of procrastination and ruin from which it seemed decent to avert one's eyes. His life grew complicated and his poetry sparse, and his achievement took forms that required sometimes unreasonable effort to value.

A judiciously abridged Coleridge, one whose exasperatingly shaggy life had been reformed along the cleaner lines of tragedy, would have been a subject more readily adapted to admiration and sympathy (or at least pity and terror) than the one his embarrassed biographers give us. Had Coleridge expired out of sight in Malta in 1805, as he and Wordsworth both expected he might, he would have avoided much of the ugly deterioration, so dismaying to his admirers, of his integrity, his personal relations, his appearance and his poetic abilities. This is not to say he would have gone out in a blaze of glory. Already his health was destroyed, his dependence on opium crippling, his marriage all to pieces, his love for Sara Hutchinson frustrated, his collaboration with Wordsworth curdling into a matter of jealous resentment, the poetry for which we chiefly remember him all in the past, his hopes and his reasons for hope decayed. He was not yet at the worst, however. His tears could still evoke answering tears, and his declarations of accomplishment and serious intent had not yet lost their credibility. The devastating hallucination in which he saw Sara Hutchinson in bed with Wordsworth was still to come; nor had he yet learned that Wordsworth, disgusted by his habitual drunkenness and lying, had begun warning friends against him. He had not yet officially given in to his tendency to domestic parasitism, or discovered that his beloved son Hartley had inherited all his own worst moral weaknesses and that his daughter Sara had followed him into hypochondria and drug addiction.

As Rosemary Ashton,[*] Richard Holmes[†] and Morton Paley[‡] remind us, Coleridge did survive the long years of estrangement, both from Wordsworth and from all he had ceded to Wordsworth; he did begin to return to himself. When the current of critical opinion reversed, he found himself the object of loud praise, the domesticated sage of Highgate whose eccentric and adenoidal monologues drew auditors from as far away as the suburbs of Boston, Massachusetts. Yet despite the successes of his later life – indeed, despite the extraordinary fecundity evident in the still lengthening shelf of his *Collected Works* – he felt his achievement to be precarious. Anticipations of his own poetic end arrive almost at once with the mature poetry. Hardly had 'The Rime of the Ancient Mariner' been published than its author announced (in May 1799) his intention 'to dedicate in silence the prime of my life' to metaphysics, a turn made necessary, as he said a year later, by his sense that his 'faculties' were 'dwindling', or at least that they would not bear comparison with Wordsworth's: 'He is a great, a true Poet – I am only a kind of Metaphysician.' In September 1800 he wrote: 'I abandon Poetry altogether – I leave the higher & deeper kinds to Wordsworth, the delightful, popular & simply dignified to Southey; & reserve for myself the honourable attempt to make others feel and understand their writings, as they deserve to be felt & understood.' In December he recognised that 'I never had the essentials of poetic Genius, & that I mistook a strong desire for original power.' By March 1801, Coleridge had decided it was all over: 'The Poet is dead in me.'

Poetry was largely crowded out by illnesses – neuralgias, mysterious swellings of the scrotum and the eye, nightmares, elaborate bowel complaints. At least some of this had to do with the opium he took and with the opium he denied himself,

---

*Rosemary Ashton, *The Life of Samuel Taylor Coleridge* (Blackwell, 1996).
†Richard Holmes (ed.), *Coleridge: Selected Poems* (HarperCollins, 1996).
‡Morton Paley, *Coleridge's Later Poetry* (Oxford University Press, 1996).

but some of it predated his addiction. Perhaps the pathology of 1834 was incapable of detecting the disease that accounted for Coleridge's distresses, or perhaps, as recent critics and biographers have suggested, the pathologists should have looked into the poet's relations with his mother, his brothers, his wife and his beloved instead of into his body. Coleridge, the inventor of the word 'psychosomatic', had wanted to believe that what he suffered from was an authentic organic disease and hoped that an autopsy might – retrospectively – establish the validity of his complaints and excuses. It did not do so.

Until very recently, not even Coleridge's sympathisers made much of an effort to rescue him from the appearance of failure. Although few went as far as Norman Fruman in condemning Coleridge as an impotent fraud and plagiarist, many reluctantly agreed with Thomas McFarland when he declared: 'Coleridge's ruin, in both life and work, is . . . the true human fact; the academic classic and the conventional achievement the illusion.' It may be that in the protracted aftermath to the much insisted on death of the author, the death of a particular author – or, rather, the dissolution of his authority and the abstraction of his agency – registers as no very terrible event, and vicariousness, marginality, diasparactivity, failures of centrality or identity or unity seem not so much defects as marks of the literary condition. Accordingly, we have had Coleridge the perpetual usher, the marginal man, the abject whose writing is simultaneously a mutilation, a mourning and a suicide. But although the fragments, the quasi-Bakhtinian dialogics, the recursive metalanguages he produced might almost have been made for postmodernist appreciation, Coleridge would not willingly have accepted redemption on those terms. Ambivalent towards his own labile genius, craving the apparently organic authenticity he saw in other writers, he loathed himself as a prodigy of ruin and, in his worst moments, would have traded all his tormentingly prodigal imagination for Southey's dully regular industry.

The referred torments and hysterical agonies that prevented Coleridge from writing the sorts of poem he wanted to write functioned as the psychic, literary and physical equivalent of an auto-immune disease, a morbid self-misrecognition or mutant Socratism in which self-knowledge is disabling and identification toxic. 'In *exact proportion* to the *importance* and *urgency* of any Duty was it, as of a fatal necessity, sure to be neglected . . . In exact proportion, as I *loved* any person or persons more than others, & would have sacrificed my Life for them, were *they* sure to be the most barbarously mistreated by silence, absence, or breach of promise,' Coleridge wrote. It was true. Kind to other men's children, he neglected Hartley, Derwent and Sara; he would wear himself out seeing Wordsworth's poems through the press but was incapable of making any but the slightest exertions on behalf of his own. All his life he got into awkward situations over men (and sometimes women) whose identities he could only imperfectly distinguish from his own: his plagiarisms may stem from this, as may his chronic suspicion that others were plagiarising him or those around him. His loathing of Sir James Mackintosh ('the great Dung-fly') and of William Pitt are the clearest expressions of self-contempt; his troubles with Charles Lloyd and Thomas de Quincey stem from a mutual or compound confusion of identities; and he inspired the same bitter disillusionment in his quondam admirers (most spectacularly William Hazlitt) that he felt towards his own fallen idols.

He felt the disease of his selfhood as a moral idiocy, an imbecility of the will, a haunting, an emptiness or poverty or unreality, a lack of solidity, an incurable loneliness, a posthumous state, a writing block. His purposes had to be borrowed, or else got up for the occasion; so did his funds and his domestic arrangements. His life, shaped by his accommodation of the unreal, required a suspension of disbelief from even its chief inhabitant, who habitually regarded his reflection with the absorption one might accord a play, treated his birthdate as a revisable fiction, and was persuaded (temporarily) to believe or act as though he believed that he loved a woman from whom all his instincts urged him to flee. An intellectual understanding of the pathological nature of his need to borrow reality from others did nothing to mitigate that need; he remained vulnerable to men of stronger will than himself, whose self-assurance or self-righteousness he interpreted at least initially as spiritual superiority. Everyone sneers at Mrs Coleridge, jealous of Wordsworth's influence, trying to snatch her husband out of his orbit, but her dismay was shared by Coleridge's friends, many of whom felt his idolatry to be a pernicious thing. And Coleridgeans, following their subject, blame Wordsworth for his exploitation of Coleridge's devotion. But the idolatry and the exploitation would have happened even without Wordsworth; the same thing had happened a few years before, with Southey, as it had happened and would go on happening all Coleridge's life. Imaginative death, literary failure and increasing numbers of non-believers required miracles of revival, redemption and conversion – required, it seemed, messianic beings like Wordsworth, by whose side Coleridge thought himself impaired.

Coleridge portrayed himself as a victim, but in many respects he was responsible for creating what injured him. In particular, he was responsible for creating the expectations of achievement by which we now measure his failure – one that might not register as failure on another scale. Naming and offering details of the works he was just about to begin or just about to complete, he converts innocent and abstract white space into the site of humiliatingly specific failure: 'The Origin of Evil, an Epic Poem' does not exist; neither does the 'Logosophia', nor the eight-volume history of English poetry and poets (together with metaphysics, theology, surgery, medicine, alchemy and chemistry, navigation, exploration and law – common, canon and Roman). Surely no one would blame him for having neglected to solve the mysteries of cosmic order and human consciousness had he not pretended to have 'completely extricated the notions of Time and Space' and to have been on the verge of being able 'to evolve all the five senses, that is, to deduce them from *one sense* & to state their growth, & the causes of their difference – & in this evolvement solve the process of Life & Consciousness'. And his claims to have worked out Goethe's theory of colours before Goethe himself did, and to have anticipated Kant, succeed only in forcing us to strip him of his borrowed glory. It is the same story with the works he did write. Representing the results of his careful and prolonged labour as products of accident or prodigy or spontaneity or derangement, he slandered them (and himself) for the sake of exemption from critical evaluation. Thus he presented 'Kubla Khan' as a fragment of a much greater piece destroyed by amnesiac distraction, perhaps in order to glorify the unrecoverable, perhaps imaginary, and certainly unjudgable original, perhaps in order merely to confound detractors, themselves in part figments of a preveniently guilty imagination.

The most self-destructive (though gorgeous) of Coleridge's strategically ambiguous metafictions is his poetic theory. The author of fragments, collaborative experiments, extratextual conversations and overgrown marginalia – works that notoriously decline to remain within their proper boundaries – insists that 'nothing can permanently please, which does not contain in itself the reason why it is so, and not otherwise,' that 'the definition of a *legitimate* poem' is that 'it must be one, the parts of which mutually support and explain each other,' and that the purpose of all poems is 'to convert a *series* into a *Whole*'. So oddly does the critical language of unity and organicism sort with the poetry of uncanny disruption that you wonder whether the incongruity can have been accidental. The criticism is to the poetry as requirement is to failure – not a mere antithesis but a typically Coleridgean idealisation of the negative of his achievement, an attempt at self-transcendence fallen into self-condemnation.

The space of that fall is the space of Coleridge's poetry. Sometimes, as in 'Dejection: An Ode', Coleridge represented the fall as a failure of his 'genial spirits' at the grim recognition of the provenance of the hope that 'grew round me, like the twining vine,/And fruits, and foliage [that], not my own, seemed mine' – a recognition that moved him to a confused attempt at rescue, wishing 'haply by abstruse research to steal/From my own nature all the natural man'. But the chronology of anagnorisis and catastrophe in 'Dejection' fails to account for the intimations of failure present from the beginning, without which even the greatest of Coleridge's poems could not have come into being. The self-doubt, the surrender of hope explicit in 'Dejection' and 'To William Wordsworth' were implicit in the moving but otherwise mysterious generosity of the so-called conversation poems, including 'Frost at Midnight' and 'This Lime-tree Bower My Prison', in which the poet wishes that others may find joy where he himself must not; despair is veiled only by the conventions of fiction in 'The Rime of the Ancient Mariner', 'Kubla Khan' and 'Christabel', all tales about loss of imaginative and linguistic control. Peripeteia occurs not only between the early poetry and the later but also within the poems themselves, both early and late.

This is not to say that all Coleridge's failures are really successes in disguise. By the standards of his greatest work, most of his verse is of minor value, either too much in the mode of what Harold Bloom called 'whooping' or else mere occasional verse, poetastry. But many of even the least ambitious poems, as Holmes and Paley show, are fresh and sharp and witty, and within the shadow of the much anthologised pieces a reader can find poems which, though lacking the extraordinary power of engagement that Coleridge's best work commands, exert a kindred fascination. These second-rank poems, unlike the masses of newspaper verse and trifles he wrote to amuse acquaintances, inhabit an emotional desolation or devastation at once more immediate and more abstract than anything one encounters elsewhere in Coleridge. Loneliness and despair remain naked, untransfigured. Preoccupied, like consciously and uneasily posthumous things, with the work of agglomeration and decay, they often inhabit provisional forms and provisional titles, so that despite their strongly autobiographical cast, they behave with the irresponsibility and sometimes the freedom of anonymous texts.

One of these, already familiar to many readers, is the emblem originally published under the title 'Time, Real and Imaginary':

> On the wide level of a mountain's head,
> (I knew not where, but 'twas some faery place)
> Their pennons, ostrich-like, for sails outspread,
> Two lovely children run an endless race,
>   A sister and a brother!
>   This far outstripp'd the other;
> Yet ever runs she with reverted Face,
> And looks and listens for the boy behind:
>   For he, alas! is blind!
> O'er rough and smooth with even step he passed,
> And knows not whether he is first or last.

In the longer version of this, 'Hope and Time', the poet identifies the sister with Hope, the brother with Time. These identifications have puzzled critics, who note the oddity of Hope's backward gaze and the impossibility of aligning either Hope or Time with either real time or imaginary time. Paley, working carefully through the text, its variants and its contexts, doubts the emblem's solubility. It probably is insoluble, for the poem behaves less like an explication of the relationship of Hope to Time, or of time real to time imaginary, than like an expression of the poet's unhappy sense of self-division. The blind innocence is his own, or was; so is the pity and yearning after the self that ran along in brave ignorance; so is the ironic knowledge that this anxious remorseful nostalgic self-love blinds its subject to all but the loss that it doubles. Here as elsewhere in Coleridge, hope is inextricable from pathos because a function of retrospection.

The imputation of a blindness that disrupts a symmetry of gazes had been present since almost the beginning of Coleridge's poetic career. In the great con-versation poems it seems an index of the power of sympathy, which can overcome even unconsciousness or inanimacy. The 'silent icicles,/Quietly shining to the quiet Moon', the child's tears that 'Did glitter in the yellow moon-beam', figure the serene ideal that begins to dim in Coleridge's surrender before Wordsworth's greater powers:

> In silence listening, like a devout child,
> My soul lay passive, by thy various strain
> Driven as in surges now beneath the stars,
> With momentary stars of my own birth,
> Fair constellated foam, still darting off
> Into the darkness; now a tranquil sea,
> Outspread and bright, yet swelling to the moon.

After 'To William Wordsworth', the image comes to seem more unnerving than affectionate, an uncanny resurrection of sympathy in the form of intolerable indif-ference. There is the transmogrification in 'Limbo' of the 'unmeaning' of 'moon-light on the dial of the day' into moonlight on the eye of the blind man who

> stops his earthly task to watch the skies;
> But he is blind – a statue hath such eyes; –
> Yet having moonward turn'd his face by chance,
> Gazes the orb with moon-like countenance,
> With scant white hairs, with foretop bald and high,

He gazes still, – his eyeless face all eye; –
As 'twere an organ full of silent light,
His whole face seemeth to rejoice in light! –
Lip touching lip, all moveless, bust and limb –
He seems to gaze at that which seems to gaze on him!

Blindness – a sublime blindness with Wordsworthian overtones – becomes (in such poems as 'The World that Spidery Witch') blankness, a reflexivity that repels finally even the abstract otherness that is its own image:

I speak in figures, inward thoughts and woes
Interpreting by Shapes and outward shews:
Where daily nearer me with magic Ties,
What time and where, (wove close with magic Ties
Line over line, and thickning as they rise)
The World her spidery threads on all sides spin[s]
Side answ'ring side with narrow interspace,
My Faith (say I; I and my Faith are one)
Hung, as a Mirror, there! And face to face
(For nothing else there was between or near)
One Sister Mirror hid the dreary Wall,
But that is broke! And with that bright compeer
I lost my object and my inmost all –
Faith in the Faith of THE ALONE MOST DEAR!

'What no one with us shares,' Coleridge had written in 'The Blossoming of the Solitary Date-Tree', 'seems scarce our own' – 'What then avail those songs, which sweet of yore/Were only sweet for their sweet echo's sake?' Bereft of his sociable voices (echoes or not), Coleridge was diminished as a man and as a poet; and, as Michael Macovski has suggested, the absence of conversation affected him as a terrifying internal silence. Even after the conversations for which we chiefly remember him, however, his poems kept up a murmuring, an internal monologue that at times approaches the kind of conversation his earlier poems were wont to have with Wordsworth's.

The violent division between Coleridge the success and Coleridge the failure has made for both convenience and embarrassment. The obvious superiority of his best work simplifies and justifies, even naturalises, the work of the anthologist. In the presence of any half-dozen of Coleridge's strongest poems, merit seems a matter of simple self-evidence. (The same cannot be said of all great poems: look at Wordsworth's, for instance.) But the simplicity has a troubling aspect, for Coleridge's anthology pieces are not, as we expect such pieces to be, fully representative; *hapax legomena*, false synecdoches, they are too few to be other than suggestive singularities. In any case, it is no longer done to rejoice in the plums at the expense of the pudding.

These four new volumes from Rosemary Ashton, Richard Holmes, Morton Paley and Ted Hughes* work to restore the plums to their proper context. Ashton's biography reminds us how thoroughly and often unhappily the poet was also the son, the brother, the orphan, the husband and the father; she weighs neurotic disability against freedom and comes up with a figure much battered, deeply fractured, but not a helpless victim. Holmes, whose own earlier half-life of the poet anticipated Ashton's in its balance of sympathy and informed scepticism, now offers a selection of poems well-known and unknown, neatly annotated and presented under new headings designed to remind us of how many more contexts the real Coleridge occupied than his myth ever seemed to. Some of the same poems make an appearance in Morton Paley's admirable study of Coleridge's 'later' poetry, which, Paley argues, declares its difference and independence from the poetry Coleridge invented with Wordsworth and returns to Coleridge's native, pre-Wordsworthian sensibility. This poetry, which Paley concedes to be less ambitious than what preceded it but which he believes is valuable nonetheless, he reads with miraculous care, insisting that the poems can 'be *fully* discussed only in relation to their textual matrices'. These matrices vibrate, like intelligent concordances, to the merest echoes of texts themselves often fragmentary or ephemeral or remote – the most ethereal of puddings.

The oddest of these volumes is Ted Hughes's collection of poems drawn together to support his contention, set forth in an exceedingly long introductory essay, that Coleridge's greatest poems (and a fair number of his lesser poems as well) allegorise the poetically lethal contest between Coleridge's repressive Protestant intellect and his passionate pagan imagination, his 'Unleavened Self'. This Unleavened Self was devoted to the Great Female who was the mythic form of Coleridge's unresponsive mother and who sometimes appeared as a bellowing maternal alligator and sometimes as an albatross. In this reading all the female characters turn out to be the same female character, and all the poems that matter turn out to be the same poem. It is a little difficult to understand just what this poem ('a single Tragic Opera') is about, but it has something to do with oaks (*not* with birches), and the

*Ted Hughes (ed.), *A Choice of Coleridge's Verse* (Faber, 1996).

moral of it seems to be that Coleridge should have had the courage to follow the wailing woman down the alligator hole.

Coleridge does give the appearance of one appalled by his perilous altitude and his perilous descent. Courage might have helped. Yet how easy for us to say that, who have only to witness the plummet and, as we choose, retrieve and pronounce on the fragments. What, however, to save? What to sacrifice? At what cost does this writer survive his own apparent extinction, and what is his survival worth?

Coleridge feels more real, rounder, both more connected and more lonely as a result of Ashton, Holmes and Paley's work of retrieval and appreciation. It is clear that he was more robust and wrote more good poetry than most of us suspected. But the ratio of sublimity to mere pleasure or worse, always in Coleridge's case somewhat hard to calculate, has dropped a little below the point at which ardent Coleridgeans had hoped it might be set. Certainly 'The Ancient Mariner' is no less wonderful for having been followed by 'To Two Sisters' and 'Lines Composed in a Concert-Room'. But now it is the brilliance that seems the aberration, and not its dimming.

19 June 1997

SHORT CUTS

Thomas Jones

COD ETHNOGRAPHY IS A less popular subject in primary schools these days than it once was, but not so many years ago a surprising number of seven-year-olds seemed to 'know' that Red Indians would say 'How' when greeting each other, and that Eskimos kiss by rubbing noses. (In a recent poll of under-tens, three out of three had no idea about either of these things; one, when given a clue – a raised hand salute – ventured that Red Indians might greet each other with 'Heil Hitler.') An equivalent factoid I picked up in elementary geography lessons is that there are sheep farms in Australia the size of Wales. I wondered if Australian schoolchildren learned that there are countries in Europe the size of sheep farms. Knowing Wales is a valid unit of area (equivalent to 20,770 km^2) is much more useful than being prepared to rub noses north of the Arctic Circle. Here are some uses: the Amazon rainforest is being cleared at the rate of a Wales a year; the largest crater on the Moon is three times the size of Wales. When that piece of Antarctica came adrift earlier this year, it was immediately, automatically even, said to be the size of Wales, and only later revealed to be closer to the size of Cambridgeshire (about a sixth the size of Wales). So it comes as no surprise to learn that a nature reserve for woolly mammoths, in order to sustain a viable population, would have to be the size of Wales. A handy website, www.users.globalnet.co.uk/~kelky/sizeofwales.htm, has a 'Walesometer' for converting hectares/acres/square miles/square kilometres into Waleses. It shouldn't be too long before EU harmonisation will necessitate replacing Wales with Belgium, which will give Europhobes something else to grumble about over their black pudding. Outside the UK, multiples of Wales aren't very meaningful; Americans, for example, are more likely to speak in terms of fractions of Texas, a place which has the very great advantage of being bigger than everywhere else.

If you took every unread copy of *Don Quixote* in the world and laid them all out on the ground, they would cover an area the size of Wales. Nonetheless, Cervantes's romance has been voted the best book ever by a bunch of writers – a hundred or so well-known authors from 54 countries, not including Isabel Allende, Bob Dylan or Gabriel García Márquez, who admirably declined to vote. The *Guardian* did a vox pop. New Puritan about town Nicholas Blincoe rather proudly let slip that he's read 81 of the top 100, smashing Mark Lawson (69) into a measly second place. 'I think the list is pompous,' Blincoe said. 'Authors really do think they are fantastically clever and I think this list reflects the high opinion they have of themselves.' Indeed. Chris Woodhead is 'surprised by *Don Quixote*. I don't think it's as good as many of the others on the list.' Perhaps even more surprising than *Don Quixote* topping the bill is the former Chief Inspector of Schools casting doubt on the validity of a league table. No one seems to have questioned the point of compiling the list, but that's probably because there isn't one. At least, there isn't one so long as we discount the logic of publicity and sales. Announcing the results in Oslo, where the thing was organised, Ben Okri told his audience: 'If there is one novel you should read before you die, it is *Don Quixote*.' Particularly if you're a moribund Norwegian, since Okri has contributed an introduction to the latest Norwegian edition of the book. Still, if the poll prompts more people to pick up one of those unread copies of *Don Quixote* and read it – enough people, say, to reveal a patch of earth the size of Cambridgeshire – then that would be no bad thing.

23 May 2002

SEE YOU IN COURT, PAL

John Lanchester on Bill Gates

HERE ARE PEOPLE WHO use computers. That is most of us. Above them on the informational equivalent of the Great Chain of Being are the people who know about computers: the people who can tell us how to stick an unbent paper-clip into the hole above a wonky disc drive to make the floppy pop out etc. All of these people are now on the internet. Above them are the bona fide geeks, who are either people who have things professionally to do with computers, or who are far-gone in hobbydom. These people can write code (which is geekspeak for 'write computer programs'), mark up HTML to create web pages, and know not only what's going on, but also what's about to go on. Above them are the übergeeks, the illuminati of the digital revolution: the kind of people, to use one example from Po Bronson's entertaining Silicon Valley collage *The Nudist on the Late Shift*,* who reprogram their BMW's chips to make the car 40 per cent more powerful, the kind of people who, in computer terms, can routinely achieve the impossible.

Bear in mind that even in this group there are sharp differences in ability. As Robert X. Cringely, a (pseudonymous) commentator on the computer business who in 1991 published *Accidental Empires*, the first and still the best book on the growth of the industry, explains:

> at the extreme edge of the normal distribution, there are programmers who are 100 times more productive than the average programmer simply on the basis of the number of lines of computer code they can write in a given period of time. Going a bit further, since some programmers are so accomplished that their programming feats are beyond the ability of their peers, we might say that they are infinitely more productive for really creative, leading edge projects.

Infinitely more productive. It's hard to think of another field of human endeavour in which you can say that about the difference between the extraordinarily gifted, and the next level up.

And then, above the übergeeks, in the pure empyrean of ultimate geekdom, is the cynosure, the observed of all observers, owner of arguably the best-known

---

*Po Bronson, *The Nudist on the Late Shift* (Secker, 1999).

entirely plain face in the world, the richest man on the planet: Bill Gates III. According to Cringely, top-level computer jocks are always, without exception, either
hippies or nerds; the lank-haired, anal-retentive, oversized-glasses-wearing, non-
fantastically-good-at-teeth-brushing Gates is the apotheosis of the nerd type. In
the country which gave us the rejoinder 'if you're so smart, why ain't you rich,' he
has revolutionised the status of the nerd. Estimates of his wealth vary. His share of
the company he co-founded, Microsoft, was in the middle of this summer worth
$72 billion; the Internet's 'Bill Gates Personal Wealth Clock' puts the figure of his
net worth at $108 billion. It's worth looking at that written out: $108,000,000,000.
Even taking the lower of those figures as the base, if Microsoft continues to grow at
the rate it has hitherto, Gates will in 2004 become the world's first trillionaire. That
means he will be worth a thousand billionaires. As John Allen Paulos demonstrated
in his book Innumeracy, most of us have a poor grasp of what numbers on this scale
mean; so take a second to guess, intuitively, what you think the difference in time
is between a million seconds and a billion seconds. Ready? A million seconds is 11
days; a billion is 32 years. A trillion is 32,000 years.

Microsoft is so important to the American economy, and therefore to the whole
world, that any news about it tends to appear on the front pages. In August we
learned that Gates had just given away $15 billion in Microsoft stock to his chari-
table foundation, thus instantly making it the second biggest in the world. (The
biggest is the Wellcome Foundation, at $19 billion.) This is a tempting way into the
Microsoft story, since it takes us to the subject of the anti-trust trial which has been
launched against the company by the American government. The Department of
Justice is contending that Microsoft is a monopolist, using its domination of the
operating systems market – that's the ubiquitous Windows – to bully companies
into using other of its products, at the expense of its competitors. The trial could in
theory lead to the break-up of Microsoft, just as an anti-trust trial led to the break-
up of Standard Oil, the progenitor of all the modern American oil firms. During that
earlier trial the head honcho of Standard Oil, John D. Rockefeller, made a regular
point of giving enormous amounts of money to his personal charitable foundation, by way of ameliorating his reputation. Gates is a keen student of history, especially American industrial history. Hmmm. Still, deeds should be separated from
motives, in the field of philanthropy maybe more than anywhere else.

So perhaps the most promising front-page lead in the last few weeks has been
that provided by the news of a hackers' attack on the Microsoft e-mail service,
Hotmail. The early story of this company is told by Po Bronson. Two young would-
be entrepreneurs, Jack Smith and Sabeer Bahtia, 'had been brainstorming possible
business ideas for a few months'. One of their problems was not being able to

exchange information over e-mail while at their respective workplaces, because they didn't want their bosses to find out they had been moonlighting. Both had work-based e-mail, which, as John Sutherland pointed out, is notoriously prone to employer surveillance; both also had AOL (America Online) accounts, but these weren't accessible via their respective office computers. Then one day, on the way home, Smith called Bahtia with an idea so compelling that Bahtia's first words were: 'Oh my! Hang up that cellular and call me back on a secure line when you get to your house!'

The idea was for a free anonymous web-based e-mail service. In other words, a service that would allow e-mails to be stored and sent over the world wide web rather than via a specific internet access provider, so that customers would be able to send and receive e-mails in complete confidence from anywhere in the world they could find a computer terminal. It would be like having a PO box number that travelled everywhere you went, which could be accessed instantaneously. This service's revenue would come from advertising, and it would be self-evidently useful to businessmen, travellers, adulterers, cheapskates – pretty much everybody, in short.

The first emblematic thing about this notion is that it was based on an idea pure and simple, a piece of intellectual property which popped into existence ex nihilo. As Bronson says, 'any disgruntled employee worried about an employer reading his e-mail could have had the idea.' The idea was so powerful that the new company grew its customer base faster than any media enterprise in history: within 30 months Hotmail – for this is they – had 25 million users, signing them up at a rate of 25,000 per day. Second, the idea was self-referential, even postmodern, in that it was based on the difficulty the two hotshots were having in developing an idea. Third, Hotmail invented the contemporary phenomenon of 'viral marketing', whereby the product is its own advertisement – so that an e-mail sent from a Hotmail account is in itself an ad for Hotmail. (The first few users found Hotmail by themselves on the day of its launch, 4 July 1996. By the end of one hour 100 were using it; 200 more joined in the next hour; 250 in the third. It was two years before Hotmail needed to spend money on marketing.) Finally, the idea, like so many hot new notions in cyberspace, ended with the people who had it being bought out by Microsoft. The price was a wallet-thickening $400 million.

When Hotmail came under attack last month, with the news that a group of computer hackers had found a way to break into any and all of its customers' accounts, most non-geeks – at least, non-geeks who don't use Hotmail – would have seen the story as yet another niggling item about internet security. (A non-issue, many geeks argue, since the net is much more secure than the post or the telephone.) But the story has more sting to it than that, since Hotmail isn't any old internet service, but one whose existence is predicated on the need for absolute security. So this was a damaging act with an ad hominem feel; and the people it was meant to damage were the owners of Hotmail, Microsoft. This is the last and main reason why the Hotmail story is emblematic: because it shows the burningly intense, personal hatred in which many people – especially geeks – hold the world's most successful company. A tempting place to begin . . . But the best place to begin the story of Microsoft is probably at the beginning.

Most people, including most people who know a bit about computers – though not most geeks, the next level up – think of the personal computer as a big machine which gradually grew smaller and smaller until we could all fit one on our desks. Thus, thirty years ago, when men flew to the Moon, computers took up whole rooms, and had flashing lights and whirling tape thingies on the outside. Clever people then somehow shrank everything, and the PC industry was born. Not so. Big, 'mainframe' computing was and remains a different type of business. The PC came from the opposite direction, as a small thing that gradually got bigger and bigger, more and more powerful: it began life in the semiconductor industry, which in turn grew out of the transistor industry. In 1971, a scientist called Ted Hoff, working at a now world-famous company called Intel, invented the first microprocessor, a single silicon chip – a piece of silicon, on which fine lines of silicon oxide were printed in a photographic process. The microprocessor was effectively all the working bits you needed to make a computer on a single chip, and despite that – or, more accurately, because of that – the big computer companies didn't want to know. They couldn't or wouldn't know what Robert Moore, one of the co-founders of Intel, had already shown, which is that the density of circuits on the chips would double every 18 months. That axiom, enshrined as 'Moore's Law', has held good throughout the three decades of the microprocessor's existence. The resulting growth in computational power is hard to grasp. In the course of my writing this piece my computer has performed more calculations than have been done by hand in the whole of human history.

It took nearly four years for someone to base a machine on the new invention. The January 1975 issue of the magazine *Popular Electronics* published a piece about a new microcomputer called the Altair 8800. Walking across Harvard Yard in December 1974, a young geek called Paul Allen – a quarter of a century before his newsmaking dates with the freshly de-Jaggered Jerry Hall – waved a copy of the magazine in the face of his good buddy, 19-year-old sophomore Bill Gates. Gates was the son of a big-shot Seattle media lawyer, Bill Gates II. (His father, who now runs Bill Gates III's charitable foundation, has said that if he lived his life over again he would call his son something else. He has tired of telling people his name and

being told 'yeah, right.' In the family, the Microsoft tycoon is known as 'Trey'.)
The young Gates wrote a scheduling program for his school at the age of 12, and a
traffic-logging system for Bellevue, Washington at the age of 16. He was a 100 per
cent, bottled-at-the-place-of-origin geek, and he saw the implications of the new
technology so quickly that his first thought was he and Allen might be too late. 'We
realised that the revolution might happen without us,' he has said. 'After we saw
that article, there was no question of where our life would focus.' Gates and Allen
soon started a company whose stated objective was to put 'a computer on every
desk and in every home, running Microsoft software'. At the time, that seemed like
a joke.

The fox knows many things; the hedgehog knows one big thing; the 800-pound
gorilla doesn't give a shit what anybody knows. Gates's great strength was in com-
bining all these attributes. He was fox-like in his omniscience about the details of
computing, and his ability to write code, and to supervise other people who wrote
it. (Since the Altair 8800 didn't exist when he and Allen saw the *Popular Electronics*
piece, the first thing they did was write a program for a larger computer duplicating
the workings of the non-existent machine, so they could then write software for it.)
He was hedgehog-like in his grasp of the single biggest fact about the – to make
the point again – as yet non-existent personal computer industry. This was, and
is, that it is dominated not by hardware but by software: it is the stuff you put into
your computer to make it do things which matters, not the computer itself. This, in
hindsight, is such a glaringly obvious no-brainer of a self-evident truth that we need
to remind ourselves about the fact that no one saw it that way. At the time, it was
perfectly clear to everybody that the real money was in the machines. Software was
just stuff run up by smelly hobbyists. Finally, Gates was the 800-pound gorilla in his
determination to dominate the industry, irrespective of any opposition. He saw all
interactions in terms of winning and losing, and he was determined always to win.
The demonic competitiveness was a symptom of a disconcerting form of megalo-
mania: Gates didn't want to own the world, he assumed that he already did.

The central principle in Gates's business career has been the insight that the real
money in computing comes by owning de facto standards. That's how you get to
be the gorilla – by owning the software which everybody uses, or at the very least
refers to as a benchmark, whether they want to or not. His big early break was in
doing a deal with IBM, the giant company which dominated the mainframe and
business computer market and which finally, against many of its own instincts and
institutional pressures, went into the personal computer market in late 1981. The
IBM personal computer came to set the standard for the PC industry; hereafter,
PC meant IBM-compatible PC. Up until this point, Microsoft wasn't in operating

systems. Its business had been in writing programming languages, such as Basic, Cobol, Fortran and C. Nonetheless, Gates saw the importance of what the IBM PC could become, and did a deal to provide the operating system for the machine. As for the operating system itself, that is, er, a hotly contested point. Basically, Gates bought it from someone else, a local firm called Seattle Computer Products who had already rustled up a program called QDOS, short for Quick and Dirty Operating System. A quick wash and brush-up later, and QDOS became MS-DOS, the operating system which is still running on every single computer on the planet which uses Microsoft software – that's to say, over 90 per cent of them. It is DOS, lying underneath Windows, which helps to make the ubiquitous Windows so unloved. (One geek name for the stuff Microsoft makes is 'crapware'. The next release of Windows, Windows 2000, will finally break with the underlying DOS architecture. It should be a much less bad operating system, but because it will not be 'backwards compatible' with the old software, it will also royally piss off a great number of reluctant Windows loyalists.)

The IBM PC did well, but not freakishly so, at first. More or less overnight, it set a standard in the fledgling industry – and therefore so did Microsoft – but the machines did not fly out of shops on their own. All of the things you could do on it were versions of things which could be done on a bigger computer – complex maths, word-processing, organising your files. For the PC to take off, it took the invention of an irresistibly compelling application, a 'killer app', which would make everyone who saw the program foam at the mouth with envy until they had it set up on their own machines. That killer app arrived in January 1983, and it was called Lotus 1-2-3.

The killer app was a spreadsheet. This is a kind of software which allows the user to enter a range of numbers, connect them into a series of calculations, and then fiddle about with them. In other words, it lets you crunch data in new ways; calculations which would have taken days can now be done in seconds – in particular, calculations of a type which involve finely tweaking figures. 'What if we put in 6 per cent for inflation, 20 per cent for annual growth and 10 per cent for growth in costs; how does that look?' Those sorts of fiddle-and-jiggle calculation were suddenly made easy by the spreadsheet, which only existed on the PC. The combination of a new type of software running on a new type of hardware made for explosive growth: PC sales began to rocket, and haven't yet started to slow down.

So what did Gates do? Having gone into the applications language business to create software for the Altair 8800, and the operating systems business to create software for the IBM PC, he now went into the applications business to create software for, well, everyone. Microsoft followed what has become its standard procedure: lag behind as a new market comes into existence; throw all its weight behind catching up and duplicating the first-comer; use the enormous leverage of the operating system monopoly to have its new software adopted by everyone; and bingo, celebrate the creation of a new de facto standard. Microsoft did it with its programs Excel (the spreadsheet), Word, File, and then with Office, the suite of software, including all the above, which now utterly dominates the PC industry. Above all, it did it with Windows, which copied the Apple Macintosh's desktop-and-files metaphor for the working environment of the PC. Then it won the inevitable huge lawsuit with Apple. When Steve Jobs, the semi-sociopathic visionary who drove Apple, accused Gates of stealing the idea of a GUI (Graphical User Interface, pronounced 'gooey'), Gates replied that Apple had in turn stolen the idea from Xerox's research institute, PARC. There was no little truth to this, but Gates's exact words are still quite something. 'No, Steve,' he told Jobs, 'I think it's more like we both have this rich neighbour called Xerox, and you broke in to steal the TV set, found I'd been there first, and said: "Not fair, I wanted to steal the TV set."' The striking thing about this – as Michael Malone points out in his ultra-detailed history of Apple, *Infinite Loop*[*] – is that there isn't a shred of truth in the idea that Gates had the GUI first. It was pure gorilla-think. 'In his peculiar and dangerous manner, Gates didn't look upon the Mac OS as competition, but as an intruder into a world that was rightfully his.' Clunky, buggy, crash-prone, counter-intuitive to use, creakily resting on top of its antiquated DOS shell, Windows became the most successfully revenue-generating piece of software there has ever been.

By the mid-1990s, with his vision of a Microsoft-using computer on every desk almost a reality, Gates was in a position of near-total domination of his industry. From this perch he made his first big mistake, one which may yet prove, in business terms, fatal. The mistake was one which almost everybody in the business made: they missed the significance of the internet.

The story is told in Michael Woolf's entertaining exposé of 'the Gold Rush years on the Internet', *Burn Rate*.[†] (Woolf is an entrepreneur who had a set of hairy experiences trying to go into business as a content provider on the net.) Nowadays, when everybody and his mum knows that the internet is the Next Big Thing, when internet stock flotations routinely make millionaires of all concerned – nowadays, hindsight makes it perfectly clear what was going to happen. At the time, it was a great shock even to the most *au courant* geek.

---

[*]Michael Malone, *Infinite Loop: How Apple, the World's Most Insanely Great Computer Company, Went Insane* (Aurum, 1999).
[†]Michael Woolf, *Burn Rate: How I Survived the Gold Rush Years on the Internet* (Orion, 1999).

Travelling in our time-machines back to the almost inconceivable distance of 1990, we arrive at the crucial moment in the birth of the net. The National Science Foundation wanted to get out of the expensive business of subsidising the increasingly complex and rapidly growing infrastructure of the academic computing network. The network had grown out of Arpanet, a matrix of computers designed to link university researchers, government defence labs and the military. (The growth of the net is one of those phenomena equally describable in opposite terms, as a triumph of lavish government subsidy or a great victory for the free market.) The NSF did a deal to wind down its subsidy over two years in return for allowing commercial use of the infrastructure. The domain names .org, .gov and .edu already existed; the deal marked the birth of .com. Nobody, but nobody, foresaw the explosion of network growth that this minor piece of 'policymaker's administrative tinkering' would cause.

'How many people knew about the Internet in late 1991?' Woolf wonders. 'More than five thousand but possibly less than 25,000.' Through 1992 and 1993, a few online services grew up, companies such as Genie and Compuserve. Some of these companies offered access to the internet, but more of them did not; they were there to allow customers to talk to each other over their services, not to throw themselves over the Niagara of unregulated sleaze which to their minds was the internet. At this point, wags were describing the whole phenomenon as 'CB radio for the 1990s'. As late as 1994 and 1995, most people in the business thought that the internet was a distraction from the main business of online services, which was allowing customers of the service to look up information on the proprietary network and to chat to each other (mainly about sex). This is the business that Microsoft was trying to get into, via its MSN network.

One übergeek in particular saw things differently, however. Marc Andreesen was a gifted programmer – a 'code god' – whose interest was in laying out visually the data on internet pages. He wrote Mosaic, the first program which enabled users to see graphics on, as opposed to just read text on, a web page; he then set up a company called Netscape with the intention of bringing such a product – now dubbed a 'web browser' – to market. In October 1994, Netscape Navigator was launched. Everyone in the computer industry studies Bill Gates closely, and by now his dictum about setting de facto standards was not a well-kept secret. In startling accordance with this axiom, Netscape didn't try to sell their browser: they gave it away. Anyone could download it for free. At a stroke Netscape achieved instant domination of the net; quite simply, every single person on it was using Netscape Navigator. Internet use took off exponentially, and even the online services which had defined themselves precisely by not being the internet started to repackage themselves as internet access outfits – the most spectacular success in this area being that of AOL, who in the process gave away literally a billion free software CDs.

Netscape's idea was to focus on what Woolf calls 'razor blade marketing' – give away the razor, sell the blades. The blades would be the inevitable software patches and upgrades to come; the all-important thing was market share. But Netscape, having made their own luck, also got lucky. When you turned their program on you found yourself taken to their home web page, which therefore immediately found itself to be the most visited page on the net. This was serious advertising power; before long, the going rate was $.02 per click (i.e. per pair of eyes to see the page).

In 1995, Gates, hitherto preoccupied by the MSN network and the launch of the insanely overhyped Windows 95, finally got it. He wrote a now-famous company-wide memo called 'The Internet Tidal Wave'. 'I have gone through several stages of increasing my views of its importance. Now, I assign the internet the highest level.' (Notice how grudgingly he defers to the existence of an external reality.) Chairman Bill threw the entire weight of Microsoft at the internet; from now on, Microsoft was to be an internet company, indeed the internet company. 'I just want them to get that we're hard-core about the internet,' Gates was saying, with a note of desperation, by the end of 1995. Gates does such a good job of regarding himself as a sage and genius that one is always reluctant to join in, but it must be said that there is something heroic about the way in which he decided he had been wrong and forced a giant multi-multi-billion-dollar company into an overnight reversal of direction. If Microsoft had been a normal company, rather than an absolute monarchy, they could never have done it.

Gates hurled Microsoft at the problem, and Microsoft came up with its own web browser, Internet Explorer. This was the birth of the 'browser wars', in which Netscape and Microsoft slugged it out for market share. At the time of writing, a scant four years after starting from nowhere with 'The Internet Tidal Wave', Microsoft has just over 50 per cent of the web-browser market. This is no small feat, but they had to give away many millions of copies of software in the process ('We don't need to make any revenue from internet software,' decreed Chairman Bill), and step very hard on very many toes. In practice, that meant issuing threats – always part of the Microsoft way of doing business.

This is what has landed Microsoft in court, as the subject of an anti-trust suit from the Department of Justice. The company is now in the greatest peril it has ever been in. The gist of the DoJ case is that Microsoft told people in the business that if they didn't make Internet Explorer their web browser, at the expense of Netscape Navigator, they couldn't have Windows. Furthermore, by making Explorer the core of the forthcoming launch of Windows 98, they were further extending and exploiting their monopoly power. What 800-pound gorilla would even contemplate doing different?

Federal Judge Thomas Penfield Jackson is showing clear signs of believing the case against Microsoft, helped by their courtroom combination of ultra-aggression and shiftiness, and also by their mountains of self-incriminating e-mails. (The overfrank internal e-mail being one corporate artefact which this trial will make extinct.) Members of the public, according to a Gallup poll, take the other view, only one in four supporting the government's case. I have never met a geek who does not believe the charges against Microsoft, but there is a range of opinion as to whether or not they matter, and what should be done about them.

For one thing, monopolies in the software industry are not necessarily such a terrible idea. Look at it another way: how would you create a monopoly if you wanted to? (All cant aside, any rational businessman wants to own a monopoly. What's the alternative – selling something that somebody else sells too? Which of those seems to you a better idea?) In the software business, you would do it by writing a program which is so useful that everybody who tried it would want other people to use it too; and then the more people who used it the more useful it would be, since files and information would be more easily exchangeable, and the larger the installed base of users the more upgrades, support systems, add-ons and other goodies; until, finally, everybody would be using your product, which would be all the more useful because everybody was using it. Whoops, you've become a monopolist – see you in court, pal. The paradox is that software is an industry where a monopoly can, to some extent, be beneficial. Or, as a Microsoft spokesman puts it, gorillaishly but with some truth: 'The laws exist to protect consumers, not competitors.'

There is also some truth to the central plank of Microsoft's defence, which is that the computer business is so competitive that the company is at full stretch trying to keep ahead of its rivals – hardly the position that John D. Rockefeller, say, was in. There certainly are a lot of very, very intelligent people out there trying as hard as they can to destroy Microsoft; a state of affairs which is of the company's own making. One of the most potent threats – in the opinion of many geeks, the single biggest danger in the longish run – is that offered by the very unlikely story of a Finnish übergeek called Linus Torvalds.

In 1991, the 21-year-old Torvalds (whose wife is the six-times winner of the Finnish national karate championships) used his free time to write an operating system, which he dubbed Linux. The system was based on an OS called Unix, a geek favourite since Arpanet days. So far so fairly unremarkable; but it's what Torvalds did next that was really new. He published all the code for his operating system, and invited people to amend and extend it as they wished. He made it into a collaborative project in which everyone could take part, and which would be free to all, thus instantly creating a worldwide community of Linux geeks.

At the moment, about seven million people use Linux. This might sound a smallish number, but the philosophy of 'open source' computing, as it's called, is reaching critical mass in the computer world. An essay on the subject by Eric Raymond,* 'The Cathedral and the Bazaar', has had enormous influence in disseminating the ideas and values of the open source; it persuaded Netscape to make available the code of its latest version of its software. Torvalds and others argue that free software is almost always better than the stuff you pay for: for one thing, it's never released before it's ready, since geek pride is at stake rather than any commercial considerations. For another, it's constantly being improved.

The threat to people like Microsoft is that Linux will destroy the cash value of the operating system; why pay several hundred dollars for something when you can get an equivalent product for free? This idea doesn't have to catch on with all that many people before it will do horrible damage to Microsoft's revenue stream. And because Microsoft has an extraordinarily high price/earnings ratio, any marked downturn in its income will have a catastrophic effect on its stock. As a result, Microsoft's attitude to Linux is hilariously two-faced. Most of the time they act as if it's strictly chickenfeed: who wants to use some cobbled-together piece of software bodged into existence by bug-eyed know-nothing hobbyists? For the purpose of the trial, however, they cite Linux as an example of the scary ultra-competitiveness of the computer business: the kind of industry where a Finnish geek barely out of his rompers can in a few spare hours write a program which threatens the very existence of a trillion-dollar corporation. The joke or irony is that it's probably this second view which is closer to the truth.

As for the trial, the geek consensus is that nothing will change. This judge will rule against Microsoft, who will appeal, and do much better in the more right-wing appellate court. The Department of Justice will appeal again, and so on. Fantasy scenarios, such as a federally mandated break-up of the company (to rival those of the oil and phone monopolies, Standard Oil and AT&T), are just that, fantasies. The real deals will happen behind the scenes. Microsoft offered an out-of-court settlement before the trial began, but the DoJ rejected it. At some point they will offer another; then – perhaps when Wall Street has hit its long-overdue speed-bump, and the idea of the federal government going after the country's most successful company is even less popular – they will offer a deal which Justice, as opposed to

*Eric S. Raymond, *The Cathedral and the Bazaar* (O'Reilly, 1999).

justice, accepts. The deal will allow the government to claim victory while leaving all essential points about Microsoft's business unchanged. The trial(s) will make it harder for Microsoft to threaten people, and they'll start encrypting their internal e-mails, but that's about it. The real, long-term threat to Gates and his company comes not from the Department of Justice but from that funny shape on the horizon, a cloud no larger than a Finnish übergeek's head.

30 September 1999

WHAT'S LEFT OF HENRIETTA LACKS?

Anne Enright

I DON'T KNOW WHERE I heard of her first: a woman whose cells are bred in culture dishes in labs all over the world; a woman whose cells were so prolific that there is more of her now, in terms of biomass, than there ever was when she was alive.

It seems to me that she is one of the saints who multiplied in reliquaries after their death, to produce, as Ian Paisley's website reminds us, the many prepuces of the infant Jesus, and the variously coloured hair of His madly trichogenous mother. Perhaps, in these days of cloning, or in future days of cloning, we will look to the evangelical Protestants and say that they were right all along: no miracles please, scientific or otherwise, no icons, no reproducing relics.

Is there such a thing as an unconscious saint – a saint who didn't know that she was in some way chosen, or even holy? I would like to put this woman and her cells in a story, but what kind of story would it be? What kind of epiphany would grace her ordinary afternoons?

My-sister-the-doctor says that what I heard was a reference to the HeLa cell line – a popular choice with medical researchers. They are, disgustingly enough, the cells of a woman's cancer. What is the difference between a woman's own cells and the cells of her cancer? They are normal body cells that have suffered a genetic alteration, that is all. The question is moot: the closer you get to the body, the harder it is to see. On a cellular level, we are each a community, or several communities, and the relationships are not always clear: some cells 'commit suicide', for example, but the question of intention must be a false one. Under the microscope, the question of 'self' is so diffuse and so complicated that it might as well not arise.

This is all unlucky talk. I am pregnant for the first time, the bump just beginning to show. I don't know what my pregnant self is, either. The pregnant body has been through a lot of law courts but I have never seen it properly discussed or described. I don't know what I am. Am I twice as nice? Am I twice as alive now as I ever was?

On the internet, I look up 'HeLa' on Yahoo and find, within minutes, that the woman's name was Henrietta Lacks. So what is she missing, I wonder, what does Henrietta lack? What does she want *now*? I type her name into AltaVista, and get 52 replies. The first site, 'The Immortal Cells of Henrietta Lacks', is illustrated with a photograph of a cell. It looks like a ball of maggots. Is this her?

No. It is a duly credited picture of a 'cultured rat bone marrow cell', magnified 19,500 times.

According to the anonymous author, the HeLa line was begun when cells were taken from the cervix of a 31-year-old Baltimore woman, for tests. The woman died of cancer eight months later but in the meantime some of the cells found their way to the lab of John and Margaret Gey of Johns Hopkins University. They were trying to find a method of keeping human cells dividing in a culture outside the body and had turned to cancer cells for their ability to divide essentially unchecked. These particular cells, named HeLa for the first two letters of the first and last names of the 'patient', proved spectacularly successful. Henrietta's cells were the first human culture to survive beyond the 50th generation and they are still growing: 'Although Henrietta is dead her cells live on in research labs around the world! In fact, some biologists believe that HeLa cells are no longer human at all and consider them to be single-celled micro-organisms!'

The exclamation marks are some kind of exhortation – but to what? The webpage goes on to say that HeLa cells grow so aggressively they cause problems by invading other cultures during routine lab transfer procedures. The result is a lot of bogus data – papers written on the biology of various cell types are in fact about the biology of good old HeLa. I'm delighted, of course, and note the recommended book by Michael Gold, *A Conspiracy of Cells: One Woman's Immortal Legacy and the Medical Scandal it Caused* (1986).

As so often on the internet, the easy information comes first. This is perhaps all I need to know about HeLa, but if I want to get a fix on Henrietta I will have to pick through the rest of the websites the search engine has thrown up, in all their glorious irrelevancy. I will have to judge by the quality of the writing whether the people who wrote them are educated or intelligent or honest. Through various inaccuracies, I will arrive at a sort of consensus of fact – these facts will probably be the same ones as on this first website, but somehow richer and more known. And somewhere along the line, an accident will give me my own fictional Henrietta, or the relentless concatenation of near-relevance and irrelevance will steal her from me. There is a danger that information will kill Henrietta Lacks. I sit at the computer, growing all the while, wondering about the differences between reproduction and creativity; between either of these and what you might call *spawning*.

Click. The same rat bone marrow cell, this time tinted sepia, with a drop-shadow added for dramatic effect. It is not credited, and the (of course, anonymous) author claims it to be 'a HeLa cell'. This is a typical infiltration of electronic content from one site to another – until everyone has a scanner, they will steal their illustrations and graphics from other websites, and the same pictures will turn up again and again. Everyone robs on the internet. The more often a piece of information is used, the more likely it is to mutate: I suspect, though, that it mutates towards, rather than away from, the expected. ('Of course it's not a rat, why would we put a picture of a rat cell on a page about HeLa?')

I'm in a series of sites that show me, if I want to know, how to detect the papillomavirus type 18 DNA in HeLa cells (using some nifty gel and a PCR machine). I think this means that Henrietta Lacks had genital warts. I think this means that she slept around.

Click. A picture of Henrietta Lacks. A woman looks down at the camera: hands on hips, smiling, as if to say: 'Is this the way you want me?' It is a confident, intimate picture. She has a strong chin, her hair is in a Victory Roll, she is wearing a short fitted jacket and is standing in front of a brick wall. The text announces a documentary called *Ihre Zellen leben weiter* ('Her Cells Live On'), to be shown on Swiss television. In the accompanying blurb, Margaret Gey is dropped from the Johns Hopkins research team, leaving 'Dr Gey' to lonely late nights in the lab, watching the petri dish where Henrietta Lacks's cells were nurtured in a solution of placenta (it doesn't say whose) and hen bone marrow. HeLa was apparently vital in the development of the polio vaccine; it was used to test cosmetic products and the effects of the atom bomb. Henrietta's cells were the first 'piece of human life' ('das erste Stuck menschliches Leben') in space. Go girl.

Click. Wait. Wait. Error.

I don't know where dead websites go. Perhaps they are not dead in any real sense, just lost, or inaccessible. This worries me – if the internet is to evolve, surely it must both reproduce and die. Do websites do either? They certainly cross-fertilise, or cross-infect. But when people say 'what will the internet turn into' maybe it won't 'turn into' anything, it will just spread (get less accurate at the edges, more stodgy in the middle).

Click. High School Biology. Students are asked what they would do if they were dying of cancer and a doctor asked them to donate some cells. 'Your cells are the first success! This could be a medical breakthrough – your approval could allow researchers to evaluate drugs in a test tube before administering them to patients.' More exclamation mark ethics. No one asked Henrietta Lacks for permission, that much seems clear.

Click. Wait. Another biology module, a different school, or college. 'This is not so much concerned with the choice HL made, but with the speed at which information flows. The actions of the editors of scientific journals, the interaction of politics and science.' There follows an interesting list of words. 'Money. Mistakes. Contamination. Spontaneous transformation. New parameter. Invalid data. Tainted literature.'

The class will work from a copy of a *Reader's Digest* article, which I do not have. At this point I should look up the *Reader's Digest* site. It takes an effort to be passive on the internet, but I hold the line. I am pregnant. I am not looking for information, I am looking for Henrietta Lacks. I am looking for an accidental insight into her red-brick, Baltimore, smiling afternoons.

Click. 'Dresses for Henrietta Lacks', an installation by Brisbane-based artist Jill Barker. 'Dresses made of silver contact paper have been adhered to the windows. Each contains intricate structural patterns, like the DNA and other molecular structures of which we are all composed.' A picture of a metal dress. In the text, John Gey has mutated to John Grey and Henrietta, for the first time, is black. (I do go back now, in a hurry, to the photo and find that this is indeed so.) Furthermore, 'Henrietta's family were never told of the research. Dr Grey [*sic*] claimed the donor's name was Helen Lane or Helen Larson (supposedly in order to protect her anonymity). In the 1970s Henrietta's name was released and the Lacks family were shocked . . . to them a part of their mother is still living and is being made to live on.'

Click. 'Behind the façade of big hospitals, many African Americans can only see one big medical experiment.' The internet often provides its own narrative like this: the story 'becomes' one about race and therefore starts to move away from me. The cells in the petri dish are black cells, they are no longer universal, they are certainly not Irish (as I am). It bothers me that I did not notice what colour she was, it makes me feel foolish, or virtuously blind.

The website brings us on a quick trot through, among other outrages, the Tuskegee experiment, where, between 1932 and 1972, in a study funded by the US federal government, 400 black men were intentionally denied treatment for syphilis so researchers could track the effects of the disease.

Click. For sale: various growth media and cultures. For a mere $55 I can buy a litre of media for Chinese hamster ovary cultures. There are also 'various magnetic goat antibodies' for $79-$89 (50 ml) and 'a laser tweezers micromanipulator' for $25,000-$40,000. Snap on those latex gloves.

Click. 'Why Cells Die'. A very technical discussion. As far as I can make out, the problem is this: free radicals are generated in the mitochondria as part of the normal metabolic process. They cause somatic mutations and deletions of mitochondrial DNA, which in their turn produce more free radicals. An overload contributes to cellular necrosis and apoptosis. The cells die or self-destruct, in other words, and other cells replicate in order to replace them.

Every time a cell replicates, its telomeres get shorter. Telomeres bind the bottoms of chromosomes together, like the aglets on shoelaces, and after, say, fifty replications they wear out. This is called the Hayflick Limit. After it is reached, the cell can't replicate and simply dies. Cancerous cells somehow 'express' telomerase and therefore avoid this problem – but don't ask me how. As I say, this was a very technical essay, complete with footnotes, which, in the world of the internet means that every single word is True True True.

Click. A personal diary. A trip to the Blijdorp Zoo to visit the Surinam Toad. Some musings about small information appliances (like an intelligent fridge) and how attached people still are to their large information appliances (like their computers). A discussion of difficulty and reward (the VCR v. the violin). A description of the sense of foreboding the writer had before witnessing an accident. Entry ends: 'Took half a melatonin before I went to bed and slept very soundly.' There is no mention of Henrietta Lacks.

Click. The American Congressional Record.

In Memory of Henrietta Lacks –

Hon. Robert L. Ehrlich, Jr

(Extension of Remarks – 4 June 1997)

Henrietta Lacks was born in 1920 in Clover, Virginia. At the age of 23 she moved to Turner's Station, near Baltimore, Maryland, joining her husband David. She had five children, four of whom – Deborah, David Jr, Lawrence and Zakariyya – still survive. Ms Lacks was known as pleasant and smiling, and always willing to lend a helping hand.

Because it is the Congressional Record (unless it is not) we know that John Gey, or Grey, is in fact Dr George O. Gey, though his wife Margaret (though perhaps she was called Mary, who is to say?) has gone the way of all female scientific flesh. The citation ends: 'I sincerely hope her name will also be immortalised as one of courage, hope and strength, and that due recognition will be given to her role in medicine and science.' Well so do I. But what was extraordinary about her particular courage, and in what sense was this unknowing contribution to science 'hers'?

Click. Click. Click. Repeat of Swiss TV timetable, more biology classes, mitosis, meiosis, all that. Click. *Der Tanz ums Grab*. Henrietta reminds someone of the 'Toraja', a tribe perhaps, who carry their dead around with them for many years, like so much hand luggage. Click. Causes of cancer: 1. Infection by an oncogenic virus. 2. Chromosomal abnormalities. 3. Exposure to chemical carcinogens. Click. 'How to use micro-organisms as vector cells in genetic engineering'. A fairly detailed guide. This, along with 'Nuclear Bombs Made Easy', I download and save for later.

Click. Error. Click. A man in California, I am warned, sued his doctor for marketing a cell line derived from his cancerous spleen. Click. 'Twenty years later a disturbing factor came to light, the HeLa cells had the ability to infiltrate and subvert other colonies of alien cells.' Now this is my favourite space on the internet, the paranoid place, where people use words like 'infiltrate' and 'alien' to produce questions like: 'Would the human immune system be capable of dealing with such an invader? Could the tales of vampire and werewolf bites have some basis in fact?' I didn't trust this site to start with because the background was pink. I think this means that I didn't trust it because I knew it was written by a woman. Oh well.

Click. 'Diana's Bodyguard Conscious and Well Enough to Talk'. Scroll down through a local newspaper to find 'Cancer Victim's Family Receives Plaque'. Good old Congressman Ehrlich has awarded the Lacks family a plaque recognising her contribution to science. 'A foundation named for Lacks plans to build a $7 million museum in her honour.' I wonder what will be in the museum. Horrors, I assume.

Click. 'Death Wish – Do Our Cells Want to Commit Suicide?' A harmlessly inaccurate essay about living for ever. Of Henrietta Lacks the writer says: 'We want the immortality of a god, not of a tumour.' Quite. He hints at future resurrections: 'Each cell contains a genetic blueprint for constructing Henrietta Lacks – who died back in 1951.'

Click. But – and there are often 'buts' in the gaps between websites – 'by now the cells have mutated so much that it's questionable whether they can still be considered "human" tissue.' So if our previous author got his wish and reconstructed Henrietta, then the human being cloned from the cell would be perhaps unpleasantly different from the original, perhaps unpleasantly different, indeed, from the human.

Click. Wait. Now what? On the internet, the meaning is so often in the gaps, and poor, mutated Henrietta is slipping between the cracks. I am waiting for the argument to continue; for something unexpected to clinch it or make it silly. This is the pleasure of browsing, and probably the trap. I used to teach multimedia students and found that they were almost exclusively interested in synchronicity and the random. This is not a kind of meaning that can be generated by a single author, it exists between authors. These students had plenty to say, they just thought it uncool to say it – all significance had to come from the group. There is nothing new about this, but it will always be frightening (and this time the group is global).

Click. 'Life Itself. Exploring the Realm of the Living Cell'. By Boyce Rensberger. There is nothing better than coming across a whole chapter of a book on the net, a proper book, especially on a page reassuringly hosted by washingtonpost.com.

The story of the American Type Culture Collection, where 20,000 frozen ampoules hold about 40 billion human cells in suspended animation. These cultures are routinely 'resurrected' and shipped off to researchers around the world.

They include skin cells taken from a little girl who died of a birth defect in 1962, and brain cells of a 76-year-old man.

Rensberger quotes the cell biologist Matthias Schleiden's insight into what we are, what our cells 'are' – they 'lead double lives, their own and that of the organism of which they are a part'. He goes on to say that 'the human body is a republic of cells, a society of discrete living beings who have, for the good of the society as a whole, sacrificed their individual freedoms.' I am not sure what individual freedoms my cells possess, though I know they can go on strike, especially the ones in my ex-smoker's lungs. But my child, when still very small, made itself known to me – first in a dream (this is only true, I am only reporting what is true) when it was under a hundred cells 'big', and then in a craving for Japanese seaweed. I have no idea how small a hundred cells are, but their impulse was, from the very start, not so much republican as despotic.

As evidence of this cell 'republic', Rensberger cites the mechanism known as 'programmed cell death'. If a cell goes 'wrong' its neighbours will order it to self-destruct. This is what is supposed to happen with cancer cells, but sometimes, of course, doesn't. It also happens to the webbing between my child's fingers. At least I hope it does.

Rensberger worries that we may find the world of cells 'miraculous' – though he allows wonder. Most wondrous of all is the cells' tendency towards self-assembly. Skin cells will form a sheet in the dish, breast cells will manufacture and secrete milk protein, and 'muscle cells will sometimes weld themselves into large fibres that spontaneously begin twitching in the dish. When cells of the heart muscle do this, they begin twitching rhythmically.' Perhaps the body is just a yearning. Every good scientist tries to rid his prose of all hint of intention, and fails. They love their cells and molecules as fiction writers love their characters, they watch them and will them on. Rensberger celebrates the 'glory' of a mechanistic view of life, quoting Jacques Monod, another important cell biologist, who says: 'No preformed and complete structure existed anywhere: but the architectural plan for it was present in its very constituents.' It seems that what molecules, and later cells, contain is information. This is not how I understand the word 'information', which, after all, can be either correct or incorrect. It is information as an imperative, information as a seed. 'The necessary information was present, but unexpressed, in the constituents. The epigenetic building of a structure is not a creation; it is a revelation.'

So I am pregnant. I am busy building bones, in an epigenetic sort of way. The child is being revealed inside me, but not yet to me. The child is being revealed to itself, but slowly. I wonder if it is lonely: I find pregnancy to be a vastly lonely state. This child cries already, or so I am told. I fancy that it likes the sound of its father's voice, that it kicks at songs by Nina Simone. I have no idea what might cross its mind, as different expressions cross its face. I have no idea what it is like to be of recently specified sex, to have webbing between my fingers and toes and then to lose it. And of course I have every idea what these things are like.

I surf the net and grow, my belly pushing towards the keyboard. I should work, but I would rather lie on the sofa and be. Sometimes, for hours at a time, I do nothing but exist. I find it quite tiring. I say to my-sister-the-doctor that my brain is gone. She laughs and says: 'You'll never get it back.' I panic and download an IQ test from the internet. I have never done an IQ test before, I don't believe in them. The test tells me that, on its terms, I can think perfectly well. It is just, perhaps, that I can't be bothered. I grow large and swim like a whale through all this information. There is a part of me now that is entirely happy. I sit and listen to my own blood, or to someone's blood. 'I am no more your mother,' said Sylvia Plath. 'I am no more your mother than . . .'

As for Henrietta – I am pregnant. I cannot conclude. I am lodged at Alta-Vista 44, a site called 'What Happens': it's the story, among other things, of her revenge. Everything on the internet is about what someone else said. There are so few primary sources, I sometimes feel that the whole thing is just a gossip factory. 'What Happens' contains a summary of Michael Gold's *A Conspiracy of Cells*, which is, of course, unfindable, out of print.

The book says much about HeLa's ability to overwhelm other tissue cultures in the lab and how it led to widespread and unacknowledged contamination of data. Researchers shared their cultures around like gardeners do clippings, and as HeLa took over in dish after dish, papers about skin cells and lung cells were in fact based on the cancerous cervical cells of Henrietta Lacks. The problem reached unbelievable proportions – in 1966 Stanley Gartler compared 17 cultures of ostensibly different tissue types and found that they were all, in fact, HeLa. In 1968 the American Type Culture collection tested all its line of human cells, and 'of these 34 cell lines, 24 proved to be HeLa.' In 1972 Russian scientists supplied American scientists with six different cancer cells taken in different parts of the Soviet Union and 'all six turned out to be HeLa.'

The author of this site, Louis Pascal, is more interested, however, in the refusal of the scientific community to acknowledge that mistakes were made. He traces the relationship between the whistle-blower, Walter Nelson-Rees, who worked at the cell bank at the University of California, and the various journals who refused to publish him. Nelson-Rees, he says, was 'effectively forced to retire' in 1981. Pascal claims a similar history for his own attempts to expose the truth about the source of HIV. There follows a passionate and plausible essay about the possibility that HIV crossed over from SIV (a variation of the virus in chimpanzees) via the polio vac-cination project in Central Africa in the 1950s – in which HeLa also played its part. This is the earlier, underground version of the argument put forward by Edward Hooper in *The River: A Journey back to the Source of HIV and Aids*, but when I stumble across it, it's all news to me.

Here is the apotheosis of the internet: forbidden information, a conspiracy against the truth. Overturning my prejudices, Pascal is all content and fiercely political. But the fact that he uses copious footnotes and is prefaced with a note written by a professor from the University of Woolagong does not mean that I know he is sane. I find myself involved in a drama of verifiability. My ignorance makes the information urgent. I have no scientific training, I am ordinary and sometimes frightened and I have no reason, finally, to disbelieve him.

Click. 'A Crime of Manners'. Blurb for a romantic fiction with a cast that includes a Lady Fuddlesby and a parrot called Sir Polly Grey. The hero, Giles, Duke of Winter-ton, decides to pay attention to an earl's daughter who has many bountiful charms that the heroine, 'Henrietta, lacks'. So here is my saint: a woman who, according to the Congressional Record, was like all saints in that she 'was known as pleasant and smiling, and always willing to lend a helping hand'. A woman whose womb carried five single cells that became children and one single cell that killed her. A minor martyr in an as yet unspecified cause. I think I should leave her alone.

Out at my sister's I ask a dinner table of doctors who owns the placenta, me or the child. Legally, I am told, it is a 'waste product'. Hospitals sell placentas all the time, sometimes to the cosmetics industry. This seems all right to me, though I worry about the lipsticks. Everyone loves scaring me about having babies. There is much gleeful talk of epidural and episiotomy. When it came down to it, none of the men actually wanted to be in the labour ward with their wives, but they gritted their teeth and sat it out anyway. All of them play golf.

13 April 2000

YOU MAY!

Slavoj Žižek on the Meaning of Viagra

'RULE GIRLS' ARE HETEROSEXUAL women who follow precise rules as to how they let themselves be seduced (accept a date only if you are asked at least three days in advance etc). Although the rules correspond to customs which used to regulate the behaviour of old-fashioned women actively pursued by old-fashioned men, the Rule Girls phenomenon does not involve a return to conservative values: women now freely choose their own rules – an instance of the 'reflexivisation' of everyday customs in today's 'risk society'. According to the risk society theory of Anthony Giddens, Ulrich Beck and others, we no longer live our lives in compliance with Nature or Tradition; there is no symbolic order or code of accepted fictions (what Lacan calls the 'Big Other') to guide us in our social behaviour. All our impulses, from sexual orientation to ethnic belonging, are more and more often experienced as matters of choice. Things which once seemed self-evident – how to feed and educate a child, how to proceed in sexual seduction, how and what to eat, how to relax and amuse oneself – have now been 'colonised' by reflexivity, and are experienced as something to be learned and decided on.

The retreat of the accepted Big Other accounts for the prevalence of code-cracking in popular culture. New Age pseudo-scientific attempts to use computer technology to crack some recondite code – in the Bible, say, or the pyramids – which can reveal the future of humanity offer one example of this. Another is provided by the scene in cyberspace movies in which the hero (or often the heroine), hunched over a computer and frantically working against time, has his/her 'access denied', until he/she cracks the code and discovers that a secret government agency is involved in a plot against freedom and democracy. Believing there is a code to be cracked is of course much the same as believing in the existence of some Big Other: in every case what is wanted is an agent who will give structure to our chaotic social lives.

Even racism is now reflexive. Consider the Balkans. They are portrayed in the liberal Western media as a vortex of ethnic passion – a multiculturalist dream turned into a nightmare. The standard reaction of a Slovene (I am one myself) is to say: 'Yes, this is how it is in the Balkans, but Slovenia is not part of the Balkans; it is part of Mitteleuropa; the Balkans begin in Croatia or in Bosnia; we Slovenes are the last bulwark of European civilisation against the Balkan madness.' If you ask, 'Where do the Balkans begin?' you will always be told that they begin *down there*, towards the south-east. For Serbs, they begin in Kosovo or in Bosnia where Serbia is trying to defend civilised Christian Europe against the encroachments of this Other. For the Croats, the Balkans begin in Orthodox, despotic and Byzantine Serbia, against which Croatia safeguards Western democratic values. For many Italians and Austrians, they begin in Slovenia, the Western outpost of the Slavic hordes. For many Germans, Austria is tainted with Balkan corruption and inefficiency; for many Northern Germans, Catholic Bavaria is not free of Balkan contamination. Many arrogant Frenchmen associate Germany with Eastern Balkan brutality – it lacks French finesse. Finally, to some British opponents of the European Union, Continental Europe is a new version of the Turkish Empire with Brussels as the new Istanbul – a voracious despotism threatening British freedom and sovereignty.

We are dealing with an imaginary cartography, which projects onto the real landscape its own shadowy ideological antagonisms, in the same way that the conversion-symptoms of the hysterical subject in Freud project onto the physical body the map of another, imaginary anatomy. Much of this projection is racist. First, there is the old-fashioned, unabashed rejection of the Balkan Other (despotic, barbarian, Orthodox, Muslim, corrupt, Oriental) in favour of true values (Western, civilised, democratic, Christian). But there is also a 'reflexive', politically correct racism: the liberal, multiculturalist perception of the Balkans as a site of ethnic horrors and intolerance, of primitive, tribal, irrational passions, as opposed to the reasonableness of post-nation-state conflict resolution by negotiation and compromise. Racism is a disease of the Balkan Other, while we in the West are merely observers, neutral, benevolent and righteously dismayed. Finally, there is reverse racism, which celebrates the exotic authenticity of the Balkan Other, as in the notion of Serbs who, by contrast with inhibited, anaemic Western Europeans, still exhibit a prodigious lust for life. Reverse racism plays a crucial role in the success of Emir Kusturica's films in the West.

Because the Balkans are part of Europe, they can be spoken of in racist clichés which nobody would dare to apply to Africa or Asia. Political struggles in the Balkans are compared to ridiculous operetta plots; Ceausescu was presented as a contemporary reincarnation of Count Dracula. Slovenia is most exposed to this displaced racism, since it is closest to Western Europe: when Kusturica, talking about his film *Underground*, dismissed the Slovenes as a nation of Austrian grooms, nobody reacted: an 'authentic' artist from the less developed part of former Yugoslavia was attacking the most developed part of it. When discussing the Balkans, the tolerant multiculturalist is allowed to act out his repressed racism.

Perhaps the best example of the universalised reflexivity of our lives is the growing inefficiency of interpretation. Traditional psychoanalysis relied on a notion of the unconscious as the 'dark continent', the impenetrable substance of the subject's being, which had to be probed by interpretation: when its content was brought to light a liberating new awareness would follow. Today, the formations of the unconscious (from dreams to hysterical symptoms) have lost their innocence: the 'free associations' of a typical educated patient consist for the most part of attempts to provide a psychoanalytic explanation of his own disturbances, so we have not only Annafreudian, Jungian, Kleinian, Lacanian interpretations of the symptoms, but symptoms which are themselves Annafreudian, Jungian, Kleinian, Lacanian – they don't exist without reference to some psychoanalytic theory. The unfortunate result of this reflexivisation is that the analyst's interpretation loses its symbolic efficacy and leaves the symptom intact in its idiotic *jouissance*. It's as though a neo-Nazi skinhead, pressed to give reasons for his behaviour, started to talk like a social worker, sociologist or social psychologist, citing diminished social mobility, rising insecurity, the disintegration of paternal authority, the lack of maternal love in his early childhood.

'When I hear the word "culture", I reach for my gun,' Goebbels is supposed to have said. 'When I hear the word "culture", I reach for my cheque-book,' says the cynical producer in Godard's *Le Mépris*. A leftist slogan inverts Goebbels's statement: 'When I hear the word "gun", I reach for culture.' Culture, according to that slogan, can serve as an efficient answer to the gun: an outburst of violence is a *passage à l'acte* rooted in the subject's ignorance. But the notion is undermined by the rise of what might be called 'postmodern racism', the surprising characteristic of which is its insensitivity to reflection – a neo-Nazi skinhead who beats up black people knows what he's doing, but does it anyway.

Reflexivisation has transformed the structure of social dominance. Take the public image of Bill Gates. Gates is not a patriarchal father-master, nor even a corporate Big Brother running a rigid bureaucratic empire, surrounded on an inaccessible top floor by a host of secretaries and assistants. He is instead a kind of Small Brother, his very ordinariness an indication of a monstrousness so uncanny that it can no longer assume its usual public form. In photos and drawings he looks like anyone else, but his devious smile points to an underlying evil that is beyond representation. It is also a crucial aspect of Gates as icon that he is seen as the hacker who made it (the term 'hacker' has, of course, subversive/marginal/anti-establishment connotations; it suggests someone who sets out to disturb the smooth functioning of large bureaucratic corporations). At the level of fantasy, Gates is a small-time, subversive hooligan who has taken over and dressed himself up as the respectable chairman. In Bill Gates, Small Brother, the average ugly guy coincides with and contains the figure of evil genius who aims for total control of our lives. In early

James Bond movies, the evil genius was an eccentric figure, dressed extravagantly, or alternatively, in the grey uniform of the Maoist commissar. In the case of Gates, this ridiculous charade is no longer needed – the evil genius turns out to be the boy next door.

Another aspect of this process is the changed status of the narrative tradition that we use to understand our lives. In *Men are from Mars, Women are from Venus* (1992), John Gray proposed a vulgarised version of narrativist-deconstructionist psychoanalysis. Since we ultimately 'are' the stories we tell ourselves about ourselves, the solution to a psychic deadlock resides, he proposes, in a 'positive' rewriting of the narrative of our past. What he has in mind is not only the standard cognitive therapy of changing negative 'false beliefs' about oneself into an assurance that one is loved by others and capable of creative achievements, but a more 'radical', pseudo-Freudian procedure of regressing back to the scene of the primordial traumatic wound. Gray accepts the psychoanalytic notion of an early childhood traumatic experience that forever marks the subject's further development, but he gives it a pathological spin. What he proposes is that, after regressing to, and thus confronting, his primal traumatic scene, the subject should, under the therapist's guidance, 'rewrite' this scene, this ultimate phantasmatic framework of his subjectivity, as part of a more benign and productive narrative. If, say, the primordial traumatic scene existing in your unconscious, deforming and inhibiting your creative attitude, is that of your father shouting at you, 'You are worthless! I despise you! Nothing good will come of you,' you should rewrite the scene so that a benevolent father smiles at you and says: 'You're OK! I trust you fully.' (Thus the solution for the Wolf Man would have been to 'regress' to the parental *coitus a tergo* and then rewrite the scene so that what he saw was merely his parents lying on the bed, his father reading a newspaper and his mother a sentimental novel.) It may seem a ridiculous thing to do, but there is a widely accepted, politically correct version of this procedure in which ethnic, sexual and other minorities rewrite their past in a more positive, self-assertive vein (African Americans claiming that long before European modernity, ancient African empires had a sophisticated understanding of science and technology etc). Imagine a rewriting of the Decalogue along the same lines. Is one of the Commandments too severe? Well then, let's regress to Mount Sinai and rewrite it: adultery – fine, provided it is sincere and serves the goal of profound self-realisation. What disappears is not 'hard fact' but the Real of a traumatic encounter whose organising role in the subject's psychic economy resists its symbolic rewriting.

In our post-political, liberal-permissive society, human rights can be seen as expressing the right to violate the Ten Commandments. The right to privacy is, in effect, the right to commit adultery, in secret, without being observed or investigated.

The right to pursue happiness and to possess private property is, in effect, the right to steal (to exploit others). Freedom of the press and of expression – the right to lie. The right of free citizens to possess weapons – the right to kill. Freedom of religious belief – the right to celebrate false gods. Human rights do not, of course, directly condone the violation of the Commandments, but they preserve a marginal 'grey zone' which is out of the reach of religious or secular power. In this shady zone, I can violate the Commandments, and if the Power catches me with my pants down and tries to prevent my violation, I can cry: 'Assault on my basic human rights!' It is impossible for the Power to prevent a 'misuse' of human rights without at the same time impinging on their proper application. Lacan draws attention to a resistance to the use of lie-detectors in crime investigations – as if such a direct 'objective' verification somehow infringes the subject's right to the privacy of his thoughts.

A similar tension between rights and prohibitions determines heterosexual seduction in our politically correct times. Or, to put it differently, there is no seduction which cannot at some point be construed as intrusion or harassment because there will always be a point when one has to expose oneself and 'make a pass'. But, of course, seduction doesn't involve incorrect harassment throughout. When you make a pass, you expose yourself to the Other (the potential partner), and her reaction will determine whether what you just did was harassment or a successful act of seduction. There is no way to tell in advance what her response will be (which is why assertive women often despise 'weak' men, who fear to take the necessary risk). This holds even more in our pc times: the pc prohibitions are rules which, in one way or another, are to be violated in the seduction process. Isn't the seducer's art to accomplish the violation in such a way that, afterwards, by its acceptance, any suggestion of harassment has disappeared?

Although psychoanalysis is one of the victims of reflexivisation, it can also help us to understand its implications. It does not lament the disintegration of the old stability or locate in its disappearance the cause of modern neuroses, compelling us to rediscover our roots in traditional wisdom or a deeper self-knowledge. Nor is it just another version of modern reflexive knowledge which teaches us how to master the secrets of our psychic life. What psychoanalysis properly concerns itself with are the unexpected consequences of the disintegration of the structures that have traditionally regulated libidinal life. Why does the decline of paternal authority and fixed social and gender roles generate new guilts and anxieties, instead of opening up a brave new world in which we can enjoy shifting and reshaping our multiple identities?

The postmodern constellation in which the subject is bent on experimenting with his life encourages the formation of new 'passionate attachments' (to use Judith

Butler's term), but what if the disintegration of patriarchal symbolic authority is counterbalanced by an even stronger 'passionate attachment' to subjection? This would seem to explain the increasing prevalence of a strict and severely enacted master/slave relationship among lesbian couples. The one who gives the orders is the 'top', the one who obeys is the 'bottom' and, in order for the 'top' to be attained, an arduous apprenticeship has to be completed. This 'top/bottom' duality is neither a sign of direct 'identification with the (male) aggressor' nor a parodic imitation of the patriarchal relations of domination. Rather, it expresses the genuine paradox of a freely chosen master/slave form of coexistence which provides deep libidinal satisfaction.

Everything is turned back to front. Public order is no longer maintained by hierarchy, repression and strict regulation, and therefore is no longer subverted by liberating acts of transgression (as when we laugh at a teacher behind his back). Instead, we have social relations among free and equal individuals, supplemented by 'passionate attachment' to an extreme form of submission, which functions as the 'dirty secret', the transgressive source of libidinal satisfaction. In a permissive society, the rigidly codified, authoritarian master/slave relationship becomes transgressive. This paradox or reversal is the proper topic of psychoanalysis: psychoanalysis does not deal with the authoritarian father who prohibits enjoyment, but with the obscene father who enjoins it and thus renders you impotent or frigid. The unconscious is not secret resistance to the law, but the law itself.

The psychoanalytic response to the 'risk-society' theory of the reflexivisation of our lives is not to insist on a pre-reflexive substance, the unconscious, but to suggest that the theory neglects another mode of reflexivity. For psychoanalysis, the perversion of the human libidinal economy is what follows from the prohibition of some pleasurable activity: not a life led in strict obedience to the law and deprived of all pleasure but a life in which exercising the law provides a pleasure of its own, a life in which performance of the ritual destined to keep illicit temptation at bay becomes the source of libidinal satisfaction. The military life, for example, may be governed as much by an unwritten set of obscene rules and rituals (homoerotically-charged beatings and humiliations of younger comrades) as by official regulations. This sexualised violence does not undermine order in the barracks: it functions as its direct libidinal support. Regulatory power mechanisms and procedures become 'reflexively' eroticised: although repression first emerges as an attempt to regulate any desire considered 'illicit' by the predominant socio-symbolic order, it can only survive in the psychic economy if the desire for regulation is there – if the very activity of regulation becomes libidinally invested and turns into a source of libidinal satisfaction.

This reflexivity undermines the notion of the postmodern subject free to choose and reshape his identity. The psychoanalytic concept that designates the short-circuit between the repression and what it represses is the superego. As Lacan emphasised again and again, the essential content of the superego's injunction is 'Enjoy!' A father works hard to organise a Sunday excursion, which has to be postponed again and again. When it finally takes place, he is fed up with the whole idea and shouts at his children: 'Now you'd better enjoy it!' The superego works in a different way from the symbolic law. The parental figure who is simply 'repressive' in the mode of symbolic authority tells a child: 'You must go to grandma's birthday party and behave nicely, even if you are bored to death – I don't care whether you want to, just do it!' The superego figure, in contrast, says to the child: 'Although you know how much grandma would like to see you, you should go to her party only if you really want to – if you don't, you should stay at home.' The trick performed by the superego is to seem to offer the child a free choice, when, as every child knows, he is not being given any choice at all. Worse than that, he is being given an order and told to smile at the same time. Not only, 'You must visit your grandma, whatever you feel,' but: 'You must visit your grandma, and you must be glad to do it!' The superego orders you to enjoy doing what you have to do. What happens, after all, if the child takes it that he has a genuinely free choice and says 'no'? The parent will make him feel terrible. 'How can you say that!' his mother will say. 'How can you be so cruel! What did your poor grandma do to make you not want to see her?'

'You can do your duty, because you must do it,' is how Kant formulated the categorical imperative. The usual negative corollary of this formula serves as the foundation of moral constraint: 'You cannot, because you should not.' The argument of those who oppose human cloning, for example, is that it cannot be allowed because it would involve the reduction of a human being to an entity whose psychic properties can be manipulated. Which is another variation on Wittgenstein's 'Whereof one cannot speak thereof one must be silent.' In other words, we should say that we can't do it, because otherwise we may do it, with catastrophic ethical consequences. If the Christian opponents of cloning believe in the immortality of the soul and the uniqueness of the personality – i.e. that I am not just the result of the interaction between my genetic code and my environment – why oppose cloning? Is it possible that they do in fact believe in the ability of genetics to reach the very core of our personality? Why do some Christians oppose cloning with talk of the 'unfathomable mystery of the conception' as if by cloning my body I am at the same time cloning my immortal soul?

The superego inverts the Kantian 'You can, because you must' in a different way, turning it into 'You must, because you can.' This is the meaning of Viagra, which promises to restore the capacity of male erection in a purely biochemical way, bypassing all psychological problems. Now that Viagra can take care of the erection, there is no excuse: you should have sex whenever you can; and if you don't you should feel guilty. New Ageism, on the other hand, offers a way out of the superego predicament by claiming to recover the spontaneity of our 'true' selves. But New Age wisdom, too, relies on the superego imperative: 'It is your duty to achieve full self-realisation and self-fulfilment, because you can.' Isn't this why we often feel that we are being terrorised by the New Age language of liberation?

Although submission within a lesbian sado-masochistic relationship and the submission of an individual to a fundamental religious or ethnic belief are both generated by modern reflexivisation, their libidinal economies are quite different. The lesbian master/slave relationship is a theatrical enactment, based on accepted rules and a contract that has been freely entered into. As such, it has a tremendous liberating potential. In contrast, a fundamentalist devotion to an ethnic or religious cause denies the possibility of any form of consent. It is not that sadomasochists are only playfully submissive, while in the 'totalitarian' political community, submission is real. If anything, the opposite is the case: in the sadomasochistic contract, the performance is definitely for real and taken absolutely seriously, while the totalitarian submission, with its mask of fanatical devotion, is ultimately fake, a pretence of its opposite. What reveals it as fake is the link between the figure of the totalitarian master and the superego's injunction: 'Enjoy!'

A good illustration of the way the 'totalitarian' master operates is provided by the logo on the wrapper around German fat-free salami. 'Du darfst!' it says – 'You may!' The new fundamentalisms are not a reaction against the anxiety of excessive freedom that accompanies liberal late capitalism; they do not provide strong prohibitions in a society awash with permissiveness. The cliché about 'escaping from freedom' into a totalitarian haven is profoundly misleading. Nor is an explanation found in the standard Freudo-Marxian thesis according to which the libidinal foundation of totalitarian (fascist) regimes is the 'authoritarian personality' – i.e. someone who finds satisfaction in compulsive obedience. Although, on the surface, the totalitarian master also issues stern orders compelling us to renounce pleasure and to sacrifice ourselves in some higher cause, his effective injunction, discernible between the lines, is a call to unconstrained transgression. Far from imposing on us a firm set of standards to be complied with, the totalitarian master suspends (moral) punishment. His secret injunction is: 'You may.' He tells us that the prohibitions which regulate social life and guarantee a minimum of decency are worthless, just a device to keep the common people at bay – we, on the other hand, are free to let ourselves go, to kill, rape, plunder, but only insofar as we follow the master. (The Frankfurt School discerned this key feature of totalitarianism in its theory of repressive desublimation.) Obedience to the master allows you to transgress everyday moral rules: all the dirty things you were dreaming of, everything you had to renounce when you subordinated yourself to the traditional, patriarchal, symbolic Law you are now allowed to indulge in without punishment, just as you may eat fat-free salami without any risk to your health.

The same underlying suspension of moral prohibitions is characteristic of postmodern nationalism. The cliché according to which in a confused, secular, global society, passionate ethnic identification restores a firm set of values should be turned upside down: nationalist fundamentalism works as a barely concealed 'you may'. Our postmodern reflexive society which seems hedonistic and permissive is actually saturated with rules and regulations which are intended to serve our well-being (restrictions on smoking and eating, rules against sexual harassment). A passionate ethnic identification, far from further restraining us, is a liberating call of 'you may': you may violate (not the Decalogue, but) the stiff regulations of peaceful coexistence in a liberal tolerant society; you may drink and eat whatever you want, say things prohibited by political correctness, even hate, fight, kill and rape. It is by offering this kind of pseudo-liberation that the superego supplements the explicit texture of the social symbolic law.

The superficial opposition between pleasure and duty is overcome in two different ways. Totalitarian power goes even further than traditional authoritarian power. What it says, in effect, is not, 'Do your duty, I don't care whether you like it or not,' but: 'You must do your duty, and you must enjoy doing it.' (This is how totalitarian democracy works: it is not enough for the people to follow their leader, they must love him.) Duty becomes pleasure. Second, there is the obverse paradox of pleasure becoming duty in a 'permissive' society. Subjects experience the need to 'have a good time', to enjoy themselves, as a kind of duty, and, consequently, feel guilty for failing to be happy. The superego controls the zone in which these two opposites overlap – in which the command to enjoy doing your duty coincides with the duty to enjoy yourself.

18 March 1999

WHEN THE SANDWICH WAS
A NEW INVENTION

Jenny Turner on Thomas Pynchon

'**S**NOW-BALLS HAVE FLOWN THEIR arcs, starr'd the Sides of Outbuild-
ings, as of Cousins, carried Hats away into the brisk Wind off Delaware'
– that's what it says right now in the window of my local bookshop. It's
been painted on the glass by hand. It's from the first sentence of *Mason & Dixon*.*

Thomas Pynchon was born on Long Island, New York in 1937. He studied engineering, physics and, later, English literature, at Cornell University, then worked as
a technical writer for Boeing until 1962. Not long after that, he more or less disappeared from public view. His fame rests primarily on what can for convenience be
thought of as his three great novels of the 1960s, *V* (1963), *The Crying of Lot 49* (1966)
and *Gravity's Rainbow* (1973), though he has also published *Slow Learner* (1984), a
collection of his early short stories, and another novel, *Vineland*, in 1990. He started
work on *Mason & Dixon* just as *Gravity's Rainbow* was winning the US National Book
Award. It has taken him a quarter-century to cross the t's and dot the i's.

Pynchon is famous for three main novels, and for three main things. His novels
are legendarily huge and 'difficult', and have a reputation for being prophetically
hip. His avoidance of publicity has caused him to be known as a reclusive writer,
although when recently a US magazine writer 'unearthed' him, she found him
living quietly but openly in New York City, complete with wife and small son, and a
very strange-looking hat. Both the hip factor and the hermit factor, whether legiti-
mately or illegitimately, feed into the third and overweening Pynchon fame-aspect:
people seldom think of him as just an author, in the way they think of authors even
as popularly eminent as Salman Rushdie or Philip Roth. He's a trendy-essay-topic
catch-all, a figure half fact and half popular-culture fantasy, forever turning up in
conspiracy theories and comic strips and on the World Wide Web. He's an enigma,
a beatnik hero. He is, in short, a cult.

'Learned diversions, paranoid transitions, hip coincidences and conspiracies', I
read in the TP entry in my useful *Cultural Icons* encyclopedia. 'The reclusive Pynchon
writes as if everything is connected to everything else, and detours so obsessively en route that even the revelation that there is actually no revelation seems

---

*Thomas Pynchon, *Mason & Dixon* (Cape, 1997).

extraordinarily significant.' It goes on to speak of 'the necessary futility of reading', 'the astonishing proliferation of codes', and, with a final dialectical flourish, 'the difficulty of pleasure, and the pleasure of difficulty'. So there you have it. Gosh.

It is true that Pynchon's novels are formidably learned. But they are also intellectually with-it and sophisticated, which is much more interesting. They negotiate complex questions in the sociology of knowledge, across both natural science and social science, in highbrow registers and lowbrow ones, with what appears to be equal ease. When people go on about Pynchon as a 'prophetic' writer, it is really this intellectual sophistication to which they refer. Prophetic writers at bottom are only writers who handle abstract concepts as easily as they do all the other stuff. They thus have a solid purchase on intellectually privileged forms of knowledge – i.e. the world of ideas. It says something not entirely complimentary about most novelists that we get all gee-whiz and overexcited whenever we come across a writer like Pynchon, who is only a novelist who has bothered to make the bread-and-butter of the serious thinker an aspect of his creative bread-and-butter, too.

But back, for a moment, to these curious Snow-Balls. They did not, I imagine, make you eager to read on. You might expect the beginning of a Pynchon novel to be 'difficult' – which is to say, stylistically packed. But the beginning of *Mason & Dixon* is forbidding, even so. It's busy, it's dense, and it's in 18th-century macaroni, full of oddly torqued inflections and hard-on-the-eyeballs initial caps. Plus, it looks like it's all about Christmas, which isn't enticing. It's worth the effort, however. Get to page 18 of *Mason & Dixon*, and a Learnèd English Dog comes in. First off, he's a talking dog. ''Tis the Age of Reason, rrrf?' he asks. 'Grrr! and your deliberate use of "drooling", Sir, is vile.' Even better, he bursts into song:

> I quote enough of the Classickal Stuff
> To set your Ears a-throb,
> Work logarith-mick Versèd Sines
> Withal, within me Nob . . .

Pynchon included a song-and-dance number in his first novel, *V*. There are more of them in *The Crying of Lot 49*, and *Gravity's Rainbow*, monumentally fearsome though it looks, concludes with one. Imagine how Pynchon must grin to himself, as he jots his awful verses down. That's artistic exuberance for you. That's artistic vitality in the raw.

Usually, when you read one of those fancy-looking magic-postmod metafictional thingies, you start scraping along the bottom of their 'prodigious' learning and creativity by the time you hit page 10. But Pynchon's learning really does seem deep enough to sustain him as he does his bathtub caterwauling, wearing his horrible hat, I don't doubt, even as he writes. Pynchon, it isn't worth for a millisecond forgetting, is a completely hilarious writer. Like all the very coolest of cultural icons, he couldn't care less about shallow things like whether he's fashionable, or whether he's singing in tune. He's cool in the manner of the very coolest of refrigerators. He's blasting with warmth out back.

Mason & Dixon is the story of two men, Charles Mason (1728-86) and Jeremiah Dixon (1733-79). Both are drawn from history, as is the outline of their doings, and as are many of the acquaintances they happen upon en route. Mason begins the tale as an astronomer at Greenwich; Dixon as a journeyman land-surveyor in the North-East of England. In 1761 they join forces to observe the Transit of Venus from the Cape of Good Hope. Thus 'Latitudes and Departures', the first part of what turns out to be a mischievously unsymmetrical three-parter of a book. Two years later, M&D accept a commission to run a boundary line eight yards wide, dividing the states of Pennsylvania and Maryland as far as the borders of Ohio. The job involves four years of laborious fieldwork, with a team of workmen in attendance to clear the 'Visto' of trees. This is the middle part. It is baldly entitled 'America', has the most bewilderingly picaresque of narrative structures, and is more than four hundred pages long. Then, finally, in a coda of less than a hundred pages, it's time for the 'Last Transit' of 1769. Mason travels alone to observe the silent planet from Ulster. Dixon voyages alone to the North Cape.

Mason and Dixon's great projects were, as a friend says, 'brave, scientifick beyond my understanding, and ultimately meaningless'. Each job, owing to forces beyond the control of our heroes, ends under something of a cloud. Directly after the Mason-Dixon Line was completed, America had its Revolution and the Line fell into neglect. It did, however, attain great symbolic force from the Civil War onwards. Proverbially, and to some extent in fact, it marked the border between the cotton-pickin' southern slave states and the northern Yankee country, in which a black man might be free.

In form, and in content also, *Mason & Dixon* is many things rolled into one. It's an epic in ways both obvious and not-so-obvious like the *Odyssey*, and it's a simple-hearted buddy story, too. It's a burlesque musical – there are many more songs – and it's a Tex Avery cartoon. It's a treatise on the Enlightenment view of scientific progress, written from a late 20th-century non-linear-dynamical point of view. It's a funny book, *Time Bandits* crossed with Douglas Adams. And it's an enormous, systematic study of order and disorder, which moves to the strange, slow rhythms of what historians call the longue durée. Although the bulk of its action seems to happen in North America, it is also about 18th-century England, and land enclosure and colonialism, and patterns of global trade. It also makes an especially jaunty excursion to Scotland. 'These people are strong, shrewd,' warns a certain Dr Johnson. 'Be not deceiv'd by any level of the Exotick they may present you, Kilts, Bag-Pipes sort of thing. Haggis. You must keep eternal Vigilance.' Mason considers himself warned.

But what actually happens in it? Well. Dixon is a rollicking country lad, a Quaker from County Durham ('Why, aye!'). He's Enlightenment Man in his Tom Jones aspect, a bright, good-natured extrovert who wags his tail at all that interests him, like a friendly dog. Mason, on the other hand, is Enlightenment Man in his sombre, 'Gothickal' aspect. He is haunted by the ghost of his dead wife, Rebekah. He dreams repeatedly of 'a night-time City, – of creeping among monuments of stone perhaps twice his height, of seeking refuge from some absolute pitiless Upheaval in relations among Men'. He's a decent chap, but regretful and prone to resentment. As a team, M&D are a bit like Eric and Ernie, as comic, as equally matched and with a similarly tender depth. 'You've no concept of Temptation,' Mason sighs at Dixon at one point. 'You came ashore here looking for occasions to transgress. Some of us have more Backbone, I suppose.' 'A bodily Part too often undistinguish'd,' says Dixon, 'from a Ram-Rod up the Arse.' Much later, M&D dream of winning the Copley Medal, the British astronomer's highest imaginable prize.

> 'Eeh!' Dixon amiably waves his Hat. 'Which half do thou fancy, obverse or reverse?'
>
> 'What?' Mason frowning in thought, 'Hum. Well, I rather imagin'd we'd . . . share the same side, – a Half-Circle each, sort of thing.'

Only, they never actually win the Medal. And so the issue is resolved.

It doesn't sound especially hip or difficult or paranoid, does it? It isn't that the trendy critical appropriations of Pynchon are inaccurate exactly, it's more that they are inappropriate to the experience of actually reading a Pynchon novel, and also a little bit vain. It would, however, be just as wrong to come away with the impression that M&D is only an Eric and Ernie with knobs on, or merely a postmodern romparama of the sort Umberto Eco managed so elegantly in The Name of the Rose. It's much more densely webbed with allusiveness. And its mood is far more rigorously subjunctive: it's an open network of potentialities, like a mutating spreadsheet or grid. It is all these things because it is at bottom a historical novel, and one premised on an extreme sense of critical scepticism about the things that seem to change through time and history, and the things that seem to stay the same.

The America of Mason & Dixon is not like any of the ones familiar from popular culture. It's an America in which the wilderness begins just west of Philadelphia.

It's the America of the Thirteen Colonies, before the formal union of any of the states, in which it is unclear to anyone whether land-claims will finally be settled by kings, or governments, or the chartered companies grown as strong as states themselves. I was reminded of the shock I got when I saw the film of Edith Wharton's *The Age of Innocence*, with much of Manhattan still, towards the end of the last century, a muddy building-site. The America of *Mason & Dixon* is more than a century more inchoate, and so is the world around it. The 'self-evident truths' that codify the Rights of Man would not be declared on that continent until 1774. They would not be declared in Europe until 1789.

Over the entirety of the novel, barely a line sets out to delineate a sense of historical period in the way I have just tried to do. Barely a line attempts to reconstruct one in any detail either. And there is no weak irony to Pynchon's handling of this huge historical distance. There's no idle fiddling about between what the narrators don't know about their future and what we, from our godly late 20th-century heights, know about them. The sense of contingency is total, and awesome. The future is completely opaque and empty, like the Enlightenment heaven and hell.

And so, for long stretches of the book which tells their story, M&D are tramping the open country, or taking measurements with their instruments, or voyaging to places in ships. Yet there is notably little concrete description of such things. Where M&D really has its setting is in the new civil society of the mid-18th century, in coffee-houses and pubs. 'One may be inches from a neighbour, yet both blurr'd past recognising, – thus may Advice grow reckless and Prophecy extreme given the astonishing volume of words moving about in here,' Pynchon writes of one coffee-house in Philadelphia. This image points up the method of the novel as a whole. Huge chunks of it are written in direct-quote dialogue, and even the omniscient-narrator parts are angled through a particular voice. The entire book is an elaborate chiaroscuro of knowledge and ignorance. Only none of the ignorance is left at all empty or dark.

Instead, every single ignorant patch is stuffed to bursting with 'Advice grown Reckless and Prophecy extreme'. The novel is stuffed, in other words, with fallacies and mistakes. There is the great Eleven Days controversy, for example, when the people of England arose in anger after losing a week and a half of wages to the Popish Gregorian calendar in 1752. There are flat-earthers and there are hollow-earthers, and an extremely funny strand involves the progress of Nevil Maskelyne – the Royal Astronomer who features centrally and villainously in Dava Sobel's top-selling pop-science book, *Longitude* – from part-time astrology buff to full-fledged Merlin lookalike, dressed in his tailor-made tartan 'Observing Suit' with co-ordinating pointy hat.

The position of our heroes among this mayhem is strategic. Both, we already know, are basically good guys, and first-generation professional 'men of Science' from the soles of their rural-artisan boots. But they don't know what they can't know, and so are as comically embroiled and mistakenly invested as everyone else. Dixon, for example, has been blessed – or cursed – by an intellectually dubious mentor figure with the gift of a watch which never stops, thus disproving the ancient adage, 'prandium gratis non est'. 'When you accept me into your Life,' the watch murmurs, '– you will accept me . . . into your Stomach.' And as it speaks it assumes 'a shape indisputably Vegetable'. 'Vegetables don't tick,' a kindly soul reminds poor Dixon, who is becoming most distressed. 'Why aye, those that be *only Vegetables* don't. We speak now of a *higher form of life* – a Vegetable with a Pulse-beat!' Is it the laudanum, is it the coffee he's constantly drinking, or is it the Daffy's Elixir he consumes in the most enormous quantities for his bowels? Or might this not indeed be a Vegetable on the move towards a state more animal, or a Clock which has begun an adaptation towards organic life? It is, please remember before you consign poor Dixon to Bedlam, a man of Science's job to come up with possible hypotheses to explain whichever phenomena appear to cross his path. It is thus the job of a man of Science to spend at least half his time in the pursuance of hypotheses that fit the available evidence, even though he kind of knows as he's doing this that they are most likely wrong.

As the novel proceeds ever further in its westerly direction, Pynchon throws stranger and stranger shadows along the Visto through which our men must go. There's a land of Giant Vegetables, and a lovelorn robot duck. And I particularly liked the Welsh-stroke-Native-American burial mound, designed like a gigantic Leyden jar, with, inscribed across the front of it, in Welsh-Indian runes: 'Keep away. Especially surveyors. This means you.' Unlike your usual look-at-me-mum magic-realist author, Pynchon pretty well never makes anything up. The ancient Welsh presence in North America, I am told, is now thoroughly established in archaeology, like the friendly visit from the Norsemen from which Pynchon's last novel, *Vineland*, took its name. The Giant Beetroot comes straight from something in David Hume.

This method, it should be obvious, has nothing to do with the weakly whacky. It caricatures, it counterfactualises and it reductio-ad-absurdums. But it does so in strict relation to real historical sources, in an oddly angled, yet almost geometrically measurable, way. What look like antihistorical anachronisms turn out on closer inspection to be aspects of a historically precise strategy. They are instruments for measuring similarity and difference, ideological clocks. They tick and tock and sometimes judder rather strangely as they attempt to bind and bridge the historical distance between the dawning of the Age of Reason and the author's – and his readers' – late 20th-century sense of the here and now.

Like the luckiest of world travellers, M&D are forever running into major historical celebrities. They have barely set foot in Philadelphia before they bump into Benjamin Franklin, posing around in 'Spectacles of his own Invention, for moderating the Glare of the Sun'. And then of course they are asked round for tea by Col. George Washington, you know, the land-surveyor and real-estate speculator, eager for his own reasons to network with these overseas visitors, whom he plies with kasha varnishkies and hemp. The delicacies are fetched by Gershom, Washington's Jewish-African slave. 'Gershom is presently telling King-Joaks – "Actually, they're Slave-and-Master Joaks, re-tailored for these Audiences. King says to his Fool . . . "'

I started looking in my wonderful *Brewer's Dictionary*. I discovered, among many other things, that Franklin really did do a lot of work on optometry (and on electricity, and he did write his ghastly Poor Richard advice column, as becomes increasingly significant as the novel goes on). And Washington really was a surveyor and land-speculator, though I wouldn't like to say about the kasha varnishkies or the hemp. Even Gershom, who must be a total invention, is an invention with resonance and point. He's bricolage in motion, a cultural syncretism on legs; a comic inversion of the master-and-slave relation delineated by Hegel and Fanon and Jean Rouch. Even the straightforward-looking way in which these guys are coded as funny characters is not, when you think about it, straightforward at all. It is itself yet another historical reference, to the Beatcomic tradition of Krazy Kat and Lenny Bruce.

This is not a naively comic Pritt stick job, like calling the alien in *The Hitch-Hiker's Guide to the Galaxy* after a Ford Prefect car, but a painstakingly careful dovetailing, in which you must mark all the detail of the separations even as you marvel at the join, and one which is replicated across the structure of *Mason & Dixon*. This is done zeugmatically, halfway through single sentences, fully exploiting the magnificent Augustan caesura that dots the novel across its entirety, along with all those rhythmically capital-lettered Nouns. It's done in the most elegant off-the-cuff one-liners, like the one about the Irish fish-pond from which the Romans learned the wisdom of carpe carpum, viz, seize the carp.

Then perhaps halfway through the novel it dawns on you that this dovetailing is the very key to the novel's narrative structure, and the friendship at the centre of it, and its wider historical plan. The last time we looked at M&D, they were contemplating the Copley medal – whether to split it obverse and reverse, or to take halves of the same side. The image is typical of the way their mutually grudging friendship is dramatised. It holds strictly to 18th-century rules of decorum, while introducing a note of sweetness and self-awareness which is unmistakably new. From the beginning of the novel to the end, not a word is said about either man to break the period conventions. And yet, it is impossible not to start liking and caring about them enormously, in a curiously modern and at first sight unaccountable, category-mistaken way.

It helps that Pynchon has borrowed his protagonists from history, which means he can't indulge his usual weakness for lumbering his characters with gross-out names like Tyrone Slothrop or Hubert Stencil. (Though he does sneak in a sailor called Bodine. And there's a whole family of Dutch Cape Colonists who go by the charming name of Vroom.) It's also true that Pynchon knows he can call on a certain readerly nostalgia to do more than half the work for him. To begin with, it seems so refreshing to meet a couple of heroes who are free of all the usual post-Nietzschean subjectivity problems, all that tedious ambivalent agony. They're such decent guys, and they seem to have no side to them. All they want is all that you and I want: life, liberty and the pursuit of happiness. At the same time, preferably, as doing the right thing. So why can't they manage this? Why do all their best-laid plans turn to failure? And why do aporia and antinomy creep into their maps like an infestation, the minute their attention is drawn elsewhere?

> 'Christ, Mason.'
> 'Christ what? What did I do?'
> 'Huz . . . '

You can't say it's just human nature or the human condition. That's far too sloppily metaphysical for a writer like TP. Except that this is exactly what Pynchon himself seems to be saying, only in a more historically grounded way. Set amid the primordial caffeine-laced chaos out of which the modern sense of democratic humanism would shortly drag itself on its stumpy constitutional legs, the action of *Mason & Dixon* emerges from the culture of the coffee-house. It is sparked by the very crack of the dawning Enlightenment: have the courage to use your own understanding! – which is an old-fashioned version of the 1990s exhortation to do the right thing. So here we have two guys in all the nicest people's favourite century, before the revolutionary Terror came along and suggested that Reason in itself would never be quite enough. They have coffee aplenty, and the sandwich is still an excitingly fresh invention. So what can it be that seems to be going wrong?

Pynchon, beautifully and directly, allows the foot-soldiers of Enlightenment to tell us in their own words. It may help to remember that Dixon, who speaks first, does so as a Geordie and a Quaker, and is thus a voice well-used to calling a plough-share a ploughshare when occasion makes the need.

'Ev'rywhere they've sent us – the Cape, St Helena, America, – what's the element common to all?'

'Long Voyages by sea,' replies Mason, blinking in Exhaustion by now chronick. 'Was there anything else?'

'Slaves. Ev'ry day at the Cape, we lived with Slavery in our faces, – more of it at St Helena, and now here we are again, in another Colony, this time having drawn them a Line between their Slave-Keepers, and their Wage-Payers, as if doom'd to re-encounter thro' the World this public Secret, this shameful Core . . . '

'Christ, Mason.'

'Christ, what? What did I do?'

'Huz. Didn't we take the King's money, as here we're taking it again? whilst Slaves waited upon us, and we neither one objected, as little as we have here, in certain houses south of the Line, – Where does it end? No matter where in it we go, shall we find all the World Tyrants and Slaves? America was the one place we should *not* have found them.'

'Yet we're not Slaves, after all, – we're Hirelings.'

We have already observed Mason losing a bar-room argument by making this distinction about his own early life in Stroud.

In 1756, the British Army declared war on the Gloucestershire weavers. 'Wages were all cut in half, and the master weavers began to fiddle the Chain on the Bar, and a weaver was lucky to earn tuppence for eight hours' work.' Mason, a baker's son, was just getting ready to leave for his great new job in London 'as Soldiers were beating citizens and slaughtering sheep for their pleasure, fouling and making sick Streams once holy'. 'Contemptible cowardly dogs who fall down dead in their own Shit', cried the infantrymen's leader, James Wolfe, the future Martyr of Québec. Years later, Mason still feels bad about abandoning his village at this moment. He's just one of those guys with a guilt-ridden nature. Unlike Dixon, who leaps in to beat up a passing Slave-Driver, without a thought as to the consequences of his actions for the slaves who find themselves so unexpectedly liberated, or indeed for himself.

At first sight, the ideas Pynchon is developing in this passage may seem too obvious to be worthy of much note. It's obvious that all the places an 18th-century traveller would visit would turn out to have been opened up in the first place to expedite the global trade in slaves. It's obvious that there's an awkward problem there for the raising, about the chattel slavery of overseas colonialism and the wage slavery both Mason and Dixon experienced as young men, with the beginnings of the Industrial Revolution kicking in at home. And it's obvious that we have a contradiction between M&D's basic well-meaningness as human beings, and their passive collusion in 'this Shameful Core'. And yet none of this was obvious to Mason or Dixon. The sophisticated understanding of history which allows us to view the globe so glibly is pretty much a high-tech, late 20th-century thing. And does it especially help us to resolve the moral problem? I'll take a quick running jump at this one and hazard an answer of No.

It is a monumental achievement, what Pynchon in *Mason & Dixon* has done. You will not know what has hit you until you are flat out on the floor. You start the book bewildered, then slowly ease into its curious patternings of order and disorder, its utterly idiosyncratic sense of rhythm and pace. By the time you get to the Talking Dog, your face will be cracking into the nicest of new-dawn smiles. 'Nice guys,' you'll be thinking of Mason and Dixon. You'll be reminiscing fondly about all your other favourite nice guys, Tristram Shandy and Leopold Bloom. And then you start fantasising about getting them all together, like Flann O'Brien does with all his big favourites in the Dalkey cave. You wonder whether the period conventions would allow for it. Is being a nice guy enough of a transhistorical quality to let the party go with a swing?

To which the answer seems to be: yes it is, quite possibly. Humanism – the philosophically fetishised version of everyday nice-guy emotion – is all we've really got to bind us, and it's also our topmost asset. And yet it has no power to address the 'public Secret' which blights the very origin of its optimism. It is powerless over the transhistorical omnipresence of its 'shameful Core'. 'Unfortunately, young People, the word *Liberty*, so unreflectively sacred to us today, was taken in those Times to encompass even the darkest of Men's rights, – to injure whomever we might wish, – unto extermination, were it possible,' comments the omniscient narrator. 'This being, indeed and alas, one of the Liberties our late War was fought to secure.'

So what of the Snow-Balls with which we started? Well, the ballad of *Mason & Dixon* is not presented unmediated. It is told by the Reverend Wicks Cherrycoke, an Anglican minister who pops up all over the main narrative, and who contributes his ecumenical homilies to many a chapter's head. It's Christmastide 1786, just after the War of Independence. Cherrycoke has been tending his old friend Mason's grave. He's allowed to room with his brother-in-law's family for as long as he can entertain the in-house tribe of teenagers – 'too much evidence of Juvenile Rampage at the wrong moment, however, and Boppo! 'twill be Out the Door with him'. There are Dough-Nuts and Buns, and Fritters and Crullers. It's like *The Waltons* or *Little Women*. It's a completely shameless feast-in of a bourgeois family Christmas.

Except of course that it is and it isn't, and it is also other things. A winter's tale which goes on for 773 pages, and will take the normal reader a solid week to read? The joke is declined in all manner of ways delicious as the novel proceeds. Sometimes, Cherrycoke disappears for ages. Then, there's page after page about the family orrery, family flirtations, family tales. There's one particularly elegant prestidigitation, in which the Mason and Dixon narrative melds with a yellow paper which is being read by a sexually frustrated college-boy. It happens over the token bit of porno-sadism Pynchon usually slips into a novel somewhere (necessity being the mother of invention, it would be hard to squeeze a bit of porno-sadism into the story of Mason and Dixon in any less protuberant a way). The name of the yellow paper is wonderful, and I'm glad to say it turns up often. It is called the *Ghastly Fop*.

The Christmastide setting – and the sprightly tenderness with which it is evoked – adds something yet richer and stranger to the long, slow patternings of the *Mason & Dixon* plot. It offers a spurious-and-yet-not-entirely-so conclusion to a story whose integrity depends on its own non-closure, allowing for an illusion – which is not entirely an illusion – of redemption and return. In its duration and in its festivity it very much brings to mind the movement of *Fanny and Alexander*, Ingmar Bergman's mighty final film. Both works bespeak great mellowness and maturity, and an enormous generosity of mind. The warmth, the optimism, the commitment to reason is unflinching, even as either piece busily depicts the innumerable ways in which reason is an exasperating business, prone to sudden slippages and with a tendency to break down.

It isn't true, as some reviewers have suggested, that *Mason & Dixon* represents a radical break with Pynchon's earlier big books. He was never much of a bug-eyed weirdo in the first place. He was just a good bit younger in the 1960s, and so both willing and able to slam-dance straight into his lifelong preoccupations, getting on down with all the crazy people in the cultural havoc at the front. To prove it, I'll say something more about those Snow-Balls. They seem deliberately to echo the beginning of *Gravity's Rainbow*. The first time as rocket science and apocalypse. The second time as eternal recurrence and fun.

'What Phantom Shape, implicit in the Figures?' Mason asks feebly of his attendants as he is about to die. ''Tis a Construction, a great single Engine, the size of a Continent . . . Our Bible is Nature, wherein the Pentateuch, is the Sky. I have found there written evr'y Night, in Astral Gematria, Messages of Great Urgency to our Time.'

'Since I was ten,' Mason's eldest son says at his graveside, 'I wanted you to take me and Willy to America. I kept hoping, ev'ry Birthday, this would be the year.' The boy's name is Doctor Isaac, after Newton. 'The Fish jump into your Arms,' he continues a little later. 'The Indians know Magick.'

'We'll go there. We'll live there,' butts in his younger brother.

'We'll fish there,' Doc says, in the last line of this wonderful novel. 'And you too.' It's the purest, naivest dream of America. And it's a sceptical critique of that continent's epistemological foundations, and so of the moral and perceptual foundations of the modern world.

17 July 1997

SHORT CUTS

Thomas Jones

THE FIRST RECORDED USE of the word 'freedom' in English comes in the penultimate chapter of Alfred the Great's translation of Boethius' *De consolatione philosophiae* (c.888), in a discussion of free will: 'thu segist thæt God sylle ællcum freodom swa god to donne swa yfel' – 'You say that God gives to everyone the freedom to do both good and evil.' 'Boethius' goes on to ask why God allows men to be wicked and make evil choices. Ah, that old chestnut, 'Philosophy' thinks. (I make no apology for being so free in my translation: it's got nothing on the freedoms that Alfred, his purposes as much political as scholarly, took with the original, such as bringing God into it.) Imagine a king, Philosophy says, whose subjects were all slaves, with no free men in the kingdom: that wouldn't be very good now, would it? Indeed not, Boethius agrees. Well then, continues Philosophy, in that case it certainly wouldn't do for God's kingdom to have no free creatures in it, would it? Quite so, Boethius says, before going on to ask: but how do you reconcile free will with divine omniscience? (Tony Blair must be relieved that Boethius doesn't sit on a House of Commons select committee.) Philosophy has a pretty decent answer. (The prime minister must long to have someone like that on his side.)

Anglo-Saxon chiefs have changed over the last millennium or so: it's easy enough to imagine George W. Bush falling asleep and burning the cakes; harder to see him taking time off from ruining the country to translate a little Neoplatonist philosophy. Not that that stops him bandying the word 'freedom' around as if it were a tax break for his buddies. 'Free' is derived from an Indo-European root meaning 'to love'; it's related to 'friend'. 'The primary sense of the adjective,' the OED explains, 'is "dear"; the Germanic and Celtic sense comes of its having been applied as the distinctive epithet of those members of the household who were connected by ties of kindred with the head, as opposed to the slaves.' More recently, 'free' has come to be used by the leaders of the 'free world' to signify simply the world that they lead. This shift can be seen as a reversal of the process described by the OED, a return to the earlier meaning: the 'free' now are those dear to the Bush administration. 'Freedom' has come to denote, quite precisely, 'the government of the United States and its supporters and allies': those who are famously 'for us', as opposed to those others who are by default 'against us'. The notorious introduction of 'freedom fries' and 'freedom toast' to the congressional canteen established one sense of the word as being the opposite of 'French': and, even if you think they're cheese-eating surrender monkeys, you can't say the French aren't, in the pre-9/11 sense, at least as free as Americans.

There are people out there who still understand the word as meaning something other than 'patriotic', such as the US army sergeant in Iraq who told the *Economist*: 'It sucks. You promise freedom. They get martial law.' In the last frame of the most recent instalment of 'In the Shadow of No Towers', Art Spiegelman riffed on the first line of the chorus of 'Me and Bobby McGee', 'Freedom's just another word for nothing left to lose': 'I thought I'd lose my life on 9/11 . . . I lost my mind soon after, and lost my last speck of faith in the USA when this cabal took over – I guess this really is the land o'th'free!' One might add that freedom in the Kris Kristof-ferson sense is what has been brought to Iraq, even if many people there had little left to lose long before the invasion. Anyway, the more you hear about 'freedom' from the powers that be, the harder it is to hold onto the sergeant's meaning. The word appears 2210 times on the official White House website, www.whitehouse.gov ('democracy', to give a sense of scale, crops up 577 times; 'oil', 537; 'tax cuts', 311; 're-election', a modest 49), but only 134 times on the more illuminating – and certainly more amusing – parody, www.whitehouse.org.

With fearful symmetry, 'terror' has acquired a new meaning, too. When President Bush or one of his followers repeats the mantra that 'freedom shall prevail over terror,' he can only mean, if the implied clash of abstractions is to have any meaning at all: 'We shall prevail over them.' In the 'war against terror', the referent of 'terror' is whomever we are fighting: the focus of the war is not determined by who the enemy is, as would be reasonable to expect, and as those waging it claim; rather, the nature of the enemy is determined by the focus of the war. Or, as one of the 'patriotic posters' on offer at www.whitehouse.org puts it, 'Saddam? Osama? True patriots just split the difference and aim for the towel.'

24 July 2003

SLOWLY/SWIFTLY

Michael Hofmann on James Schuyler

NOT FIRST SIGHT, often enough, but a second look – it is a mysterious thing with poetry that it finds its own moment. The poets that have meant most to me – Lowell, Bishop, Schuyler – all, as it were, were rudely kept waiting by me. I had their books, or I already knew some poems of theirs, but there was no spark of transference. Then it happened, and our tepid prehistory was, quite literally, forgotten beyond a lingering embarrassment at my own callow unresponsiveness. It was as though they had always been with me, and I found it difficult, conversely, to remember our first encounter. It is a slight relief to me that James Schuyler, who writes about reading almost as much as he writes about seeing, confesses to a similar sluggishness of feeling:

> Twenty-some years ago, I read Graham Stuart Thomas's
> 'Colour in the Winter Garden'. I didn't plant
> a winter garden, but the book led on to his
> rose books: 'The Old Shrub Roses', 'Shrub Roses
> of Today', and the one about climbers and ramblers.
>
> ('Horse-Chestnut Trees and Roses')

It is this dilatory or sidelong compliance I am talking about. Here follows my own belated winter garden to the American poet James Marcus Schuyler, pronounced 'Sky-ler', 1923-91.

The first time I was aware of James Schuyler was in one of those rather windy American 'Best of' annuals. At the back of the book, the poets comment on their own poems, in every shade of vainglory and modesty, pretentiousness and Aw shuckery. The only comment I can remember from a decade's worth of these books is Schuyler's, to the effect that while his poems were usually the product of a single occasion looking out of a window (his version of the unities), the poem in question (I think it was 'Haze') departed from this by using more than one window and more than one occasion. 'I do not normally permit myself such licence,' the poet sternly ends. This stood out: for its idiosyncrasy and scrupulousness, for its thoughtful rebellion against unthinking unassumingness, for its (I am somehow convinced) borrowed plumminess. There's something enjoyably performed and bewigged about it. That was in 1990. From then I date my public espousal of the 'poem out of the window' – though that's an old cause with me – and a little later, I finally began to read Schuyler.

It was on a morning in Manhattan, the book was *The Morning of the Poem* (typically, I don't know how it came to be in my possession), and the poems that convinced me (it's unusual to remember this) were a sequence of 11 short pieces called 'The Payne Whitney Poems'. The Payne Whitney, I knew from reading about Robert Lowell, was a New York mental hospital, in the same way I knew from reading *Lunar Caustic* that the Bellevue was a New York mental hospital, and here was a clutch of texts fit to set beside Malcolm Lowry's book, or Lowell's 'Waking in the Blue' or his sequence 'Hospital'. Intact records of damage, frail hints at a central neural mystery, words newly out of bandages:

> **Arches**
> of buildings, this building,
> frame a stream of windows
> framed in white brick. This
> building is fireproof; or else
> it isn't: the furnishings first
> to go: no, the patients. Patients
> on Sundays walk in a small garden.
> Today some go out on a group
> pass. To stroll the streets and shop.
> So what else is new? The sky
> slowly/swiftly went blue to grey.
> A grey in which some smoke stands.

Typical of Schuyler are the adjustments and corrections – like Bishop's, only more sweeping (and yet just as mildly carried out, 'no, the patients', 'slowly/swiftly'). Also the small thoughts and whimsical, half-experimental notations, before they are countermanded: 'This/building is fireproof'; 'Today some go out on a group/ pass' – this last reminding me unfortunately of someone's altogether more robust sneer (is it Berryman?), 'nuts in groups about the room'. There is a clear and real external scene, a view or 'subject', and yet always stronger is one's sense of the poem as being made, like a painting: the quick, nervous applications of paint, and the quick taking of it back. Schuyler is a painterly poet, descriptive and objective, and at the same time he uses all the subliminal, microbial quirks of language.

The poem attempts perhaps to find something to affirm, but everywhere there is either fear or envy (of the patients on their exeat) or a crippling feeling of fatuity. Something as 'normal' and ordinary as 'To stroll the streets and shop' can rarely have sounded as hesitant and borrowed and speculative as it does here. The infinite wistfulness of the infinitive. To know her is to love her. To walk and chew gum. To pass through the eye of a needle and enter heaven. No wonder it takes the patients straight out of the poem, leaving the speaker with the self-interrogation which, one senses, he has been avoiding as hard as he can. From shame, from weakness, from 'shakiness' – a condition referred to in one of the other poems – or perhaps from lifelong aesthetic preference, the speaker, it seems, would prefer to stick to external, middle-distance things. His speech feels like remedial speech, the words sound odd and insecure. Having asked his question – doesn't it sound like a visitor's, easy to ask, hell to reply to, that he's unhappily parroting to himself? – he heroically interposes 'The sky', so perhaps as not to have to offer information about himself. Unluckily, 'The sky' sounds like a play on the poet's name, and the predicate may perhaps offer clues about his condition (I have seen both the following ascribed to Schuyler): the schizophrenic 'slowly/swiftly', or else the bipolar 'went blue to grey', a past verb – more, painful, relearning of language – suggesting the change, which of course the speaker has no hope of quantifying, from depressed, 'blue', to medicated, 'grey'. 'A grey', the information carries on, in a rather unlooked for way, 'in which some smoke stands'. The last word, wholly unexpected, makes the poem. Not that one had any doubts about the poem being made – it makes itself through-out – but such an ending, dutiful, dominant, at no stage seems remotely within its reach. Here is the unlooked for affirmation, a new physics in which smoke 'stands' while windows 'stream' and brick is 'white' and 'fireproof; or else/it isn't'. And of course, there is the platitude: 'no smoke without fire'. The patients are the first 'to go', and so this one, humorously, has 'gone'.

What looked like a static scene – a view out of the window – is instead a little drama. The interest of the poem – fully held by the minutely controlled to and fro, paint and scrape of the sentences, its terrible, casual sensitivity – is in its naked tact and its secret optics. The form of the arch had Kleist's admiration for being kept up by the desire of every individual part of it to fall. 'Arches' is the poem of someone with his glasses off, or his brain decoupled, of the infinitely delicate return of matter, manner, humour, humanity. What we think of as a 'journey', Kafka said, is a 'wavering' or 'dithering'. 'The Payne Whitney Poems' (*pace* Heaney) waver into sense. They take very small steps tremendously irresolutely. At the beginning of 'Arches', the speaker recognises or discerns nothing; by the end, he sounds wise. Not just that, he seems to be under very low pressure. There is painfully little forward momentum. Most rhetoric is based on repetition: Schuyler uses repetition that is only repetition, that is without rhetoric. The title – ironically – falls into the poem, and the poem shuffles from 'buildings' to 'building', from 'frame' to 'framed', from 'the patients' to 'Patients'. If Lowell or someone had written within such parameters, it would have had tremendous power (say, 'tops of the moving trees move helter-skelter') – no power accrues to it here. Rather, the miracle is that the frailty, even the lightness of the thing is not impaired. It is someone taking these tiny steps, backwards and forwards, and not treading on anything, not hurting anything.

However halting, impaired, almost uncommunicative the poem, I still have the perverse sense that the station to which it is tuned, however low, is merriment. The sentences may be mumbled and reluctant and short and full of wrong turnings, but there is still a low ebb of wit in them – in the macabre speculation, in the observation of others like or unlike himself, in the unexpectedly fluent linkage of smoke and fire. It is, in other words, and perhaps again unexpectedly, literary; and I have come to think that Schuyler is everywhere literary. It seems to me not inappropriate to be reminded of other poems and poets by 'Arches', by the other 'Payne Whitney Poems', by Schuyler passim. 'Her hair dressed with stark simplicity' (from 'Let's All Hear It for Mildred Bailey!') is Horace. 'Buried at Springs' anticipates Bishop's 'North Haven', and there is no shortage of other 'Bishop moments', such as 'More litter, less clutter' from 'The Man with the Golden Glow' or 'The bay agitatedly tries to smooth itself out./If it were tissue paper it would need damp and an iron' – which then corpses into 'It is a good deal more than damp./What a lot of water' ('The Edge in the Morning'). 'An Almanac' is Brodsky, but in 1969, before there was Brodsky: 'Shops take down their awnings;/ women go south;/few streetlamp leaners;/children run with leaves running at their backs./In cedar chests sheers and seersuckers displace flannels and wools.' Rilke is a pervasive presence: 'men with faces like happy fists' ('Scarlet Tanager'), or the thought in 'The best, the very best, roses. After learning all their names – Rose/de Rescht, Cornelia, Pax – it is important to forget them' and 'When I/was born, death kissed me. I kissed it back' (both in 'Hymn to Life', which is like a stray elegy). Frank O'Hara, Schuyler's friend and sometime flatmate, is very obviously there (I'll keep myself therefore to one example): 'Look, Mitterrand baby' ('Simone Signoret'). O'Hara aside, this is not a matter of being influenced – or influential. The quotations are not borrowings, but convergences or congruences: they affirm a conventionality that, with all their wacky freedoms, Schuyler's poems also satisfy. It's not that they are touchstones – something I had thought of saying about 'Arches' – but that although they are not conceived as touchstones they are every bit as good as touchstones.

When I began reading Schuyler, I thought it wasn't possible for anyone to occupy so much of O'Hara's territory without looking pallid; then I thought I liked him better than O'Hara: less strenuous, less riotous, more depth and stamina in the personality, more like that 'something to read in normal circumstances' (Pound) that I generally crave in poetry. After a while, I thought I hadn't liked anyone this much since Lowell; then I had the (for me) heretical thought that perhaps I even liked it better than Lowell. Still, Lowell is part of my picture of Schuyler, who is, I think, or can be, Lowell by other means. This is an inconvenient or irregular thought: a distaste for Robert Lowell and all his works seems to be axiomatic for Schuyler's admirers. There is a reflex opposition to Lowell in O'Hara and the New York School that seems to me only partly just, and I don't think they can take Schuyler with them on this. Their view of Lowell seems to be stuck in 1955 and their (unsuccessful) espousal of Schuyler, who is almost unknown in England and underappreciated in the States, rarely goes beyond perplexity and adulation. A typical sentence is Howard Moss's 'How Schuyler manages to be absolutely truthful and an obsessed romantic at the same time is his secret.' Well, perhaps the critic should have tried harder to get it out of him. Lee Harwood in his afterword to Schuyler's *Last Poems* enthuses about 'poems where the poet is not an isolated heroic figure but a social creature enjoying or enduring the "ordinary" experiences of life'. Harwood doesn't mention Lowell by name, but it's easy to imagine he's thinking of him in that 'isolated heroic figure'. But what is the speaker of 'Arches' if not 'an isolated heroic figure'? And how 'ordinary' an experience is hospitalisation anyway? I read and admire Schuyler with the same part of me that reads and admires Lowell. To make sense of 'The Payne Whitney Poems', I contend that it helps to have read 'For Sale', 'Waking in the Blue', 'The Mouth of the Hudson', 'Myopia: A Night', perhaps even 'Waking Early Sunday Morning'. Yes, Schuyler has a different register, his words emerge either slower or faster than Lowell's, more sparingly or more drenchingly (in 'Arches', it is slow and spare), but both are in the same business of forging a written voice or making print that sounds. It doesn't seem to me justifiable to set the author of 'I keep no rank nor station./Cured, I am frizzled, stale and small' against the author of 'Arches' – besides, Elizabeth Bishop was a great admirer of both.

From 'The Payne Whitney Poems', I ranged happily over the rest of *The Morning of the Poem* (1980), and then the *Selected* and *Collected Poems* of 1990 and 1993. The *Collected* was never published in the UK, but the large and late and very good *Selected* was done by Carcanet in their 'beautiful hardback' period: copies are available, and I earnestly recommend it. Schuyler readers have fared rather well since his death, in 1991. Black Sparrow brought out *The Diary of James Schuyler* in 1996 and the *Selected Art Writings* in 1998; in 1999 Slow Dancer published as *Last Poems* those pieces that had been included in the American *Collected* but not the *Selected*; and the New York Review of Books Classics series adopted a delightful novel called *Alfred and Guinevere*, his first book, from 1958, and republished it in 2001, with an introduction by his friend John Ashbery.

Schuyler is first and last a poet, but the other books shed interesting light on the poetry. 'For readers of his poetry, the idea of the *Diary* of James Schuyler might almost seem like too much of a good thing,' begins Nathan Kernan's introduction – too much because the poems have so much of the particular and the quotidian about them. The *Art Writings* – Schuyler followed Ashbery and O'Hara to *Art News*, and wrote for it, off and on, from 1955 to 1978 – show a well-tempered, diversely appreciative critic, with an apparently inexhaustible range of ways of saying things (on Alex Katz: 'the first in the "allegorical" style that showed the painter and his wife Ada and small son striding smiling out of a summer landscape; like the end of a Russian movie when the wheat crop has flourished') and an unexpect-edly fervent commitment to a minor-Ruskin aesthetic that also informs the poems (on Jane Freilicher: 'that passion for prettiness that can charge a lyric gift with the greatest potency of beauty'). One thinks of the New York poets as associating with the Abstract Expressionist painters, but a lot of Schuyler's enthusiasms – not to mention his book-jackets – tend to be for rather pretty and watery figurative work. O'Hara may have claimed not to be able to enjoy grass or trees 'unless there's a subway handy', but Schuyler was a rather more wholehearted visitor to Long Island, a long-time resident of Vermont and Maine and Upstate, and in many of his New York City poems celebrates a *rus in urbe* pleasantness. The novel, finally – Schuyler wrote a couple of others, one with Ashbery, but I haven't read them – is quite an extraordinary piece of work, chronicling an uneasy period in the life of a brother and sister, seven-year-old Alfred and 11-year-old Guinevere. There is no narra-tion, beyond 'he said' or 'she said'; the whole book is kept in speech, occasional letters (Alfred has to dictate his), and Guinevere's monstrously precocious diary entries ('When I take up smoking remember about lemon juice removing stains'). It lives in the frighteningly accurate contrast between the two voices (two ages, two sexes, but also two individuals) and, almost more, in that between written speech and writing (which, to me, is also an area where Schuyler's poetry makes a great showing). Rather remarkably, *Alfred and Guinevere* was originally published, mistak-enly, with illustrations, as a children's book.

Talking about the poetry of someone like Schuyler – almost devoid, I sometimes think, of any exterior mannerisms – is nearly as difficult as talking about an entire person. What can you say? There is the jagged early poetry, the exceedingly narrow middle poetry (one or two words a line in 'Buttered Greens' or 'Mike' – as though done with masking tape) and the wide, Whitmanish lines of the long poems, 'The Crystal Lithium', 'Hymn to Life', 'The Morning of the Poem', 'A Few Days'. Over time, I suppose he became more subdued. A sense of style is all-pervasive, but nothing is determined or excluded, it seems, on stylistic grounds. It's as though everything has been read or played through, but also let stand; typical of this are the geometrical line-lengths, where some breaks are interesting and suggestive, and many are not.

There seems to be nothing that Schuyler cannot or will not say, but he is not a *provocateur* like O'Hara. Most characteristically, he is a sweet, decorous and witty writer: but he is just as capable of being the opposite. Whichever, he seems not to have to operate under any imperative – no 'I must make this charming/characteristic/peculiar/off the wall'. He often writes, as I noted of 'Arches', under very low pressure, with minimal invention and exuberance – which is one of the things that makes him hard to quote from. There are wonderful jokes and moments of outrage, but in a sense they are untypical, and I certainly wouldn't want to pretend he's all like that. He has that extremely rare thing, the ability to write interesting description. The 'Andrew Lord Poems' is a sequence in *Last Poems* about pottery, not a subject to set the pulses racing, but the reader doesn't take against it here. Nor, conversely, is a subject used to sell a poem: 'Buried at Springs' is Schuyler's elegy to O'Hara, but one almost wouldn't know it. Even irrelation, in Schuyler's hands, becomes a form or type of relation, and informality is a version of formality, inaccuracy of accuracy:

> There is a hornet in the room
> and one of us will have to go
> out the window into the late
> August mid-afternoon sun. I
> won. There is a certain challenge
> in being humane to hornets
> but not much . . .
>
> ('Buried at Springs')

> Look, Mitterrand baby, your telegram
> of condolence to Yves
> Montand tells it like it is
> but just once can't some high
> placed Frenchman forget about the
> *gloire de France* while the world
> stands still a moment and all
> voices rise in mourning

a star of stars:
Simone Signoret was and is
immortal
(thanks to seeming permanence
yes the silver screen l'*écran*?)
Simone Signoret, a.k.a.
Mme Yves Montand, is dead . . .
                ('Simone Signoret')

All the leaves
are down except
the few that aren't.
                ('Verge')

These carelessly chosen quotations – they could be varied by hundreds, thousands of others – all have in common the idea of impermanence ('immortal' gets a line to itself). Schuyler, it seems to me, responds to the challenge of impermanence, accommodates impermanence, sings impermanence more than any other poet, and that's why he's a classic. In the long, tangent-driven poem-fleuve 'Hymn to Life', Schuyler finds himself suddenly remembering Washington, where he spent part of his boyhood:

Odd jobs, that stretch ahead, wide and mindless as
Pennsylvania Avenue or the bridge to Arlington, crossed and recrossed
And there the Lincoln Memorial crumbles. It looks so solid: it won't
Last. The impermanence of permanence, is that all there is?

There is a sort of drollery here, beginning with 'crumbles'. Schuyler has lost the thread of his thought, the boring vistas of odd jobs, and has allowed himself to take up – perhaps through aesthetic animus – almost a contrary position. Much dearer to his heart always is the opposite: the permanence of impermanence.

Hence the importance of tone in Schuyler (often wit), and of surface detail (prettiness). Both are secondary qualities, emanations like Yeats's 'wine-breath' in 'All Souls' Night', and both, in a sort of mathematical way (not change, but change in the rate of change), exhibit a constancy in inconstancy, like the revolutionary 'grey in which some smoke stands'. Ephemeral things are sung in the most ephemeral way, and the effect is of permanence (though not the dreary permanence of the Lincoln Memorial). And here, too, is Schuyler's literariness, *aere perennius*. Poem after poem – utterly variable, unpredictable, scatty meanderings, often on next to nothing, or on the most inconsequential things – is, in fact, a *monument*: 'Milk', 'Now and then', 'A blue towel', 'Korean Mums'. Instability of language, of level, of approach, of attention ('Dining Out with Doug and Frank' begins, 'Not quite yet'; its second section begins, 'Now it's tomorrow,/as usual') seems to be the response, instead, of a vast style. There is no gilding or freeze-drying, no E-numbers, the perishability is in the language. You wouldn't say, I wouldn't say: Schuyler is a proponent of 'the best words in the best order'. And this freedom of address is actually – as I don't think it is in Ashbery and not often in O'Hara, apart from 'The Day Lady Died' – responsibility.

Where it shows most, and most surprisingly, is in the endings of the poems. Again, this is hard to show by quoting, but time and again a poem that looks to be this, then that, then the other thing, will have a proper ending. A knock-out, a result, a return to the beginning, a few 16ths of an inch along a light-meter, a colour chart, a diary or a biography. The effect is terribly moving. It unexpectedly restores the personal, the artistic, the controlling hand. It's at times as though there was one sideways genius ramifying, digressing, surprising – and then another intervened, with an implacable insistence on pushing the whole thing forward. While looking like our jumble and our aporia, a Schuyler poem is always an advance. The short poem 'Closed Gentian Distances' begins, in the way dozens of Schuyler poems seem to do, 'A nothing day', and ends with two lines that Heraclitus or Heaney (the pun on 'stream') would have been proud of (as well as a different version of *simplex munditiis* – this one goes 'crisp in elegance'): 'Little fish stream/by, a river in water.' So much, then, for nothing. 'The Night' begins, 'The night is filled with indecisions/To take a downer or an upper', and ends: 'It's true/We do we/Love each/ Other so.' The first stanza of 'October' goes: 'Books litter the bed,/leaves the lawn. It/lightly rains. Fall has/come: unpatterned, in/the shedding leaves'; and the last sentence is: 'The books/of fall litter the bed.' An extraordinarily slight, deft and lovable piece of patterning. An alternative type of ending, just as conclusive and controlled, is when Schuyler reaches a point so bizarre, often, or so delicately foolish, that it makes further writing impossible. It sounds strange, but I can think of no better way of describing the ending of, say, 'The Walk':

> I love
> their white
> scuts when they
> bound away,
> deer at horseplay.

Or 'Today':

> Everything chuckles and creaks
> sighs in satisfaction
> reddens and ripens in tough gusts of coolness
> and the sun smites.

After 'smites' *rien ne va plus.*

7 February 2002

WHY ALL THE HOOPLA?

Hal Foster on Frank Gehry

FOR MANY PEOPLE, Frank Gehry is not only our master architect but our master artist as well. In the current retrospective which is about to transfer from the Guggenheim in New York to the one in Bilbao, he is often called a genius without a blush of embarrassment (Thomas Krens, Guggenheim director and Gehry 'collaborator', can't get enough of the word). Why all the hoopla? Is this designer of metallic museums and curvy concert halls, luxury houses and flashy corporate headquarters, truly Our Greatest Living Artist?

The notion that he might be points to the new centrality of architecture in cultural discourse, a centrality that goes back to some of the early debates about postmodernism in the 1970s, which were focused on architecture. But it also looks forward to contemporary crossings of art and architecture in installation art, fashion display, museum design and so on. But it's also the case that to make a big splash in the global pond of spectacle culture today, you have to have a big rock to drop, maybe as big as the Guggenheim Museum in Bilbao, and here an architect like Gehry, supported by clients like the Guggenheim and the DG Bank, has an obvious advantage over artists in other media. Such clients are eager for name recognition, or brand equity, in the global marketplace – in part the Guggenheim has become brand equity, which it sells on to corporations and governments. This, too, favours the architect who can deliver a building that will also serve as a logo. (Bilbao uses its Gehry museum this way: it appears on the first sign for the city you see on the road, and it has put Bilbao on the world-tourist map.) But why is Gehry singled out?

His beginnings were humble enough, and he has retained a rumpled everyman persona. Born in Toronto in 1929, he moved to Los Angeles in 1947, where, after stints at Harvard, in Paris, and with various firms, he opened his own office in 1962. Influenced by Richard Neutra, the Austrian emigré who also practised locally, Gehry gradually turned a Modernist idiom into a funky LA vernacular. He did so primarily in domestic architecture through an innovative use of cheap materials associated with commercial building – exposed plywood, corrugated metal siding and chain-link fencing. As is often the case with architects, his first landmark was the renovation of his own home in Santa Monica (1977-78), which has functioned as a laboratory-cum-showroom ever since (he redesigned it again in 1991-92). He took a modest bungalow on a corner lot, wrapped it in layers of corrugated metal and chain-link, and poked glass structures through its exterior. The result was a simple house extruded into surprising shapes and surfaces, spaces and views. It is justly admired, but it also serves strategically as the primal scene of his practice: 'The House that Built Gehry', as Beatriz Colomina puts it in the catalogue.

Gehry extended the lessons of this house to other designs, in which Modernist geometries were also disrupted – the plan rotated off axis, the skin pierced by wooden bridges, pavilions made of chain-link and the like. The unfinished look of this early style seemed right for LA: provisional in a way that was appropriate to its restless transformations, but also gritty in a way that resisted the glossier side of Tinsel Town. In effect Gehry devised a 'critical regionalism': even as he used new materials, he rejected the formal purities of modern architecture, burst open its abstract boxes and plunged the rearranged fragments into the everyday ground of Southern California life. But this LA vernacular needed the foil of a reified International Style to make its points, and with the prominence of postmodern architecture in the 1980s, full of classical symbols and Pop images, his style began to lose its edge. Gehry came to a subtle compromise with the new postmodern order: though he never fell into the historical pastiche of Michael Graves or Charles Moore, he did become more imagistic in his design. The great interest of this retrospective is to trace his passage from the early grunge work, through an elliptical Pop style, to the lavish 'gestural aesthetic' of the present. For throughout the 1980s and 1990s Gehry went upscale in materials and techniques, clients and projects – from the improvised chain-link of Santa Monica to the recherché titanium cladding of Bilbao, from unbuilt houses for local artist-friends to mega-institutions for multinational elites.

Such repositioning, in which reception feeds back into production, is neither immediate nor final, but its trajectory is clear enough. Take the cardboard furniture that Gehry designs from cut-out sheets stacked, laminated and shaped into chairs and divans. When it first appeared in the early 1970s, it was edgy, materially and formally inventive, and potentially cheap. But as it became more studied as design, the populism of the cardboard began to look fake or worse, a kind of homeless chic, attractive only to people far removed from any actual use of the stuff. His Pop tendencies also became more pronounced as the 1980s progressed. In his Indiana Avenue Studios (1979-81, in Venice, California), he had already made imagistic use of materials and elements: he defined the first studio, in blue stucco, by a big bay window; the second, in unpainted plywood, by a huge chimney; and the third, in green asphalt, by giant steps cut into the roof. Typological signalling can be effective as an architectural language, and Gehry often makes it witty. But it can also be manipulative in its Pop imagery and inflated scale.

Gehry's work of the mid to late 1980s moves back and forth between a material-formal inventiveness and a Pop-imagistic obviousness, and often resorts as a compromise to a collage of forms and images. On the one hand, there are projects like the Winton Guest House (1983-87, in Minnesota), in which separate rooms are cast in bold shapes, sheathed in striking materials and set in a dynamic 'pinwheel plan' that Gehry has often used since. In such domestic projects he composes the house as a kind of intimate town; and when he turns to commercial projects, such as the Edgemar Development (1984-88, in Santa Monica), he reverses the process, and treats the urban complex as a sort of extended house. This is imaginative and, as Jean-Louis Cohen demonstrates in the catalogue, it can be contextual. On the other hand, there are projects that simply go Pop, such as his Chiat/Day Building (1985-91, in Venice), where, under the influence of Claes Oldenburg, Gehry designed a monumental pair of binoculars as the entrance to the offices of a large advertising agency. This may suit the client, but it manipulates the rest of us, and reduces architecture to a 3-D billboard. The Pop dimension remains strong in his work, even when disguised as a symbolic use of otherwise abstract materials, colours and forms; and it came as no surprise when Gehry began to design for the Disney Corporation in the late 1980s.

There's a big difference between a vernacular use of chain-link in a house, or of cardboard in a chair, and a Pop use of giant binoculars as an entrance, or of a fighter jet attached to a façade (as in his Aerospace Hall, 1982-84, in LA). There's also a big difference between a material rethinking of form and space, which may or may not be sculptural (Gehry is influenced by Richard Serra), and a symbolic use of a ready-made image or commercial object (in which he is influenced by Oldenburg). The first option can bring elite design into contact with common culture, and renew stale architectural forms with fresh social expressions. The second tends to ingratiate architecture, on the model of the advert, to a public projected as a mass consumer. It is this dialectic that Gehry surfed into the early 1990s, and it swept him from LA architect to international designer.

His finessing of architectural labels helped, too: for all that Gehry first extended Modernist structures and then dallied with postmodern symbols, he is not saddled with the stigmas of either. In effect he trumped both movements in a crafty way that might be understood by reference to *Learning from Las Vegas* (1972), the principal manifesto of postmodern architecture. There, in a famous opposition, Robert Venturi and Denise Scott Brown distinguished Modernist design, in which 'space, structure and programme' are subsumed in 'an overall symbolic form', which they called the 'duck', from postmodern design, in which 'space and structure are directly at the service of programme, and ornament is applied independently of them': they called this the 'decorated shed'. 'The duck is the special building that is a symbol,' Venturi and Scott Brown wrote; 'the decorated shed is the conventional shelter that *applies* symbols.' And in an argument that supported the ornamental basis of postmodern architecture, they insisted that, however appropriate the formal duck was to the object world of the machine age, the decorated shed was only fitting for the speedy surfaces of the car-and-television age. Since Gehry privileged neither structure nor ornament, he seemed to transcend this opposition, but it is more accurate to say that he collapsed it, and often combined the duck with the shed. His 'sculptural' architecture is not really that, for it breaks down into front and back more often than it reads in the round. Furthermore, his interiors are difficult to decipher from his exteriors and vice versa, whether they are read structurally as with the Modernist duck, or ornamentally as with the postmodern shed. This disconnection between inside and outside can be beguiling, as it is in his Vitra International Headquarters (1988-94, in Switzerland) or his EMR Communications and Technology Centre (1991-95, in Germany). But as his 'duck sheds' expanded in scale – as he slouched towards Bilbao – so did the liabilities of this combination, for it risked the most problematic aspects of both Modernist and postmodern architectures: the wilful monumentality of the first and the faux populism of the second.

Gehry combined duck and shed almost literally in his huge Fish Sculpture for the Olympic Village in Barcelona in 1992, a work at once eccentric and central to his career (he has adopted the fish, the catalogue tells us, as his 'private totem'). If the Santa Monica house was the primal scene of his early career, this gold-ribbed leviathan is the primal scene of his later career, for it marks his first use of a technology that has guided his practice (and many others) ever since – computer-aided design and manufacture (a.k.a. Cad and Cam), in particular a program called Catia (computer-aided three-dimensional interactive application). Developed first in the motor and aerospace industries, such programs are also used in film animation, and Fish Sculpture does indeed suggest a futuristic fossil version of the dinosaurs of *Jurassic Park* (maybe it can serve as a prototype when Disney animates *Moby-Dick*). A trellis hung over arched ribs, the Fish is equal parts duck and shed – a combination of Serra and Oldenburg, it is at once all form and all surface, with no functional interior. And yet Gehry's Catia-designed buildings also privilege shape and skin, the overall exterior, above all else. In large part this is because Catia permits the easy modelling of non-repetitive surfaces and supports, of different exterior panels and interior armatures, which has encouraged Gehry to play with wacky topologies that overwhelm straight geometries – the non-Euclidean curves, swirls and blobs that became his signature gestures in the 1990s. These effects are most evident in the Guggenheim Bilbao (1991-97), 'the first major project in which the full potential' of the Catia program 'was realised'. (Cad and Cam are said to be cost-effective, but they are not necessarily so, and their use is as much rhetorical as actual; for example, the thin titanium panels in Bilbao were partly cut on site and manually bent into place.) A cross between an ocean liner run aground and a spaceship landed in the Basque country, the Bilbao museum is deemed the masterpiece of his 'sculptural' style, and it has served as the model for his subsequent mega-projects, the Walt Disney Concert Hall in LA (under construction), the Experience Music Project in Seattle (1995-2000), and the proposed Guggenheim near Wall Street.

So what of the claim that Gehry is Our Greatest Living Artist, or at least our great sculptor? First we need some definition of modern sculpture, and a good one (certainly a laconic one) comes from Carl Andre, a Minimalist sculptor of the sort said to have influenced Gehry. 'I want to give you the three phases of art as I know it,' Andre remarked in a 1970 radio interview, with the Statue of Liberty as his test case. 'There was a time when people were interested in the bronze sheath of the statue . . . And then there came a time when artists . . . were interested in Eiffel's iron interior structure, supporting the statue. Now artists are interested in Bedloe's island' (the site of the statue). Andre sketches a particular passage in modern sculpture from an academic modelling of the human figure supported by a hidden armature (most statues are like the Statue of Liberty in this regard), to a Modernist exposure of the 'interior structure' of the object (think of the open framework of Constructivist sculpture of the 1920s), to a contemporary interest in a given place – the expanded field of sculpture that extends from earthworks in the 1960s and 1970s to site-specific projects of various sorts today.

How does Gehry the architect-sculptor fit into this history? In a kind of time-loop. Like many other new museums, his colossal spaces are designed to accommodate the expanded field of postwar art – of Andre, Serra, Oldenburg, and assorted descendants. In fact, these museums trump the art: they use its great scale, which was meant to challenge the museum, as a pretext to inflate the museum itself into a gigantic spectacle-space that can swallow any art, let alone any viewer, whole. In short, museums like Bilbao use the breaking-out of postwar art as a licence to corral it again, and to overwhelm the viewer as they do so. At the same time, considered as sculpture, the recent Gehry buildings are regressive: they reverse the history of the medium sketched above. For all the apparent futurism of the Catia designs, these structures are akin to the Statue of Liberty, with a separate skin hung over a hidden armature, and with exterior surfaces that rarely match up with interior spaces. Again, Gehry is frequently associated with Serra, but Serra exposes the construction of his sculptures for all to see, while Gehry is often tectonically obscure. Some of his projects resemble the baubles set on corporate plazas in the 1960s and 1970s blown up to architectural scale, and some look as though they could be broken into with a tin-opener.

With the putative passing of the industrial age, Modernist architecture was declared outmoded, and now the Pop aesthetic of postmodern architecture looks dated as well. The search for the architecture of the computer age is on; but, ironically, it has led Gehry and others to use academic sculpture as a model, at least to a degree. (Imagine a new ending to *Planet of the Apes* where, instead of the Statue of Liberty being uncovered as a ruin in the sand, the Guggenheim Bilbao pokes through, or the Fish Sculpture in Barcelona.) The disconnection between skin and structure represented by this academic model is at its most radical in Gehry's work in the Experience Music Project, commissioned by the Microsoft billionaire Paul Allen because of his love for Jimi Hendrix (a fellow Seattleite): its six exterior blobs clad in different coloured metals have little apparent relation to its many interior displays dedicated to pop music. Just as Gehry wanted to make Bilbao legible through an allusion to a splintered ship, here he makes an allusion to a smashed guitar (a broken 'fret' lies over two of the blobs). But neither image works, even as a Pop gesture, for you have to be well above the buildings to read them as images at all, or you have to see them in media reproduction – which is indeed a primary 'site' of this architecture.

Don't get me wrong: I'm not pleading for a return to a Modernist transparency of structure (that was mostly a myth anyway, even with such purist architects as Mies van der Rohe). I'm simply suspicious of a computer-driven version of a Potemkin architecture of conjured surfaces. For the disconnection between skin and structure that one often senses in Gehry can have two problematic effects. First, it can lead to spaces that are not surprising (as in the early houses) so much as mystifying (as in Bilbao or Seattle) – a strained disorientation that is frequently mistaken for an Architectural Sublime. (Sometimes it is as if Gehry and others have taken the famous critique of delirious space in postmodern architecture, first presented by Fredric Jameson in the early 1980s, as a guideline for practice – as if they designed expressly to suit what Jameson calls 'the cultural logic of late capitalism'.) Second, it can lead to a further disconnection between building and site. 'The great strength of Gehry's architecture,' the catalogue insists, 'lies in its response to existing conditions.' But this insistence suggests that the reality is otherwise, and his sensitivity to context is exaggerated. The Bilbao museum, we are told, 'adapts to its setting with billowing forms that face the river and evoke marine imagery'. Likewise, the metallic curves and swirls of the proposed Guggenheim near Wall Street are said to mediate, like so many waves and clouds, between the East River in front (the museum is to span three piers) and the downtown skyscrapers behind (it includes its own tower). But this isn't description, much less analysis: it's Whitmanesque gush about New York warmed over as press copy. And it's simply not true: the Wall Street Guggenheim is even more anti-contextual than the Bilbao – swollen to twice the size and propped up on super-pylons like a giant metal dodo.

An obvious point of comparison is the Frank Lloyd Wright Guggenheim, built in 1959. It, too, is often seen as a sculptural object, but has a formal logic (the whitish spiral), as well as a programmatic conceit (the museum as continuous ramp), that the Gehry Guggenheims do not possess. Moreover, the Wright uses its difference from its context smartly: it breaks with the line of Fifth Avenue and bows into the greenery of Central Park. Its form is expressive because it appears motivated in different ways. Can the same be said of the 'gestural aesthetic' of Gehry? The gestures of his early houses were often idiosyncratic, but they were also grounded in two ways – in an LA vernacular of common materials and against an International Style of purist forms. As these gestures began to lose the specificity of the former and the foil of the latter, they became not only more extravagant (almost neo-Expressionist or neo-Surrealist) but also more detached: they became signs of 'artistic expression' that could be dropped, indifferently, almost anywhere – in LA, Bilbao, Seattle, Berlin, New York. Why this curve, swirl or blob here, and not that one? If there is not much in the way of apparent constraint – of formal articulation derived from a resistant material, structure or context – architecture quickly becomes arbitrary or self-indulgent. (Here again part of the problem might be the technical facility of Catia, which is said to translate 'the gestural quality from model to built work' all but directly.) The great irony is that Gehry fans tend to confuse his arbitrariness with freedom, and his self-indulgence with expression. The *New York Times* greeted the retrospective with the banner 'Gehry's Vision of Renovating Democracy'.

So what is this vision of freedom and expression? Is it perverse of me to find it perverse, even oppressive? In one sense – the sense of Gehry as Our Greatest Living Artist – it is oppressive because, as Freud argued long ago, the artist is the only social figure allowed to be freely expressive in the first place, the only one exempted from many of the instinctual renunciations that the rest of us undergo as a matter of course. Hence his free expression implies our unfree inhibition, which is also to say that his freedom is mostly a franchise in which he represents freedom rather than enacts it. Today this exceptional licence is extended to Gehry perhaps more than to any other artist – certainly with greater consequences.

In a related way this vision of expression and freedom is oppressive because Gehry does indeed design out of the 'cultural logic' of advanced capitalism, with its language of risk-taking and spectacle-effects. In 'The Social Bases of Art', an essay published in 1936, Meyer Schapiro argued that the Impressionist painter was the first artist to address the new modern world of speed and glitz. 'For this individual,' Schapiro wrote, 'the world is a spectacle, a source of novel pleasant sensations, or a field in which he may realise his "individuality", through art, through sexual intrigue and the most varied, but non-productive, mobility.' So it is still today – for our privileged artists, architects and patrons – only more so. Yet 'such an art cannot really be called free,' Schapiro cautioned, 'because it is so exclusive and private': to be deemed free at all, its 'individuality must lose its exclusiveness and its ruthless and perverse character'.

I was reminded of this old warning at the Gehry retrospective, for the individuality of his architecture does seem more exclusive than democratic. Rather than 'forums of civic engagement' (the catalogue again), his cultural centres appear as sites of spectacular spectatorship, of touristic awe. Thirty years ago Guy Debord defined spectacle as 'capital accumulated to such a degree that it becomes an image'. With Gehry and other architects the reverse is now true as well: spectacle is an image accumulated to such a degree that it becomes capital. Such is the logic of many cultural centres today, designed, alongside theme parks and sports complexes, to assist in the corporate 'revival' of the city – its being made safe for shopping, spectating and spacing out. 'The singular economic and cultural impact felt in the wake of its opening in October 1997,' the catalogue says of 'the Bilbao effect', has 'spawned a fierce demand for similar feats by contemporary architects worldwide'. Alas, so it has, and it is likely to come to your hometown soon.

23 August 2001

SHOE-SHOPPING

Jenny Diski

I N SPITE OF THE V&A's Versace Festival, and books like *Fashion Statements: Archaeology of Elegance 1980-2000*,* I've never been convinced by the idea of fashion as art. I don't see why it has to be; it has so much else to do. When culture and art swan up and down the catwalk bedecked in 'fashion', I find myself scrummaging around in the oversized wardrobe in the spare room at the back of my mind, thinking about my lifelong romance with what I can't help calling 'clothes'. Call them 'clothes', and what some people think of as art and cultural studies become for me private history, memory and a grossly overspent youth and middle-age in search of the perfect garment. I recall a much-published novelist claiming in an interview that she would rather never have written a word than have lost the husband who divorced her a dozen years before. I gasped to read this. Give up writing for love? Really? World peace, maybe, social and educational equality, possibly – though I would demand firm guarantees. Then an image slithered into my head of a cupboard – let's call it a closet – stuffed with slinky Galliano slips of dresses, a handful of witty Chanel suits, a selection of madly deconstructed Margielas and Demeulemeesters, a St Laurent smoking section, an unworn sprinkling of sparkling Versace, an almost invisible beige shimmer of Armani, and beneath, all in neat array, row upon row of Blahnik, Miu Miu and Jimmy Choo kitten heels. Well, would I have traded work for frocks? Certainly I'd give my right arm for such a wardrobe (I'm left-handed). My soul, without doubt (but then before the tragic days of giving up, I once offered up my soul in return for a late-night cigarette when I'd run out). My integrity you could have for a song, though I value it enough to demand lyrics by Cole Porter or Lorenz Hart. My sanity I gave up long ago when I discussed with a friend whether it was preferable to be mad or fat. But I wouldn't give up writing. At least I don't think so . . .

But it isn't really fashion that has such a hold on me. It is (like the ultimate book in my head, which is storyless, characterless and perfect) an image, without any detail, of the perfect outfit, the one that slips over my frame and drapes itself around my contours in a way that finally defines me – look, this is what I am – just

---

*Marion de Beaupré et al (eds.), *Fashion Statements: Archaeology of Elegance* (Thames and Hudson, 2002).

as my flesh defines the boundaries between myself and the world. And it's a private thing essentially, not primarily about being seen in or envied for a fashionable look: indeed, I generally imagine wearing these incomparable outfits in the privacy of my own home. It's stuff to sit on the sofa with that I'm after first of all; then it's OK to go out and flaunt the frocks. Fashion statements and identity statements are much of a muchness as far as I'm concerned. To look like, to feel like and to be like are as close as flesh and bone.

The crucial encounter with fashion occurred when I was 12. Until then I had put up with whatever my mother considered respectable, an accurate mirror of the life she wished to be perceived as having. I baulked loudly, it is true, at discomfort, which came mostly in the form of woollen vests that she told me were as soft as butter (meaning expensive and imported from Belgium) but which were actually as scratchy as barbed wire. But by the time I was 12 the family fortunes had taken such a severe downturn and swerve away from the Belgian imports that Social Services had issued her with a voucher to buy me a pair of shoes to wear at my new secondary school. This was a matter of desperate shame for my mother, returning her to a poverty she had devoted her life to escaping. The idea of handing over – in public – vouchers from the state instead of crisp currency agonised her. Worse, the vouchers were rejected with the disdain she feared at all the shops she usually went to – Daniel Neal did not X-ray any old child's feet. The only place that accepted them was a gloomy little cobbler's shop which, as I remember it, was hidden away under a near derelict railway arch in the fashion wasteland of King's Cross. The Dickensian and mawkish nature of the occasion as I recall it, the drab light and huddled aspect of the shoe shop, suggest that this may be one of those false memories you hear so much about, conjured up to match the dismal mood of the event. The old man who owned the place, unshaven, bent, gruff and wheezing – the Victorian workhouse vision just won't go back in its box – inspected the voucher, measured my feet, and without a word shuffled to the back of the shop. He returned with a single shoe box.

'See if these fit,' he said to my mother.

Taking off the lid, he brought out a pair of the grimmest black lace-up school shoes I had ever seen in my life. 'Sturdy' doesn't even get close to describing their brute practicality. In today's fashion-diverse world it is hard to imagine the despair I felt at the sight of what he expected me to put on my feet. And then greater despair yet as it occurred to me that I would be expected actually to wear them out in the world. They were so blankly, stylelessly sensible that they might have been orthopaedic appliances (poverty and disability perhaps being seen as equally reprehensible). Great clumping virtuous blocks of stiff leather with bulbous reinforced toecaps, designed (and I use the word loosely as a small bubble of ancient hysteria wells up) never to wear out. The best that could be hoped for was to grow out of them, after which they would still be sound enough to be passed down to generation after generation of the undeserving poor. Probably today they would be at the more moderate end of chunky footwear. I confess there have been times when I've rejoiced in wearing very similar things with an incongruously delicate little number in chiffon – though Doc Martens are ladylike in comparison. But back then – think 1959, the burgeoning of youth culture, rock and roll, multilayered net petticoats, ponytails – I only had to take one look at them, to see myself arriving at my new school with those on my feet, to know and feel, gut and spine, head and heart, the shame of becoming an instant fashion (and therefore everything else) pariah in the cruel girls' world of T-bars, flatties and slip-ons. The shoes would stand for my entire character, my class, my race, my lack of nous, and for ever after my almond-toed peers would deem me a sad case to be avoided and sniggered at as I clunked my solitary way around the playground. But it wasn't just the social disaster of such unfashionability that froze my heart: it was the fear that appearing to be the kind of person who wore such shoes might mean that that was the person I actually was. It wasn't just that my peers would despise me: I would despise myself. I didn't even dare risk seeing my reflection in the mirror in the empty shop.

I said, politely, that I didn't like them, thinking he had mistaken me for someone who might be happy to help him get rid of his unsaleable items and that he must have kept back his stock of fashion footwear. He showed no sign of having heard me. He was not impressed, he wasn't interested in an opinion: he just wanted to know if he needed to bother to get another size. These, it was made clear, were the shoes you got in return for vouchers. Take them or leave them, he told my mother, not so much as glancing at me. Though I sensed that the world was about to end (in the way it often did when things went wrong for my mother) I shook my head firmly. I refused even to try them on. I would simply not have them on my feet. His lip curled at my bad character. My mother's embarrassment redoubled at having to be embarrassed in front of this miserable old man. It was bad enough having to be on the receiving end of charity without having to suffer the charity-giver's contempt. But I shook my head steadily from side to side and kept my toes curled tightly so that even if they used force they would never get those clodhopping shoes on me. I ought to be grateful that taxpayers were providing me with any shoes at all, the shopkeeper rasped. (Was he really wearing a food-stained, cigarette-burned buff cardigan and checked felt slippers?) It was these, or it was nothing.

'Then it's nothing,' I said, quite prepared for whatever civic punishment befell ungrateful children who didn't know their place (though I looked forward less to the moment when my mother got me home). I would wear my present shoes down to a sliver. If necessary I would go to school barefoot. My mother didn't bother to wait – she shouted at me all the way home. I slunk along beside her in silence. How could I do this to her, she screamed. What did a pair of shoes matter? In fact, they mattered more than her wretchedness, even more than my loved, lost and delinquent father who had put us in this situation. They mattered like life itself. More, perhaps. Now, I am somewhat ashamed of having been obdurate when times were bad, but the truth is that even as I write I flush at the imagined ignominy of wearing those shoes. It was, as it were, my first fashion statement.

Between then and now fashion and my fortunes have been up and down and back again, but at no point have clothes been secondary. In the 1960s, I was in cheap frock heaven, alternating between instant fashion (skirts the length of a window pelmet, crushed velvet bell-bottoms, fishnet tights and purple boots with platform soles from Biba and Granny Takes A Trip) and wild antique fantasies (Victorian lace nighties and velvet frockcoats, original 1940s working-girl bias-cut dresses and moth-eaten movie-star fox-fur jackets) culled for shillings from Portobello Road. Later, it was the denim and boiler-suits of the school-teaching radical 1970s (Camden Market), then the swagger of big-shouldered jackets and snappy high heels, followed by loose, soft, draping viscose (how I thank the gods for letting me be born into the era of viscose) and silk, layer on layer of it (beloved Nicole Farhi), or parodic mannish suits (Emporio).

Buying clothes is an act of bewitchment. As soon as I stand in front of a rail of garments, a trance descends on me. My consciousness rises slightly above my corporeal body so that I seem to be looking down on myself (a near clothes-buying experience) as my hand reaches out and slides the hangers along, one by one (small grating noises, wooden clicks), my fingers twitching the fabric, feeling its texture and weight (no hint of Belgium wool), my eyes drawing a bead on each item, assessing it to see if it belongs in my life. No, no, no: and then – yes! This is the one. I've found it. It has found me. As if I had been drawn into the shop by its presence. As if getting up that morning and leaving the house had been a response to the whispering in my sartorial soul of this garment, reaching out to find me as it waited, created as it was, destined as it was to be mine. I try it on only for the pleasure of seeing myself for the first time exactly as I should look and feel. At last, after all these decades, after all that shopping, I have the garment I was always meant to wear. It's a silk shirt, a linen skirt, a pair of jeans, a sharp suit, a wispy frock, a pair of pink kitten heels, a sweatshirt, a pair of pull-on baggy trousers: but what it really is, is perfect. And (almost) whatever the cost, no matter the state of my bank balance or the condition of my house and car, however many remarkably similar – similar but not *perfect* – things I may have in my cupboard at home, I buy it knowing that now at last I will be content.

And for a while, I am. Yes, of course all the skirts, shoes and dresses in my bulging wardrobe were each the perfect garment when I bought them. And so they remained for days, weeks, occasionally even months, as I existed at last in the world looking exactly like I wanted to look, just right: until I began to feel that scratchy need somewhere in my solar plexus and it seemed to me that I heard a susurration in my inner ear, telling me that something, somewhere was hanging on a rail waiting for me to meet it. The next siren call comes, the last thing bought seems somehow not quite right. And, sleuthing around the shops, I discover once again a garment that in my mind balances perfectly on the narrow boundary between inner and outer definition, which I have been looking for, doubtless, since the day of the implacable black school shoes. That's why fashion as culture, fashion as art, leaves me cold: I'm too preoccupied with clothing myself to pay it proper attention.

14 November 2002

PARADISE SYNDROME

Sukhdev Sandhu on Hanif Kureishi

HANIF KUREISHI GOT ME beaten up. Admittedly it was by my dad. At home, as at the factory where for more than half of his life he had been a semi-skilled machine operator, he preferred to communicate with his hands. Yet as his fists whacked into my face I thought, then as now, how right he was to do what he was doing.

He had come to England in 1965, spurred by the promise of quick wealth and the chance to flex his masculinity. Sikhs have traditionally been among the most enterprising, far-travelling people in India. At the end of the 19th century my father's grandfather had sailed to Australia, where he worked for twenty years. Now it was his turn to assert his independence, to nudge at the frontiers of possibility. Squeezed into a tiny box-room in the Hounslow house of his elder brother, working 16-hour shifts in the local Nestlé factory, he didn't quite achieve this. These were frugal, unswinging times. Most of his scanty earnings he handed over to my venal uncle. The rest he sent to the wife and daughter he had left behind in India. Shortly after they joined him here in 1969 they all moved to Gloucester, a small and unglamorous town known these days as Kwik Save Central. Its main claim to fame is Fred West, whose home I jaunted past to and from school for seven years and which has recently been turned into a memorial garden.

My father's fall from grace was one that many immigrants suffer when they arrive in a new country. His shrunken status compared unfavourably with the respect enjoyed back home by his father, who had served as a police officer for the British in Hong Kong during World War Two. In 1945 my grandfather returned to the small feeder village in the north-west district of Punjab where, tall and stentorian, he owned much land and was deferred to by the local community. Even village hoolies bantering and mischiefing on dusty track roads used to stand to attention as he marched past them on his way to catch the bus to the nearest town, at whose savings bank he deposited the profits he made from his tenants' wheat and cotton crops. Nobody ever genuflected to my father. Kids in the park used to flick rubber bands at him as he stood guarding me from falling off the swinging tyre. Bored punks made monkey noises as he lugged home sacks of chapatti flour from the local continental foodstore.

In his early twenties my father had had a minor stroke. It twisted his jaw slightly and made it rather unnerving to watch him smile. Not that he did too often. Throughout the 1970s and 1980s, he lived out another form of paralysis. Each morning he would get up at five o'clock, pack luncheonmeat sandwiches and a flask of sugary tea into his bag before leaving to catch the works minibus. For ten hours he would silently load pallets and heave filthy crank cases. He'd return at five, smothered in oil and grease, and sit blankly in front of the telly or roam the house looking for woodlice to stamp on. Gloucester had a tiny Asian population and there was no gurdwara where he could gossip and politick and complain about women with other Sikh men. He spurned introspection – like most Indian men he preferred to beat his wife or his children than assail himself with self-doubt – yet he had neither friends nor social outlets. He never went to the cinema, to restaurants, on holiday. He became, gradually, inevitably, trapped in his own private universe. As emotionally parsimonious as he had to be financially, he broke his silence only to regale the family with anecdotes he'd overheard from workmates or catchphrases from ITV quiz shows.

The only change to this joyless and dulling regime, one which gave him ballast and security – and a habit shared by all my relatives – came about after the death of his father. Forsaking *Family Fortunes*, he began belatedly to seek refuge in the homiletic verses of the Ghotka, a slim abridgement of the Sikh holy text, the Guru Granth Sahib. After a lifetime of turbanless beer-drinking my father suddenly got God. He would retreat to his bedroom, where he would place a crumpled handkerchief on his balding head, cross his legs, and recite devotional verses. Night after night, across the landing, and above the slapping noises made by my mother washing the family laundry in the bathroom next door, I would hear him susurrating the same passage over and over again. Then he'd get up, belch, and go and pick a fight with his wife.

He was, in short, a not untypical working-class man. I myself was a typical stroppy teenager who liked to retreat to my own room to write florid homosexual poetry and listen to jangling indie miserabilisms on a tiny transistor – 'bah bah' music, he called it. Even so I longed to have something in common with him other than our big noses.

The opportunity to forge a tentative East-West alliance seemed to arise when *My Beautiful Laundrette* was shown on TV. The film, written by the Anglo-Pakistani Hanif Kureishi and directed by Stephen Frears, told the story of Anglo-Pakistani Omar (played by Gordon Warnecke) who, tired of being patronised and bullied by his family, decides to get ahead by opening a gleaming new laundrette in South London. Having acquired the necessary start-up cash by conning a family friend in a drug deal, he employs as his partner a former schoolfriend, Johnny (Daniel Day-

Lewis), from whom he had drifted apart after Johnny joined a gang of skinhead racists. While they busy themselves disavowing their cultural obligations and falling in love, all around them is chaos – Omar's uncle's mistress is poisoned by his wife, Johnny's abandoned cronies go ballistic.

Comic and knowing, socially engaged without lapsing into earnestness, the film was a great success on its release in late 1985. It was seen as a welcome riposte to the heritage cinema of *Chariots of Fire* and *A Room with a View*. An ironic critique of Thatcherite entrepreneurialism and individualism, it seemed to open up the possibility of a popular and oppositional British film culture. Indeed, its cast of gays, blacks and young characters made it seem a product of a hypothetical GLC film unit. Small wonder that Norman Stone bemoaned 'the overall feeling of disgust and decay' conveyed by the film and complained that Kureishi was inciting a 'sleazy, sick hedonism'. Audiences disagreed. Costing £600,000 to make, the film grossed $15,000,000 and earned the young Kureishi an Oscar nomination for best screenplay.

All this passed me by at the time. Like my parents I never went out. All I had seen were the tantalising trailers: the film looked youthful; it was about people like me. The night it was on TV, I swept the carpet, prepared snacks – some Nice biscuits and a mug of hot milk each – and sat my parents down. On the wall of the sitting room was the obligatory picture of the Sikh holy shrine, the Golden Temple in Amritsar; the photo's bright colours were fading, its silver-plated frame was garlanded with tinsel. The Temple told us where we came from and where we might one day return. Next to the photo hung one of the free calendars that all Sikhs used to display in their houses – a garishly colourful drawing of Guru Nanak, bearded and reproachful, above an equally loud banner advertising 'Dokal and Son Cash and Carry – Wholesale and Distribution'. A happy marriage of culture and commerce.

Everything was perfect except, it turned out, the film itself. It was being screened by Channel 4, a station known then for its obscurity (it was so little-watched that a common joke went: 'Where do married couples go when they want to elope? Channel 4') and its liberal attitude towards the depiction of sex and nudity. The opening scenes, which featured rundown London squats and tenement blocks, were far too dingy and parochial for people accustomed to the technicolor fantasies of Bollywood. My mother, who had to be up at six the next morning to catch the bus to the sewing factory where she worked, started muttering discontentedly. By the time the camera showed Omar's uncle in his garage office humping away with his half-undressed, red-corseted mistress I was having doubts. '*Bakwas!*' shouted my father. (Bollocks!) His milk was untouched. When we got to the scene in which Omar's cousin, Tania, is so bored at a family get-together that she decides to liven up the evening by flashing her breasts my father flipped. 'Why are you showing us such filth? Is this what you do at school? Is this the kind of thing you listen to on the radio?' he yelled before lunging at me. Just as well we never got to the scene where Omar and Johnny start fucking in the laundrette.

My father was right to be appalled. The film celebrated precisely those things – irony, youth, family instability, sexual desire – that he most feared. It taught him, though it would take years for the lesson to sink in fully, that he could not control the future. And control – over their wives, their children, their finances – was what Asian immigrants like him coveted.

Most of them had come over to England in the wake of the Commonwealth Immigrants Act of 1962, which restricted entry to those citizens who carried work vouchers issued by the Ministry of Labour. They found that their farming backgrounds were useless. Poor spoken English meant that, unlike Jamaican and Barbadan immigrants, few of them could get work in public transport or in nursing. Unskilled industrial jobs were also scarce, in London especially, following the postwar decline in manufacturing. They were forced to head for drabber, greyer cities like Bradford, Leicester and Birmingham, whose foundries, steel mills and textile factories offered them ready, if menial employment and where rent and travelling expenses were low.

Here in the back-to-back terraced houses in which they lodged, and which they later bought, they ground out the lifestyles that were to characterise Asian life in Britain for the next twenty years. Pleasure was renounced. They worked all the double shifts and overtime slots they could grab. They pennypinched and hoarded. They rarely went out after work: they were too tight, too tired. Their broken English discouraged them from mingling with white communities which increasingly resented their cheerless, yapping ways. This austere work ethic continued long after they had paid for their families in India and Pakistan to join them. They prized money, not culture. Asian mothers would drag their kids around town for hours looking for distressed fruit to buy at reduced prices; they would eradicate all traces of grass in their back gardens in order to plant cash-saving spinach and spring onions; their houses were littered with bargain basement junk and commemorative mug sets they'd bought at car boot sales. Meanwhile shoals of silverfish skated across their bathroom floors; their toothbrushes, unreplaced for years, turned into candyfloss.

Homes were important to Asian parents not just as cost-cutting warehouses but as places for indoctrination. If many of them had only a limited grasp of English, and through suspicion and timidity shied away from the exigencies of social life, then at least they knew that on returning home they were entering a controlled, less complicated zone where they could impress on their children their religious, matrimonial and educational values. They assured them that English women were floozies who liked to lie across car bonnets and get pregnant, that English men were smooth-tongued predators eager to fleece them of their savings. All contact with the outside world was potential contamination. They were instructed never to share anything – sweets, toys or, most important, information – with white people. It wasn't just yashmaked Muslim girls who were being veiled from society. All Asian kids had to be on their guard. They were in England – and needed to do well there – but, at the same time, they should never think of themselves as English.

This doubleness was obvious in the way that Asian mothers dressed. They would go out draped in beautiful, riotously coloured fabrics, sequinned and beaded, hairbuns scrupulously in place, kohl applied to their eyes, lovely *chuplia* on their feet, their cracked nails layered with vivid polish. Yet these colours were muffled by the dull grey overcoats they always wore and which made them look dowdy, rather absurd. At first I thought the reason Asian women wore them was because they weren't used to needing warm coats. But it was more than that. They didn't bother to co-ordinate colours because they didn't care about their cheap coats, which they felt belonged to the white world. Indians could wear them without really wearing them. What they were to be judged on was their Indian clothes.

Such a bifocal outlook could easily descend into hypocrisy. Asians liked to trade anecdotes about the grossness and immorality of Westerners. Yet they still sold them pornography and alcohol in cornershops. Their piety was subordinated to the demands of the weekly balance sheet, the cash till's huge appetite. Never did they see themselves as two-faced money-grabbers. As long as they stayed clean and (largely) sober the white world, they reasoned, could go hang.

Asian parents craved stillness, the faithful replication of ancestral ways of thinking and behaving. Migration had made no difference. The future was to be the past, a few years on. Daughters could look forward to their fingers being chapped by decade after decade of peeling sticky chapattis from the flaming *tuvva* pans in their poky kitchens; buttery diets later to send them to premature graves would form tyres round their middle-aged waists; they'd not be able to sleep at night because of the back trouble they had developed from stooping over Singer sewing machines both at work and at home. As a reward for these sacrifices they would be shunted into the back room whenever guests came to their home and be expected to emerge sporadically to proffer rounds of milky tea and Indian sweets for fat men in pullovers to tuck into.

Pustular teenage boys, meanwhile, knew it wouldn't be long before they were married off, occasionally by means of adverts their parents had placed in the matrimonial columns of the ethnic press. 'Respectable family seeking suitable match for their son: sincere, clean-shaven, fair, chemical engineering MSc, enjoys his fitness routines and believes in high moral values, exporter of garments in Dubai. Girl must be beautiful, family-orientated, vegetarian.' Soon their mothers would be wearing out the lettering on the rewind button of the remote control as they played back their sons' wedding videos for the tenth successive time to satisfy the family's appetite for uxorious images.

Sometimes it seemed as if these were reasonable destinies to live out. Mostly, though, it didn't. Asians who, like me, grew up in areas of England such as Horsham or Cheam or Gloucester, where brown faces were scarce, became increasingly embarrassed by our parents' accents, by their insistence that we wear outdated polyester clothes and drench our hair in coconut oil before going out. It was easy to forget the love and care that made them do this. We walked fifteen feet ahead of them when out shopping, dreading the moment when they'd call out to us in loud Hindi or Urdu. We rechristened ourselves – Davinder became Dave, Baljit Trevor. We learned Joyce Grenfell comic monologues off by heart, read short stories by Arthur Quiller-Couch – anything we thought would make us truly English. Not only would we laugh at malicious jokes – 'Why do Pakis never play football? Because every time they get a corner they build a shop on it' – but, eager to ingratiate ourselves, we'd try to trump them: 'What's the difference between a Paki and a bucket of shit? The bucket.' White kids would laugh – not with us, but at us. Deep down we knew this.

We were, then, in timid turmoil. And Kureishi's work – particularly the Frears films My Beautiful Laundrette and Sammy and Rosie Get Laid (1988) and his first novel The Buddha of Suburbia (1990), but also plays such as Outskirts and Borderline (both 1981) – not only captured these anxieties, but offered for the first time a recognisable portrait of British Asian life. Previously we had made do with sitcoms such as It Ain't Half Hot Mum and Mind Your Language, in which Asians wore comical headwear and were the butts rather than the tellers of jokes. The BBC broadcast the odd native-language series which, well-intentioned but sombre, featured wailing classical musicians from the Subcontinent or vinegary crones knitting baby clothes in front of the camera. Mainstream news and current affairs coverage was in those days negligible apart from the occasional exposé of the barbarism of arranged marriages or footage of disputes involving Leicester textile workers.

Kureishi's Asians were more varied. They included pushers, tyrannical ex-foreign ministers, bogus mystics, brutalising landlords, togged-up likely lads, sex-hungry cripples. They duped and slagged off one another. They argued constantly. They also exploited or augmented their ethnicity at will: in My Beautiful Laundrette Omar is sent to a flash new hotel where he is due to pick up an unspecified consignment on behalf of his business associate Salim. The hotel room door is opened to reveal an elderly looking Pakistani whose sprawling white beard makes him resemble a devout mullah. Suddenly, to Omar's astonishment, the 'mullah' peels off his beard which, it turns out, he uses for smuggling sachets of heroin. Equally revelatory is the moment in The Buddha of Suburbia when Karim, the novel's Bromley-born hero, attends the funeral of a family friend: 'I did feel, looking at these strange creatures now – the Indians – that in some way these were my people, and that I'd spent my life denying or avoiding that fact. I felt ashamed and incomplete at the same time, as if half of me were missing, and as if I'd been colluding with my enemies.' Karim decides that 'if I wanted the additional personality bonus of an Indian past, I would have to create it.' The key word here is 'create'. A sense of culture is no longer a curse, no longer a birthmark that you carry with you all your life. Rather, it may be fashioned from nothing: it's a 'personality bonus' – words straight out of an Argos catalogue. And if Indianness is addable, it's also subtractable. Karim, an aspiring actor, is keen to exploit this insight. Since childhood he's been a fan of another chameleon and shape-shifter, David Bowie, who was raised, like the author, in Bromley.

Similarly, Kureishi's next novel The Black Album was named after a bootleg LP by Prince to whom the main character, Shahid, is devoted. Prince plunders freely from various musical genres, from rock or disco or funk or rap. To popular amusement he is forever adopting new personae: a satyr, an androgyne, a symbol – the latter, along with 'The Artist Formerly Known as Prince', being one of the numerous names by which he has at times insisted on being known. Polymorphous, perverse, self-transforming, limitless in ego and imagination (although increasingly limited in genius), Prince was an understandable idol for Asians who felt themselves constrained by the order of things.

Allusions such as these highlight Kureishi's pivotal role in helping second and third-generation Asians think of themselves – and be thought of – as young people. Throughout the 1960s and 1970s white people regarded us as a prematurely middle-aged race with no interest in contemporary fashion. We were thought to take after our fathers, who venerated Magnus Magnusson and Peter Jay, anybody who looked like the besuited officials that a century of colonial education had taught them to defer to. On Friday nights, when many teenagers were out necking bottles of cheap cider or haggling for lovebites in discos, we would be at home hoping the immersion tank wouldn't run out before we could have our bath. Those crucial years of idling and experimentation, of lying in graveyards striving to be profound, of throwing bricks at passing trains – we missed out on all of that. Small wonder that nobody aspired to be like us. Our demeanour was too courteous, our hairstyles rank, our dialects too foreign for anyone to want or be able to filch our slangy in-terms.

In these respects we were very different from young blacks, whose cultural capital we envied with a passion that contrasted with the caste-driven snobbishness of our parents, who condemned them as ganja-smoking layabouts. What we wouldn't have given to have sporting heroes such as the Three Degrees: West Bromwich Albion's Cyrille Regis, Brendan Batson and Laurie Cunningham. Vicariously we clutched our hairbrushes and mimed along in our bedrooms to joyful reggae anthems such as 'Uptown Top Ranking' and 'Young, Gifted and Black'. But we failed to forge musical alliances along the lines of those between rudeboy ska and skinhead stomp at the end of the 1960s, or 1976's reggae-punk axis. These marriages encompass-ing fashion, music, sex and shared attitude helped shape today's multiracial, urban culture which, thanks to such media-hyped epiphenomena as 'bhangramuffin' and 'the future sound of India', Asians are only belatedly entering. For most of the last thirty years the only 'Sounds of the Asian Underground' we'd ever heard were our classmates yelling, 'The light's going out! We're going Paki-bashing!' as they spotted us entering the subway on the way home after school.

Like his heroes the Beatles and Bowie, Kureishi believed that only London could provide his characters with the stimulation and excitement they craved. His met-ropolitan landscapes are populated by young people who have abandoned their scabby rooms to cruise through the streets, past myriads of multi-ethnic shops, restaurants and diversions; they'll smile, laugh, absorb both high and low culture, usually to the accompaniment of pumping dance music which captures the skelter and dense medley of young London. In *The Black Album* Shahid and Deedee giggle their way through Islington; they kiss, wander past the shops selling Indian-print scarves or punk bootlegs, buy Greil Marcus and Flannery O'Connor books, visit pubs. 'It was rare to see anyone over forty, as if there were a curfew for older people.' This, for Shahid, is the life – the clamour and congestion for which an Asian upbringing had left him gasping.

Perhaps the most charming scene Kureishi has ever written comes in *Sammy and Rosie Get Laid*, when Sammy enthuses to his baffled father about the joys of kissing and arguing on the Hammersmith tow-path, strolling through Hyde Park, watching alternative comedians in Earl's Court abuse the government and attending semi-otics seminars at the ICA where Colin MacCabe discusses 'the relation between a bag of crisps and the self-enclosed unity of the linguistic sign'. This rhapsody emerged at a time when metrocentric lifestyles were not so routinely cannibalised by Lottery-funded film-makers and late-night TV schedulers. It anticipated – and is far superior to – those luridly packaged paperbacks with titles such as *Skunked* or *Shagging Darren* which reel off tedious tales of clubbing, copping off and charlie-snorting.

Kureishi cherishes London's ability to disrupt and upheave. Its chief glory is that it isn't home. The attack on the cult of home is one of the most compelling aspects of Kureishi's early work, in which the sophistication of a character's interior decor is an index of their moral stature. The more sophisticated the furnishings the more vile the character. Tending to the honeysuckle along the back wall or hanging tasteful Indian friezes in a four-storeyed St John's Wood mansion are the pursuits of reactionaries and manipulative control freaks. The cosmetic is opposed to the ethical. In *Sammy and Rosie Get Laid*, the only way for Rosie to convey her hatred for her 'crude, vicious, racist and ignorant' father – a former Mayor of Bromley – is to announce that he runs a furniture store.

Kureishi's first three screenplays featured young, enterprising characters being evicted from their squats or the ramshackle dwellings they'd managed to construct under motorway arches. His heroes lived in dilapidated bedsits, in communes full of rotting tarpaulins and leaking pipes, which they shared with radical lawyers, intellectual lesbians and jazz lovers. Blood ties mattered less than collective goodwill and mutual commitment. To some extent these degentrifications were lifestyle choices, the traditional messiness that is the luxury of well-connected dropouts and would-be bohos. Still, by depicting – with sympathy and approval – crumbling households, unorthodox communities and designs for living that were contingent and slung together, Kureishi offered a vision of domesticity hateful to both Thatcherite and traditional Asian notions of propriety.

His second-generation protagonists regarded home as an 'octopus', something that squeezed their brains into 'a tight ball', and which they feared would swallow them up 'like a little kebab'. Home had to be fled, quickly. It was their love of speed, the sense that their lives didn't have to be provincial and piecemeal that aerated Kureishi's Asian readers. His characters were on the make, ambitious upstarts with nothing to lose except a constraining familial rootedness. We identified with their youth and their desire to do something, anything. They were always on the move, dashing to places they didn't yet know. That didn't matter: escape was all. In *The Buddha of Suburbia* Karim is so keen to escape the plod and atrophy of life back home that he cycles into South London, 'nipping through traffic, sometimes mounting the pavement, up one-way streets, braking suddenly, accelerating by standing up on the pedals, exhilarated by thought and motion'.

Speed replaced stasis in the heterotopia that Kureishi devised for us. Happiness would no longer be sacrificed at the altar of atavistic religions. It seemed that we could have it all. These themes resonated not only with us but with a white audience once defined by Kureishi as 'aged between 18 and 40, mostly middle-class and well-educated, film and theatre-literate, liberal progressive or leftish'.

What, above all, made Kureishi a talismanic figure for young Asians was his voice. We had previously been mocked for our deference and timidity. We were too scared to look people in the eye when they spoke to us. We weren't gobby or dissing. (If this got us little respect from our peers, it did at least help us academically. My own experience is not untypical: there were three Indians in my year at school, and to everyone's amusement, and our own embarrassment, we were, term after term, the top three performers in our English class.) Kureishi's language was a revelation. It was neither meek nor subservient. It wasn't fake posh. Instead, it was playful and casually knowing. Rafi, the avuncular, murderous Third World tyrant in *Sammy and Rosie Get Laid*, says: 'For me England is hot buttered toast on a fork in front of an open fire. And cunty fingers.'

Kureishi's public persona wasn't too dissimilar from that of his lead characters. We cut out articles he'd written in newspapers and read and reread them. He seemed to lack all fear. He didn't try to be liked. He'd assume the estuary drawl of Mick Jagger and 'do' cocksure and bored. Sarky and sussed to the point of being obnoxious, he'd lay into Norman Tebbit, cheer on Poll Tax rioters and celebrate orgiastic youth. Embodied on screen by Tania's display in *My Beautiful Laundrette* and Vivia and Rani's aggressively self-conscious clinching in front of Rafi in *Sammy and Rosie Get Laid*, Kureishi's provocation made us laugh, confident, fighting fit.

A casual flick through *Midnight All Day*,* Kureishi's latest collection of short stories, gives the impression that it is exactly like the books he wrote in the 1980s. Inventories of metropolitan pleasure pile up: characters are shown dawdling along Kensington High Street shopping for drugs, sex toys and Al Green records. They dream of driving through the metropolis in a taxi – through the West End, down the Mall and past the Minema screening arty Spanish films. The characters, too, are the usual band of artists and Lotharios who pass their time reading hardback fiction, dropping E and having noisy sex. Their obsessions, other than finding more drugs and more sex, still have to do with the need for greater freedom and less domestic responsibility.

A closer look reveals subtle but important changes. Where once Kureishi's heroes were scrambling towards material and creative prosperity, they now tend to dwell on the right side of affluence. Squatting and communal living have been replaced by luxury pads and invitations to private parties at the ICA. They run film production companies, lecture on human rights in the States, write

---

*Hanif Kureishi, *Midnight All Day* (Faber, 2000).

zeitgeisty novels. They holiday in the Hamptons. They eat humous and floren-tines. When they feel intellectually undernourished they turn to Nietzsche and Pascal rather than to Kerouac and Eldridge Cleaver. And when they feel a bit rotten, as they often do, they like to compare themselves to figures in paintings by Lucian Freud. Like anorexic film stars and rock musicians writing their not-so-difficult fourth album, it appears that Kureishi's characters are suffering from a low-key form of Paradise Syndrome.

Relationships have become the main source of angst. Some, like Marcia in 'Sucking Stones', who has regular assignations with a Bulgarian former Olympic cyclist in his shabby bedsit, are stuck in company they're not sure they want to keep any longer. Others, like Rob, a successful working-class actor from South London, are distraught that their partners are about to leave them. Infidelity is rife. Husbands scramble to hold onto wives. Ex-wives hiss at the men who abandoned them. Ex-girlfriends do their best to drag their former partners into bed. Those who are in relationships nurse dark fears about the future.

Sex used to offer joys of Lucullan excess in Kureishi's work. Wishing to coun-terblast what he believed to be the state-sponsored repression of the 1980s, the original title for *Sammy and Rosie Get Laid* was 'The Fuck'. Sex was joy, intentionally gratuitous. However bizarre and squalid, it was a form of liberation. No longer. In place of unfettered sexual activity there is only bruised pensiveness. Characters see themselves as too old to be bohemian. Though they're rich and adulated, they worry incessantly about the greying hair behind their ears, their failing eyesight. They feel estranged from themselves as much as from others. Where they used to be dazed and confused by the vertiginous possibilities for self-transformation London offered, now they wander the capital perplexed by what's happened to their lives and how they have become so congealed. The titles of the short stories – 'Strangers When We Meet', 'That Was Then', 'Morning in the Bowl of Night' – catch the mood of crepuscular resentment.

'It has come to this,' says one of the characters self-reproachfully. The reader of *Midnight All Day* might be tempted to say the same. The book represents – along with *Love in a Blue Time* (1997) and *Intimacy* (1998) – the third instalment in the ongoing decline of a once vital writer. The problem resides not so much in the cosseted and unlikable characters, nor in the stagnation of the stories, but in Kureishi's inabil-ity to exploit his form. Short stories require a metonymic imagination, a desire to distil experience. Kureishi, however, thrives on aggregation and accumulation. He is essentially a metropolitan writer and the urban aesthetic, as Jonathan Raban has argued, is noun-orientated, always striving to catalogue the density of new infor-mation that the city spews out. Kureishi's soft-porn rites-of-passage movies and novels involve multiple pile-ups of disparate characters and social worlds. Such constant hustling – upwards! onwards! – is not well suited to the short story.

For a book which dwells on the fraughtness of human relationships and the difficulties of communicating, it seems odd that everyone is able to express their confusion in meticulous sentences. Rob, the narrator of 'Strangers When We Meet', accidentally bumps into the husband of the woman he has been seeing for a year. They discuss, he says later, 'the emptying out; the fear of living; the creation of a wasteland; the denigration of value and meaning'. Idling in a friend's apartment in Paris to which he has escaped with his pregnant lover – this is in the title story – Ian explains his decline in relation to Thatcherism: 'Following her, they had moved to the right and ended up in the centre. Their left politics had ended up as social tolerance and lack of deference.' These lunges towards portentousness are greedy and inelegant. They are so simplistic that one is tempted to assume that Kureishi is being ironic. In 'Meeting, At Last', Eric asks his wife's lover to tell him what he thinks about deception: 'Your demeanour suggests that it doesn't matter, either. Are you that cynical? This is important. Look at the century! . . . I work in television news. I know what goes on. Your cruelty is the same thing. Think of the Jews.'

The attempts to yoke the priapic to the political in the style of Roth or Updike also fail on linguistic grounds. Kureishi is not a prose writer of any distinction. For all their grousing and despair none of his characters is capable of producing the 'jeroboams of self-absorption' found in *American Pastoral*. They explicate rather than illuminate. One announces that 'When I am depressed I shut everything down, living in a tiny part of myself, in my sexuality or ambition to be an actor. Otherwise, I kill myself off.' Another declaims: 'Falling in love was simple; one had only to yield. Digesting another person, however, and sustaining a love, was bloody work, and not a soft job.' But this bloodiness never crosses over into the words. The idiomatic, suited-and-booted dialogue of his early work has disappeared. Prim, medium-lengthed, stiff-backed, shorn of excess, his prose – as well as his characterisation – lacks warmth.

Like his characters, Kureishi seems to have reached an impasse. All the body-rocking brio of old has waned. His work is sapped and weary. It hasn't even the passion or swagger to merit the accusations of misanthropy and misogyny that have recently been hurled at him. In his earlier writing he captured and defined a precise historical juncture. He changed the lives of many young Asians. He also inspired a lot of them to become artists. Now times have changed and everywhere one turns there's a new magazine, conference or club night dedicated to staging the antics of young Asians in Britain. Ayub Khan Din, who in 1988 played opposite Frances Barber in *Sammy and Rosie Get Laid*, has gone on to write *East Is East*: it packed out the

Royal Court Theatre in 1997 and was made into a slightly inferior film which has, nonetheless, just become the highest-grossing fully British-funded movie. Chart-topping Cornershop had a song called 'Hanif Kureishi Scene' on the B-side of their curry-coloured first single; the posters for *My Son the Fanatic*, Kureishi's last movie, boasted that the soundtrack album featured the band even though they weren't heard in the film itself. Meera Syal, one of the sour-faced lesbians in *Sammy and Rosie Get Laid*, is well-known as a writer and as one of the stars of *Goodness Gracious Me*, the all-Asian television comedy series which sends up – without too much venom or subtlety – Asian, British and Anglo-Asian culture. The work of these artists is saturated with the optimism that is missing from *Midnight All Day*.

18 May 2000

COMMANDED TO MOURN

Adam Phillips

OTHER PEOPLE'S MOURNING – like other people's sexuality and other people's religions – is something one has to have a special reason to be interested in. So to write a book,* as Leon Wieseltier has done, about the mourning of his father is asking a lot (and to write a book of 585 pages is asking even more). One of the ironies of the so-called mourning process is that it tends to make people even more self-absorbed than they usually are; in need of accomplices, but baffled about what they want from them. In actuality what the mourner wants from other people is so obscure, so confounded that religions are usually still needed to formulate it. Even secular therapies – which are all, one way or another, forms of bereavement counselling – are keen to offer us guidelines about how to do it, and how to know if it isn't going well. Because mourning can make fundamentalists of us all, because grief (like sexuality) can seem like a cult that could kidnap us, there is always a great deal of social pressure on the grief-stricken to conform, to observe the protocols, to believe in the process (and that it is a process). And so recover sooner rather than later. But what would recovery be, what would have been recovered?

If grief doesn't have a shareable story, if there is no convincing account of what happens to people when someone they know dies, grief will always be singular and secluding: as close as we can get to a private experience without it sounding non-sensical. When someone dies something is communicated to us that we cannot communicate. Hence the urgency that goes into making death a communal experience. The fact that all cultures have been so determined to ritualise this experience reflects just how socially divisive, how maddening the experience of death is considered to be. The only taboo, where grief is concerned, is on not experiencing it: not feeling it and performing it appropriately. There are no grief scandals in the way that there are sex scandals; there are only scandalous absences of grieving.

'What death really says is: THINK,' Wieseltier writes in one of the many arresting sentences in this book. The problem, as he well knows, is that death says nothing to us except what we make it say. And 'we', in this context, are the people (in our

---

*Leon Wieseltier, Kaddish (Picador, 1999).

various cultural traditions) who have gone before us in dealing with this unusually common experience. When his own father died Wieseltier found himself returning to the religion of his forefathers, which involved the observance of a year's mourning and a complementary enquiry into the provenance and meaning of the Jewish prayer known as the mourner's Kaddish. This book is at once a journal of that year and a kind of theological meditation on Judaism and grief. So it inevitably raises the question whether it is still possible to write an inspirational classic – a curiously nostalgic ambition in itself – without sounding like pastiche Kierkegaard, or indeed Woody Allen's *Death Notebooks*.

One of the most dreaded eventualities in a man's life has overtaken me,' Wieseltier writes, 'and what do I do? I plunge into books! I can see that this is bizarre. It is also Jewish. Anyway, it's what I know how to do.' And what the books do, among other things, is tell you that this is the most dreaded eventuality in a man's life. The books tell you to open the books so that you can find out beforehand what will be the most significant events in your life. Above all, they confirm for Wieseltier the value of the books; and the books he writes commentaries on, at some length, are mostly works of Biblical or Talmudic exegesis. So the exclamation-mark here is either self-delightedly smug or genuinely puzzled by these old-fashioned reflexes. That he finds himself, at this most unsettling moment of his life, doing exactly what the books would want him to do is both reassuring and an inspiration. The problem is the pragmatic shrug: 'Anyway, it's what I know how to do.' He knows how to study these books, but he doesn't know how to miss his father. He doesn't know what to do with a death. And what he wants from the books becomes inextricable from what he wants out of the death. In the interesting twist that provides the drama of *Kaddish*, Wieseltier's natural naivety about the effect of his father's death gets displaced onto his religious tradition. He is suddenly confronted with his ignorance about the mourner's prayer. 'I was struck almost immediately by the poverty of my knowledge about the ritual that I was performing with such unexpected fidelity . . . A season of sorrow became a season of soul renovation, for which I was not prepared.' His father's death makes him enact something that he then needs to know about. *Kaddish* is about the importance such knowledge came to have for Wieseltier. Not how or why it worked – his chosen texts are not treated as sophisticated self-help books – but the fact that his father's death made a certain kind of enquiry into the past imperative. It is not, of course, uncomplicated that such deaths are often renovations.

Kaddish is not the record of somebody's attempt to get over something. Wieseltier is not trying to find a way out, or even a way through, but a way into what has happened and is happening to him, through the tradition he was born into. Every death is a crisis of continuity; and Wieseltier's father's death is superimposed on family deaths in the Holocaust. So the people who are burying their dead are, at the same time, people who have been unable to bury their other dead. *Kaddish* is knowingly haunted by those who were deprived of their rightful death. In writing of these things, it is a notable difficulty to avoid the sanctimoniousness that is always a loophole for the soul; or the kitsch inner superiority of those who are deeply moved by the sensitivity of their own response. Atrocity doesn't bring out the best in people because, faced with it, people no longer know what the best in people is. One of the things our traditions are there to do is to remind us what the best things about us are.

In search of the history of the mourner's Kaddish – of ways the Jews have observed their deaths and the invocations and hopes buried in their prayers – Wieseltier kept a journal which, like many such 'journals', must have always half-wanted to be a real book. That is, to be read by people Wieseltier doesn't know. 'I recorded the ancient, medieval and modern sources that I found, and the speculations that they provoked. This volume is that journal. It is not exactly a work of scholarship.' But it is exacting partly because the scholar is so obviously Wieseltier's kind of hero. Not exactly a work of scholarship is certainly a nod to those scholars for whom nothing could be inexactly scholarly. *Kaddish* is straight-faced about scholarship – though not quite straitlaced: it sometimes sounds like a Jewish *Anatomy of Melancholy* but clearly dreads turning into a Jewish Rabelais – because it is essentially a tradition of scholarship that Wieseltier is after. But the unembarrassed ways in which he flaunts his piety, his being so staunchly undaunted by the antic disposition of his readers, sometimes makes *Kaddish*, with its devoted and devotional scholarship and its harsh critique of contemporary life, seem the blithest of provocations. It is a solemn book that asks to be read in exactly the spirit in which it is written. Or, to put it another way, Wieseltier is artful in creating the illusion that he would be the best reader of this book, which is best read, I think, as an occasionally remarkable philosophical meditation, often poignant in its belatedness; and as a letter to Philip Roth.

'The history of Jewish literacy: now there is a delicate subject!' Wieseltier exclaims. 'It turns out that rabbis have been complaining for centuries that the book has often been closed to the people of the book.' It might seem a bit offhand in this context to say that now books might just be for the people who like them (there will be no people of the video); or to speak up for the Golden Calf side of the tradition; or even to suggest that *Kaddish* would have been a better book – a more hospitable book, less proud of its restrictiveness – if Jewish literacy had been considered to be a more indelicate subject. Wieseltier is on the side of the rabbis and is not keen to countenance the ironies that attend the wholehearted promotion of virtue. To promote virtue, of whatever kind, forces people to be more of a piece, to be more consistent, than they can bear to be. For Wieseltier it is the great boon of the tradition that it effectively tells its members who they are. 'For ancient Jews and medieval Jews,' he writes, 'there was no escape from Jewishness, and this was their happiness. Can modern Jews understand such happiness?' Could those ancient and medieval Jews understand it? Did they understand it as happiness exactly? Was that always (often?) their word for it?

It is perhaps not entirely surprising that Wieseltier is unimpressed by revolutions. 'The voluntarism of modern Jewish identity,' he writes, 'was one of the great revolutions of Jewish history. Like all revolutions, however, it exaggerated. It made foolish Nietzschean demands of ordinary men and women. But most people do not invent themselves. Most of them choose to be what they already are. This is a kind of honour, too.' So-called ordinary people are always the fodder for these kinds of views, which can only be made to seem sensible, and even kind, by obfuscating the whole notion of choice. The fact that some things in life are unchosen doesn't mean that nothing can be chosen or that a lot of people aren't keen to make choices, and aren't happily enlivened by doing so. I can choose to go to bed, but not to go to sleep; I can't choose to fall in love but I can choose to make a pass; I can't choose not to be Jewish, but I can choose to go to synagogue, and so on. There is revolution when what is deemed to be ordinary is put into question, when what is considered to be beyond the realm of choice is discovered not to be. One may think, as one reads Wieseltier's book, that what people are capable of doing, or indeed should do, to improve their lives has already been decided. So *Kaddish* is often driven by an exhausted realism, a seeing through modern life which is presented as the rediscovered wisdom of a tradition, rather than the sadness of a bereft son.

'The ideal of epiphany,' Wieseltier writes, 'the thirst for what Americans call "peak experiences": all this is a little cowardly, an attempt to escape the consequences of living in time . . . The peak experience will peak. And there will occur, in the most quotidian way, an experience of eschatological disappointment.' These Americans, like those ordinary men and women, just don't know what's good for them. But what is it that Wieseltier is trying to secure for himself and his fellow Americans? Perhaps they should have eschatological disappointment counselling; after all, not being able to bear disappointment is hardly a good reason to avoid, or contemptuously dismiss, peak experiences. The unremitting fact of his father's death and the unthinkable fact of the Holocaust are then pretexts, licences for another contemporary jeremiad. And, like most jeremiads, this one has no misgivings about its own genre. 'In the company of death,' Wieseltier writes with that astringent clarity that is the best voice in the book, 'subjectivity is wild. So subjectivity must be tamed.

The taming of subjectivity is the work of the Kaddish.' One sign that subjectivity is wild is when it starts speaking with too much conviction, on behalf of too many people.

'It is almost impossible,' Wieseltier writes, 'to think unsentimentally about continuity.' Sentimentality is one risk, but stridency is another. Imposing a pattern or form on experience over long stretches of time tends to make people very impatient because the material is always so recalcitrant. Continuity is always at war with circumstance, and the contingency of events. If a religion wants to be more than a refuge it has to develop, but if it adapts too eagerly it runs the risk of dissolving. At what point do you stop calling it Judaism and start calling it something else (literature, politics, obsessional neurosis)? It is the threats to continuity, the attempted redescriptions, that make people despondent or violent or write books like this one. The death of a parent is bound to leave one to wonder, one way or another, about parenting; about who, if anyone, one belongs to or wants to belong to; and where, if anywhere, one needs to imagine oneself coming from. For Wieseltier it is the notion of a Jewish tradition that holds it all together. That parents all the parents. And it is about the notion of tradition – and custom and ritual and observance – that he is at his most engaged, if not always at his most engaging. In so far as more and more people now believe in history but not in character – or at least find it easier to describe a person's history than who they are – *Kaddish* is very much of its time. As it is in its rather gleeful acceptance of its chosen determinism. What is more alarming is Wieseltier's wish that people should be, as it were, buried alive in their traditions.

'The right response to tradition is vertigo,' Wieseltier writes in knowing combat with the Existentialist's vertigo of freedom. For Wieseltier, it is the dizzying release from choice that engenders vertigo. Tradition is like the stern parent everyone needs to deal with the unbounded ecstasies of pain (and pleasure). 'Since death is final, grief is final. Since death will never end, mourning will never end. That is why the tradition must intervene to end it.' If tradition is the great punctuator that saves us from ourselves it also usefully cuts us down to size, reminding us that we're not that special, that our supposed uniqueness is trivial in the grand scheme of things. 'Tradition is the opposite of identity,' Wieseltier writes, relishing what he has been chosen to speak up for. 'Identity is an accident. There is no need to ready yourself for your identity, because it is your inheritance. And that is its scandal.' The portentousness of this final flourish could be exhilarating were it not for the snarl-ups along the way. Tradition must be the opposite of accident (whatever that might be: presumably design by God). But your identity, which is an accident, is in fact your inheritance (your tradition), which is not. Leaving aside what it might mean to ready oneself for one's identity – it's fortunate one doesn't need to do this because it isn't obvious how one would go about it – this does seem a misleading way of putting it all.

'Insofar as civilisation is a communion with the past,' Wieseltier writes, 'and regards an absence as a presence, it is mysticism.' But it is rather important – as Burke, among too many others, unwittingly showed – to sort out the mysticism from the mystification. Real mysticism never seeks to convert others, real mystification always does. The trading in absences as presences is something to be vigilant about. And pragmatism, which has always been usefully attentive to such metaphysical conceits, is almost for this very reason anathema to Wieseltier. 'Pragmatism is such a puny theory,' he writes. 'There are so many questions for which the pragmatists have no answers. Human transformation is not a "practice". There are changes for which we have no rules and conventions. That is why we fear them and honour them; they are accomplishments for which experience cannot have been a guide.' Wieseltier's grief for his father is never proffered in this honourable book as a device for the abrogation of serious argument – rather the opposite, in fact. But, like many of Wieseltier's pronouncements about the even vaguely modern, his remarks about pragmatism are more prejudicial than anything else; righteous indignation that produces more righteous indignation. Human transformation may not always be a practice, but to assert that it never is, or can be, is to replace politics with mysticism.

Wieseltier is particularly alert to other people's failures of rigour. Mourning brings one up against the question of what it is to do things properly; and why doing things properly might matter. What, if anything, does one owe a dead parent, and how is it to be given? If one's life as a child is at least in part organised around what one imagines the parent wants of (and from) oneself, then the death of the parent might leave one stranded with unmet obligations. Wieseltier is averse to anything that smacks of modern psychological explanation – for him, not unreasonably perhaps, psychology is what happens when the tradition becomes decadent – but one of the book's consistent laments is that people, most often himself, are never doing enough. They are never sufficiently thorough, or penetrating, or committed, unlike the Jewish theologians he prizes. ('Why,' he asks, 'is egalitarianism so often accompanied by a general slackening?') It is the sly evasions, the falling short that is so pernicious. And so, like the many Jewish prophets who turned their competition with God into a speaking on His behalf, this slack Golden Calf mentality, which seems to be everywhere, makes him want to lay down the law; or rather rule the roost. 'Whenever I read Kafka,' he writes, 'I wonder: what sort of dejection is this, that leaves one the strength to write, and write, and write? If you can write about the wreckage the wreckage is not complete. You are intact. Here is a rule: the despairing writer is never the most despairing person in the world.' Was Kafka lying or, even worse, boasting? Kafka may have lost the despair competition, may not have gone the whole way, but what is the game Wieseltier's rule lets us play? Given Kaddish's Talmudic urgings, it would be churlish not to quibble.

It is a book in which doors keep slamming in the reader's face. 'When Nietzsche lost his faith, he concluded that God is dead. This is not critical thinking. This is narcissism.' This is not critical thinking either. And that in itself doesn't matter – a lot of so-called critical thinking is *Dunciad* material – if the sentences work (work something up), and the author doesn't humourlessly and endlessly advocate the necessary virtues of such thinking. 'The tradition,' Wieseltier writes, 'reveals an admirable indifference to psychology.' But the problem with 'the tradition' as presented (and represented) by him is that it seems self-admiringly indifferent to anything that might make it think otherwise. The mourning of his father that might have made him wonder about the tradition and his place in it told him what his mourning was: 'You do not mourn only because he died. You mourn also because you are commanded to mourn. There is your heart, and there is the Torah.'

Kaddish makes one wonder whether it is as much the function of a 'tradition' to distract the mourner from his grief – by talking him into a specific version of it, or by not allowing for its absence – as to console him. It is possible that we have no idea what secular grief is; what grief unsanctioned by an apparently coherent symbolic system would feel like. It may, for example, be possible to miss people when they die without feeling that there is anything to be sad about. 'When you mourn for your father you serve things larger than him,' Wieseltier writes. The interesting question is why we think we need things larger than 'him'. It is a mystery why we should still be so daunted by our insignificance. Why we can't find the right size to be in the universe. In Wieseltier's tradition the will-to-meaning too often does the work of the imagination. If this is what Wieseltier calls the 'charisma of learning', we should forget it.

18 February 1999

SAVING MASUD KHAN

Wynne Godley

THIS IS THE STORY of a disastrous encounter with psychoanalysis which severely blemished my middle years.

I was about thirty years old when I found myself to be in a state of terrible distress. It was the paralysis of my will, rather than the pain itself, which enabled me to infer, using my head, that I needed help different in kind from the support of friends. A knowledgable acquaintance suggested that I consult D.W. Winnicott, without telling me that he was pre-eminent among British psychoanalysts.

I don't think that living through an artificial self, which is what had got me into such an awful mess, is all that uncommon. The condition is difficult to recognise because it is concealed from the world, and from the subject, with ruthless ingenuity. It does not feature in the standard catalogue of neurotic symptoms such as hysteria, obsession, phobia, depression or impotence; and it is not inconsistent with worldly success or the formation of deep and lasting friendships. The disjointed components of the artificial self are not individually artificial.

What is it like to live in a state of dissociation? In a real sense, the subject is never corporeally present at all but goes about the world in a waking dream. Behaviour is managed by an auto-pilot. Responses are neither direct nor spontaneous. Every event is re-enacted after it has taken place and processed in an internal theatre. On the one hand, the subject may be bafflingly insensitive but this goes with extreme vulnerability, for the whole apparatus can only function within a framework of familiar and trusted responses. He or she is defenceless against random, unexpected or malicious events. Evil cannot be countered because it cannot be identified.

The short personal story which follows is so familiar in its outline that it may seem stale, but I cannot explain how I allowed such strange things to happen to me unless I tell it.

My parents separated from one another, with great and protracted bitterness, at about the time I was born, in 1926, and I hardly ever saw them together. In infancy I was looked after, in various country houses in Sussex and Kent, by nannies and governesses as well as by a fierce maiden aunt who shook me violently when I cried. My mother, though frequently in bed with what she called 'my pain', was a poet, playwright, pianist, composer and actress, and these activities took her away from home for long and irregular periods of time. When she rematerialised, we had long goodnights during which, as she sang to me, I undid her hair so that it fell over her shoulders. She used to parade naked in front of me, and would tell me (for instance) of the intense pleasure she got from sexual intercourse, of the protracted agony and humiliation she had suffered when giving birth to my much older half-sister, Ann, who grew up retarded and violent (screamed, spat, bit, kicked, threw), and of her disappointment when my father was impotent, particularly on their honeymoon. The intimacies we shared made me love her 'over the biggest number in the world'.

My father was shadowy to begin with; he was an elderly man – always approaching sixty. I first perceived him as an invalid – disturbingly unlike other children's fathers. But he had great personal authority, distinction and charm, which I could identify in the responses of other people to him. Occasionally he gave me superlative presents – a toy launch which got up its own steam, a flying model of a biplane.

Neither of my parents had a social circle. No one came to stay. There were no children next door to play with.

As a young child I believed myself to be special, endowed with supernatural, even divine, powers which would one day astonish the world. I also knew that I was worthless, with no gifts or rights, and that I looked fat, dull and unmanly. The achievements of others, particularly those of my older brother John, stood in for anything that I might achieve myself, and afterwards a series of distinguished men were to step into John's shoes. I acquired a spectacular ability to *not* see, identify or shrewdly evaluate people or situations. Although passive and sickly, I enjoyed secret fantasies of violence. When asked what I was going to be when I grew up, I replied that I was going to be 'a boy actress'.

When I was six, an abscess developed in my inner ear which eventually, in a climax of torture, burst through my eardrum. For years afterwards I often had to wear a bandage round the whole of my head to contain the discharge. I became 90 per cent deaf in one ear; I also started to get short-sighted and wear spectacles.

When just seven years old I was sent to a boarding school, for eight solid months of each year, without the elementary social or other skills that were needed. I could hardly read and had never dressed myself, so that doing up my back braces was painful and nearly impossible; it never occurred to me that I could slip them off my shoulders. The little boys were often beaten and kicked by the masters and I found this extremely frightening; one child was severely caned in front of the whole school. Lessons were an impenetrable bore. Occasionally I had severe panic attacks associated with strange fantasies – for instance, that I would soon die and be reincarnated as a rabbit in a hutch, unable to communicate with my parents or siblings.

When I was ten, my father, having inherited a peerage and a great deal of money, remarried and recovered a family estate of unsurpassable loveliness in a remote part of Southern Ireland. My stepmother, Nora, created a luxurious and beautiful home, full of light and flowers, in a mansion house which overlooked two large lakes with woods running down to them. With John and my sister Katharine I was cocooned, during the school holidays, in total complaisance by a full complement of servants, gardeners, handymen and farm hands, of whose irony I was never conscious. On the morning of my 11th birthday my father walked into my bedroom, still wearing his pyjamas, with a 20-bore shotgun under his arm. I learned to shoot snipe and play tennis.

Around this time, my mother revealed that for years and years my father had been 'the most terrible drunkard'. In response to my anxious enquiry she emphasised that he drank 'until he became completely fuddled'. Meanwhile she had taken as a lover an ebullient young man, 15 years younger than herself, who emanated genius. This was William Glock, later to become the most versatile and influential musician of his generation. It was through his ears that I first heard and loved music and therefore started to learn the oboe. He soon fell in love with Katharine, and, sort of, with me (now aged 14), and we three drank a lot of rum and lime, with enormous hilarity.

When I was about 15, while John was fighting a gallant war over the Atlantic, my father started to drink again.

Heavy drinking is often associated with boisterous behaviour in a social context. My father never drank publicly at all and, drunk or sober, was never boisterous. He saw himself as a nobleman; and his style was that of a distinguished barrister, which is what he really was. But having suffered previously from delirium tremens, one or two shots caused him to collapse into bestial incoherence. He had convinced himself that if he was alone when he put the bottle to his lips no one would notice what was going on. I colluded with him in this, never referring to his drinking in any way. His drunkenness, when it occurred, was conspicuous and desperately embarrassing, whether he was in residence as a grandee in the Irish countryside or asleep in the Chamber of the House of Lords or visiting me at school. When he was not drinking, he recovered his authority completely. He was a fine violinist and during his abstinent periods, with Katharine at the piano, we played the great Bach double concertos together.

As my father started to deteriorate in earnest he became violently anti-semitic and, just as the war was ending, he used to say: 'Would it really have been so bad if the Germans had come here?' My stepmother confided to me, as my mother had done, that my father had generally been impotent and that she had a lover in Dublin.

For all the confidences I had received, for all my precocity and sense of having been through more than my contemporaries, I did not know, at the age of 17, that the vagina existed, supposing that childbirth was painful because it took place through the urethra. Nor did I know that men ejaculated.

I spent four supremely happy years at Oxford and owe my higher education entirely to Isaiah Berlin, who taught me philosophy, tête-à-tête, through 1946-47. I designed my first essay for him with a conscious intent to please but he was not to be seduced; he interrupted me at once and tore my work to pieces. A week later I adapted my first philosophical position to one which, so far as I could infer, must be closer to his, but he left me in shreds again. In response to his seemingly inconsistent criticisms, I invented ever more complicated structures which must, I supposed, be getting me closer to what he really thought. One day he asked me to repeat a passage and when I did so he burst into merry laughter exclaiming: 'How gloriously artificial!' I was deeply hurt but impelled thereafter to make the stupendous effort which, over a period of 15 months, was to transform my intellect.

All my old people faded away very sadly. Nora shot herself in the head with a shotgun; my father, his entire fortune squandered, died alone in a hospital where the nurses were unkind to him; my half-sister was committed to a high security mental institution at Epsom; my mother had a bad stroke and lived out her last six years hemiplegic and helpless, her mind altered. She told her nurses that they were 'lower-class scum' and complained that I was 'marrying the daughter of a New York yid'. This yid was Jacob Epstein.

Soon after my mother died I had a dream. I saw her in a bathtub in which there was no water. She was paralysed from the waist down and instead of the pubic hair I had seen as a young child there was a large open wound. Through the upper part of the room there was a system of ropes, pulleys and hooks. Although the lower part of her body was inert, she could operate the ropes skilfully with her hands and arms in a way which enabled her to get her body to move, with extreme agility, about the bathroom. She was confined to the room because the whole contraption was slung from the ceiling and attached to the walls. Her lower half sometimes got left behind or forced into strange shapes against the walls or over the edge of the tub as she moved around.

Winnicott's elegant white suit was crumpled; so was his handsome face. He reminded me of a very frail Spencer Tracy. His sentences were not always coherent but I experienced them as direct communications to an incredibly primitive part of myself; I want to say that we spoke to one another baby to baby. The crumpled face was a tabula rasa, impassive but receptive.

I described my impasse to Winnicott, adding that 'my tears were tightly locked into their ducts.' After desultory responses he asked me whether I had any 'cot' recollections. 'Yes,' I replied, scouring my mind and recollecting myself in a pram in a place where it could not, in reality, have stood – in the middle of a main road.

'Was there an object with you?' he asked.

'Yes,' I replied, 'there was a kaleidoscope.'

'What a hard thing,' was Winnicott's comment.

Winnicott next asked me if I would have any objection to seeing a Pakistani analyst. As I left he said, very kindly, 'You have been very frank with me,' adding: 'I think you were a lonely child.'

I arranged an appointment with Masud Khan from my office in the Treasury, where I was now an economic adviser, and he met me at the foot of the stairs leading to his attic apartment in Harley Street. He was in his mid-thirties, a tall, erect and substantially built man with beautiful Oriental features. He had abundant black hair swept back over his ears and was slightly overdressed in the style of an English gentleman.

I repeated to Khan the story of my impasse and in the course of telling it mentioned that I read a lot of newspapers. He looked up and asked me whether, if I read all these papers, I hadn't read something about him. When I said that I hadn't he assumed an expression of mock disbelief. A little later he broke into my narrative and asked irrelevantly: 'Haven't you got some connection with Epstein?' At this I checked, expressing concern about the confidentiality of what I was telling him, since his question implied that he already knew something about me and perhaps that we had social friends in common. Khan did not answer directly. He grunted and tried to look impassive.

Khan next explained that he was going to get married to Svetlana Beriosova, the loveliest of the Royal Ballet's ballerinas, in about ten days' time; this was why I might have read about him in the press. At the end of the interview, he drove me slowly part of the way home in his Armstrong Siddeley. In the car he produced a book of poems by James Joyce from the pouch in the door and told me that he read them when he was stuck in traffic jams. He asked, 'Did you never think of killing yourself?' but answered the question himself: 'You would not know whom to kill.'

It is astonishing to me, with the knowledge I now have, that Khan so intruded himself into that first interview, which should have held out the promise of a safe, private and neutral space in which a dialogue with its own dynamic could take place. Yet within minutes of our first meeting, as I can now clearly see, the therapeutic relationship had been totally subverted. He needed my endorsement, as will become increasingly clear; he also needed to intrude on me. I had no way of registering that there was something amiss in his expecting me to know about his forthcoming marriage (which implied that he would be leaving me for his honeymoon almost as soon as we had begun work) or in his showing me that he was a literary man who drove a smart car. But I did know that there was something completely wrong about the Epstein question; it had given me a sense of contamination, which I suppressed in a sickeningly familiar way.

Khan now distanced himself. I referred the following day to his 'girl' and he corrected me, 'my future wife . . . ' adding: 'You thought you were going to cuddle up with me, didn't you?' I did not, by a very long way, have the understanding or presence of mind to reply that this was an expectation which he himself had created; and I felt that it was, indeed, I who had intruded.

During the next few days my artificial self came, in stages, completely to pieces although my adult mind continued to function in a completely normal way; for instance, I continued to work in the Treasury without a break. The meltdown, which took the form of a series of quasi-hallucinations accompanied by storms of emotion, all took place at home, although I reported them to Khan. These waking dreams came to a climax after about three days. I 'saw' a blanket inside my skull which was very tightly wrapped around my brain. And it began to loosen! First intermittently, then decisively, the blanket came right away like a huge scab and I reached, as it seemed, an extraordinary new insight. My father had hated me! By appearing at my school when obviously drunk, he had maliciously used my love for him as a weapon against me! And he had cruelly separated me from my sister by sending me away to school. These 'perceptions' generated an outburst of infantile rage. While in this strange condition I saw, as in a vision, a sentence which was lit up, flickering and suspended in the air. The words were:

UNLESS HE JUSTIFIES HIMSELF I MUST SAVE HIM

The meaning I attributed, with partial understanding, to this sentence was that unless the parent is perceived by the infant as strong and self-sufficient, the caring process will go into reverse with the force of the ocean bursting through a dam.

No one, as I now know, has written with more penetration about the genesis of the artificial self than Winnicott. The birthright of every child is to receive, starting from the primal union, a uniquely empathetic response which nurtures its growth and establishes its identity. If this does not happen, the infant may come under an overpowering compulsion, as a condition for its very survival, to provide whatever it is the parent needs from the relationship. An incredibly destructive but deeply concealed reversal of roles then takes place.

My cathartic explosion was perfectly sincere and real. A fantastic distortion of my character that had governed my life up to that point, a bizarre mushroom growth, had been clearly revealed to me and I experienced a feelingfulness which had been blockaded for as long as I could remember.

By the time Khan returned from his honeymoon in Monte Carlo, I was having dreams about cars slipping backwards down icy pathways in the darkness. But I clung to the firm belief that another emotional breakthrough would soon occur.

It never did. What followed was a long and fruitless battle culminating in a spiral of degradation.

A crucial component of the analytic process resides in the patient's ability to articulate thoughts, fantasies or images as they occur to him or her, especially any hostile thoughts he or she may have towards the analyst. Unless this happens, the primitive reversal of roles can never be undone. But it is extremely difficult, requiring great concentration, courage and trust, to express murderous thoughts and insults to their object. The way such insults are negotiated is one of the keenest measures of an analyst's skill, character and fitness to practise; the artificial self knows all too well how to make others bleed.

As I come to describe Khan's failure to pass this elementary test, I realise that I am in danger of making him seem a mere figure of fun. There was indeed something wholly ridiculous about him – as there was about Adolf Hitler. But he had a formidable and quick-acting intelligence, astonishing powers of observation and an unrivalled ability straightaway to see deeply below the surface. He was impossible to worst. He knew how to exploit and defy the conventions which govern social intercourse in England, taking full advantage of the fact that the English saw him instinctively as inferior – as 'a native' – and tried to patronise him.

When I asked Khan why he wore a riding jacket which had a silly slit in the middle of his behind, he replied stiffly: 'Ask the man who tailored it.' When I said his flat was furnished like a hotel he referred reproachfully to 'my wife's superb style', which I had failed to recognise, turning the flat, in my mind, into 'a shabby hotel'. I didn't have the presence of mind to tell him that what I objected to was that his flat was like a *smart* hotel. Khan told me that he 'wanted to give me a good start' and went on to explain how the infant eats the breast but that the breast also eats the infant. Summoning up my courage (for I was also afraid of hurting him) I said: 'This silly buffoon is talking drivel.' To this Khan replied that, unlike some of his colleagues, he believed in paying back aggression from his patients in kind. And I was presuming to look for help 'from the man whom in your mind you call a buffoon' in a clipped, whispered and venomous tone, adding that I lived 'like a pig' in my own home. He wasn't going to pretend, so he said, that things were other than they were; he had been sadistic towards me and for days and months afterwards he referred to this as 'the sadistic session'.

Beriosova was often featured, scantily dressed, in press photographs. I wanted to know which bit of her was grabbed by her partner when he held her on top of a single outstretched arm, as well as other more intimate things. Khan told me that I was 'using the analytic situation as a licence to articulate [my] intrusive fantasies'. And he soon became enraged. 'You say that to me to annoy me,' he said and then, after a pause: 'Which it does.' He then went into a tirade about my crude assault ('You Englishman!') on a being so precious to him. 'I do know how to protect my wife,' he said as though I had attacked her. At the least slight it was Khan's invariable response to deliver a righteous speech, often finishing up with some withering coda such as 'And to think you people ruled the world!' Only now can I see how easy it was to bait him.

We hardly ever spoke of my childhood. Khan preferred, he said, to 'work out of' the material which was thrown up by contemporary experiences. Everything of significance that had happened in the past could be reinterpreted in terms of what was happening now. This gave him a licence to interfere actively, judgmentally and with extraordinary cruelty in every aspect of my daily life.

We entered a long period of painful stasis. 'When is something going to happen?' I would ask and he would reply: 'I wonder too when something is going to happen. I have exhausted' – these were his exact words – '*every manoeuvre that I know*. You are a tiresome and disappointing man.'

How did I account to myself for what was happening? I thought that everything unkind Khan said to me was justified and that I was learning to accept home truths; that this was extraordinarily painful but the essence of what a good and true analysis should be. We weren't having one of those soppy analyses that the ignorant public imagines, where a pathetic neurotic talks about himself and is passively listened to, and endlessly comforted. The characteristic sensation I experienced was a smouldering rage which carried me from session to session. I felt like a kettle that had been left on the flame long after the water had boiled away.

Khan liked it when I moved up through the Treasury ranks, greatly overestimating the importance and significance of the positions which I held. Meanwhile he began increasingly to fill the sessions with tales about his own social life in London or, occasionally, New York. The stories were not good ones. Many were obscene and many were flat, but there was one feature common to every one of them: Khan had got the better of someone. He had rescued Mike Nichols from a man with a fierce dog in New York. He had fought physically with Peter O'Toole, using a broken bottle. He had got the overflow from his lavatory to pour a jet of water onto the head of a woman who was making her car hoot in the street below. Often it would be nothing more than an ugly exchange at a drinking party for which he needed my approval and endorsement. The following characteristic tale, being brief, must stand in for a limitless number of other stories that I can immediately recall.

A man comes up to Khan at a party and says: 'Every night I go to bed with two beautiful women. I make love to one of them and then, if I feel like it, I turn over and make love to the other. Sometimes I make love to both of them at once.' 'Yes,' Khan says, 'but by the laws of topology there must always be one orifice which remains vacant.'

Very occasionally he appealed to me for sympathy. Princess Margaret had tripped him up over the way he had pronounced something. Lord Denning (it was Profumo time) had not replied to his invitation to come to dinner.

Khan always answered telephone calls during sessions. When Winnicott rang up I could clearly hear both sides of the conversation, so presumably he angled the phone towards me. Winnicott spoke respectfully to Khan, for instance about a paper which he had recently published. 'I learned a great deal from it,' Winnicott said deferentially. This particular conversation ended with a giggly joke about homosexual fellatio – the final two words of the conversation – accompanied by loud laughter.

A gynaecologist rang up during one of my sessions to enquire about a patient of Khan's whom I shall call Marian and who was expecting a baby. Khan spoke harshly about her to the gynaecologist, closing the conversation with the advice: 'And charge her a good fee.' Khan kept me in touch with the progress of Marian's pregnancy. She was not married, and as her confinement approached he referred to it bitingly as 'the virgin birth'.

After the child was born, Khan started speaking of Marian as a suitable partner for me – although I was happily married and although, as I much later discovered, he had secretly invited my wife Kitty to an interview with him. Marian and I were 'handmade for one another'. Khan induced me to take her out to lunch. 'If she's not really beautifully dressed, but really beautifully dressed, give her hell.' I took her to Overton's in Victoria where we ate seafood and had an amiable conversation without there being any spark between us.

We now started meeting à trois, Marian, Khan and myself. On one occasion we went to a literary group in Battersea where Khan gave a talk on 'Neurosis and Creativity'. On another, Marian watched from the gallery while I trounced Khan at squash, breaking his nose with my racquet in the process; immediately following which Khan, bloody nose and all, insisted on playing, because he could win, a game of ping-pong. And the three of us spent a whole evening playing poker for matchsticks. Khan cheated; he grabbed half my growing pile of matchsticks when I wasn't looking, although I didn't allow myself to realise it at the time. He chortled that with the power he possessed over each of us he could 'orchestrate the conversation at any level he chose'. At my next session he told me that this had been the happiest evening he had ever spent in his life.

At my next session! I was still seeing the man five times a week and paying him large fees. And I went on doing so until the end, although it is inconceivable that any therapy was taking place; for a long time now I was the one who was looking after him. Paying fees was part of keeping up the absurd fiction that a great patient was having a great analysis with a great analyst. 'I have the virtues which are the counterpart of my defects,' he was fond of saying. He had saved my life, the story went – and no one else could have done it. About this time Khan began to shower me with presents. He gave me a silver pen, a complete *Encyclopaedia Britannica*, a signed lithograph of sunflowers by Léger, an Indian bedspread, a Nonesuch Bible in three volumes, and several books, including *The Naked Lunch*.

Sometimes Beriosova was the hostess. Her physical movements were light and regal though she smoked heavily and drank a great deal of gin. On one occasion there were other analysands besides me present. Beriosova drank more gin than usual, retired to the Khan bedroom and screeched: 'Get them out of here, get them out of here.'

One evening I found myself alone with Khan and Beriosova in their flat. Both of them were drunk. They left the room separately so that I was alone for some minutes. I heard a faint moan which was repeated more loudly; the moan turned into my own name – an inarticulate appeal for assistance from someone helpless and in severe pain. Going into the hall, I saw Khan, lying full length and motionless on the ground. In agony he whispered: 'My wife has kicked me in the balls.' As he slowly recovered his wind I supported him back to the drawing-room. Re-entering the hall I found Beriosova lying full length on the floor exactly where Khan had been. I tried to lift her up. (It must be easy to pick up dancers – they have no weight – I somehow thought.) But Beriosova was a substantial woman, inert and apparently insensible. I left the hall and on my return a few moments later she had disappeared. At the next session I observed to Khan that I might, at some stage, have to say that things had got so far out of hand that I would have to break off the analysis. His reply was that if it got that far, *he* would break off the analysis 'one day' before I did. So he won that trick too.

Eventually Khan irrupted into my home. He rang up announcing that he and Beriosova were going to call on us within the next few minutes. Khan fidgeted about the house and made a lot of suggestions as to how we should manage our minor affairs (I should mow the lawn diagonally, for example, or set the lamp which hung low over the dining-room table upside down). He teased Kitty's younger daughter, then a patient of Winnicott's, by doing a ludicrous imitation of her. For this he 'got a tremendous rocket from Winnicott' he later recounted with loud laughter.

We now started to meet quite frequently, and go to parties, as two married couples. It is part of the story that we often met celebrities and that I found myself in conversation with, say, Rudolf Nureyev and François Truffaut.

As a prelude to the final tale, I must record that Kitty, having had a miscarriage a year or two before, had reached the third month of an exceptionally difficult pregnancy in the course of which all hope of saving the child had been given up more than once. We had not yet had a child.

We went out to dinner à quatre to a Chinese restaurant in Knightsbridge. Khan outdid himself in a tour de force of meaningless aggression. The only precise things I can remember are that he bullied and insulted the Chinese waiters, for instance by openly 'imitating' them. (I use inverted commas because it was not a genuine imitation, but a high-pitched whine appropriate to a schoolboy joke.) Although I was incapable of any vital response, Khan's behaviour was so extreme and unremitting, and there was so little space in which to move, that I began at last to feel something curdling deep within myself.

The next day Kitty came into the room and told me that Khan had rung her up and torn into her. She had a sharp pain in her womb.

The perception that, at the level of reality, Khan had made an attempt on the life of our unborn only child was painful beyond anything I can convey. I believe that one of the Nazi medical experiments was to inject ammonia into victims' veins. I felt that the living, if deformed, armature inside myself was corroding.

I rang up Winnicott and said, 'Khan is mad,' to which he said emphatically, 'Yes,' adding: 'All this social stuff . . .' He didn't finish the sentence but he came round to our house immediately, saying that he had told Khan not to communicate with me again. As he said this, the telephone rang and it was, indeed, Khan wanting not only to speak to me but to see me, which I refused to do.

And that was the end of my 'analysis'.

Ten years after the Chinese meal, having had an operation for cancer of the throat, Khan made a direct appeal to me, in a hoarse whisper, to visit him. When I arrived at his flat in Bayswater, a small Filipino servant pointed towards his drawing-room door saying: 'The prince is in there.' Khan had entirely changed his style; he had lost his beauty and now wore a black tunic and a necklace with a heavy ornament hanging from it. He was very drunk and insisted on talking pidgin French, which was completely incomprehensible. His companions were sycophants but there was one beautiful and elegant woman among them. From time to time he pointed to me and said: 'He and I the same. Aristocrats.'

I hear that Khan slept at will with his female patients, became an even more serious drunkard and shortly before he died was struck off. And that Beriosova appeared drunk on the stage at Covent Garden, faded away and died, first separated then divorced from Khan. I have also discovered, to my astonishment, that throughout the whole time that I was seeing Khan, *he was himself in analysis with Winnicott*. And this has led me to reinterpret some letters which I sent to Winnicott at Khan's instance, and the replies I received from him, as an aggressive flirtation between the two of them, using my body as unwitting intermediary.

It is now perfectly clear to me that, after seeing Khan daily for several years, and after untold expense and travail, no therapy whatever had taken place. What a trap! He had reproduced and re-enacted every major traumatic component of my childhood and adolescence. The primal union had been ruptured. The confidences which he reposed in me had made me special, just as my mother's had; he had the same need as she to perform and be performed for. And the same destructive gymnastics that I had once had to negotiate, given the deep attachment I had to my deteriorating father, were played out all over again. For the second time, I was overcome by a compulsion to attempt the transformation of a drunken, anti-semitic, collapsing wreckage into a living armature on which to build myself.

HE COULD NOT JUSTIFY HIMSELF SO I WAS COMPELLED TO SAVE HIM

What I have written is not an attack on psychoanalysis, for which, as a discipline, I have the utmost respect. I could not have gained the insight to write this piece, nor could I have recovered from the experiences I have described, if they had not at last been undone at the hands of a skilful, patient and selfless American analyst beside whom the conceited antics of Khan and, indeed, Winnicott seem grotesque beyond words.

But what recommendation could I now make to someone in need of help? One answer might be: 'Ask the president of the British Psychoanalytic Society.' But this, it turns out, is precisely what I did, without realising it. And Khan himself was training analysts for years after my break with him. Yet his personal defects were so severe that he should never under any circumstances have been allowed to practise psychoanalysis. I understand that his disbarment, when after twenty odd more years it came, was the consequence not of psychoanalytic malpractice, but of his outspoken anti-semitism. This, it seems, was more important than the deep, irreparable and wanton damage he wrought, from a position of exceptional privilege and against every canon of professional and moral obligation, on distressed and vulnerable people who came to him for help and paid him large sums of money to get it.

22 February 2001

READING THE SIGNS

Peter Campbell

I N A PHOTOGRAPH I N Friday's evening paper, behind the firemen and the
flames rising out of an old oil-drum, I recognised the relief lettering: L.C.C.
FIRE BRIGADE STATION EVSTON 1902. I know the sign well. Above it is a
little enamelled badge: that of the old London County Council. Their architect was
W.E. Riley. The lettering is part of a very good piece of integrated Arts and Crafts
design. In Riding House Street, north of Oxford Street, a building by H. Fuller Clark
of 1903 announces in gold and green mosaic, over a couple of floors, that it was the
premises of Boulting & Son, Sanitary and Hot Water Engineers. Another of Clark's
schemes, the ground floor of the Black Friar beside Blackfriars Bridge, sets out the
name in the same green and gold.

Such inscriptions, literally embedded in the façades, are among architecture's
most fragile elements. The fire station owes the preservation of its lettering to
the vigilance of a printing historian, James Mosley, and an architectural historian, Andrew Saint; and to the fact that the building is still a fire station. When
the clothing store Simpson of Piccadilly became a Waterstone's bookshop a more
painful battle of badges took place. Inside, mounted on an upstairs wall you can
still find the old Simpson sign – a good piece of Art Deco lettering. It has been
replaced on the front of the building with WATERSTONE'S in their undistinguished
house style. On black stone, to either side of the façade at street level, 'W, formerly'
has been added to the existing 'Simpson Piccadilly'. It looks like the bodge it is. But
you can't expect a shop to wear a false livery – even English Heritage can only insist
on the preservation of discarded pieces. The result is that a building of great style
has lost an element which was to it what Lautrec's monogram, say, is to his posters:
a signature that is part of the work of art.

All this is symptomatic of a change in the way we get to know what a building
is for. You used to know a church, theatre, school, almshouse or railway station
when you saw one. A projecting sign differentiated one craft from another and, on
grander buildings, a motto like the lettered band across Roger North's gateway to
the Middle Temple was all the written direction you got – such inscriptions in any
case celebrated what the building was rather than directed you to it. But over the
years the identity of buildings with owners and functions has become weak. Words
are now temporary, like notes stuck on a computer screen. Take the case of bank

buildings. Many grand ones have become bars. The message the banking hall once gave (probity, substance) is now written into advertising copy and it turns out that banker's pomp fits brewer's cheer well enough. The architectural message of Victorian pubs was glitzier and on a smaller scale (less marble, more mahogany and cut glass), but at bottom both offered reassurance. For pubs, judging by the number of fake Victorian refurbishments around, the style still works. Banks, on the other hand, now need to say not just 'this is *the* bank' but 'this is *our* bank,' and to say it in odd places like shopping malls. So a corporate identity is applied to branches, cheque books, stationery: the lot.

When bank buildings are older than the latest affiliation, look for redundancies (on a grand Lutyens bank building in the City a discarded name – THE MIDLAND BANK – is still carved into the rusticated stonework by the entrance, while the red and white diapers of HSBC are hung out to catch the eye) and palimpsests (in Fleet Street you can still read 'National Westminster' on the granite, under the perkier 'Natwest'). Badging is, of course, much cheaper and easier to apply than a deeper architectural identity. You can put a badge on any structure, and take it away painlessly, if expensively (the re-signing of a large corporation costs millions). But when a characteristic building becomes redundant – take the little Lutyens Midland Bank in the corner of the churchyard of St James's Piccadilly – it is, like a dismissed servant who still wears your livery, a reminder of other, more solid days, even if pale patches where signs were are the only direct evidence of lost rank.

Because a corporate badge or logo has become the norm, the older signals – from the architecture itself or from integrated words – seem to need re-emphasis. So the new Somerset House logo, a little purple and white plaque, now hits you at eye-level as you turn in below Chambers's entrance from the Strand. The finest and most assured entrance in London (although, I admit, one easy to miss) is thus given the equivalent of those designer labels which are placed on the outside of a piece of clothing.

There are, though, still buildings which have no words on them at all. The clubhouses of Pall Mall and St James's, for example, where the stranger invited to lunch at the Travellers must ask which it is, or remember that it is 106 Pall Mall and stands between the stucco one (the Athenaeum) and the bigger Florentine palazzo (the Reform). You can tell that the RAC, on the same street, is not a club for gentlemen because it has a whopping great flag outside. The next step up from this assumed domestic status is collegiate identity. Most of the staircase entrances of the Inns of Court have lists of names painted by a sign-writer – as do (or did) those of Oxbridge colleges. But now that typeset signs are so easily produced, handmade one-offness is becoming rare – the latest fashion in the Middle Temple seems to be to have the names printed on a sheet of milky-green glass. Sign-writing may in the end become an amateur craft, one which distinguishes the independent sandwich bar from Starbucks.

The ability to print type, photographs or drawings on plastic and stick the result over a whole building, a bus or a taxi has eroded the distinction between solid structures and scene-painting. The city has become a print-substrate, an almost anonymous structure which you read by way of notices, badges, signs, logos and banners. The battle between one message and another has escalated. There is a descending order of seriousness from the permanent to the ephemeral, and an order of conspicuousness running in the opposite direction. Cut in stone, your name will last. Serious donors to museums get that treatment: the British Museum has nothing on its front façade to say what it is, but the frieze of the east wing records the name of the man who gave the money to build it. Metal and terracotta also speak of permanence. But they are easy for the eye to slide over, to see as being of the building, not about it. Paint is brighter and easy to paint over. Plastic is cheap. Glass (painted on the reverse, perhaps gilded) is old-fashioned – pubs, old chemists' shops – but elegant. Light – neon, backlit panels, digital displays – transforms dirty daytime streets into mesmerising funfairs at dusk.

Over the past couple of hundred years, the possibility of a single coherent reading of what you see as you stand in any one place has become more and more difficult. Each new message shouts as loud as it can, knowing that it has to compete. Consider what you must attend to as you walk down Piccadilly. Traffic-lights to stay alive. Shop signs which identify chains and products. Banners outside the Royal Academy in case you slip past without knowing what is on. On the corner of Arlington Street, waiting to cross over to the Ritz arcade, you can scan notices about parking, note the 'no entry' sign, and pick up the connotations of 'The Ritz' in lights: the bulbs set in a channel speak of 19th-century Paris and popular amusements as clearly as the Beaux Arts architecture of the Mewès and Davis building speaks of aristocratic ones. Waiting to cross the Strand to the Middle Temple you note not only the discreet City Heritage Award plaque but the larger and bolder red and white 'CCTV cameras in operation'. Although these are things which, like other people's conversations, we are good at not attending to when they do not concern us, the chatter of signage does stand between us and the dream (not realised now, perhaps not realised even in the middle of Paris, in Bath or in Venice) of a rational city in which a hierarchy of signs, written as well as architectural, becomes a coherent statement.

12 *December* 2002

MASS-OBSERVATION IN THE MALL

Ross McKibbin on Princess Diana's Funeral

THE WEEK BEFORE PRINCESS Diana's funeral and the funeral itself were, by agreement, a remarkable moment in the history of modern Britain, but most of us, despite broadsheet press commentary which was frequently sensible and thoughtful, have found it difficult to understand or even to know what happened. And this, of course, is due to the fact that the dominant intellectual categories of the 20th century are secular and rational: we are in a sense taught not to be able to understand such 'irrational' phenomena as the reaction to Diana's death, or indeed anything to do with public attitudes to royalty, and are frequently embarrassed if asked to do so. Historians of the 20th century are particularly disabled – historians of medieval religion or Byzantinists at least know what questions to ask. Furthermore, we are compelled to measure things which are almost immeasurable. The great majority of the population, after all, did not leave flowers in front of the palaces or anywhere else. Over one-quarter of the adult population did not even watch the funeral on television. Most of those who were there were not weeping. Does that mean they were emotionally unaffected? On the other hand, many more watched the funeral on television than watched the Euro 96 England-Germany match, hitherto the record-breaker. Does that mean we feel more intensely about Diana than about the national game – or simply that more women watched the funeral than watched the football? And, in any case, can people articulate what they feel in ways we can understand? In due course we might know these things but at the moment we do not.

This is why historians and sociologists of the 20th century have approached the subject of royalty and its audience gingerly, and few have done so at all. However, by coincidence, the first and still the most sustained attempt to understand our reactions to royalty was published exactly 60 years ago; and it was, also by coincidence, a study of a single royal event. This was Mass-Observation's study of King George VI's coronation in 1937 – May 12. Two hundred 'observers' were posted about the country and instructed to note what they observed: with the exception of those who kept a record of what they themselves felt, they were not to intrude or act as mediators – simply to observe. There are all sorts of problems with Mass-Observation's techniques, as any historian knows, and they have not been universally admired – the sociologist T.H. Marshall thought them at least in part 'moonshine'. It is also true that observers, though instructed merely to record the ordinary and everyday, tended to record the extraordinary on grounds of interest and inevitably 'edited' what they saw (since 'facts' do not speak for themselves), but it is unlikely, given that they were trying to measure degrees of emotion and sentiment, that anybody will ever do much better.

The possibilities and limitations of Mass-Observation were apparent to anyone who was in London the week that Diana died, particularly in the Mall or outside the palaces. I recorded my own impressions in as mass-observant a way as I could and tried to come to conclusions consonant with what I 'saw'. In the end, my regard for Mass-Observation and what they achieved was enhanced, since I found it difficult to reach conclusions which were anything more than tentative in the face of evidence that was quite intractable. And it is the case that one tends to notice the extraordinary or unexpected: I expected, for instance, the great banks of flowers but failed to anticipate that they would produce a very pungent, sweet smell which will affect, I am sure, how everyone remembers the scene. One of my strongest memories of the Mall was of something absolutely untypical: an elderly black woman singing hymns in a cracked voice without regard for anyone else. She was singing for Diana alone. More typically, almost every bouquet was accompanied by a card, letter or poem. There was some surprise that the flowers were left in paper or cellophane. But these were individual presentations and the paper kept them individual. Not everyone gave flowers: there were many posters and manifestos attached to trees or railings – with people happy to identify themselves, in one case as 'Freddie Mercury's cousin'. A very large proportion of the bouquets and messages – probably a majority – came from children, often collectively: from playgroups, kindergartens, primary schools. Some classes sent whole books in which, presumably, every child contributed something. How far there were parental guiding hands in all this is hard to say. The language (and spelling) suggests not much. From what I saw, parents left their children to write what they wanted. At a rough guess, I would say there were an unrepresentative number of cards and letters from Asian children, though that could be wrong. What was characteristic of the letters and poems as a whole is how highly-charged and emotionally uninhibited they were. Some exceptionally so. The most common words appeared to be 'angel', 'heaven', 'soul', 'paradise', 'smile', 'cared', 'love', 'grace', 'peace' and 'at peace'. Many of the letters hoped that Diana would have the peace and happiness in heaven which she failed to find on earth: hoped that she was now 'free from her troubles'. Most, directly or indirectly, expressed a sense of personal loss. A significant number (which surprised me) were to both Diana and Dodi, and I doubt this was merely gratitude to Harrods, who were dispensing free Evian and coffee in the Mall. Many were in fractured English and I saw several in French. Very few mentioned the royal family. Some of the posters were 'political': 'Diana – the only jewel in the crown'; 'Charles, you've lost the best thing you ever had. Good luck to Wills and Harry,' said one poster stuck to the railings of Buckingham Palace.

As many people noted, the whole atmosphere was very 'democratic': rarely can the railings of our royal palaces have been treated with such disrespect. Posters, cards, letters, even rosaries were stuck in and stuck on them any old way. There were also many forms of demotic art – drawings, sketches, paintings and photo-montages. And there were gifts, mostly from children – huge numbers of teddy-bears and related comforters. But not all from children. Outside Buckingham Palace, for instance, was prominently displayed a bottle of Bailey's Irish Cream – perhaps a more effective comforter. There were innumerable candles, many intended to be votive, and some so large they could only have been bought at an ecclesiastical supplier.

As to the people, a steady day-long stream became a flood after six. Many were parents (frequently both parents) with children, but the population as a whole seemed fairly well represented. The majority were women, but only just. There were many 'businessmen' (for want of a better word), dark suits and briefcases, who were bringing flowers – and this again was a surprise. Most striking, and something confirmed on the day of the funeral, were the large numbers of young couples, with as many men as women holding flowers. The queues of those waiting to sign the books of condolence increased throughout the week until Friday, when 3 books became available. On Thursday the sign said 'waiting time 7 hours,' but the police said eight. (The police were helpful and good-humoured.) The queue, again, was pretty representative, though understandably biased towards the hale and hearty. Once more the majority were women, but not a large majority. I think the queue was disproportionately non-white, but that is said without much conviction. There seemed to be a considerable number of tourists both in the queue, Americans particularly, and in the crowd, where a great many Italians and Spaniards were taking photographs. There is a view that the reaction to Diana's death represents a 'Mediterraneanisation' of our culture, but the slightly stunned look many of these Italians and Spaniards wore suggests not. The number of photo-seekers around Buckingham Palace was so large that the police had created photographer-only queues.

Making sense of this is not easy. The tendency has been to read into these events a profound change in British life, but the evidence points in different directions. Most of the letters and poems, for example, were written in an instantly recognisable, though very heightened graveyard style which is, if anything, mid-19th century. The 20th century has been bad at devising a language of grief and mourning: the result is that the feeling for Diana has resorted to rhetorical conventions which in other circumstances we would regard as out-dated. On the other hand, there is a timelessness, too, about our responses: we are surprised that so many people seemed to have a quasi-religious view of Diana. But throughout the 20th century observers have been 'surprised'. In 1935, 1936 and 1937, years of many royal events, Kingsley Martin, the editor of the *New Statesman*, was astonished at the 'recrudescence of sheer superstition' surrounding the monarchy. People endlessly spoke of 'royal weather'; there was much publicity given to a crippled Scottish boy who learnt to walk 'after' having met George V; in 1939 it was alleged that the inhabitants of Southwold crowded around George VI to 'touch' him for his magical curative powers. These stories are very similar to those which have appeared about Diana and the effect she had on the ill. Their recovery, it is said, has been 'like a miracle'; what is 20th-century about that is the care people take not to say: 'it's a miracle.' But there is no reason, even allowing for 20th-century caution, to think that the enormous fund of popular 'religion' which surprised Geoffrey Gorer in the early 1950s has much diminished. He noted the widespread belief in astrology, spiritualism, an afterlife, in the power of prayer, charms and good luck, which he attributed to the feeling of helplessness which (he thought) so many people had about their own lives. I do not think this has much changed.

The memorial literature also underlines the extent to which people believe, as Diana herself believed, that the social good depends on individual goodness, kindness, understanding and, above all, love. Some have argued that this belief stands for progress, for the emergence of a new and gentle Britain. Certainly, humane sentiments of that kind represent a repudiation of the hard-faced values dominant over the past twenty years. That this is progress, however, is more doubtful: it is highly traditional to believe that the social good is dependent on individual goodness. Moreover this way of thinking gives Diana semi-magical qualities, thereby reinforcing the age-old notion that royalty is magical. In fact, Diana's social authority depended on political powerlessness. As Freud's biographer, Ernest Jones, argued of George V (and the argument holds for Diana), once the monarch becomes divorced from the discharge of political power, once government 'decomposes' into two persons, one 'untouchable, irremovable and sacrosanct' (the king), and the other 'vulnerable in such a degree that sooner or later he will surely be destroyed' (the prime minister), the king is held to be 'above criticism'. As such, it becomes difficult for him to be unpopular. Hence the paradox of Diana's hold on our emotions: its strength was in direct relation to her political powerlessness. It is unlikely that flowers will be strewn in the path of Lady Thatcher's coffin, and she was certainly 'destroyed', but, unlike Diana, she wielded power and achieved what she wanted.

It has been widely argued that Diana's enormous popularity is a result (perhaps even a cause of) the 'feminisation' of our values, which are now thought to be softer and less aggressive, a process accompanied by the 'Catholicisation' of our public ceremonies. There may be some truth to this and it could be related to the fact that such a small proportion of the male population has had any experience of the armed forces. One thing which does seem to be new is the willingness of young men to grieve publicly in a 'feminine' way. This was very apparent both before Diana's funeral and at the funeral itself, but was first manifested after the Hillsborough disaster, when Anfield was thick with bouquets and gifts (usually Liverpool scarves). And there was nothing very Protestant about the mourning or the funeral: not merely the lack of restraint but the fact that both Earl Spencer and Prince Charles crossed themselves – an act which would have brought the monarchy down a generation ago. I doubt, however, that this is as new as it appears: the mid-Victorians, for instance, would have found it all much more familiar than we do. My guess is that the stoicism thought to be typical of the British character is a product of the later 19th century and reached its apogee in the first fifty years of the 20th. And even this is perhaps a fiction. Mass-Observation's *May 12* describes very unbuttoned crowds whose behaviour, if not extravagant, was not restrained. In a couple of cases the lack of restraint is almost suspicious. Outsiders had two stereotypes of the British: there was the famous discipline and constraint, but there were the excitable, partisan crowds, even more excitable than the Italians, especially at sporting matches. Arguably, what is exceptional in British history is not the extravagance but the stiff upper lip.

And we should remember who was being buried. The three great public funerals within living memory – George VI, Churchill and Mountbatten – were all of heroic males intimately associated with war and empire. Diana was the reverse of this, and the kind of mourning associated with them would have been wholly inappropriate for her. Diana stood for the most traditional image of woman. The first to leave flowers, cards and letters were children and they made the running. This reinforced the picture of her not as heroic but as loving mother, and a mother who cared for the outcast – her 'constituency of the rejected', as Earl Spencer rather craftily put it. More difficult to explain, as with the whole phenomenon, was the intensity with which these traditional attitudes were expressed. It was clear from the beginning that in many people's minds the Queen of Hearts was close to the Queen of Heaven. And since this queen was wounded and vulnerable the identifications became stronger. Nor is there much doubt that Diana's physical appearance, like Eva Perón's in her last days, was what many thought the Queen of Heaven's should be: blonde, beautiful and soulful. This should not be underrated.

Although Diana's appeal is largely traditional, it is also eclectic. Who else could bring the Queen Mother, Tom Cruise and Ruby Wax to the same ceremony? Her friendship with many of the heavyweights of popular culture, and their attendance at the funeral, evoked a world of strong pleasures and emotional stimulation very attractive to young adults. Again, this is not as new as it appears: the future Edward VIII, as Prince of Wales, carefully cultivated his relationships with the stars of prewar popular culture and that – what in the interwar years was always called 'glamour' – was undoubtedly an element in his enormous popularity. Then, too, the media were problematic in his life as they were in Diana's. What role they played in the days after Diana's death is, like so much else, almost unknowable, since the relationship between the media and the audience is usually reciprocal. In this case, the first steps were taken spontaneously and it is the first steps which count. The original decision to bring flowers and cards to the palaces was not the media's, although the extent of media reporting might well have made those who had not thought of doing so feel they should. Equally, the behaviour of the huge numbers who watched the hearse on its way north might have been influenced by what they had seen on television of the behaviour of the crowds in Central London, but the applauding of the hearse and the throwing of flowers at it were also clearly spontaneous – an instinctive and moving awareness of the funeral service as a rite of passage. Although it was said that to complain of the media's excessive attention to Diana in death was risky, in practice many people did complain. A guess is that large numbers thought the press was overdoing it, but were 'drawn in despite themselves', as Mass-Observation said of George VI's coronation. Such ambivalence is what we would expect; but it would be wrong to imagine that public emotion was merely worked up by the media.

In 1953, in a famous article, Edward Shils and Michael Young argued that popular celebration of the present queen's coronation marked a 'degree of moral unity equalled by no other large national state'. Can we say the same of Diana's death? In Shils and Young's terms almost certainly not. In the first place, the popular reaction to her death was international – more intense in Britain perhaps, but definitely not confined to it. Diana really was the most famous woman in the world in life and its most famous person in death. If the reaction does mark 'moral unity' it cannot be British alone. Does it mean that Britain is now more 'democratic', less deferential; that in mourning her we were, as the *Observer* put it, 'united against tradition'? There was certainly a strong whiff of 1789 in the royal family's return from Balmoral and they had a beleaguered look throughout; while the whole tone of the funeral was a long way from the House of Windsor. Our traditional elites are now held in much less respect than they were a generation ago, and that is no loss. The country's democratic potential is greater than ever: but that potential has not been realised, and the reaction to Diana's death demonstrates the limitations as well as the strengths of modern British democracy.

When Shils and Young wrote of Britain's almost unique moral unity they meant primarily that the industrial working class was more successfully integrated in Britain than in any other major country. That class now hardly exists and the political system which integrated it has not adjusted to its political and social decay. The result is that the economically and socially deprived are relatively more deprived today than they have been for over half a century, if not longer. The decline of a particular sense of the nation which Shils and Young (rightly or wrongly) identified in 1953 has left many out in the cold and no one (including the present government) is inviting them back in. The exclusion of the poor has been accompanied by the triumph of individualist ideologies and the defeat of the idea of social solidarity. This bears on Diana: those two countries where Diana worship is most intense, Britain and the United States, are not simply the two where celebrity and glamour are most admired, but where social solidarity is now weakest and individualism strongest. In them the remedy for social failure, poverty or homelessness is to be found in individual virtue. Love, care, goodness are no less valued, indeed are perhaps even more valued, but they are not thought to be found in the social sphere. The remedy for social exclusion or distress is individual action and individual virtue; the more the possessor of such virtue is associated with women's traditional qualities the more she is cherished.

When in the 19th century the Roman Catholic Church raised the Virgin in the battle against materialist or collectivist ideologies it knew what it was about. Diana, for many of the same reasons, in her turn became 'saviour of the world', as one of the posters outside Kensington Palace put it. Much that happened after Diana's death involved powerful and generous emotions; but a democracy which admired her with such intensity is both incomplete and immature, and will always exclude those who apparently made up her 'constituency'.

2 October 1997

DROWNED IN THE DESERT

James Meek on maggots

IN BULGAKOV'S *The Master and Margarita*, the killer demon Azazello has a wonderful talent. He can shoot someone in a named part of their heart – an auricle, say, or a ventricle. He puts a bullet hole through a marked spot on a seven of spades even though the card is covered by a pillow. His skill arouses Margarita, who has 'a passion for all people who do anything to perfection'.

Lee Goff's* peculiar skill evokes the same delight and horror as that of the perfect assassin, though he is dealing with the effects of other people's murders, and not doing any killing himself (except of pigs and rabbits). It is a fine thing, rare in fiction and not so common even in non-fiction, to read an account of how an expert applies his talent. It is the nearest thing to magic in the real world, and not to be despised merely because Goff's skill lies in a place where people prefer not to look: where maggots feed on the flesh of dead people.

As a founding father of the modern science of forensic entomology, Goff is most often called on to determine the time of death of a murder victim, and his accuracy can awe. He recounts a case from 1992, when the corpse of a man was found at an airbase in California. The dead man had been stabbed several times in the chest and his throat had been cut. The body was discovered at 7 p.m. on 28 April; the autopsy was on 1 May. A week later samples and data were Fedexed to Goff's Hawaii home – crime scene photos, insects from the body, soil samples and local weather information. On 14 May, he phoned in his final conclusions: the victim had been murdered between 10 p.m. and midnight on 25 April. He spoke to two detectives in turn. Both were speechless. Eventually they told him that just before he called, a suspect had confessed to killing the victim at about 10.30 p.m. on 25 April.

Neat stuff. But not many would have had the stomach for the work Goff did in the course of the week. I was glad there were no photographs in the book, only tasteful line drawings of insects. Beetles, ants, wasps, flies, mites and a centipede all parade in Goff's bestiary, but it is maggots which rock his world. Masses of maggots. There is something reassuringly democratic about the maggot nurseries our bodies become if they are left in the open, or in a shallow grave. The insects

---

*Lee Goff, *A Fly for the Prosecution: How Insect Evidence Helps Solve Crimes* (Harvard University Press, 2000).

make no distinctions of race, rank, sex, age or wealth. We're just a place for them to grow up and feed. It's more than humbling: it's heartening – we're organic, too, and in the end nature recovers the meals we've taken from it, by eating us back. Strictly speaking, of course, we're not entirely organic, and some of the hidden chemicals we contain can have the strangest effects on creatures which consume us. A forensic entomologist was baffled by the unusual size of some of the maggots on the corpse of a 20-year-old woman found stabbed to death by a logging road. It turned out that the big maggots, which had grown more than twice as fast as they should have done, had been feeding from the victim's nose, which was suffused with cocaine from years of drug abuse. The maggots thrive on Ecstasy, too.

Goff compares the human corpse to one of the Hawaiian archipelago's islands: 'A decomposing body is in some ways like a barren volcanic island that has recently emerged from the ocean,' he writes. 'A resource . . . waiting to be colonised by plants and animals.' In Hawaii's balmy climate, the insects may set to work with more speed, but the process Goff elaborates with such enthusiasm is character-istic of anywhere that is frost-free. One local species of blow fly can locate exposed human remains within ten minutes of death. The first flies arrive, feed on blood or other fluids in wounds or natural body openings, then lay their eggs there. Twelve to 18 hours later, the eggs hatch into maggots, which immediately begin feeding. These first colonists are joined by other species of fly – including the flesh fly, which doesn't lay eggs but swoops down on the body like a dive bomber and squirts out a spray of tiny hatched larvae. Meanwhile, the corpse, inflated by gas released by bacteria working within, swells and heats up. As the maggot activity peaks, further beetles, ants and wasps arrive, some to join the feast, some to prey on the maggots. Others act as parasites, aiming to use living maggots as incubators for their own offspring. The combined efforts of maggots and bacteria breach the skin of the corpse, which deflates, releasing a foul stink. (Goff calls this the Decay Stage: his graduate students in the Entomology Department of the University of Hawaii in Manoa, where he holds the chair, have come to dread the discovery of a body in this condition.) As the corpse decays, the sated maggots drift away to pupate and hatch into flies, leaving the human remains, now largely skin and bones, to specialised beetles. Finally, when all that is left is a skeleton and hair, the beetles depart. Even this is not the end of the new world a human death calls forth: tiny carrion-linked organisms and mites can stay in the soil for years.

Beyond decay, a cleaned-out human skull still makes four walls and a roof. Goff helped identify a victim found in a metal toolbox by the side of the road on the Hawaiian island of Oahu. Nothing was left of the dead man except a skeleton, wearing a short-sleeved Hawaiian shirt, pants, short jeans, socks, steel-capped construction boots, a watch and a pager. When the post-mortem began, ants started pouring out of the toolbox. They had turned the inside of the victim's skull into a nest, and a new generation of ants was about to hatch out. Goff calculated from the head-nest that 18 months had passed since the murder – information that was key to catching the killer.

Forensic entomology dates back at least to 13th-century China, when a magistrate picked out a murderer from among a crowd of peasants because his sickle alone was attracting a swarm of flies. In the Scottish Borders in 1935, an Edinburgh entomologist provided vital maggot-based evidence in the notorious Ruxton case, involving the dismembered bodies of two women, Isabella Ruxton and her maid Mary Rogerson. Ruxton's husband, Buck, a local doctor, was convicted of the murder. Yet only in the US has the field extended to the point where it is now not unusual to have forensic entomologists on both the defence and prosecution sides.

Partly this is thanks to Goff and his colleagues, who in 1984 set up CAFE, supposedly standing for the Council of American Forensic Entomologists but actually indicating that they met in cafés. Not much more was asked of members than that they could look at pictures of decomposing corpses while eating breakfast. Partly it is thanks to the fact that America both provides the sheer quantity of dumped corpses required to sustain such a specialism, and has the open-mindedness to take a man such as Goff – first cautiously, then eagerly – into the fold of the criminal justice system.

Goff, whose university gave him tenure on the understanding he would study the effects of insects on agriculture, is a silver-haired individual with a wide beard, a diamond stud in his left ear and a fondness for the gaudy shirts of his islands. He tends to arrive at the morgue or the scene of the crime on a Harley Davidson. When he first began offering his services to Hawaiian investigators, they didn't call him: he would call them, after reading in the papers about the discovery of a badly decomposed corpse. The authorities realised he was more than a transient figure when he started bringing students along. Marianne Early, for example, joined him in 1984 to gather maggots from the 19-day-old corpse of a murdered woman found close to Pearl Harbor. Early, Goff writes with a certain pedagogic affection, 'had been conducting decomposition studies on pig and cat carcasses on various parts of the island of Oahu'.

Now that forensic entomology has become a routine part of investigations, the medical examiner calls Goff, who shows every sign of relishing the call-outs. He is the kind of man who seems to like being summoned from a family get-together on New Year's Eve for an 'enjoyable' motorbike ride along the north shore of Oahu to the scene of a horrible murder – a dead woman wrapped in two blankets with a centipede moving between them, for example – where he collects maggots, beetles and other samples, takes them to his lab, rides home, then showers and changes in time to rejoin the family for their holiday dinner.

One result of the growth of forensic entomology is the increased killing of pigs. Goff slays them to simulate the effects of decay on human corpses in different conditions. He has left trios of dead pigs all over Hawaii and watched the flies and beetles strip them down. He ran into trouble early on in his studies when the university's Institutional Animal Care and Use Committee questioned whether it was ethical to shoot three 50lb domestic pigs through the head with a .38 calibre pistol in order to simulate murdered humans. In the end it was deemed ethical enough, providing a policeman, rather than an entomologist, took the pigs out.

Since then Goff has burned pigs, hanged pigs and buried a pig in his own backyard under the curious eyes of his neighbours to try to understand decomposition in different cases. He still runs into trouble once in a while; he is indignant that he has to get the consent of eight public agencies to place a decomposing pig in the tidal area of Coconut Island, half a mile from a tourist centre. But each year he now gets to conceal five dead pigs in the woods behind the FBI Academy in Quantico, Virginia, for the benefit of student agents: a pig rolled in a rug, a pig hanged from a tree, a pig dumped in the open, a pig in a shallow grave and so on.

Goff first hanged a pig to solve a time-of-death conundrum involving a man found hanging from a tree on a Hawaii golf course. It took a long time to identify him because in life he was only five foot two, but suspended in death over what turned out to be 19 days, his body stretched till it was six feet long. That didn't explain why the body had decayed so slowly. Thanks to his pig on a gibbet, Goff discovered the simple explanation: the maggots, taking a breather on the skin of the corpse, just fell off, and couldn't climb back up.

The strangest part of the case was the behaviour of the visiting Japanese golfer who discovered the body. The tourist's ball, aimed at the 16th hole, flew into the rough, bounced off the hanging man's head and dropped to the ground directly underneath the corpse. Noting the body, the golfer nonetheless decided to play through, and finished his game before reporting the corpse at the clubhouse. Goff might not have mentioned the fact had it not made his job more difficult. Put off his game by the proximity of a dead body, the golfer had needed several swings to play the ball out of the rough, destroying the 'drip zone' under the body that is such a boon to insects.

Occasionally Goff strays a little deeply into the realm of the technical. In parts the book could almost have been written as a text for his students. Yet it is still not detailed enough for some. He received a series of disturbing e-mails from someone who demanded to know how entomological evidence might be altered to prevent accurate estimation of post-mortem interval – as if the e-mailer wanted to commit the perfect crime. Writers of murder mysteries, indeed writers of any kind, will find plenty to nourish their darkest imaginations here (the ants-in-the-skull case, and another involving a wasps' nest in the head of the corpse of a 15-year-old girl, are reminiscent of a core moment of horror in Iain Banks's *The Wasp Factory*). But as Goff points out, there are fewer murders in Hawaii than island-based TV series like *Magnum* and *Hawaii Five-O* suggest. He might have added, if the stories he tells hadn't made it unnecessary to spell it out, that for all the indifference of maggots, they seldom get to feed on the bodies of the rich and the beautiful. Just as Inspector Morse's real-life counterpart seldom comes across dead dons, aristos or corpses in cloistered quads, the corpses of Hawaii are usually of the disadvantaged, the dispossessed and the desperate, killed in rages and stupors or at the culmination of sexual frustration, petty schemes and banal grudges. Goff has the delicacy never to name victims he has worked on, like the pregnant woman strangled by her druggie husband and left in a cupboard in their flat for eight days while the man and their 20-month-old daughter went on living there. All the husband could remember was that he had strangled his wife 'a little over a week ago'. Investigation doesn't always involve corpses: the size of maggots in children's nappies or on old people is used in court to prove the scale of neglect on the part of parents or carers. One case, involving a 16-month-old girl abandoned in the Oahu bush, was appealed all the way to the Hawaiian Supreme Court on the basis that Goff's testimony about maggots was so graphic that the revolted jury would have been unduly prejudiced against the accused. At times like these, Goff's detachment breaks down. 'I imagine that it was indeed difficult to feel sympathy for a mother who had abandoned her child,' he reflects. 'Particularly if maggots were involved.'

The fresher the corpse, the worse. The more decomposed a body, the less it looks to Goff like a person:

> I try to maintain my detachment by concentrating on the intense activity taking place on and around the corpse. In Hawaii, there are over two hundred different kinds of insects and other arthropods that may be associated with a decomposing human corpse. The longer the remains have been exposed to insect activity, the greater the diversity of insects and the more complex the puzzle I have to solve. Each insect is doing something different, and I frequently become so involved in the task of interpreting their activities that I can almost forget they are on a corpse.

Goff's relatively low-tech approach to forensic entomology, with its roots in experience, observation and dead pigs, may be overshadowed by new advances in DNA analysis. Some of his students hope to begin analysing bed bugs for traces of human DNA from the blood of sleepers. The spaces in which we live are filled with potential witnesses, munching on microscopic bits we shower in our wake, and eventually science may be able to call these witnesses to the stand. Until then, insect-based justice relies on Goff and others like him, popping corpse maggots and pupae in vials, speeding back to the lab on his Harley, feeding them beef liver, studying them to see how they develop and drawing his conclusions.

Murder is not the only form of death where forensic entomology is called on. In 1992, Goff helped clear up the mystery of two hikers, a man and a woman, found a hundred feet apart, close to a trail on the north rim of the Grand Canyon. The woman had a splint on her leg. The post-mortem showed they had drowned – yet their bodies lay in an arid desert area. Goff studied weather data, soil samples and a dozen different sets of insects from the corpses which were couriered to him in an extremely smelly package. Examining the maggots of three species of blow fly and of one species of flesh fly, together with adult maggot-eating rove beetles, he came up with a time for the deaths: the evening of 21 August, five days before the hikers were found. It turned out, when weather records were checked, that there had been heavy rain in another part of the Canyon that night, enough to cause flash flooding in the place where the bodies were discovered. The couple appeared to have left the marked trail and been forced to spend the night on the canyon floor after the woman fell and broke her leg. The flood hit them without warning and swept them downstream before the waters dispersed and evaporated, leaving their bodies a hundred feet apart. The heat of the day quickly dried them out and the insects arrived – the insects which were later to tell Goff the story of how a man and a woman drowned in the desert.

20 July 2000

TOO BAD ABOUT MRS FERRI

August Kleinzahler

O N A F I N E, late October afternoon in 1957 I came home from school to a great commotion at the foot of the block where we lived. TV trucks and news reporters were clustered at the gates to the long drive leading up to Albert Anastasia's enormous Spanish Mission-style home. The Palisades section of Fort Lee, New Jersey, then as now, was a sleepy, leafy enclave, overlooking the Upper West Side, a mile or so across the Hudson.

My mother came out the front door of our house, walked up to me, knelt down, and said: 'Augie, Gloriana's daddy got very, very sick, and Gloriana and her mommy are going to have to go away for a while, so Gloriana won't be coming over to play.' Gloriana's daddy sure did get sick. Albert Anastasia, head of Murder Incorporated and capo of the Mangano family, had been assassinated that morning at 10.20 while getting a shave at the Park Sheraton Hotel on Seventh Avenue.

The Gallo brothers made the hit: Joseph 'Crazy Joe', Larry, and Albert 'Kid Blast'. They were accompanied by an ugly little torpedo named Joseph 'Joe Jelly' Giorelli, who finished the job with a bullet to the back of Anastasia's head. These four were the aces of Joseph Profaci's hit squad. But the order had come from higher up, from Vito Genovese himself. Anastasia was whacked because he was too dangerous. His appetite for killing had made him reckless and a liability, and the other mobsters had called him (behind his back of course) the 'mad hatter'.

It wasn't very considerate of him to kill our plumber, Mr Ferri. Reliable plumbers are hard to come by; they were then, they are now. Mr Ferri was Anastasia's plumber as well and he must have seen something he wasn't supposed to see. The Feds put Mr Ferri and his wife in the witness protection programme, down south in some Miami suburb. Ha, ha, ha. Who the fuck did they think they were dealing with, huh? Too bad about Mrs Ferri. But on balance my folks found Anastasia an exemplary neighbour. He minded his own business and was very polite when their paths crossed. I'm not sure when that was, given that Anastasia tended to keep odd hours and spent a lot of time in his Oldsmobile luxury sedan going back and forth between Jersey and New York, driven by his most trusted bodyguard, Anthony 'Tough Tony' Coppola. 'Courtly', was how my parents described Anastasia.

I don't suppose it was Tough Tony who brought little Gloriana to my parents' house every day and baby-sat for the two of us while my mother went off shopping or visited friends. It was some other affectless gorilla with a shoulder-holster. 'Play-a nice children,' he would say if things started going to hell in the sandpit. Apart from Gloriana and her mommy it was my mother who was most saddened by Anastasia's untimely death. For with him went the best baby-sitter on earth. Mother knew that if anything, anything at all, happened to either of us, the baby-sitter would have his dick shot off.

New Jersey was famous for gangsters way ahead of *The Sopranos*, and Fort Lee most famous of all. Like Walt Whitman before them, a number of enterprising souls had come over to the 'Left Bank' from Brooklyn. Guys like Willie Moretti, Tony Bender and Joe Adonis, né Doto, who took the name Adonis on account he was so fucking good-looking. The 'Al Capone of New Jersey' was another good-looking guy named Longy Zwillman, whose favourite party trick was to produce from his wallet a pubic hair belonging to Jean Harlow, with whom he'd had a hot affair.

The local headquarters for these men was an Italian restaurant called Duke's Place in Cliffside Park, the next town south from Fort Lee. My folks went there quite often because it was close by and the food was good. That is, until my mother, who is given to irrepressible asides about people's appearance and speculation about their personal lives, remarked to my father one evening at Duke's: 'How old could that little blonde number be over there with those two hoods?' My mother does not have a small voice and this met with a poor, but not fatal, response. My father was not given to asides, but tended in his younger days to grow very agitated in restaurants when he felt the service was lackadaisical. This is a circumspect way of putting it, but my father is still alive and reads this journal. One evening at another local hood joint, probably Joe's Elbow Room, my parents hadn't even received a menu after sitting there for twenty minutes. The place was empty aside from a plenary council of silk suits involved in a confab over some ziti. Having enjoyed many episodes of my father's behaviour in such situations, I shudder to think what might have happened next. Fortunately one of those silk suits belonged to Mr Anastasia. The folks were served with remarkable dispatch, and the pasta was *al dente*, as my father liked it.

Fort Lee was, in those days, a vivid little town, not the usual American suburb. My family lived at the southern end, a couple of blocks from Cliffside Park and only three blocks from one of the largest amusement parks in America, where for six months of the year you could hear the screams of people riding the Whip or the Cyclone, the giant roller-coaster.

At the north end of town was the George Washington Bridge and just above the bridge a famous hood nightclub called the Riviera, which always booked star entertainers and put on gala floor shows. But it was more famous for its plush gambling casino at the back, the Marine Room, which was off-limits to ordinary patrons. The Marine Room was run by the Zwillman-Moretti syndicate. One of the star acts at the Riviera was Frank Sinatra, a skinny Jersey boy from down the road in Hoboken. Moretti took a shine to Sinatra, whom he probably first saw perform as a singer-waiter at a little roadhouse called the Rustic Cabin in the next town north, Englewood. He helped the youngster get some band dates. Later on, Sinatra signed with Tommy Dorsey, became a star, and then wanted out of his contract. Dorsey wasn't having any of it, however, at least not until Moretti jammed a gun down his throat, petitioning the band-leader to exercise reason and good judgment.

Twenty years ago, shortly after I came to live in San Francisco, my cousin Seymour, who lived in Mill Valley and for a time had been Sinatra's agent, or one of them, took me to dinner at the Fairmont Hotel on Nob Hill. Seymour was showbiz and liked to make a flash impression. After dinner he made me drink a sambuca with a coffee bean in it. He told me this was what classy guys drink. I asked him if Sinatra was Mob. Without missing a beat, Seymour laughed and said: 'Are you kidding, Frankie's a pussycat; he couldn't hurt a fly, even if he tried. He just likes to pretend he's a gangster.' Which is presumably what he was doing in 1946 when he posed in Havana for a photo-op with his arm around Lucky Luciano's shoulder. Another nice picture shows him with Carlo Gambino, who was the intermediary between Vito Genovese and Joseph Profaci in the Anastasia hit: Frankie-boy is smiling in his dressing-room at the Premier Theater in Westchester, New York, next to Carlo and the hit-man (later informer) Jimmy 'the Weasel' Fratianno and three other hoods later convicted and sentenced for fraud and skimming the theatre's box office.

Frank, who was a good son, bought a lovely home for his mother, Dolly, in Fort Lee. I'm sure Dolly enjoyed her stay, even if she missed some of the gang from her local ward in Hoboken, where she did quite a few favours for the local big shots. Fort Lee in those days was about 98 per cent Italian. There were a few Jewish families, like mine, a couple of Greek families, an Irish family, an Armenian family, but everyone else was Southern Italian. You might as well have been in Palermo, except the buildings were newer.

David Chase, *The Sopranos*' creator, grew up in Essex County. Fort Lee is Bergen County, but never you mind. I played as a child with Tony Soprano and his pals, if you can imagine them as eight-year-olds. During recess and the lunch hour the schoolyard at #4 Elementary School in Fort Lee was like a theme park for Tourette's Syndrome. There is a scene in *Scarface*, the movie by Brian De Palma (born Newark, NJ, Essex County), in which Al Pacino is sitting in the bath, cranked up on coke, and launched on a rant, when his ice-goddess new wife, played by Michelle Pfeiffer, says something like: 'Are you capable of finishing a whole sentence without repeating the word *fuck*?' Sometimes there was a bit of *va fungule*. Other popular terms of abuse were 'faggot' and 'douche'. The use of the latter is somewhat mysterious: it was directed exclusively at other males and no one had any idea what a douche-bag was. It was also bellowed out in a particular fashion, in order to achieve maximum release for the diphthong. Duckie Juliano was a master of this art. One time I called someone a son of a bitch, which must have sounded preposterously foreign and Noël Coward-like. All activity ceased, and I was viciously assaulted by Tommy Grumulia and Anthony Delvecchio. Boys are formed by the playgrounds they come from. Ours was violent, noisy and profane, somewhat operatic in the Italian manner. But there were no guns or knives and no one ever got seriously hurt, except when Louis Boccia tore off most of his ear after running too close to the cyclone fence during a game of *salugi*. But it got sewn back on, almost like new.

Not long after Mrs Anastasia and Gloriana went away, the big house was bought by Buddy Hackett, a fat little funny-man who had a successful TV and lounge act. He looked rather cherubic, in a greasy way, with his button nose and chubby cheeks, and this allowed him to get away with stories and jokes that were quite blue for the time. Also, he had a peculiar way of speaking, almost a speech defect. He had a thick Brooklyn accent and his voice seemed to live moistly in the back of his throat, the effect much compounded by what seemed to be marbles or acorns or jelly-beans in his mouth. Each word or phrase had a messy, difficult birth. His pièce de résistance was his Chinese waiter routine, in which he put a rubber band over his head and face so his eyes narrowed like a Chinese. In the sketch Hackett took an order from a table at a restaurant, and when it was time for dessert, he would intone, in his Brooklyn-Chinese accent: 'OK, who the wise-guy with the kumquat?'

After dinner one night my parents told me to go get Buddy Hackett's autograph. My parents had no interest in Buddy Hackett's autograph. They hardly ever watched TV and were convinced I was mildly retarded because I did. No, they were sending me forth, in their endearing Jersey City way, as a trial balloon.

I had never been to the big house. Gloriana and the gorilla always came to me. But I knocked at the door. A frightened, bewildered Hispanic maid in uniform opened it. I gave my little talk: 'I'm Augie Kleinzahler from down the street and I would like Mr Hackett's autograph, please.' The maid, looking stricken, disappeared, and next up was a woman I took to be Mrs Hackett. She said something mildly discouraging but I didn't budge, knowing better than to return home without a result. At which point Mrs Hackett disappeared.

I immediately registered the cause of their apprehension when the famous entertainer himself came waddling to the front door. He was barely taller than I was, and I was seven years old. He was red-faced and breathing moistly and with some difficulty, like a toy bulldog on a sultry day. 'Whuh da you want, kid?' he asked in one of America's most distinctive voices. I identified myself, told him where I lived and asked for his autograph. He glared at me, incredulous, for a few moments (I could sense the wife and maid cowering inside) and said: 'Fuck you, kid; talk to my agent!' And slammed the door in my face.

I stood there briefly, considering my options, then turned and walked down the long driveway. It was a pleasant summer evening, fragrant, the maples in leaf, and the air filled with cries of terror from the nearby amusement park. I found my parents where I had left them, on the back porch, reading. My mother looked up from her book and smiled. 'Well?' she said. 'He said: "Fuck you, kid, talk to my agent."' My father went back to his book. My mother, for what seemed a long time, stared at me over her reading glasses. 'Well,' she asked, 'did you at least get his agent's name and phone number?'

20 September 2001

NO BAIL FOR MR X

John Upton

To enter Greenwich magistrates court you must first go through an airport-style metal detector which squeals at the slightest provocation. The court is a small Victorian building with wood-panelled courtrooms that lead off a waiting area with a mosaic floor. A few rows of green metal seats are bolted to this floor and there is a drinks machine in one corner. To find out which courtroom you are appearing in, you have to look at the printed lists which are pinned up on one of the walls. There are no specific times given for hearings so when you get to appear in court is a matter of luck, persistence and whether your client (or lawyer, if you're a client) turns up early or not. The atmosphere in an old court like this is best likened to that of an understaffed Accident and Emergency Department in which none of the patients wants to be treated.

I am here to represent a man who is already serving a custodial sentence for burglary. He is being 'produced' from his prison today to appear in court for the first time for another burglary, allegedly committed at around the same time as the one for which he has served almost a year. Forty minutes ago, I was sitting in my chambers reading a novel, unemployed for the day. Now, furnished only with the above information which has been phoned in from Mr X's solicitors, I begin a routine which is typical of many days in my working life.

Fifteen minutes of questioning various court officials establishes for certain that Mr X is actually going to arrive at this particular court on this particular day.

Eventually the list-caller in Court Number One, the woman who decides on the order that cases appear in court, comes to see me as I sit in the waiting area and tells me that the police officer in the case of Mr X is here. The policeman comes out of the courtroom. His head is shaved and he is wearing a shirt and tie and suit trousers. He is in his thirties and has the hard look of a Met CID man. Immediately he begins to explain that the reason this matter has taken so long to come to court (the point he thinks I'll be raising in front of the magistrate) is that they have been waiting nearly a year for forensic evidence taken from the scene to come back from the laboratory. It's certainly not the first time I've heard this one. It is frequently used by the prosecution as a catch-all excuse for being unprepared and it's a sure-fire adjournment-getter. It just so happens, however, that Mr X has only two weeks of his current sentence left to run, so this fresh allegation, brought at this time, will ruin any chance of Mr X being released in the near-future.

The morning list of cases is almost finished. The CID man outlines the basis of the charge: the burglary, the threats to shoot (although he admits that no gun has ever been found) and the million-to-one chance that the DNA is not that of my client. I thank him and go to the cells.

To get to them I press a doorbell and am let into a small holding chamber. I identify myself to a guard who is sitting behind a perspex screen and another door opens automatically. I enter a waiting area with a reception desk. There are a number of guards standing around in their green shirts and trousers. They attempt to intimidate. They stare and smirk and make comments under their breath. The atmosphere is unhealthily confrontational and it seems that my client is in large part responsible for this. He is a violent man, I'm told. The staring continues and I try to make small talk as I sign the visitors' book, in which I have to list my client's name, the time of my arrival in the cells and the name of the solicitor's firm to which I belong. (In a reflex act of snobbery I write 'Counsel' in the last column, an indulgence which will antagonise the guards who seem to have a Khmer Rouge-like capacity for hatred of anything they perceive to be too bourgeois.) My efforts are met with further hostility. A number of guards are chewing gum with an air of casual aggression.

It isn't the same in every court cell area. Once, on a visit to another set of cells, I listened to the guard at the reception desk singing Irish folk songs that echoed down the corridors where the prisoners were being held and were painfully poignant. In another, one of my clients had been awarded the unofficial freedom of the jail. The guards did not lock him into his cell, allowed him unlimited use of the telephone and made sure he received enough visits from his fiancée and friends. Given that it was strictly forbidden to have any visitors other than lawyers this was quite an achievement. What had he done to receive such treatment? He was, I gathered sub-sequently, supplying the chief jailer at court with drugs that he was bringing with him from prison.

Here, at this court in a high crime area, dealing with all manner of 'real villains', as the argot has it, things are different and the cell staff have managed to perfect an ambience of barely restrained thuggery in an attempt, no doubt, to meet fire with fire. Incongruous in all of this, an island of oestrogen in a turbulent sea of testosterone, is a heavily made-up woman who is in charge of the signing-in book. In contrast to the short haircuts of her male colleagues, she sports a teased, hennaed, lacquered concoction and long varnished nails. Instead of their Doc Martens, she wears Cuban-heeled suede pixie boots and trousers tapered to lie flatteringly along the line of her leg. I am pleased to note, however, that she has not dispensed with the sneering unhelpfulness which makes theirs and everybody else's job that much more difficult.

To her left is a whiteboard with the names of prisoners written in felt-tip against the number of the cell in which they are being kept. She writes my name up against that of my client. Then I walk further along the corridor to a wall of bars which fills the space from floor to ceiling. A number of guards stand on the other side of this obstacle and I shout: 'To see Mr X, please.' One of the guards pushes himself off the wall on which he is leaning like a schoolboy told to stop hanging about in the playground and get to lessons. He unlocks a section of the bars. They swing outwards and I step through the entrance, then it is locked behind me. He points to one of the cells but does not speak. The cells have small blackboards fastened to the wall outside them with the names of the prisoners chalked up. The wicket of Mr X's cell is pulled up fully: I press the catch to release the plate covering the hole in the door, which is at head height, and it slides down. Mr X is pacing up and down his cell furiously.

'All right mate, all right mate. Let's go to the interview room, let's go to the interview room, let's get into that fucking interview room.'

Mr X's eyes are wide open with annoyance. He is a small man with a lean face and a wiry, strong frame. He has the instantly recognisable look of the incarcerated, an inner shadow which shows through the pallid skin of the face and flickers in the eyes. It is strange to be part of a prisoner's world, for however brief a time; to have to ask whenever you want a door opened or a petty request granted, to have to beg repeatedly for a light for a fag or to use the toilet. It is disturbing to witness an adult reduced to a state of dependence which we are used to seeing only in young children and the elderly. I turn to the guard.

'Can we use the interview room?' He shrugs his shoulders and unlocks the interview room door across the corridor from the cell. Then he unlocks Mr X and stands aside to let him go by, rather like a matador allowing a fresh bull to charge past his arched body.

The interview room is ten feet square. There is a table bolted to the floor and fixed benches on either side of it. One of the benches runs the length of the wall, the other is smaller, extending no further than the edge of the table. The smaller of the benches is for the lawyer. There is a panic button at shoulder height on the wall next to this seat. The guard locks us in. Mr X holds an envelope stuffed with papers, which he immediately spreads on the table. He sorts them into well ordered piles with the precision of a croupier dealing out cards in a casino. 'The cozzas tried to take these off me this morning.'

Again, it is difficult to imagine just how hard it must be to keep a collection of belongings together in prison, especially when those belongings are documents compiled in order to assist one's defence. The fact that he has these papers here today signifies a triumph over random searches, sudden transfers and beatings – all the harshness of prison life. Mr X has been a heroin addict, it was the fuel on which his offending ran. But here is a certificate to show that he has passed random drug tests, correspondence with drug counsellors and, most important, a letter stating that he has been accepted onto an intensive treatment programme which is due to start the week after his release from prison.

Mr X also has a notebook in which he has painstakingly recorded the chronology of his case. His handwriting is like that of a six-year-old. Each one of the characters in that notebook must have been a source of immense effort to Mr X and he is determined to vent his frustration. He is not aggressive. I feel no threat because he is not communicating with me: he is reciting a piece that has been rehearsed over many months. It is a litany of delay and obfuscation on the part of the prosecuting authorities: Mr X suspects that they have allowed this matter to lie dormant until now so that his dreams of liberty will be dashed, and the drug placement that he has gone to such lengths to arrange will be lost.

When he has finished, he tells me that he would like a bail application made on his behalf so I take some personal details about his wife, his children, the fragmented home life of the professional criminal; then he thumps the door and the guard unlocks it. 'See you up there, mate,' he says to me and is locked back in his cell.

The prosecutor crosses the deserted waiting area holding his packed lunch. I call him over. He is thin with a wispy beard, black-framed spectacles and a dusty, ill-fitting pinstripe suit. From behind the front-of-house information desk, he fishes out the prosecution file on Mr X.

'He's a nasty man,' he says. 'He dangled a policeman by his legs over the side of a multi-storey car park.' The prosecutor produces Mr X's previous convictions. The list runs to four pages dating back to 1995. All the offences are either for violence or theft. 'I haven't got his entire record.'

The prosecutor tells me that if we are successful in winning bail today, which will of course be merely technical until his release on the other charge, he is going to appeal the decision. End of conversation. The prosecutor walks off. I realise that Mr X is correct, that his attempt at redemption will not be allowed to succeed.

'Anyone here for Mr X?' I call out in the waiting area. Sitting near the entrance are two women and a girl of about fourteen. I know that I have seen the girl somewhere before.

'Yes.' The younger of the two women raises her hand. She is dressed in a black leather jacket, trousers and cowboy boots. Her skin is taut over high cheekbones and she looks a little like Billie Whitelaw. This is Mr X's wife and the older woman is his mother-in-law who is to stand as surety for him this afternoon. I tell them that he's bearing up and Mrs X says: 'He hasn't done this. He always puts his hands up to anything he's done.' She asks me whether I've heard about the police-dangling incident, and when I express surprise at how lenient the sentence was (he received six months in the magistrates court) she tells me it's because they had photographs taken of Mr X chained to a hospital bed after being beaten senseless by the cozzas.

'Of course,' she says, 'he was on the gear at the time so he looked even worse.' The photos had been shown to the magistrate, who had sentenced him there and then, rather than sending the case to the crown court. She says that Mr X's bark is worse than his bite and how he's always (well, almost always) managing to give Old Bill the slip.

'That's why they hate him so much.' She laughs, the mother-in-law laughs and the girl laughs. Mrs X tells me about the time Mr X hid underwater in a stream to avoid being tracked by a police helicopter. To her he's a hero.

'Where do I know you from?' I ask the girl. She is one of Mr X's daughters.

'You represented my boyfriend last week.' She tells me his name and it comes back to me. I acted for him in the youth court, where he was charged with an offence of violence.

We are all in court. Mr X is in the dock surrounded by guards and his family are sitting in the public gallery behind him. I am sitting next to the prosecutor in the well of the court and the stipendiary magistrate is giving Mr X some bad news. He indicates that it will be a waste of my time making an application for bail because no matter how sympathetic he may be to the arguments advanced on behalf of my client, he is not prepared to grant it, even technically, because Mr X is a serving prisoner. His decision is expressed in fluent legalese with mention of statutory powers and sub-sections of the Bail Act and is muttered rapidly to his clerk, the prosecutor and me. Mr X, who clearly hasn't understood or probably even heard a word of this, spits, 'Let him do what he has to do,' and eyeballs the magistrate like a gunfighter in a Western. The magistrate formally remands him in custody to appear here again in seven days' time. There's a momentary calm before the storm and then Mr X lets out a guttural, now wailing, now snarling, 'Fuuuuuuuuuuuck.' It is a call to arms, a summoning of strength. I turn round but the guards have already bundled him out of the dock and into the cells.

The magistrate looks embarrassed. For a moment, the ordered world of British

Justice and the violent reality of the people who inhabit the system have collided. I bow and utter the stock response of the unsuccessful advocate.

'I'm grateful, sir,' I say automatically and walk out of the court. Moments later, the detective in the case comes for me, looking flustered.

'He wants to see you.'

This time when I enter the cell area, all the guards are massed around the reception desk. The detective stands with them. It seems they have had a struggle and they are flushed and out of breath. No one speaks. They stare at me but this time without the studied arrogance. Violence is near at hand and it has concentrated their minds. It is very tense. I look around for some indication of what I should do but none comes. Eventually I speak. 'I'd better go and see him.'

Two of the guards walk down with me to his cell. Before we reach it, one of them says: 'Remember, you can speak to him through the wicket. You don't have to go into the room if you don't want to.' And now, having lit the touchpaper, he stands well back and waits for the fireworks. I pull down the plate and, recalling the various horror stories about people leaning too far through the wicket hole and having their noses bitten off or turds stuffed in their mouths, keep my head well away from the opening. Mr X looms large. 'I want to go into that room, into that fucking room. NOW.'

I am scared. 'Are you sure you're all right?' is all I can think of to say.

'Yes. I'm sure.'

I turn to the guards who have retreated up the corridor. 'I'll see him in the interview room.'

As he lets me into the room, the guard says: 'Sit by the panic button. Use it if you need us.'

And then Mr X is in and the door is locked.

'I didn't even get a chance to smile at my wife,' he shouts. 'I didn't understand a fucking word of that.' I explain to him what has happened and his angry eyes whip over my features, sizing me up. In desperation I ask him about the dangling policeman. Suddenly he lets out a rueful laugh.

'How do you know about that?' he asks, chuckling despite himself.

'I've seen your form.' He asks to have a look at his record and I show him the four sheets.

'Have they got my whole life here?' he asks. I tell him they haven't.

'If he fucking tries to talk to me on the journey back, I'm going to punch his fucking head,' he says about his police chaperone and, because he seems to have decided not to punch mine, I agree that this would be a perfectly reasonable course of conduct. I tell him that he can go for bail next week – 'when the position is clearer,' I waffle. We don't mention the drugs programme. There is a tacit under-standing between us that it has gone and suddenly he seems diminished: where there was aggression there is now only a bitter acceptance of what has happened, and for the last few moments of our meeting he disengages from me entirely, as if pushing off from the shore on a long winter journey.

As I leave the cell area, the guards and the policeman once again stare, this time with curiosity. The CID man asks, 'Everything all right?' and as nonchalantly as I can, I reply: 'Yep. He's fine now.' But my voice is shaking.

Mr X's wife and daughter are the only ones left in the waiting area. A muted light filters through the windows. Mrs X is anxious to leave as she has to pick up her other children from school in half an hour. They will be back next week.

'Say hello to your boyfriend from me,' I say to the girl as they get up to leave.

'He's up for a burglary next Thursday,' she replies and her mother laughs.

'Don't do what I did,' she says. 'Get rid of him.' But her daughter isn't listening. She is smiling with pride at the thought of him. Then the two of them walk under the arch of the metal detector, out into the full light, ready to stand by their men. Again.

29 October 1998

HOW'S THE EMPRESS?

James Wood on Graham Swift

RUMMAGING AROUND, in a notebook entry of 1896, for the properly grim place to deposit his unfortunate heroine, Maisie Farange, Henry James alights on Folkestone, and with grey satisfaction asks himself: 'Don't I get an effect from *Folkestone*?' James does indeed get an 'effect', in *What Maisie Knew*, from Folkestone: from the name, from the town, from its seaside hotel, from the 'cold beef and Apollinaris' consumed by Maisie and her stepfather.

There is a kind of Folkestone tradition: Eliot with Margate in *The Waste Land*, Pinter with Sidcup in *The Caretaker*, Ian McEwan with Dollis Hill in *The Innocent*. Graham Swift knows all about such effects, and knows – as Pinter does – that they will probably now be self-conscious, deliberate dives into the sublime banal. Nowadays a novelist's characters may themselves be knowingly aware of the effects of place. Swift's new novel* returns to the South-West London of his first two books. It is set in Wimbledon, but ventures, if that is the word, to Putney, to Hammersmith, to Chislehurst, even to Broadstairs. His two chief characters, George Webb, a private detective, and Sarah Nash, his client, grew up in Chislehurst, and are much taken with the apparently true fact that the Emperor Napoleon III and the Empress Eugénie lived for many years on the site of what is now the Chislehurst golf club. (Forget the Napoleon of Notting Hill.) In a novel intensely and explicitly interested in cliché and banality, it is hard not to hear an ironic grimace in a passage like this: 'Putney High Street: the blaze of shops. Superdrug, Body Shop, Marks and Spencer.' These particular shops a blaze? Only to a suburban fire-eater. This passage continues, daring the reader to rebel against its flatness: 'Past the station, through the traffic lights, the climb up Putney Hill. Then the roundabout at Tibbet's Corner and the turn for Wimbledon. Less than a mile from Putney Vale.'

This is how, chapter after chapter, Swift's new novel is written, and there may be readers so incredulous at the even grey of its stylistic climate that they feel the need to take a warmer holiday after only a few pages, convinced that some cold literary game is being played on them. They would be mistaken, because the novel's commitment to ordinary speech only shows what games most literary novels really are. *The Light of Day* is narrated by George Webb, a bent (though honourably bent)

---

*Graham Swift, *The Light of Day* (Hamish Hamilton, 2003).

ex-policeman, now a private eye with an office in the middle of Wimbledon. First-person narration (and its posher cousin, stream of consciousness) is almost always a giant fudge. A novel's narrator, supposedly 'speaking' to the reader, generally writes to the reader, since few writers dare to smother their only eloquence; even Faulkner's narrators, particularly in As I Lay Dying (a novel that had some influence on Swift's Last Orders), sound little like children or illiterates. Meanwhile, stream of consciousness, apparently the most realistic of modes, is the mandarin's way of slowing down literary detail, the better to pluck its lustres; surely no one ever thought that Leopold Bloom, rather than Joyce, would notice and document 'the flabby gush of porter' and 'the buzzing prongs' of a fork in just those fine words?

But The Light of Day is as close to seeming spoken as any novel I have read. It dares the ordinariness of flat, repetitive, unliterate narration. Perhaps this doesn't sound daring; but it is certainly risky. A writer must have a very steady hand to maintain a truly flat voice over two hundred pages: 'Cooking. It was something for her too, a bit of a thing, a passion. And once life had been, maybe, a kind of constant, regular feast. I saw it, never having lived it, exactly, myself. Dinner parties, pulling of corks. Windows lit up, through the trees . . . I'd learned to cook. Discovered, in fact, a bit of a flair.' V.S. Pritchett, whose music can be heard in Swift's novel (Pritchett, like Swift, was very fond of that shy petty-bourgeois English apology, 'a bit of a'), never kept up this kind of voice for longer than a novella. And even Pritchett tended to use vernacular in a too literary way, like someone consciously trying to turn Chekhov into English. Even Pritchett would have faltered at 'Golf – it's not exactly action, but it isn't sitting on your arse.'

Swift's dare is worth the risks, however. The book's pleasures, slowly coddled, take time to mature, but in the process they teach you the art of reading slowly and carefully, of maturing with the story. And even flatness has angles. Time and again, the reader notices with what precision Swift ventriloquises his ordinary narrator. A fugitive lyricism begins to appear. 'Late October. The clocks about to go back. Now more things could happen in the dark.' Verbally, there could hardly be anything flatter than that last sentence, yet how finely it summarises a wintry resignation, combined with an almost suburban prurience (we know what kinds of thing go on in the dark). And that is exactly how a policeman might think of long winter nights: as the cover under which 'more things could happen,' more crimes. Or take the following sentence. George visits his former client, with whom he is in love, every fortnight in prison. He parks near the nick, then walks away from it, to a café where he gets his lunch before the visit proper. About this street, he comments: 'A street of houses, houses with a prison handy.' Again, the extreme vernacular relaxation. But how marvellously odd that word 'handy' is. Who would ever think of a prison as 'handy'? Yet the phrase conveys, pictorially, the view many of us have seen of a street end-stopped, as it were, by a prison (or a factory or a football ground). Such streets are completely different from their serried neighbours, since they are institutional cul-de-sacs. Such streets do indeed, in a way, have a prison handy, as one might think of a football ground or a park. And again, this is just how George might think. Most people would imagine a street with a prison at its end to be a miserable place. But George knows this street well, has been walking down it every fortnight for two years, and to him it is indeed 'handy' that the prison is there and not somewhere else. Furthermore, a policeman (or ex-policeman) might well think of a prison as handy: to a policeman, a prison is as handy as a football ground, because there are more criminals than footballers. There are many such 'effects' in The Light of Day, and if one needs a clue as to why this slender book appears to have taken Swift six years to write, it lies in such exact and pondered essences.

The novel's story elapses in a single day in November. George Webb leaves his Wimbledon office in the morning, buys some flowers, visits a man's grave, and then drives to the prison where Sarah Nash, his visitee of two years, resides. Over the course of this day, he tells us about his relationship with Sarah, who arrived in his office just over two years before the story begins, anxious to employ him to follow her adulterous husband. We learn a good deal about George, the information (like the information about Sarah's eventual crime) cleverly rationed over the span of the book. Swift has always been an exceptional narrative craftsman, adept at dangling sinister, wormy facts (in this he resembles Ian McEwan, a writer temperamentally close). George tells us, eventually, that he was pushed out of his job as a detective for over-zealous interviewing procedures, that he is divorced, and that his daughter has recently come out to him as a lesbian. If the novel has a weakness, it is the literary and cinematic familiarity of George's situation, its borrowed aspect. It is an odd paradox in a book so finely unliterary that its *mise en scène* should seem the kind of thing that one only ever encounters in novels. (The suggestion, proposed by several reviewers, that since The Light of Day shares with The End of the Affair a private eye, a triangular relationship and a woman called Sarah, it must be some sort of *hommage*, seems far-fetched to me, though it emphasises the sense of general echo that the book's plot has.)

Still, if a private eye who falls for a distressed client seems an obvious set-up, this particular private eye turns out to be less obvious as the book develops. Whenever Swift turns his acute eye on George's past, his narrator puts on quiddity. We learn, for instance, that George's father was a photographer, with a studio on Chislehurst High Street. (This is a great novel for high streets.) George's father had started out in 1946 as a beach photographer, in Broadstairs, where he snapped (in both senses of the word) George's mother. Swift perfectly captures the reticent, lower-middle-class English tone of that generation when he has George recall: 'Now and then they'd both mention, with a certain look in their eye, "Mrs Barrett's place" – "Mrs Barrett's place in Broadstairs", as if Mrs Barrett was some guard dog they'd more than once tiptoed by.' It is characteristic of Swift's technique that he refrains from expanding here; 'Mrs Barrett' was his parents' secret, and now it is George's – and now too it is ours, unamplified and implicit.

George later discovers that his father had taken a formal photograph, in his Chislehurst studio, of the five-year-old Sarah Nash – which is the right way round, because Sarah's origins (and circumstances) are fancier than George's. She is a teacher of languages (Spanish and French) at Roehampton, is married to a gynaecologist, and lives in one of the smarter Wimbledon enclaves. The marital troubles began a year before her visit to George, when she pityingly took in one of her students, a Croatian refugee called Kristina Lazic. Sarah's husband began an affair with the Croatian, and Sarah comes to George to ask him to follow the couple – specifically to follow them to Heathrow, from where Sarah fears that her husband and Kristina will elope. Of course, all this happened two years before George begins his story. It has been two years since Sarah killed her husband, and George, who fell in love with her as soon as she walked into his office, still feels obscurely responsible for the murder. And he is still in love. Sarah has eight years to serve in prison, but George intends to stay the course.

George is very likable. He is poorly educated but keen enough to learn. His daughter, Helen, had been an art student, and George had tried to keep up: 'I even went to art galleries, and looked – and yawned. I even mugged up on her favourite painter, Caravaggio (they all looked like waxworks to me). And found out he was a bit of a tearaway himself, a bit of a thug on the side, always running up against the law. (Was there a message there for me?) A bit of a nancy too.' Sarah, the language teacher, has been tutoring George in the importance of words, and George has even taken cookery classes. At the prison, during their fortnightly visits, they talk about Napoleon and Eugénie, because Sarah is spending her time translating a French biography of the empress. 'And anyway it's kept her afloat. A raft: the three of us. Her, me and the Empress Eugénie. Not forgetting Eugénie's old emperor husband. The four of us. We talk about them like people we know. "How's the empress today?"'

Contemporary novelists tend to be enamoured of random contemporary information, the more exotic the better – the geneaology of the apricot, a fact about Prince Albert's testicles, the sonics of the trombone, the financial system of Lithuania, whatever can be Googled up – and the possession of this information is, bewilderingly, thought by many to be evidence of great intelligence, now tellingly rechristened 'smartness'. Alas, bright lights are taken as evidence of habitation. Napoleon III's residence in Chislehurst is exactly the kind of glossy information that might add aimless glamour, but there are many novelists who could learn from the quiet functionality with which Swift employs his peculiar fact, the way in which Napoleon and Eugénie enter the narrative and are then naturally, not showily, appropriated by the characters. Similarly, whenever George hazards a simile or metaphor, it is the sort of likeness that this narrator – who, after all, has been trained to notice things – might have come up with; it is not Swift showing off. It is always natural. 'And now it's past mid-morning, there's even a final hint of warmth when you lift your face to the sun, like warm water in a cold glass.' Or: 'Only women smoke like that – blowing the smoke straight up – women who are angry. Like a kettle on the boil.' Or: 'The feeling of being alone in the house. Like water flooding into a ship.' In case after case (I have selected from many applicants), Swift finds the domestic, even homely image, never pushing his literary luck too far.

The Light of Day may trouble those currently engaged in 'the war against cliché'. For cliché is the very fabric and procedure of its style: 'in the fullness of time', 'memory lanes', 'I knew the ropes', 'working flat-out', 'I've read the signs' and so on. George overflows with them. The novel is a reminder of how important cliché is to a living literature. More than that, The Light of Day is explicitly an investigation into cliché, a skirmish not so much against as with cliché. As George finishes his story, it becomes clear that one fact will be revealed at the expense of the revelation of another. That's to say, we learn that Sarah killed her husband (and how she did it – she stabbed him), but not exactly why. After all, her husband had just put the Croatian student on a plane, had ended the affair, and was on his way home from Heathrow to his wife. Sarah knew this, because George, tailing him, had phoned to tell her. Sarah herself does not know why she did it. 'Something came over me,' she will tell George, who knows this cliché from his days as a detective. George himself likes to play with cliché: 'The crematorium doing a roaring trade,' he says at one moment (like Beckett in 'First Love': 'Personally I have no bone to pick with graveyards'). Sarah, he tells us, dressed up to receive her husband that night; she was 'dressed to kill'. And Sarah is a 'striking woman. If that's not an unfortunate word.' When she saw her husband enter the house, her heart at first 'leaped up'. 'It's just an expression of course, words aren't things, things aren't words,' George tells us.

But perhaps words – specifically clichés – are things, after all? For Sarah tells George, in prison, that her husband had enraged her by saying, months before the murder: 'I can't live without her.' And then Sarah darkly adds to her visitor: 'He didn't, did he?' The novel's suggestion seems to be that we might act in order to make words true, that clichés might madden us into action, trapped in that most clichéd of situations, the unfaithful marriage, that clichés might force us to vivify them and drag them out of their dead metaphoricity. If Sarah's husband tells her that he cannot live without his Croatian – well then, Sarah will make sure that he cannot, literally. And what better place, full of its own 'effects', for the literalisation of cliché, than Wimbledon?

Out of this apparently limited material and apparently limited style, Swift coaxes a novel of solemn depths. Beckett, the jester with cliché, can often be felt here: in the style's thinned repetitions, in its air of daily burden, even in one of its central themes, that of waiting and how to wait. Late in the book, standing in a queue at a café, George reflects that the advantage of such lines is that they remind you of all the much more awful lines you could be in, 'all the terrible shuffling lines'. He continues: 'Is there a life anyway which isn't half made of waiting? Studded with detentions? "Worth the wait." "Give it time." Nothing good can be hurried – like cooking.' George knows about waiting; it is his job, and now it is his life. This small dilation into the universal is uncharacteristic of George; but the novel has earned it by now, earned it by hewing so faithfully to the characteristic.

17 April 2003

BEAST OF A NATION

Andrew O'Hagan

I N WESTMINSTER ABBEY A number of years ago, I stood for over an hour talking to Neal Ascherson. It was one of those freezing January evenings – cold stone, long shadows – and we adopted our BBC faces in Poets' Corner, looking at the memorials and marble busts on the walls. I noticed Ascherson was taking his time over an inscription to the poet Thomas Campbell, and some words of Campbell's began to echo somewhere in my head, two lines from *The Pleasures of Hope*.

> 'Tis distance lends enchantment to the view,
> And robes the mountain in its azure hue.

Not good lines, but they seemed good enough as I watched Ascherson watching. He gave the impression there was something new to be said about Campbell.

'Come with me,' I said. 'I want to show you something.' Leading Ascherson across the Abbey, round an altar, down a spartan side-chapel, I pointed through some slats to the Coronation Chair. 'They took it eight weeks ago,' I said, 'the Stone of Destiny.'

'How did they remove it?' Ascherson asked.

'They gouged it out. They broke the chair. It's a 13th-century chair.'

Ascherson looked at me, then looked again at the dimly lit chamber. He was smiling but I couldn't tell if he was pleased or not. The Stone of Destiny had been taken back to Scotland, and I remember wondering, as we stood in the Abbey, if Ascherson thought the Scots would be delighted to have their coronation stone back after seven hundred years. 'It was borne on the back of a polished military Land Rover,' he writes in *Stone Voices*.*

> The onlookers on the pavement were sparse, and did not applaud. They seemed uncertain about what reaction was expected of them; whatever it was, they refrained from it ... They found this mournful pageant a bit alienating, and in a way it was meant to be. For the queen, the Stone still remains her personal property; she had sent her son the Duke of York to escort it to Edinburgh Castle

---

*Neal Ascherson, *Stone Voices: The Search for Scotland* (Granta, 2002).

where it would be deposited 'on loan' between coronations, visible to her subjects for £5.50 a peep.

Ascherson is interested in relics, interested in what they mean, and he's not short on native instinct when it comes to endowing even the most common stones of Scotland with an uncommon mystical power. This book is a haphazard work of auto-geography, one man's attempt to map his feelings about his own country, to send his affections first through the prism of history and then though the mincer, to hold up his own experience, his own devotions, to argue with time and battle with his own ambivalence, and above all, in the end, to have a go at telling a story about what it's like to spend your life married to a scenic fiction: Scotland the Brave.

'Normally, people inclined to faith rather than to reason tend to affirm the authenticity of a relic,' he goes on, 'not to deny it.'

> In Scotland, it was the opposite. It had become important and alluring to many people to believe, in the teeth of all probability, that the Stone placed in Edinburgh Castle was a fake.

Why was this? And what was the connection between the unexpected coolness displayed by the Edinburgh crowds and these compulsive denials? It was the fact that over time the Stone's importance had become essentially that of the grievance it evoked. What mattered about the Stone was precisely its absence: the fact that it had been carted off by an English king in an act of plunder which was also intended to be a symbolic act of conquest. Not the Stone, but the presence of the Stone at Westminster served to define one of the underlying realities of the English-Scottish relationship, and it continued to do so even after the 1707 Treaty of Union fused the two kingdoms into one 'Great Britain'.

A half-hearted nation will want to hold fast to its grievances, and in that sense Scotland has done well. The nation's brickwork is cemented with resentments, from ruined monastery to erupting towerblock: blame, fear, bigotry and delusion, their fragments powder the common air – and always the fault is seen to lie elsewhere, with other nations, other lives. Scotland is a place where cultural artefacts and past battles – the Stone of Destiny, Robert Burns, *Braveheart*, Bannockburn – have more impact on people's sense of moral action than politics does. The people have no real commitment to the public sphere, and are not helped towards any such commitment by the dead rhetoric of the young Parliament. Yet the problem is not the Parliament, it's the people, and the people's drowsy addiction to imagined injury – their belief in a paralysing historical distress – which makes the country assert itself not as a modern nation open to progress on all fronts, but as a delinquent, spoiled, bawling child, tight in its tartan babygro, addled with punitive needs and false memory syndrome.

Neal Ascherson has been through many long nights with this heart-scorching beast of a nation, yet, in spite of what he knows, he most often manages to play the part of the good father, coddling Scotland into a state of temporary sleep with the singing of old lullabies. As you would expect, the voice is tuneful and there is often an intelligent, estranged ring to what he writes. His book hovers over the hills and waterways of Scotland, staring down at the rutted marks of former glaciers and the footprints of deer, but all the while there are questions whispered under his breath: do I belong here? Is Scotland authentic? And most stirring of all: when was Scotland?

The first of his journeys is to mid-Argyll, the place Ascherson's family come from. At some non-negotiable level of himself, he feels connected to those Bronze Age monuments, to these standing stones and circular cairns that punctuate the fields. In the manner of Hugh Miller, stonemason and essayist, the grain of Ascherson's thinking is apt to spark off these heathen formations, these 'ritual spires of condensed fear and memory', as he calls them, and a melancholic attitude accompanies the notion that the modern age can do damage to such configurations on the headland. Some of the stones have holes in them, peepholes, you might say, into those spots of time that matter to the author. We find him stopping to look at the stones as he makes his way to the Oban hospital where his mother lies ill. Marion Campbell, the novelist, historian and poet, an old friend of the Aschersons, was lying in a bed nearby. 'Later in the ward,' Ascherson writes,

> I was talking to my mother about the Ballymeanoch stones, and the one that fell, and saying that nobody seemed sure when it had fallen. A muffled voice came from behind me. 'Well, I know!' said Marion, suddenly awake. 'It was in 1943, and a Shetland pony was sheltering up against it from the storm when it broke off. Must have terrified the poor beast.' She paused, and then said: 'Nobody would believe now that I remember the stone when it was up, and how I used to look through the hole.' She slept again, and later that afternoon they came to put screens around her bed. They tried to drain her lung, but it was too late. She must have known how ill she was.

There is a sense of belonging in all this, a sense of belonging to a place and a people, a love of nature, and one's own nature, and of what Joyce called the 'ineluctable modality of the visible'. I think Ascherson is less interested in origins, in where stones or people or nations come from, than in what happens to them, in how they are seen or how they see themselves, in what survives, and in the ways that one thing leads to another, which can become a fairly gentle way of describing your own personal history, too.

John Smith, the late Labour leader, believed a devolved Scottish parliament was 'the settled will of the Scottish people'. He died too young and is buried now on the Isle of Iona, in what is thought to have been the graveyard of the Scottish kings. There's a large oval stone lying over his grave, and it seems right, in the Ascherson way, for this man to be linked with the rudiments of some timeless, unknowable Scottish material, and tied to a notion of Providence. In 1845, just before the potato failure, the cholera epidemic reached Argyll; the village of Allt Beithe lay in the hills around Tarbert, and one day it was noticed that none of the villagers had been seen for a while.

> A rescue party set out, and went first to the hamlet of Baldarroch, where they found only the dead lying in their houses. Climbing on, they reached Allt Beithe. There 'they found everyone dead or dying except for a baby, Archibald Leitch,' a little boy of two. He was carried back to Tarbert and brought up by relatives, and in time grew up to be a boat-builder.

And, Ascherson points out, John Smith's great-grandfather.

When people write Scottish history, they do so, if they're at all sure of their market, with a certain degree of patience and hope, and with as good an eye for questions of destiny as for questions of fabulation. Scottish people respond to the idea that there is a Story of Scotland, and writers who can make that story a stormy marriage of internal and external strife – of deep feelings and strong weather, true love and ancient rocks – are answering to a need that is taken for granted in Scotland. Where documentary evidence is lacking, rocks can replace papers; people read their ancestral stories into the scattered stones, and even where there are papers, people have traditionally shown a tendency to make for the rocks if there is no supporting evidence for what is written. In this respect, Ascherson takes his cue from Hugh MacDiarmid – 'There are ruined buildings in the world, but no ruined stones' – and that is a poetic truth with a mighty appeal for Ascherson's generation of Scottish politicians. It appeals to those who are more taken with essence than experience, those who, for good reasons not bad, wish for an overarching grandeur, a galvanising truth, something in the Scottish character that can live up to the landscape. It is part of what Ibsen called 'the saving lie': the presentation of every sort of necessary, ancient virtue, which, taken together, might seem to compensate for the nation's terrible smallness of vision. Scotland is presently – and quite horrendously – failing the test of its own modernity. Much of its life is, by and large, a mean-minded carnival of easy resentments; it is a place of bigotry, paralysis, nullity and boredom; a nation of conservatives who never vote Conservative; a proud country mired up to the fiery eyes in blame and nostalgia. It's not nice to think about, but it's there, this kind of Scotland, and everybody knows it's there.

Ascherson's book is not an uprooting kind of work – it is soft, and soft-hearted, finding perfect cover in the hardness of rocks. It's difficult not to fail when dealing with the failure of Scotland, so much wells up, and one's deepest hopes are such a pitiable hindrance, but the time has surely come for calling a shovel a shovel. In place of 'Heartless Midlothian' and 'Young Mortality' – as yet unwritten accounts of the country's vast self-pity, arrested development and the way out of that – we are served with another 'Portrait of the Artist as a Reluctant Patriot'. Ascherson must know that Scotland does not live by the remnants of grandeur alone, it lives by lies, by lies stronger than truths, by fictions stranger than facts. Behind the great myth of Scottish self-observance, behind the chant of 'wha's like us?', lies the fact that modern Scots don't ever quite look at themselves, and know nothing of what they are like. Wha's like us? The answer is nobody – especially not ourselves.

Ascherson's 'Search for Scotland' has trouble with the notion of 'us', but it has just as much trouble with notions of trouble. He draws his cutlass halfway, only to put it back again, to fix his eyes on the middle distance and ruminate on the efficiency of old songs, his hands sweating as they rest on the sheath that guards his blade. He has a lot to say about his forebears, but what might his own great-grand-children contemplate when they look back to the Scotland of his day? 'Webs of mutual support', he says, the 'apparently indelible colouring of Scottish society'.

Scotland has survived and still exists as a chain of small collective loyalties: 'Society People' singing in the hills or clansmen enlisting with their chieftain, colonists on the Vistula or private partnerships in Bengal, crofting townships in Assynt or mining villages in Fife.

When Scotland's last deep coal mine at Longannet flooded and closed down for ever in March 2002, a man called George came home from the pit to find his telephone ringing. 'Dinnae worry, big man, we'll see you're no stuck for work.' This is a nation at home in hard, stony times. It will find its own way in the world.

This is a cold, hard jet of pure nonsense. I'm happy for the chieftains, and happy for George, but Ascherson has witnessed the slow altering of several European societies, and witnessed too much of Scotland, overall, to allow such fetid and unimaginative resignation to stand at the end of his inquiry. I begin to worry that the great explicator of velvet revolutions has dithered too long in the purple heather, and has forgotten to ask what life is actually like over in Greenock, Buckie, Cumnock and Cowdenbeath. A chain of collective loyalties? A nation at home? You must be joking.

A people so addicted to the notion of belonging must surely live in fear of strangers, and, even more so, in fear of the stranger in themselves. In his better pages, Ascherson knows this, and he sometimes puts his powers of clarity to the task of expressing it. One of the first pieces of business in the new Scottish Parliament was to be the repealing of Clause 2a, the one about 'promoting' homosexuality in schools and public libraries. An unholy alliance was forged in Scotland to oppose this removal, this 'routine detail of political hygiene'. With the backing of the brain-numbing *Daily Record*, the nation's tabloid newspaper, Cardinal Winning of the Catholic Church joined forces with the Presbyterians and was soon enjoying the financial backing of Brian Souter, a bus-line millionaire and born-again Christian, to Keep the Clause. Souter used his millions to petition every home in Scotland. Of the people daft enough to respond to the campaign, six people out of seven voted to keep the clause and attacks on homosexuals increased immediately. Though the Parliament held its nerve and repealed the clause, it put in a few sentences about heterosexuality and family life being the best thing since sliced bread.

Ascherson mentions Scotland's 'grim and persisting record of religious intolerance and discrimination'. He was able to say this without having the benefit of the Scottish Executive's most recent survey, which led to a leader in the *Guardian* this month, declaring that the Scots were possibly the most racist group in Europe.

> There was a dogged public assumption that racial prejudice was an English problem to which the Scots – for reasons of social history, for reasons of superior native intelligence – were immune . . .

But this was a prettified version of history. The Lithuanians had at first run into a wall of hatred from the Scottish working class who perceived them, not entirely without reason, as cheap foreign labour brought in to collapse miners' wages. The Italian community was utterly unprepared for the ferocious anti-Italian riots which flamed through Scottish towns and cities in July 1940, when Fascist Italy joined the war on Hitler's side. But the central flaw in this self-congratulatory myth, the grand denial of the blatantly obvious, was the matter of the Irish.

With some verve, and some nerve, Ascherson tells a story of his own prejudice, of how he thought his young sister might have caught impetigo swinging on the gates of a Catholic school. But there are no jokes in Ascherson's book. 'Here was

I,' he writes, 'a much-travelled journalist with left-wing opinions and a Cambridge history degree. And, nevertheless, for almost all my life I had never questioned that if you touched a railing used by small boys of a particular religion you would probably acquire a disfiguring disease.' He mentions other disfigurements along the way – murdered asylum seekers, lacerated Celtic fans, and land abuse, in one form or another – making his sonorous, ballad-singing conclusions about the strain of commonality in the Scottish seem all the more absurd.

You come to wonder why Ascherson won't attempt to understand Scotland's victimology. Why doesn't he relate the sociopathic elements in that small country to what he knows about the hungers of small nations elsewhere in Europe? These are matters most of us aren't equipped to explain. His book sets up an expectation of something new, and he is sometimes good at describing ailments, but when the call for new ideas and interpretations looms, he escapes into powerless long passages about deforestation, the Picts and the Gaels, 17th-century Scots in Poland, or the Covenanters, leading you to feel that Scotland's best journalist is becoming one of those writers whose main aim is to ensure polemic never gets in the way of positive thinking. That kind of thing is the opposite of Ascherson at his best, a fact you're reminded of when you come to passages like the following:

> The Scottish trauma is to do with self-doubt (sometimes masked in unreal self-asser-tion), with sterile speculations about national identity and – as I guess – with suspi-cions of 'otherness' which so often poison relationships between Scottish neighbours. But above all, the trauma shows itself in a chronic mistrust of the public dimension. The invitation to 'participate', especially to offer critical comment in public, touches a nerve of anxiety. This derives partly from the instinct that to disagree with another person before witnesses is to open a serious personal confrontation; the English or American assumption that 'free, open discussion' is non-lethal and even healthy is not widespread in Scotland . . .
>
> The deep geological fault running underneath national self-confidence is still there . . . and from time to time it makes itself felt. When it does, the confident few who lead political change feel misunderstood and betrayed. In Bertolt Brecht's words about the leaders of the former East Germany, they feel tempted to dissolve this people and appoint another one.

Free-falling anxiety about Scottishness has a tendency, among Scots, not only to turn into hatred of others, but into hating bad news about the country itself, and seeing critics as traitors. There are few European nations in which intellectuals are so willing to serve as soft-pedalling merchants of 'national character', handmaidens to the tourist industry: broadcasters, academics, lawyers, some of the poets too, sell pride and tears, spiritual laxity and pawky good humour in place of inquiry.

I recently went to New York to take part in something called *Distilled: Scotland Live in New York*, a business and tourist junket masquerading as an arts festival, the highlight of which was a march by five thousand kilted bagpipers up Fifth Avenue. 'We want to show our solidarity with New Yorkers in their time of terrible suffering,' said the Lord Provost of Edinburgh, 'and remind you that Scotland is an excellent place to visit and invest in.' Whisky poured from the bar, commercial blether mixed with the unruly sentiment of the expatriate, and deals were made, palms were greased. I spoke to a man who deals in computer jobs in the Clyde Valley. 'We're all New Yorkers now!' he shouted over his tumbler of Dewars.

Alyth McCormack, an amazing singer of Gaelic music, got up on stage to sing a song about the Highland Clearances. The song is grave and bleak and full of historical complications and human wrongs, but you couldn't hear the woman and the song she sang. The business crowd and the cultural delegates of Scotland and New York were shouting at one another, their red faces all compliant, their glasses full, and the volume increased, the laughter bellowed out, until it became quite a thunder of ill-consideration, and the sound of McCormack's voice just disappeared, and the business of land clearance or human loss was nowhere present in these people's minds. Meanwhile, over by the windows, in the tartan glory of 23rd Street, other people stood and they stared out at the missing towers, and some of them pointed to the view of the Statue of Liberty and the view of Ellis Island. As I made for the exit, I wondered if any of those at the windows were prompted by the drowned-out music to look for the ghosts of their ancestors standing on the quay.

'This race,' E.B. White wrote in his 1946 essay on New York, 'between the destroying planes and the struggling Parliament of Man: it sticks in all our heads.' Yes it does. And that day – Tartan Day in America – it mingled for me with thoughts of my own about what Scotland wanted to be in the world. Growing up in what the novelist John Galt wonderfully called The West – the West Coast of Scotland – we used to look from the beach at Irvine New Town as if looking towards America, and Polaris submarines would pass and we'd feel happy we were on America's side and safe in the bowl of the Ayrshire hills. Our Scottish Enlightenment had fed into their Constitution, via Francis Hutcheson and Thomas Jefferson, and the music playing on the local radio – West Sound – was all country music about personal freedom and broken trust and breaking hearts.

In *Stone Voices*, Ascherson tells of his own visit to America the year before. 'Tartan Day is about liberty,' said the right-wing Republican Senator Trent Lott on that occasion, borrowing the Braveheartish banter that now stands for modern

Scotland in Washington and Hollywood. Lott mentioned the Scottish clansmen who 'were our clansmen, our brothers', as if American kinship were the only kind that counts, the only context in which a small and ancient country might understand its own worth. The Scottish ministers (and Sean Connery) mugged for the camera, shouting 'freedom!'

Scotland should have outgrown its own pantomime by now. 'Ending the war in Ulster,' Tom Nairn wrote in *After Britain* (2000), 'entailed a fundamental rearticulation of the United Kingdom's unitarist tradition, founded on a post-Thatcher recognition that – in the language of the "Downing Street Declaration" – Britain no longer retained "a selfish strategic interest" in retaining control over any part of Ireland.' The constitutional plates have moved under Scotland, too – the nation itself has outgrown its own people – and Britain is not what is was. Some hatreds will tend to outlive their original occasions, yet traditional Scottish resentments about 'foreignness' must surely perish if the country is properly to awake in Europe.

Ascherson's most invigorating chapter is about the Scottish Empire – the subject of so much Nationalist bad faith over the years – and there can be no argument, now that the old style is gone, about how well Scotland did from the Union. All considered, it did better than England. There is, as Nairn puts it, a 'tantalising sense of redemption which always informs nostalgia', but the Scottish people cannot afford to get stuck there any longer, and Scotland must go on now to establish its role in bringing about a new United Kingdom within a new Europe. In the manner of Stephen Dedalus, we might do better to see Scotland's conscience as 'uncreated'; for while we must admit that Ascherson's stones are interesting, they are not as interesting as people. Nationalism in Scotland is a place where good men and women busy themselves shaking the dead hand of the past, but the naming of a tradition is not the same as the forging of a nation, and modern Scotland, now more than ever, needs a new way of thinking, a new kind of relation to the old, a way to live, a way to make itself better than the badness that's been and the badness to come. The question of what the past amounted to can lie about the grass.

31 *October* 2002

KOSOVO'S BIG MEN

Jeremy Harding

HISTORY, IT'S SAID AGAIN and again, is what makes the loss of Kosovo so much harder for the Serbs to entertain than any of the setbacks they've borne so far under the dark stewardship of Slobodan Milosevic. Kosovo is the geographical fundament of Serbian Orthodoxy; the site of a legendary face-off between Christianity and Ottoman incursion. Among Serbs, this past is a far more vigorous currency than the miserable Yugoslav dinar, yet very few non-Serbs recognise it, or anything minted in Belgrade, as legal tender. We, too, can invoke history to explain our hesitation. Seven hundred years ago, Dante wrote King Milutin of Rascia into the book that lies open on the Day of Judgment. Milutin's sin, the imperial eagle explains to the poet in the *Paradiso*, was to forge Venetian ducats ('il conio di Vinegia'). Today his remote descendant Milan Milutinovic, president of Serbia, is honouring the tradition by issuing one counterfeit version after another of events in Kosovo. Since Richard Holbrooke, Washington's Balkan fixer, brokered a rickety ceasefire last October, Milutinovic's arguments have come with a plausible lustre – he invokes the UN Charter, the sovereignty of member states and so on – but his latest observation, that the 45 ethnic Albanian villagers massacred in Racak by Serbian security forces on 15 January were all 'terrorists', has persuaded no one.

Milosevic is clearly the bigger figure; larger than death, you could say, and thoroughly Orientalised: the West is aghast at the federal president's 'cunning', his staying power, his hecatombs, yet over the years and around the world, we have not done badly ourselves. For some time now Milosevic has had the better of Washington. He has also stood the normal order of events on its head: in Kosovo, the last few months of 'peace' have not been the logical outcome of exhaustion, defeat or satisfaction in war, but a necessary prelude to renewed hostilities.

Late last year, the weather in Kosovo turned momentarily in favour of Holbrooke's ceasefire. In Pristina, the provincial capital, the change began with a warning volley of snowflakes just after dark. By the following morning the roads were nearly impassable. Food deliveries to the villages ravaged by the Serbian offensive – scores of villages in Kosovo – were delayed. And the low-key war, the sporadic skirmishing that has since escalated, was reduced to a minimum. A few centimetres of snow had done more than any monitors or roving ambassadors to muffle the ardours of

the Kosovo Liberation Army and the Serbian authorities. The road out west to Pec
– Peja in Albanian – was an ice rink. The villages we passed were gutted and quite
deserted: the most recent addition, and presumably the last, to a long trail of ruin,
consuming hundreds of peasant communities, which dates from the early 1990s
and curves down through much of the former Yugoslavia. Stray dogs limped across
the white fields. With the disruption of rural life, they had learned to run in packs.

We stopped in a village sacked by the Serbs during the offensive which ended
in September. The damage was near-absolute and the place was still largely abandoned. A handful of people had returned but they were now in a state of terror:
two days before, the KLA had killed two policemen and wounded four others in an
ambush in the village and the Serbian police had taken summary revenge on any
ethnic Albanians they could lay hands on. Nobody was dead, but there had been
severe beatings. Two EU staff attached to the Diplomatic Observer Mission, a fore-
runner of the much bigger OSCE verification mission now in deep water in Kosovo,
had moved in promptly to investigate the reprisals. One of the monitors had been in
Kosovo for four or five months. He sat in his armoured vehicle with the door open
and checked his ledger for details of the village: 'Originally 1861 inhabitants, 187
houses, 95 per cent destroyed in the Serbian offensive.'

He accused the KLA of irresponsibility: they must have known what would
happen to the villagers after the ambush. There was daily harassment of Albanian-
speakers by the police in this area, he told us, but reckoned that the KLA was
responsible for 90 per cent of the serious provocations. The local KLA commander
is a man named Ramush Haradinaj. 'He speaks fluent French and people say he is
a former legionnaire. His English is also good. He corrects our interpreters.' The
monitor had had several dealings with Ramush and believed he was tough, fanatical even. 'He wants to stay in the hills for ever and cleanse this whole area of Serbs.'
He answered to no one, the monitor thought; certainly not to the KLA office in
Pristina, headed by Adem Demaçi, a symbolic figure from the Parliamentary Party
of Kosovo whose links with the liberation army are not hard and fast, although
he is widely respected as a militant secessionist who spent 28 years (longer than
Mandela's term) in Yugoslav jails.

The independence of a well-equipped kaçak – or outlaw – like Ramush weakens
the chain of command that is needed to turn an assortment of dedicated maqui-
sards into the armed wing of a co-ordinated political movement and the dangers
of warlordism in some KLA sectors are correspondingly high. Yet the organisation
enjoys widespread support in the western part of Kosovo, above all in the Drenica
valley: if civilians pay a high price for KLA actions, the liberation army is recognised
as the only challenge to a minority regime that has stripped ethnic Albanians of

most rights of citizenship, deprived them of jobs, forced them to develop a parallel system of schooling and health care, lately destroyed their rural infrastructure and cast them yet again in the historical role of Muslim intruders. The KLA also receives material support from Albania (the Democratic Party of Albania has purchased weapons on their behalf or passed on the contents of the government arsenals looted in 1997) and can count on funds from the Kosovar diaspora in Germany, which has the largest community of Kosovar expatriates, and Switzerland, where the organisation holds its main bank accounts. Switzerland is a major KLA recruiting ground; many Kosovar exiles have returned to fight for independence alongside people who have remained in the province, or dipped in and out of Albania between periods of detention.

'When you meet the fighters,' a young Albanian interpreter in Pristina announced, 'you will see how they are. They are epic.' This was not a frivolous description. She meant that the fighting tradition among ethnic Albanians is long (the current bout can be thought of as a continuation of hostilities that go back 85 years or more); that it has a robust undercarriage of myth, further strengthened by fierce notions of uprightness – moral notions that lie somewhere between honour and bravado; some would say courage. She was worried that the most reckless wield great authority, irrespective of their rank, and that this could happen within any given command (just as, on a bigger scale, semi-autonomous sectors can act as they see fit). The willingness to die is also a difficult issue. Death is easily reconfigured in terms of sacrifice and heroism, but it's a setback just the same, and in war the presence of forces – living, able-bodied forces – in the field is always an asset. The statuesque figure of the KLA fighter hewn from the bones of his forebears and caked with the dust of earlier struggles is part archetype and part identikit – and mostly suspect. Yet the term 'epic' tells us something about the KLA's strengths and its weaknesses.

It also serves to distinguish their approach from the more admirable and ponderous efforts of Ibrahim Rugova's alternative administration, the government of the 'Kosovo Republic', voted into existence by the provincial chamber that Milosevic stripped of its effective powers ten years ago. Two days after our journey to Pec, I took up with another interpreter, a young journalist who supplemented her income with work at Rugova's information centre. M. had had many dealings with the KLA. She understood their impatience with Rugova, an impatience bordering on contempt, but she would not denounce the project of independence by peaceful means that he has so honourably, and hopelessly, pursued. She wanted a coherent front moving ineluctably towards an independent state of Kosovo, but she was a realist who thought better of her wishes.

M. knew a KLA base off the road leading north from Pristina to Podujevo and up into Serbia proper. We drove for forty minutes or more, the traffic decreasing as we got further from the capital. We passed a Serbian police post, continued until we were beyond sight of it and got out. The driver took off with the car. Working from memory – she had been here several months earlier – M. found a narrow track leading up to a rise, about half a mile off. On either side of it ran a low wall, and sometimes hedgerow, clotted with snow and ice. After a few hundred yards we were visible from the police post, but almost at once the track dipped and a long rampart of snow hid us from view.

M. took me to a farmstead surrounded by a palisade of rough thatch. She spoke to a man who directed us across the fields and some time later, tired now, we reached an isolated house with three pairs of frozen boots stood on the tiled floor of the porch. On the sloping roof above us, where you might have expected a weather vane, there was a white satellite dish. We knocked and an elderly man with a smattering of teeth appeared in the doorway, two younger men behind him. M. introduced us and showed them a pass she'd obtained from Demaçi in Pristina. One of the younger men came out of the house and put on his boots. The other handed him an old Kalashnikov and two magazines strapped together with masking tape. We followed our burly, convivial guide across the fields, breaking the crust of virgin snow as we went, and sinking up to our shins. He was fitter than either of us. On our way we encountered two other KLA men. He shouted to them and the sound of laughter clattered back at us through the lean air. 'He says he has two suspects from Pristina,' M. explained, 'and we're both under arrest.'

As the terrain levelled out we found ourselves in a plantation of young oak trees. M. wanted a photograph and the fighter stood motionless on the path between the trees with his gun in both hands. He could have held the posture for as long as it took a singer to recite the history of his village. 'Epic', it struck me again, was not a bad word. It was only as we left the plantation that I noticed the ground underfoot. It consisted of a thick snowfall strewn with autumn leaves. The trees, too, were still hung with straggler foliage. In Kosovo, winter had stolen a march on the fall and the normal order of events seemed once again to have been reversed.

We must have reached the village an hour or so later. It was quiet at the bottom but the path rose, and beyond that was a well-manned KLA checkpoint. We were shown into a house that M. had visited before. One of the officers recognised her. There was a woodstove burning in the front room. A big blown-up photograph of a pastoral landscape with a stream running over boulders covered the back wall: a homely, tautologous reminder of the KLA motherland that was all around them, large sections of it now under their control. The stovepipe ran up through the picture some distance from a weeping willow. The stutter of walkie-talkies, and from somewhere at the back of the house, the rasping crackle of a base-set, came and went in the room.

Our meeting was short and not very frank. We sat with three men in uniform. I'd come to Kosovo, I said, to trace the family of some refugees and knew that here only a small number of the people displaced during the Serbian offensive – 250,000 according to the UN, nearly double that by the reckoning of an American NGO – had actually left the province (which M. translated as 'republic'). The officers said that a lot of people had moved from their sector last July, and that the KLA had helped them. There were probably twenty villages in the area and around 15,000 people. Most were gone by August, when the Serbian offensive was frenzied. They said that people had left by car, on buses, in tractors, swarming into Pristina and Podujevo, and that the KLA had stuck close to them, in the rear, with the idea of protecting them if the worst came to the worst. One of the men, a short, engaging character with a deferential smile, said that he'd urged his parents to leave; reluctantly they'd agreed, but had kept coming back. The inhabitants of one village had been moved wholesale and brought under the protection of the fighters at the base.

The officers insisted they were still at war, despite the Holbrooke/Milosevic agreement. And, yes, the ceasefire was an occasion to plan and regroup – 'a good moment,' M. said, translating the words of the senior commander, chain-smoking at a desk behind a portable typewriter, 'to collect matériel. Training we have already done.' Independence was the unequivocal goal. The idea that the medium-term outcome of the Holbrooke/Milosevic negotiations would redefine the province as a third republic, along with Serbia and Montenegro, within what remains of federal Yugoslavia was addressed with serious interest. But this interest is strictly provisional. Whether Kosovo is recast as an 'autonomous region', as it became in the 1940s, or an 'autonomous province', as it became in the 1960s, or a republic in all but name, as it did under the Tito Constitution, or simply a Serbian annex, as it did in 1989, these officers – like many ethnic Albanians I met – have simply had enough of the Yugoslav project. They wanted international guarantees that the option of independence would remain open after any interim return to autonomy, in whatever guise. At the same time, they know there are no international guarantees. Disruption and violence on a scale that the West finds unsettling are the likeliest guarantors of their ambitions and these are the things they intend to call on. Complete separation from the remains of Yugoslavia is the objective.

The KLA base seemed backwoods-ish, ominously easy-going as it went about its business, preparing for the bleak days ahead. There were men chopping firewood; others attending to cars – plenty of cars, some of them four-wheel drives in good condition. It was a military version of the extended family that is everywhere in

Kosovo: an advantage in this kind of war, but yet another obstacle, perhaps, to the creation of a modern chain of command in a small world of village notables and well-respected clans. There can be few Kosovars who do not have distant relatives in the KLA and so, to the authorities (above all Milan Milutinovic), every ethnic Albanian is a terrorist suspect, which means that in Kosovo those who condone terrorism outnumber Serb citizens by nine to one.

To our hosts, the close family connections between fighters and civilians proved that the movement swam in the waters of popular support. In eight months, they had lost only seven fighters and 14 civilians. But here, the KLA had not been put to quite the same test in the eyes of their followers as units further south in Drenica, which bore the brunt of Serbian revanchisme, or the units that were active near Recak before the recent massacre. A day after leaving the base, I drove through the wreckage of Malisevo, a town in Drenica which the police and army had taken apart with all the more vigour for the fact that the KLA had occupied it and proclaimed it a liberated 'capital'. The snow looked like a demure attempt to cover the charred remains of the place, as you'd cover the dead, but it is a monument of shame, both to the Serbian army and police for what they did to it and to the KLA for having turned it into such an object of enmity, knowing full well that they could never hold it. The police were sandbagged in; there was armour half-hidden on the outskirts. Down the road to Dragobilje, the KLA had regrouped; it was a frontline of sorts, with the two sides staring one another down across a fraying cordon of foul weather and shuttle diplomacy. No one imagines it will hold.

M. had handed me a sheaf of her photographs before we parted. Most were from a recent trip in the field and, of these, the ones she urged on me showed a dead man – an ethnic Albanian – washed and readied for burial. He had been killed by the Serbian army, she said. The wounds were brutal, the post-mortem stitching was crude. The body was bluish grey. She had used up the rest of the film at a gathering of her family and friends. The prints were all poor. It wasn't the body that was troubling, so much as the business of showing the photos at all, and the fact that the shots of the dead man were on the same roll as the family snaps. I think M.'s motive was simple. I was fond of saying that I knew nothing about the Balkans and perhaps she thought the photos would illustrate how bad things had been here. But one of the distinguishing features of Kosovo seems to be the readiness with which people light on the subject of atrocity. You'll hear often, in differing detail, how one killing or another was a lingering and terrible affair, all this without a trace of the reticence you'll find in other places where things have gone equally badly. It's not simply that these horrors are fresh in people's minds and have to be exorcised. For a people at war, atrocity, like death and heroism, is always a building block in the edifice of national identity, but is there anywhere it sits so snugly in the foundations?

'The state,' a member of Rugova's Parliament told me, 'holds the monopoly of violence now' – which is how it looked last year and how it looks again since the massacre at Racak, but only at a glance. In any case, it doesn't have a monopoly on atrocity. Late one night, as the thaw came on, I walked through a marsh of blackening melt-water to the Grand Hotel in Pristina, picked up a Serbian interpreter, and made my way to the police station. It was nine o'clock. I was instructed that anything arising from this meeting should be attributed to 'official government sources'. Let's call him the Source, a stocky, intense man with a witheringly powerful stare, a profound sense of grievance and a tendency to draconian exposition. A pile of white ring-bound folders lay stacked on the table at which we sat, but these would not be broached before 'a short résumé on the situation in Kosovo'. It was, in fact, lengthy and punctuated by harsh criticisms of the Western media.

Since the Holbrooke/Milosevic agreement, the Source had lost nine policemen; another 25 had been wounded and 11 kidnapped (those figures have since risen). In the course of 1998 – with a few weeks to go – 112 police had been killed (a figure broadly consistent with the ratio of Serbs to ethnic Albanians in Kosovo, given the 1998 death toll of something between one and two thousand people) and nearly 400 wounded. The Source had a register of 1632 terrorist – that is, KLA – attacks, but emphasised that in the wake of the Serbian offensive, the authorities had decreed an amnesty for anyone handing in firearms and had so far received nine thousand weapons, manufactured mostly in Nato member-states and China.

He was speaking for the moment as a police chief, responsible for the welfare of his men, with a body of law to uphold and the integrity of a state to defend. All around him he saw terrorism in its purest form: two Serbs are abducted as profiteers for selling firewood to ethnic Albanians, then an ethnic Albanian is shot on the spot for buying the same firewood; a road is mined, a police post is assaulted, his officers die; whole villages are forced to take up arms which they're at pains to part with once the amnesty is declared. 'What,' he inquired, 'could my government do? Would the government of your country tolerate such a situation?'

We passed now to the white folders, forensic evidence of killings in Kosovo, complete with autopsy reports compiled by the office of the coroner, with poorly printed colour photographs, like M.'s, exposed on the same kind of camera as hers. 'Six corpses unidentified, in a hole, estimated to be three months old, discovered on 3 October 1998 as a result of dogs carrying human remains.' 'August 16 and 17 1998, police officers Srdan Perovic and Milorad Rajkovic tortured to death in Lausa after being abducted by men in civilian dress'; the photos show one body, severely bruised, with the hand cut into strips; the other with an ear severed, the nose cut, both arms broken and, in a picture taken from another angle, a gaping hole in place of a shoulderblade. The coroner's report advises that these injuries were sustained before death.

There were scores of cases, all of them terrible. The more eager I became to draw our meeting to a close, the more agitated and persistent the Source became, standing over me, pointing, recapitulating, insisting, enraging himself with the ghastliness of the detail until his face became ashen. The last dossier contained three photographs of an outright villain, identified as Aslan Klecka, born in 1947. He was the embodiment of everything a Serb might fear in an ethnic Albanian. The stereotype of the Muslim extremist, whose presence in Bosnia was so briskly milked for the credulous West, is once again stressed in Belgrade's propaganda about Kosovo. In one photograph, Aslan was wearing a robe and keffiyeh and posing beside an enormous mounted machine-gun. In another he was Abraham, raising the knife over Isaac, except that he was leering and the blade was already running with blood. In the third, he was at prayer in what appeared to be open countryside. Across from these photos was a forensic shot of a distended body on the floor of a garage with the head severed and blood seeping through the trousers at the crotch. The Source claimed that this was one of Aslan's last victims, that Aslan was found dead in a car, killed by a member of his own entourage – which may or may not be true – in September 1998, and that the other pictures were removed from Aslan's house during a police investigation.

The parody of militant Islam compromised the Aslan dossier. The rest of the evidence had been as credible as any allegations from the 'terrorist' side, but this looked like montage. I suspect nonetheless that it was genuine, a piece of good luck for the authorities, allowing them to tar the organisation with the Islamist brush in a way that's neither fair nor representative, despite the fact that Mujahidin elements are active in the KLA. 'Wild West,' said the Source, stubbing his forefinger on the picture of this Oriental Charles Manson posturing with a machine-gun.

The trouble with atrocity, and tit-for-tat evidence, is that it explains only the brutality of war. Neither side in Kosovo is a stickler for the Geneva Conventions, and both are deeply invested in updating their national myths. Both feel wronged by history, which is why they incline to the historical view. To inquire of someone like the Source why he has so many chilling deeds on file is to ask him to speak as an ordinary person and therefore as a Serb. He would say (as he did) that decent people don't commit such crimes; perhaps too (though he didn't) that the forces of the Serb prince, Lazar Hrebeljanovic, marshalled against the Turks on the plain of Kosovo in 1389, were defending the nearest thing to a civilisation, in the hectic world of medieval Balkan polities, against the nearest thing to barbarity; and finally that this model holds good six centuries on.

As the night grew longer, the line between the diligent policeman and the embattled Serb became harder to trace. Which of them was it who ventured the opinion that the Serbian offensive had been drawn to a close too soon last autumn? ('Three more weeks and the job could have been done.') And which of them urged me to take copies of the photos in the dossiers back to Britain? (It would be unethical on my part, and an affront to the dead, not to get them published.) I declined politely and the mood of my 'official government sources' – policeman, statistician, bureaucrat and Serb – rapidly darkened. Even so, he kept his rage more or less in check, as many Serbian policemen and soldiers do not. Their own is contracted out to the strategy of terror that now passes for law enforcement in Kosovo. But rage, as we know, is a law unto itself.

4 February 1999

SHORT CUTS

John Sturrock

S TENDHAL ONCE OBSERVED THAT to introduce politics into a work of fiction was like firing a pistol during a performance in the theatre, a loud and unwanted intrusion of the real on a setting all calculated artifice. The analogy was brought to mind two weeks ago by the death of David Kelly, a real event which intruded in a shocking way on the calculated artificiality of the Parliamentary Foreign Affairs Committee before which he'd been called, a body convened on the face of it to determine whether the government had earlier misled all of us in persuading itself there needed to be a war; or whether, less seriously and once the war was over, a BBC journalist had misled rather fewer of us about the degree and nature of the government's duplicity. It had seemed all along that to appoint a group of MPs, proportionally representative of the government majority in the House of Commons, to decide the question of whether Blair & Co. or the BBC were to be blamed for exaggerating certain details in the intelligence reports on Iraqi weapons, was quite wrong. How wrong became doubly apparent when, following all too immediately on Dr Kelly's death, our footloose prime minister paused on his way to open a new branch of Tesco's in Tokyo and announced that a 'senior' judge would now be asked to look into the circumstances which precipitated that sad event.

And all this hinging, as by the rules of our Parliamentary play-acting it had been led to do, on an assertion which in a less artificial world would have counted for nothing, that the Iraqi weapons imagined to be pointing in our direction could have been brought into use within 45 minutes, or to put that less sexily, within three-quarters of an hour. That assertion had a spurious ring from the word go, its arbitrary precision suggesting it had been elicited from, and not volunteered by whoever was its source: the age-old spinner's gambit of asking an expert whether such a thing is possible and then, on being told yes, it's possible, adopting it, expert caveats notwithstanding, for the unworthy purposes that Blair's 45 minutes were adopted – as evidence waiting to be put before an impressionable nation so that an already dodgy dossier can be made that little bit dodgier. Those of us who remember the four-minute warning, the brief window of opportunity we were told was all we would enjoy between being alerted to an upcoming nuclear attack and its arrival, might well reflect that the 45 minutes, had they been a reality, would have seemed on the leisurely side: mildly reassuring evidence that the Iraqis weren't quite as quick on the technological draw as they should have been.

Whether it was the government that spun the intelligence evidence it had received or, subsequently, the BBC that spun, should never have become the issue it has become, to the point where the BBC may suffer lasting damage at the hands of a vindictive regime. The hard fact is that the evidence, whether spun or unspun, was, we're now entitled to believe, false, and in my own view is likely to have been sufficiently negative in respect of Iraq's capabilities to smooth the way to the launching of a low-risk war. Nevertheless, the 45 minutes have been written indelibly into the script of the unholy theatrical performance which threatens to run and run, along with the deal that never was between Iraq and Niger to buy uranium, a deal which Professor Norman Dombey suggested in the LRB last year could very easily have been an intelligence sting, if a peculiarly pointless one, since Iraq already had, as Dombey pointed out, 'hundreds of tons of uranium at its disposal'. It involved what was by all accounts an elementary forgery, which should have taken in no one at all, but for which our government was happy to fall, its lack of scepticism further evidence that when you are set on having a war, you don't analyse what you learn from intelligence services too carefully in case it puts you off.

Meanwhile, the delusional cast of mind of those who ordered our armed services into action on a false prospectus appears to be spreading, no doubt being seen in high places as a sound qualification for anyone who may now be angling to land a job sorting things out in Iraq itself. Thus the man who has been put in charge of a body called the Iraq Industry Working Group was quoted last week as saying that within quite a short time – as little as three years, he thought – Iraq could be turned from the unhappy scene of murderous disorder and deprivation it currently is into a tourist venue, containing, as he reminded us, such recently overlooked destinations as the 'birthplace of Abraham' and the Hanging Gardens of Babylon, even if these particular sites might need a spot of making over by the people you see on television doing that sort of thing in the English suburbs. Why, on the other hand, wait even three years to open the country up to tourists, when you could start easyJetting them in straight away and offer them their own weight in air miles if they manage while they're there to do what no one else has done and finger the missing weapons?

7 August 2003

THE POLITICS OF
GOOD INTENTIONS

David Runciman

O N 1 APRIL 2003, the *Guardian* admonished the prime minister to remember the importance of living up to his good intentions:

> Putting Iraq to rights, in Mr Blair's view, should be the whole world's business. The more that all nations make common cause to do this, the better. The less this happens, the more vital it is to balance any absence of common cause with a sense of equitable and humanitarian initiatives – on the Middle East and on reconstruction in particular – which can help establish what Disraeli, seeking to justify the British invasion of Abyssinia in 1867, called 'the purity of our purpose'.

Disraeli is perhaps not the most obvious of Tony Blair's predecessors for the *Guardian* to summon in aid of its own, consistently high-minded opposition to creeping American imperialism. It is true, nevertheless, that the British invasion of Abyssinia, which began in 1867 but concluded only in the spring of 1868, offers some striking parallels with this spring's conflict in Iraq. Disraeli's Abyssinian adventure was, as its architect conceded in the House of Commons on 2 July 1868, 'a most costly and perilous expedition', the announcement of which was 'received in more than one quarter with something like mocking incredulity'. Indeed, 'when the invasion of Abyssinia was first mooted, it was denounced as a rash enterprise, pregnant with certain peril and probable disaster.' The risks were diminished, however, by the massive technological imbalance between the combatants, and in the end it was no surprise that, as Disraeli put it, 'the manly qualities of the Abyssinians sank before the resources of our warlike science.' The decisive battle of the war – the Battle of Arogi – lasted for an hour and a half, at the end of which the British forces had suffered 29 casualties. Of the Abyssinian force of three thousand at least five hundred were killed; many more were wounded. So the nay-sayers and doommongers at home were also routed, and Disraeli was able to tell the Commons that 'we have asserted the purity of our purpose.' 'In an age accused, and perhaps not unjustly, of selfishness, and too great a regard for material interests,' he continued, 'it is something, in so striking and significant a manner, for a great nation to have vindicated the higher principles of humanity.' The leader of the opposition, William

Gladstone, seconding Disraeli's vote of thanks to the troops who had pulled off this masterly campaign, could only acquiesce.

Unfortunately, however, Disraeli meant by the purity of his purpose precisely the opposite of the course the *Guardian* was urging on Blair. The Abyssinian war was fought to free a group of nine hostages – the British consul among them – who had been taken by the King of Abyssinia, Theodore II, to his fortress at Magdala in a fit of pique after Queen Victoria had refused his pleas for help, as a Christian, in his wars with his Muslim neighbours. The hostages were rescued, albeit at vast expense (the final bill for the expedition, at £9 million, was nearly double the original estimates), and Theodore committed suicide in his ruined fortress, shooting himself in the mouth with a pistol he had been given as a present by Victoria. The fortress was cleared, its armaments destroyed, and the town of Magdala burned. Then the British troops went home. The proof of Disraeli's pure intentions came precisely from the fact that they didn't hang around, didn't try to rebuild, or oversee, or maintain anything in the place they had sacked, but simply got out. Because Disraeli was a bona fide imperialist – a believer, like many of those around George Bush, in the principle of *Imperium et Libertas* – he could demonstrate that he had no goal other than that of freeing the hostages and punishing their captors only by sacking the place where they had been held. The 'higher principles of humanity' he sought to uphold were not what we would now call the higher principles of humanitarianism. Rather, they were the principles of biblical justice, the idea that wrongdoers would be pursued, no matter how far away, and no matter how relatively trivial the offence. Saddam Hussein could have been treated in the same way. His technical offence – the breach of United Nations resolutions – was also relatively trivial in the grand scheme of things (trivial in the sense that it happens all the time). The Abyssinian solution would have been to find Saddam's weapons of mass destruction, destroy them and those responsible for them, and then leave, in order to prove it really was about the weapons, and not about something else. It is a sign of the very different moral and political universe Blair inhabits that he can prove the purity of his purpose only by persuading the biblically-minded Bush to do the reverse – to stick around (though not for too long), spend more money and try to repair some of the damage. And it is a sign of the complexities of Blair's moral and political universe that this risks the charge that Disraeli the bona fide imperialist was able to avoid: the charge of imperialism.

Still, you can see why the *Guardian* was so desperately rummaging for some historical precedent in order to pin the government down. The New World Order is awash with good intentions, many of them Tony Blair's. Yet the suspicion remains that good intentions in politics don't count for much. One of the things that unites all critics of Blair's war in Iraq, whether from the Left or the Right, is that they are sick of the sound of Blair trumpeting the purity of his purpose, when what matters is the consequences of his actions. Yet there he stands, somewhere between Left and Right, trumpeting away. And he remains very hard to pin down, because Blair doesn't just believe in good intentions; he, too, believes that what matters is outcomes, and is prepared, as he puts it, 'to let history be my judge'. He is still, despite his new-found disdain for focus groups, a Third Way politician, and he believes in having things both ways. What, then, is the worth of his good intentions? Does history provide any sort of guide?

The most celebrated, as well as the most sceptical, historical account of the role of intention in justifying political action is the one given by Max Weber in his lecture 'Politik als Beruf' (usually translated as 'Politics as a Vocation'). It was delivered on 28 January 1919 to a group of students in Munich, and Weber used it to warn them, among other things, against politicians who come flaunting their good intentions, but leave behind them a trail of blood. Munich was not short of examples of this type in early 1919. The most prominent was the journalist turned politician Kurt Eisner, who had stumbled into power at the beginning of November the previous year when he declared Bavaria a republic, two days before a similar proclamation was made in Berlin, and four days before the official end of the war. Eisner remained at the head of the state he had brought into being, despite the fact that the elections he called to the new Bavarian Parliament in January had seen his group of Independent Socialists receive just 2.5 per cent of the vote, and three of the 180 seats available. Brushing aside this result, and the unsurprising clamour for his resignation, Eisner clung to office, on the grounds that practical politics had to give way before the purity of his purpose. His mission as he saw it was to cleanse the political life of Germany, starting in Bavaria, by embracing the idea of German war-guilt. In Eisner's world, everything that preceded November 1918 was immoral, sinful and corrupt; everything after could be beautiful, healthy and pure, if only German politicians would own up to the wickedness of what had gone before.

Eisner was not in Munich to hear Weber's lecture. He had better things to do. In fact, at the end of January he had a choice of three different conferences to attend as the representative of the new moral order in Bavaria – one in France, one in Germany and one in Switzerland. He could have gone to Paris, to witness the start of the peace negotiations that were to culminate in August in the Treaty of Versailles. Alternatively, he could have gone to Weimar, where he was expected to attend the opening of the Constituent Assembly that also produced in August a document of world-historical significance: the Constitution of the new German Republic. Instead, Eisner chose to go to Berne to attend a convention of European socialists, whose delegates included Ramsay MacDonald and Arthur Henderson, and which produced nothing.

The convention was designed as a continuation of the regular prewar gatherings of the Socialist International, at which various factions had squabbled and bickered before declaring their unshakeable class solidarity and confidence in the future. The elephant in the room this time, politely ignored by some of those in attendance, was the fact that the working classes of Europe had spent the last four years trying to blow each other to bits. Eisner was not a man to ignore an elephant in the room; rather, he dressed it up in ribbons and bows and tried to pass it off as a peace offering. Germany was to blame for the horrors of the war, he readily acknowledged. But because Germany was to blame, Germany was the best source of hope for the future. This was designed to be the beginning of a virtuous circle: expressions of guilt would mean a fresh start; a fresh start was the surest sign that the past was truly regretted. 'We want to expiate our guilt,' Eisner told his fellow delegates, 'by going ahead on the path of socialism.' What did elections, or peace treaties, or constitutions, matter in the face of moral renewal? Nevertheless, Eisner decided to return from Berne to Munich, where his absence had been much resented, in time to attend the inauguration of the new Bavarian Parliament on 21 February. Going to the opening ceremony on foot, and heedless of the repeated threats to his life he had received since coming to power, he was confronted by an embittered, anti-semitic Bavarian aristocrat called Count Anton von Arco-Valley, who shot him dead. The moral renewal of Bavarian politics was over.

The mismatch between Eisner's intentions and the unintended outcome of his brief period of prominence would be comic, if it weren't so tragic. When news of the assassination reached the chamber to which he had been heading, one of his few remaining supporters produced a pistol of his own and shot the leader of the majority Independent Socialist Party, wounding but not killing him. After that, things went quickly downhill. Within weeks a workers' soviet republic was declared, though it continued to be governed by those Weber called 'littérateurs' – 'poets, semi-poets, mezzo-philosophers and schoolteachers'. They sent an armed Red Guard onto the streets of Munich, but insisted that they mark their uncompromising opposition to bourgeois ways by pointing the muzzles of their rifles to the ground. The majority socialists fled the city, and soon more systematic killing began. This was enough for the government in Berlin, and for its nominal head, Friedrich Ebert, soon to be the first president of the Weimar Republic. He acquiesced in the suppression of the Bavarian revolution by the Freikorps, troops with mixed loyalties but united in their anti-Bolshevism and taste for vengeance. (He had earlier acquiesced in the murders of Rosa Luxemburg and Karl Liebknecht, the leaders of the short-lived Bolshevik uprising in Berlin, deaths which elicited from Weber the memorably heartless response: 'They called up the street, and the street has dispatched them.') In

Munich, Red Terror was followed by White Terror, which was worse. By May, it was all over. Many thousands of people were dead, and political life in Munich became what it was to remain for the remainder of the Weimar years, a running sore for the new Republic. Eisner had hoped to create in Bavaria a beacon for a new kind of politics, founded on goodwill and high moral purpose. After his death, Bavaria did quite quickly become the seedbed of a new political movement; it was, however, entirely malevolent. Munich was the birthplace of National Socialism.

Weber does not mention Eisner by name in the published version of his lecture, which appeared in October 1919. He probably felt he didn't need to. Nor does he refer to Friedrich Ebert, though it is possible to read parts of the text as an address to the new president, encouraging him to hold firm. Instead, Weber chooses to discuss the thoughts of Professor Friedrich Förster, a celebrated moralist and pacifist, who was his colleague at Munich University, as well as a colleague of Eisner's in the new Bavarian government. Förster also happened to be in Switzerland at the beginning of 1919: he had been sent there by Eisner as his ambassador, charged with spreading the news of Germany's rediscovered sense of its moral responsibilities, and the sincerity of its good intentions. It was Förster's belief that, in politics, only good can flow from good, and only evil from evil. For Weber, this was the political philosophy of a child. 'Not just the entire course of world history,' he wrote, 'but any unbiased examination of daily experience, proclaims the opposite.' Förster's mistake was to believe that a Christian ethic, and the benign categories of religious moral thought, could possibly apply to the world of politics. Politics is the devil's business. 'Anyone who gets involved with politics,' Weber declared in one of the best-known passages in the lecture, 'is making a pact with diabolical powers.' It doesn't follow from this that we are all damned; only that no one should get involved with politics if damnation is what primarily concerns them. Förster, Weber said, was a man he could respect 'because of the undoubted integrity of his convictions'; but for just that reason, he went on, 'I reject him unreservedly as a politician.' It was of only small comfort that if such a man was to get involved in politics, ambassador to Switzerland (a nation Weber sometimes held up as a model of what can happen if you decide to opt out of power politics altogether) was probably the best position for him.

Eisner and Förster were united by their sense that war-guilt was an essential vehicle of political renewal, and was to be enthusiastically embraced. Weber thought their fixation not only childish but perverse. In his lecture, he drew an analogy with the way some men behave when a love affair turns sour. Most men, he argues, will attempt self-justification, telling themselves that '"she did not deserve my love," or "she disappointed me," or offering some other such "reasons"'. This is a 'profoundly unchivalrous attitude', since it burdens the abandoned woman 'not only with misfortune but also with being in the wrong'. It also has a counterpart in the attitude of the unsuccessful lover, the man who takes his rejection as a sign of inadequacy, that he is of 'lesser worth'. The same kinds of thing, Weber suggests, happen after a war:

> The victor will of course assert, with ignoble self-righteousness: 'I won because I was in the right' . . . When the horrors of war cause a man to suffer a psychological break-down, instead of simply saying, 'It was all just too much for me,' he now feels the need to justify his war-weariness by substituting the feeling: 'I couldn't bear the expe-rience because I was forced to fight for a morally bad cause.' The same applies to those defeated in war. Instead of searching, like an old woman, for the 'guilty party' after the war (when it was in fact the structure of society that produced the war), anyone with a manly, unsentimental bearing would say to the enemy: 'We lost the war – you won it. The matter is now settled. Now let us discuss what conclusions are to be drawn in the light of the substantive interests involved and – this is the main thing – in the light of the responsibility for the future which the victor in particular must bear.' Anything else lacks dignity and will have dire consequences.

A preoccupation with guilt is a mark of irresponsibility, both in sexual relations and in political relations. In his lecture, Weber cautiously extends the sexual analogy, calling questions of past guilt 'politically sterile (because unresolvable)'. But he was more explicit in his private correspondence. In a letter he wrote on 13 November 1918, he complained that 'this wallowing in guilt feelings . . . is a sickness – just as flagellation is one in the religious area and masochism is in the sexual sphere.' Weber was not alone in holding this view. M.J. Bonn, another professor at Munich University during 1919, recalled long afterwards his feeling that Bavarian politics were dominated during this period by 'neurotic temperaments to whom self-inflicted tortures are a source of joy'. For some, peace without honour was too good an opportunity to pass by. 'These Germans,' Bonn wrote, 'went at it, as *flagellantes*.'

'Sterile excitement' is how Weber characterises the temptations of conviction politics. He contrasts them with what he calls an 'ethic of responsibility'. Respon-sibility does not exclude conviction, but it does presuppose a particular attitude towards it. The responsible politician knows that good does not always follow from good. Even actions undertaken with the best intentions will generate unintended consequences, and the mark of a responsible politician is how these are dealt with. The way to deal with them is to take responsibility for them, which means neither denying them nor wallowing in them, but accepting them for what they are: the unintended but foreseeable consequences of any involvement in politics. All politi-cians with real power have dirty hands, because real politics is a bloody business. The trick for Weber is not to try to hide them, nor to parade them through the streets, but just to get on with the task in hand, in the knowledge that dirty hands, and a soiled conscience, are the price that all politicians have to pay. Responsible politicians will suffer, but they should suffer in silence, because the test of politics is whether you can cope with the knowledge that you are not as good as you would like to be.

How easy, though, is it to distinguish this ready acceptance of suffering from some of the vices that Weber detects in the irresponsible politician? The American philosopher Michael Walzer, writing in 1973, in the immediate aftermath of another misjudged imperial war, detected in Weber's 'mature, superbly trained, relentless, objective, responsible and disciplined political leader' a recognisable type: the type of the 'suffering servant'. 'Here is a man who lies, intrigues, sends others to their death – and suffers. None of us can know, he tells us, how much it costs him to do his duty.' The almost teary, always steely look on Vladimir Putin's waxen face, most notably as he apologised on Russian television for the deaths of innocents after the Moscow theatre siege last year, is the perfect embodiment of this. The responsible politician can apologise, but he can't do more than apologise, because that would mean passing the burden onto someone else. As a result, responsible politics in the wrong hands can look a lot like its opposite. 'We suspect the suffering servant of either masochism or hypocrisy or both,' Walzer writes, 'and while we are often wrong, we are not always wrong.'

How can we tell? Weber does not give many examples in 'Politik als Beruf' of politicians who fit his mould of responsibility, but the one who appears most often also happens to be the most notorious self-flagellant in modern political history. Weber does not discuss, and presumably knew nothing about, William Gladstone's predilection for scourging himself with a whip after his periodic encounters with prostitutes whom he was endeavouring to 'save'. Instead, Gladstone appears as an example of two interrelated phenomena which Weber takes to be characteristic of modern, professional politics. First, Gladstone was a quintessential product of the age of machine politics, and a symbol both of its increasing prevalence and of its paradoxes. He was not a machine politician himself: he stood outside the party machine and simply required it to do his bidding. It did his bidding because he gave the machine what it required: electoral success. And he did this precisely by being more than just a machine politician in the eyes of the public. It was what Weber calls the 'ethical character' of Gladstone's personality, the sense that he was not just a vote-winner, that gave him his hold over the new breed of political professionals who were interested in nothing more than getting out the vote. His electoral success, particularly after the Midlothian Campaign of 1879-80, also exemplified another aspect of modern politics in Weber's eyes, the heightened sense of legitimacy that mass democratic politics can bestow on successful politicians, particularly in Britain and the United States. Gladstone was, for Weber, 'the dictator of the electoral battlefield', and Weber admired the British Parliamentary system precisely for its capacity to produce leaders of this type. Gladstone may have been an ethical politician, but nothing about his political ethics was straightforward. As a successful conviction politician in an age of mass politics, he was, almost by definition, not simply a conviction politician.

Tony Blair is the political leader of the last hundred years who most obviously fits the Gladstonian mould. He is, like one or two before him, the dictator of the electoral battlefield, but he is also more than anyone since Gladstone a politician of a particular ethical type: moralising, ruthless, self-serving, pious, visionary, partisan and thoroughly self-aware. He may or may not be a hypocrite – it is one of the marks of this kind of politician and this kind of politics that the charge of hypocrisy is almost impossible to prove and impossible to refute – but he is showing increasing signs of masochism. In the run-up to the war on Iraq, Blair's public performances were marked by a relish for confrontations in which he could not hope to come out on top. All he could do was show us that he was willing to suffer the barbs of his opponents, and do so uncomplainingly, because it was his lot to suffer for his beliefs. This reached its apogee in the bizarre encounter on 10 March with a group of women in an ITV studio, at the end of which he was slow-handclapped for the first time since his encounter with the Women's Institute in 2000, something he hadn't seemed to enjoy at all. This time he appeared, if not exactly to enjoy the abuse, almost to welcome it. His facial expressions – long-suffering, concerned, sincere, distressed, resolute – gave the whole thing the feeling of what Gladstone would have called 'rescue work', although in this case no one wanted to be rescued. The audience included three women who had been bereaved by terrorism, two on 11 September, and one in the attack on Bali. Unsurprisingly, Blair had nothing to say in the face of their rage and pain except to let it wash over him. No politician in their right mind would choose the recently bereaved as their interlocutors for an argument about the rights and wrongs of a proposed course of action that involved killing. But this was not an argument – it was an exchange of feelings, conducted in an atmosphere of mutual incomprehension, and barely suppressed emotion. The point, so far as one could tell, was for Blair to be able to say, as he did say, repeatedly, that just as he understood the strength of feeling of his opponents, he needed them to understand that he felt just as strongly.

The difference between Blair's rescue work and Gladstone's is that Gladstone's really was rescue work – it was private, and personal, and more or less secret. Like the self-scourging that followed it, it lay deep in the background to his politics, and though some hint of its tone may occasionally have leaked into his political rhetoric, it was not a political strategy (public exposure would have been catastrophic). Blair's masochism is a political strategy, and has, one presumes, no echoes in his private life. In this respect, Blair has more in common with Eisner than with Gladstone: he makes a parade of his guilt. Of course, he's really nothing like Eisner or Förster or any of the other moralisers who briefly and disastrously flitted across the scene of German politics in the Weimar period. He is not nearly wishful enough, and much too successful. He is also much too keen on war (five in six years, at the last count). Eisner and Förster were expressing guilt for a war they had done what they could to oppose, and whole-heartedly repudiated. Blair may have tried to prevent war in Iraq, but not even his most fervent admirers could claim he did so whole-heartedly. He is a different kind of politician, who doesn't really fit into Weber's typologies of political responsibility and irresponsibility. He seems to be both types at once.

Take Weber's injunction that responsible politicians should always weigh their intentions against the consequences, both intended and unintended, of what they do, and not simply contrast their own motives with the ill-will of their opponents. 'What distinguishes the polemics directed by most exponents of the supposedly new ethics at the opponents they criticise from the polemics of other demagogues?' Weber asked in his lecture. 'Their noble intentions, some will say. Very well. But the claim under discussion here is the means, and their enemies lay just as much claim to noble intentions, and do so with complete sincerity.' It was a distinction of this kind that even the moralising Gladstone sought to uphold. Though he made clear his personal revulsion at the antics of his Tory opponents, he was careful not to impugn their motives, for it was not motives that mattered. Gladstone made much of his principles – at Midlothian it was 'the sound and sacred principle that Christendom is formed by a band of nations who are united to one another in the bonds of right; that they are without distinction of great and small'. But he went on:

> I hold that he who by act or word brings that principle into peril or disparagement, however honest his intentions may be, places himself in the position of one inflicting – I won't say intending to inflict – I ascribe nothing of the sort – but inflicting injury on his own country, and endangering the peace of all the most fundamental interests of Christian society.

Tony Blair is not so cautious. He does not shirk from questioning the motives of his opponents, from the wicked Saddam, to the malicious French, to the self-serving Liberal Democrats, to the cynical media. Moreover, it is central to the political philosophy of Blairism that actions that may conceivably endanger the most fundamental interests of the international community can be justified by the good intentions that lie behind them. Yet, as Weber says, what matters here are the means.

Disraeli was able to show that there was no mismatch between the means and the end of his adventure in Abyssinia, because he set out to liberate only nine hostages, not a whole captive people. Blair does not have this luxury. There is an unavoidable mismatch between what he intends and the methods he employs, because he intends peace and has chosen war. Nor does he have the luxury of the 19th-century politician in the face of this paradox, which is to invoke God. Abraham Lincoln, who also fought a war for peace, and is in some ways the embodiment of what Weber meant by a responsible politician, did not have to take full responsibility for the war he fought. In a letter of 4 September 1864, he wrote to a friend: 'We hoped for a happy termination of this terrible war long before this; but God knows best, and has ruled otherwise . . . Surely He intends some great good to follow this mighty convulsion, which no mortal could make, and no mortal could stay.' Blair may think like this, but he couldn't say it, even among friends, for fear of ridicule. Lincoln also spoke of the purity of his own purpose ('Having chosen our course,' he told Congress on 4 July 1861, 'without guile, and with pure purpose, let us renew our trust in God, and go forward without fear, and with manly hearts'), but he had the further advantage of being able to prove it, in adversity. The warlike science available to Lincoln's armies, newly terrible as it was, was also available in large extent to the other side, so that neither could hope to win without being prepared for a long, hard, bloody conflict, which is what they got. Purity of purpose here meant, among other things, a willingness to fight to the end. Blair can't really talk in these terms, because the fights he picks are too one-sided. It is true that he likes to point out that in each of his major wars (Kosovo, Afghanistan, Iraq) he stayed the course when the doubters were writing his political obituary. But it was in each case just his obituary they were writing, and just a political one; the killing remained almost entirely the killing of unknowns on the other side. Moreover, staying the course meant holding his nerve for a few weeks in the face of attacks mounted in TV studios and in the pages of publications like this one. Blair has shown courage, but he has not had to show all that much courage; certainly he has not been given the opportunity to demonstrate his integrity solely by dint of what Lincoln and Weber might have called his 'manliness'.

Instead, in each conflict Blair has fought, he has been forced to offer a different kind of justification for the mismatch between means and ends. He has explicitly conflated the two types of politics Weber sought to distinguish – responsible and irresponsible politics, or the politics of unintended consequences and the politics of good intentions. He has sought to show that he is well intentioned by showing that he takes the unintended consequences of his actions seriously. In some ways, this is such a familiar argument that it is barely noticed any more. But it is only familiar because Blair has made it so. For example, speaking in the House of Commons on 28 April 1999, during one of the 'difficult' phases of the Kosovo conflict, when innocent civilians were being killed by stray bombs but little progress was being made, Blair defended himself in these terms: 'The difference' – between us and them – 'quite simply is this. Whenever there are civilian casualties as a result of allied bombs, they are by error. We regret them, and we take precautions to avoid them. The people whom the Serb paramilitaries are killing are killed deliberately. That is the difference between us and them.' This statement contains the three classic elements of Blairite self-justification in wartime. 'We' are to be distinguished from 'them', first by our 'regret', second by our 'precaution', and third by the fact that in our case the killing is not 'deliberate' – it is unintended. Of these three, the second carries least weight, both morally and politically. The best way to take precaution against the killing of innocents is not to drop bombs on them in the first place. It is perfectly possible to believe that one should do everything one can to avoid causing unintended harm or injury, but that means being willing to abjure politics, as the only certain way to avoid these things. The Kosovo war was hardly an abjuration of politics, but rather something like an attempt to adhere to what Weber calls the politician's maxim: 'You shall resist evil with force, for if you do not, you are responsible for the spread of evil.' Hence, inevitably, a limited role for precaution.

There is also something problematic about the 'we' here, since 'we' doesn't really mean us, but the Americans. The American conduct in recent wars, whether in Kosovo, or Afghanistan, or Iraq, has occasionally been cautious – the high altitude from which the bombs were dropped on Kosovo, for fear of Serb artillery; the 'operational pause' before Baghdad while the Republican Guard was pounded into dust – but this is not the same as taking precautions against the unnecessary loss of life among non-combatants. In fact, it's the opposite. Taking precautions in Kosovo would have meant flying bombing missions at a low enough height to make accurate identification of targets possible. In Iraq, it would have meant more special forces operations, and fewer large explosions. Bunker-busters, cluster-bombs and daisy-cutters are not precautionary weapons.

So, that leaves regret and good intentions. What does Blair mean by regret? Presumably he means that 'we' take the deaths of the civilians seriously, that we do not discount them or consider them nugatory in the light of the justness of the cause, that we do not simply accept that some people's lives are means while others' are ends. It is true, in war, that some people's lives will be means in the cause of saving others, but this is not a fact without moral significance; on the contrary, it is precisely because it is morally significant that these deaths are regretted notwithstanding the justness of the cause. This is the language of political responsibility, expressing a willingness to take seriously what Weber calls 'morally suspect or morally dangerous means' without being incapacitated by them. However, regret is, on Weber's account, a 'personal' matter, something that a politician will have to deal with and something from which no politician should suppose themselves immune. What it is not is a justification for political action, as it is used by Blair. This incongruity is emphasised by the fact that in the same breath as expressing his sense of responsibility, Blair also employs the argument from good intentions, by stating that these are deaths by error. In other words, if we discount the line about precaution, he is saying that the difference between him and Milosevic, or Osama bin Laden, or Saddam, is that, on the one hand, he (Blair) regrets what has happened, and, on the other, he has less to regret, because he did not mean to do the things he regrets. Which somewhat diminishes the quality of the regret.

Precaution, regret and the absence of malice have become something of a mantra for what Noam Chomsky calls 'the new military humanism', of which Blair is perhaps the leading exponent. In this philosophy the old methods of power politics are allied to a new ethic of good intentions to produce ostensibly beneficent results. This ethic is not really new, since it draws heavily on the just war tradition, with its emphasis on fighting wars for the right reasons, and with restraint. What is new, in Blair's versions of these arguments at least, is the collapse of the separate principles into each other – the collapse of the distinction between jus ad bellum and jus in bello. Too often, Blair takes restraint as evidence of good intentions, and good intentions as evidence of restraint. This is circular: you can tell we mean well from the fact that we didn't mean to kill those people; you can tell we didn't mean to kill those people from the fact that we mean well. Moreover, just war theory is not designed to help distinguish 'us' from 'them'; it is intended to enable us to distinguish good wars from bad ones. The reason that we fight a particular war cannot be to distinguish ourselves from the enemy in the way we fight it. If that were the motive, we would best distinguish ourselves from the enemy by choosing not to fight at all.

The other striking thing about these Blairite formulations of just war theory is their pervasiveness in the philosophy of New Labour. They do not just apply in the case of war. Indeed, politics in New Labour circles often looks like the continuation of war by other means. For example, Blair's defence of his Kosovo strategy found an echo in the aftermath of that war's successful conclusion in the words of Ian McCartney, then a minister at the DTI, now Labour Party chairman, when seeking to defend the government's domestic record. Speaking in an interview published on 12 July 1999, and wishing to answer the accusation that Labour had abandoned its principles in office, particularly with regard to welfare provision, McCartney said:

The difference between a good minister and one who just performs is that you have to make difficult choices. Sometimes you have to make decisions which disappoint people, but I don't think this government has made a single decision which was malevolent. Every one has been taken for the right reasons and we are really making a difference to people's lives.

There is at least no talk here about precaution, or trying to cause as little damage as possible. It is a straightforward conflation of the argument from responsibility (or in Blair's version 'regret') and the argument from good intentions. First, McCartney sets out the credentials of the responsible politician, who knows that there will be difficult choices – what Gordon Brown likes to call 'tough decisions' – and that the attainment of political ends always involves treating some people as means and not as ends (or, in McCartney's sanitised version, 'disappointing' them). In other words, New Labour understands the idea of unintended consequences. But in the second half of what he says the tone changes from one of self-knowledge to one of justification: the difference, he suggests, between us and them (i.e. the Tories, who would also treat some people as means, but would do so with 'malevolence', or, as Blair might put it, would disappoint people 'deliberately') is precisely that we do not intend these things. As a result, what were difficult choices a sentence earlier have now become easier, because each one is taken for the right reasons. Just as regret justified in terms of intention sounds less like regret, so tough decisions justified in terms of intention sound more like foregone conclusions. Because we regret, we have less to regret. Because we know the choices are difficult, they are not difficult for us. Weber warned against politicians whose saintly intentions were taken to sanctify the unforeseen results of their naivety. McCartney's is the cynic's version of saintliness – a sanctification by other means. Because we know we are not saints, he seems to be saying, you are not to judge us as though we were, and as though we were not fully aware of what we are doing. Knowing we are not saints serves to sanctify the consequences of what we do.

This line of argument can be used to defend anything, even the indefensible. The journalist turned politician Siôn Simon, once the most skilled and fearless of all Blair's polemicists, now languishing on the back benches, offered the absurdist version when seeking to justify another of Blair's pet projects, the grotesque and idiotic Millennium Dome. Writing in the *Daily Telegraph* on 13 November 2000, by which time it was quite clear that the Dome was a monstrous white elephant that no amount of bows or ribbons could disguise, Simon defended it by reminding his readers of the intentions that lay behind its creation:

Blair's decision to go with the Dome was everything it should have been. It showed the confidence that befits a British prime minister. The complaint of arrogance is irrelevant – all confident acts are called arrogant when they go wrong; the word usually employed when they go right is 'brilliant'. That the entire cabinet was against it matters even less. Since assuming the Labour leadership in 1994, Blair has been opposed by the entire shadow cabinet and 95 per cent of the party in virtually every important decision he has made. If Labour had been a democracy rather than an elective dictatorship, the party would now be on a philosophical par with the German Social Democrats. Probably in power and probably headed for another term, largely thanks to the opposition, but with no sense of purpose or direction.

Most important, the Dome was a visionary project . . . It was bold, confident, proud, unembarrassed, modern, European, grand. We were none of these things under John Major, and only partly one or two of them under Mrs Thatcher when we went to war. Furthermore, it was a very open, self-imperilling and therefore very trusting thing for a leader to do. Blair didn't just take the national mood as fixed, he set about changing it. The paradox is that although the means failed, the ends were achieved.

This is a longer and bolder version of the 'non-apology' apology that Blair himself offered at the Labour Party Conference that year, when, in a carefully choreographed moment of contrition, he said that although he took full responsibility for the fact that the Dome had not achieved what it set out to achieve, he wouldn't apologise for 'trying'. Simon's version is also explicitly Weberian. He invokes the confidence that is both a responsibility and a resource of the office of prime minister, which derives from the particular relation between party and leader within the British Parliamentary system, and which is documented by Weber in the first part of 'Politik als Beruf', culminating in his description of Gladstone's mastery of the party machine. Simon recognises, and celebrates, the fact that Blair, too, is dictator of the electoral battlefield. His dig at the German Social Democrats picks up on a further preoccupation of Weber's political writings, which was how to reconcile the Caesarist demands of modern mass democracy with the limitations placed on it by a system of proportional representation, and with the interests and principles that the so-called 'ethical' parties of the Left seek to represent within such a system. But alongside these Weberian and mock-Weberian themes Simon runs another set of claims, which are quintessentially Blairite. This is the argument that Blair's courage, the 'self-imperilling' nature of the whole enterprise, can justify it after the event, when it has gone wrong. Certainly the Dome was a very risky thing for a British prime minister to get involved with, in that it was hideously expensive, horribly managed and full of rubbish. But this can hardly serve to justify the decision to proceed.

Simon suggests that the fact that this was such a risky project should excuse its unintended outcome; but if it does excuse it, then the project turns out not to have been so risky after all. The Dome cannot both have endangered the prime minister and be cited as the reason we should give him the benefit of the doubt.

Simon takes the us/them distinction that Blair maintains in the international arena, and McCartney in the domestic arena, and runs it through the party machine. The 'them' here are the rest of the cabinet and 95 per cent of the party; above all, the 'them' is Gordon Brown, who is known to have opposed the Dome in cabinet, and would not therefore, had he been prime minister, even have 'tried'. Simon also makes explicit the connection between such self-serving visionary politics and war (as Blair's outriders periodically like to remind the press, Brown doesn't really 'do war'). But the conflict in Iraq shows the limits of this kind of self-justification. Not even Blair would have been able to save himself, if the military campaign had gone wrong, by claiming to take responsibility for the failure, but refusing to apologise for 'trying'. He would have had to resign (as, in a perfect world, he should have had to resign over the Dome, which was the biggest public accounting scandal of the last fifty years). What's more, Blair has now hitched his wagon to an American president who, unlike his predecessor, doesn't really do philosophical contortion ('although the means failed, the ends were achieved'). George Bush is more like a cowboy version of Friedrich Förster, who believes that good will follow from good, and evil-doers will pay the price of evil. In a sense, this has allowed Blair to be more straightforwardly moralistic about this war than he was about Kosovo, where he was hedged in by the caution of his allies. It is also true that in this war the moral equation was simpler, in utilitarian terms at least: it may be true that it would have done more harm to leave Saddam's regime in place than to remove it by force (this was also true of the Serbian regime in 1999, but complicated by the fact that regime change was not the aim of that war, and much of the visible harm inflicted by Milosevic in Kosovo took place after the allies started dropping their bombs). But if Blair is more straightforward about his claim that this war is a good war, he is also more straightforwardly hypocritical. His insistence, for example, that he could ignore a veto by one of the permanent members of the UN Security Council if that veto was 'capricious' makes a mockery of the international legal system he also wishes to uphold. If French vetoes are 'capricious', and American and British vetoes are not, then we are back in a world where intentions count more than outcomes. If this is true, then no vote on the Security Council or anywhere else carries any weight, because what matters is not the show of hands but the presence or absence of malice among those who raise them. This is the same reasoning that led Eisner to refuse to accept the outcome of elections to the Bavarian Parliament in 1919, and the reason it was hypocritical (and foolhardy) of him to attend its opening ceremony.

Some commentators have taken the new-found brazenness of Blair's hypocrisy as evidence that he is not simply foolhardy, but has gone mad. Matthew Parris, writing in the *Times*, has cited Blair's serene attitude to his rebuff in the Security Council, along with his increasing self-righteousness, his Iraq fixation and the strange look in his eye, as symptoms of mental unbalance, and possibly the beginnings of mental collapse. Weber warned in 'Politik als Beruf' that mental breakdown is the risk that all conviction politicians run, because the dirty reality of politics always chafes against the clean, straight lines of conduct they try to follow. As these become blurred, the temptation is to go into denial, and to declare: 'The world is stupid and base, not I. Responsibility for the consequences does not fall on me but on the others, in whose service I work and whose stupidity and baseness I shall eradicate.' Anyone who believes this is indeed mad. But Blair is not mad, at least not in this way. He knows that because the world is stupid and base, it doesn't pay to think in these terms. He also knows that madness is not an attractive quality in a responsible politician. Indeed, just as it is part of the intellectual architecture of Blairism to equate political responsibility with an absence of the malice that marks one's opponents, so it is traditional to question their sanity as well. The Blairite response to the charge of mental unbalance is to say: 'Look, we know politics is a devilish business, which is what distinguishes us from our enemies – the "mad" and the "crazy", like Milosevic and Saddam; the simply "weird", like most of the Tory front bench; or just poor, troubled Gordon with his "psychological flaws". Seeing what it does to other people is what keeps us sane.'

What is distinctive about Tony Blair's version of political responsibility is that he takes what is 'internal' in Weber's account – that is, what belongs to the interior life of the politician, or the party machine – and plays it out on the surface of politics, so that the inner workings of his political conscience are laid bare. Gordon Brown's problem, and before him Gladstone's – another Iron Chancellor who was thought by many even in his own party to be mentally unbalanced, and therefore unfit to become prime minister – is that they keep it all buttoned up inside. Blair is able to talk about his good intentions by making a parade of his awareness of their limitations. This is not a tactic that would work for everyone – George Bush, for example, prefers to make a spectacle of his own personal limitations, his very 'ordinariness', in order to highlight the strength of his convictions – but it works for Blair. What it does not do is justify any particular course of action. Knowing that good intentions aren't enough isn't enough.

8 May 2003

SEEING STARS

Alan Bennett

IN THE 1940S WITHIN a mile or so of where we lived in Armley in Leeds there were at least half a dozen cinemas. Nearest was the Picturedrome on Wortley Road but others were just a walk or a tramride away – the Lyric down Tong Road, the Clifton at Bramley, the Palace off Stanningley Road and the Western a bit further on. And without ever being a dedicated filmgoer I could have graded them all from flea-pit upwards in their degree of comfort and sophistication just as, a little later, I would be able to grade the neighbourhood churches in terms of high and low, many of the churches and cinemas since sharing a common fate, conversion to carpet warehouses, second-hand furniture marts and, nowadays, health clubs.

Programmes changed twice a week and we generally went on a Monday and a Saturday. Comedies were best, particularly George Formby, but we took what was on offer, never knowing whether a film had any special merit. Some came with more of a reputation than others, *Mrs Miniver* for instance with Greer Garson, *Dangerous Moonlight* (with the Warsaw Concerto) and *Now, Voyager* with the famous cigarettes. But I'm sure I must have seen both *Citizen Kane* and *Casablanca* on their first time round with no notion that these were films of a different order from the usual twice-weekly fare. It was only towards the end of the war that more of a fuss started to be made over forthcoming films, so that I remember reading in *Picture Post* (and probably at the barber's) about *The Way to the Stars* with the young Jean Simmons, and the making of Michael Powell's *A Canterbury Tale*, and the first Royal Command Performance, another Powell film, *A Matter of Life and Death*.

Suburban cinemas were often pretty comfortless places. While the entrance could be quite imposing, with the box office generally at the top of a flight of white marble steps, presumably to accommodate the rake, the auditorium itself was often not much more than a hangar, the aisle carpeted but the seats on lino or even bare concrete. Wartime meant there was no ice-cream but en route to the cinema we would call at a sweet shop and get what Dad called 'some spice', provided, of course, we had the points, sweet rationing the most irksome of wartime restrictions and still in force as late as 1952, when I went into the army.

As a family we always went to the first house, which ended around 8.10, with the second-house queue waiting as we came out, scanning our faces for a clue to the experience we had just had, much as, I imagine, soldiers did when queuing outside a brothel. The second-house crowd seemed to me more loose-living than we were, raffish even. It certainly included more courting couples and folks who liked a drink (and who might even have had one already), none of whom minded rolling home at the to us unheard-of hour of half-past ten.

The waiting (and the Second World War involved a good deal of waiting in every department) was generally done up the side of the cinema in a grim open-sided arcade that today would be drenched in urine but wasn't then. If the cinema was full and the performance continuous the commissionaire would come down the queue shouting: 'Two at 1/9'; 'A single at 2/3.' Or (very seldom): 'Seats in all parts.'

We always called it 'the pictures', seldom 'the cinema' and never 'the movies'. To this day I don't find it easy to say 'movies', 'going to the pictures' still the phrase that comes to me most naturally, though nowadays I'm not sure that 'the pictures', like 'the wireless', aren't among the self-consciously adopted emblems of fogeydom, the verbal equivalent of those smart Covent Garden establishments that do a line in old luggage. But calling the pictures 'the movies' went with calling cigarettes 'fags', beer 'booze' or girls 'birds'. It signalled a relaxed, unbuttoned approach to things, life led with more of a dash than I was ever going to manage.

Picture-going was generally a family affair, but when we were still quite young, at eight or nine, say, we were allowed to go to U films by ourselves and (with a bit of nagging) to A films too. Since the A signified that a child could only see the film when accompanied by an adult this meant hanging about outside the cinema accosting congenial-looking cinema-goers, preferably women, with 'Can you take us in, please?' Warning us often, every time we left the house it almost seemed, against 'stopping with strange men', my mother never liked my brother and me to go to the pictures on our own, but only once did I come to any harm and then not really.

In 1944 we had moved, disastrously as it turned out, from Leeds to Guildford, where we stayed for a year, so at that time I would be ten, and had persuaded my mother one afternoon to let me go see Errol Flynn in *The Sea Hawk*, which I'd seen in Armley but was now showing at the Palace in Onslow Street (closed in 1956 to become a bingo hall and currently a nightclub called The Drink). I hung about for a bit until a genial middle-aged man in glasses came along with one boy in tow already. This seemed to indicate respectability and I was about to ask him if he would take me in when he got in first, even taking my hand before shepherding us both past the box office; he may even have paid.

The film had already started, Errol Flynn flirting with Flora Robson as Queen Elizabeth while the usherette showed us down the aisle and before we had even sat down the man was pinching me and remarking on my nice chubby legs. This seemed fairly boring to me as, so far as I was concerned, they were just legs, but I put up with it for the sake of Errol Flynn, who soon after we sat down was away on the Spanish Main. However, the clutching and the pinching was getting more urgent until, innocent though I was, it dawned on me that this must be what Mam's mysterious warnings had been about.

The sight of Errol Flynn now chained to an oar in the Spanish galleys seemed to bring these claspings to a new pitch of urgency and I decided, as they moved higher up my legs, that I ought to make a break for it. So I got up and, foolishly, headed not up the aisle to the foyer but down the aisle to the Gents where, not surprisingly, my admirer followed. Once there, I didn't hide in a cubicle but just stood waiting, not knowing what to do.

I see myself standing in that cinema lavatory and hearing the bang of the swing-door as this kindly, bespectacled man, now suddenly sinister, comes through the door in pursuit. The entrance to the Gents was also the back door to the Exit and my admirer stood there for a second, obviously wondering if I had fled the cinema altogether. There was a moment, which in a film would hardly seem credible, when he stood with his back to me trying to decide if I'd gone. Had he turned and looked down the steps to the lavatory he would have seen me. But he didn't turn, and obviously deciding it would be prudent to leave, he pushed the bar and went out through the exit door.

I wish I could record that I went back and watched the finish of the film but I just hung about for a few minutes until the coast was clear, then (though nothing had happened to me) ran home in mild distress. I told my mother, who became satisfyingly hysterical, but Dad, a shy and fastidious man who I knew regarded me as a liar and a show-off, was just made angry, refusing even to believe anything had happened and, if it had, 'It was all nowt.' Certainly I hadn't been damaged, and if damage was done at all it was only in Dad's refusal to acknowledge the situation. As it was, the only lasting effect of the incident was to put paid to any further lone visits to the cinema and to teach me to keep quiet. One's legs often got felt up as a child. Dad's old headmaster, Mr Alexander, used to give us lessons in algebra and he was a great stroker and clutcher, though only of the legs and not the parts appertaining. Vicars did it too, without seeming to want to take it further. It was something I came to expect, and just another of the ways in which grown-ups were boring.

The stars of the films seen in childhood had an unreality and a glamour no stars have ever had since. It was inconceivable that their world should ever impinge on ours, though occasionally, almost miraculously, it did. That I can remember the deaths both of Leslie Howard and of Carole Lombard chalked up on the newspaper-sellers' boards in City Square hardly counts. But there was the afternoon sometime in the 1940s when I was out shopping with Mam and we were walking up Thornton's Arcade and saw coming down a vast man with a much smaller friend in tow, like a whale and its pilot fish. He was wearing his coat slung around his shoulders just as I'm sure we'd seen him in the cinema when he was the Gestapo chief in *Pimpernel Smith* and, if it was in the late 1940s we would have seen him as Mr Bumble in *Oliver Twist* and Jaggers in *Great Expectations*. It was Francis L. Sullivan, whose huge bulk must have been gracing the stage of the Grand that week, though we did not know it, thinking only that a creature from the celestial realms of film had materialised in, of all places, Leeds. We rushed home to tell Dad, who, predictably, was not much impressed.

Another brush with Hollywood came one morning in Manfield's Shoe Shop on Commercial Street, where Mam's older sister, Kathleen, was the manageress (this was what she claimed anyway, though she may just have been the oldest female assistant). An urbane figure slipped into the shop (and I see him, too, with a camel-hair coat draped round his shoulders and even a cigarette-holder). Aunty (or 'Miss Peel', as she was known in the shop) took charge, and I see her perched sideways on one of those low pentagonal stools on the sloping rubberised side of which the customer placed his or her foot, over which Aunty's head would be reverently bent about to unlace the shoe. Coyly she looks up. 'Have I,' she says in those exaggeratedly correct tones of which she was so proud and which marked her out as a professional woman, 'Have I the pleasure of serving Mr Ronald Colman?'

Whereupon Mr Ronald Colman (and God forgive him) looks most put out, says 'No,' and strides out into Commercial Street. Of course had Aunty had more sense she would have waited until she had his shoe off, then his departure would have been necessarily less prompt. But there was no disguising the awfulness of the rebuff; it was so unmistakable that I'm surprised she was ready to retail the circumstances. But she had seen – and indeed touched – Ronald Colman and there was no gainsaying that. Still, I think even Dad, who was her sternest critic, felt a little sorry for her, believing that the Ronald Colman whom we had seen on the screen (in *Lost Horizon*, for instance, or *Random Harvest*) would have had more manners.

Except that now, telling the story, I can't be sure that it was Ronald Colman and not Robert Donat, who was certainly more likely to be in Leeds and indeed in England and who was known to be shy (and, as Mam said, 'a martyr to asthma') and therefore more likely to bolt from the shop.

Cherished and admired as a local boy was Eric Portman, who had made good while playing with 'the amateurs'. More robust than Donat, he was always said to have worked at a gents' outfitters in Halifax where the aunties may even have claimed to have seen him behind the counter. Then he'd joined the Rep before becoming a star. James Mason was another local boy who had made good, though from what beginnings I wasn't sure: maybe he'd worked in a gents' outfitters too.

'Making good' meant getting out, as you would have to do if you were going to be a film star, but which applied to literature too, the success of J.B. Priestley and, at a later date, John Braine evinced by their brisk departure from their Bradford birthplace. In this respect the Brontë Sisters (Mam had seen the films, though she'd not read the books) were thought to be tragic figures, not on account of their bleak upbringing or their short lives, but because, so far as Mam knew anyway, they had never escaped from that terrible parsonage and stayed put in Haworth all their lives. For both Mam and Dad there was always a sense in which success could be summed up as a one-way ticket to King's Cross.

Film actors inevitably came trailing remnants of their previous roles, memories of other films in which they had figured and the inclinations of the characters they usually played. For a child at the cinema this was a help; there was not much ambiguity to be had and certainly with the masculine roles whether this was a goody or a baddy pretty soon became apparent, or was apparent already because the actor concerned had played more or less the same part in a film one had seen the previous week. Female roles were less easy to assess because love or passion were often motivating factors and at the age of ten both were a bit of a mystery to me. Generally, though, where the actors stood on the moral scale was as plain as if they were characters out of a fairy story. We knew what they would do long before they did it, whatever the plot their roles in it fixed and immutable; they had no need to unpack their belongings: as soon as they showed their faces on the screen one knew what they had brought. There was a certain leeway in the details: the wicked but outwardly respectable businessman might be fond of art or dote on his pretty daughter, the lawyer a bit of a dandy, the killer fond of cats, but these were ornaments, decorations, and in the fixed moral scheme of films in the 1930s and 1940s they did not alter the story but were just the accessories to costumes that were always off the same peg.

What puzzled me about villains was why, when they were masquerading as respectable citizens, their essential no-goodness wasn't as obvious to people on the screen as it was to me in the stalls. How could Pinocchio be so stupid as to be led astray by the patently wicked Fox, or Snow White not know the Queen was up to no good? Had the Queen been flesh and blood and not a cartoon she might well have been played by Joan Crawford, who was always something of an enigma to me. I never liked her, and with her gaunt face, protruding eyes and instinct for melodrama she seemed the embodiment of evil, yet she was often cast in the role of heroine. Even if she managed during the span of the film to convince me of her goodness and all ended happily I felt it was only a matter of time before somewhere in the film's after-life she would emerge in her true colours, grasping, selfish and (because she was like a man) a thoroughgoing rotter.

Claude Rains was another puzzle. He was determinedly silky and seldom unsmiling, sure signs that he was a baddy, though not always. There was the analyst in *Now, Voyager* or, more ambiguously, the Vichy police chief in *Casablanca*, ironic, twinkling and an advert for pragmatism. I wish the lesson I derived from these divergences from what I saw as the norm had been that people weren't always what they seemed, but probably I just wished they'd make their minds up.

Old Mother Riley apart, there weren't many funny women. I didn't go for Gracie Fields nor did I understand why when she appeared everybody suddenly burst out singing – songs in films always something to be endured rather than enjoyed. Still, Gracie Fields in her Northern-mill epics and excursions to Blackpool was preferable to those gloomy, haunted heroines racked by passion and driven by concerns I didn't understand and who cropped up far too often for my taste. There was Ida Lupino, who always seemed to be either blind or confined to a wheelchair; Barbara Stanwyck, who seemed to want to be a man and certainly behaved like one; and the wholesome but plain Jane Wyman, who, on account of the plainness and wholesomeness, could be relied on in the end to get her man, homespun values always winning out against brittle sophistication.

The supreme exponent of brittle sophistication was Bette Davis, and for my aunties in particular she was someone to emulate. With her clipped tones, raised eyebrow and mocking smile Bette was a standard-bearer for shop assistants everywhere and in the 1940s you could find her presiding over the counters of the smarter shops – Marshall and Snelgrove, Matthias Robinson or, in my aunties' case, Manfield's Shoe Shop and White's Ladies Gowns. The Davis manner, bored, sceptical, sarcastic, was particularly effective when 'chalking people off', as Mam called it. It was something she never had enough self-confidence to do herself but which her worldlier sisters saw as their professional duty, some sheepish Hunslet housewife trying to force her bunioned feet into a narrow 7 finding herself hardly helped by Aunty Kathleen doing her Manfield version of Bette Davis as Mrs Skeffington. When Aunty Myra joined the Waafs and went off to India that was Bette Davis too, a Leeds version of *Now, Voyager*, though I doubt that Aunty Myra ever had her Craven A lit by someone as refined as Paul Henreid, Australian lance-corporals more her line of thing.

If not quite on the same footing as Davis or Crawford there were a whole string of tall, elegant 'professional women' who were stars in their own right: Alexis Smith, Rosalind Russell, Eve Arnold – women who could perch casually on the edge of an editorial desk, toss one long silk-stockinged leg over the other while lighting a cigarette or consulting a powder compact. Graceful and expensive as racehorses, they were amused, ironic and sceptical; they wrote columns in papers, edited magazines and were funny about love and romance with men just their playthings.

Mam can scarcely have thought she inhabited the same universe as these seen-twice-weekly stars and that any of us would ever come across them in the flesh was as unlikely as coming across Gulliver pegged out in Gott's Park or Horatio keeping the bridge over the Leeds-Liverpool Canal. When, years later, I was playing in *Beyond the Fringe* on Broadway and wrote home to say I had actually met Rosalind Russell and Alexis Smith and a host of others besides, my weekly letters listing these encounters must have seemed like a reprise of those dark, wet wartime nights twenty years before when we all used to go to the pictures together.

Sometimes the setting of these encounters was backstage at the Golden Theatre on 45th Street, where *Beyond the Fringe* was lodged for its Broadway run, but more often than not it was the Central Park West apartment of Arnold Weissberger, partner in the firm of Weissberger and Frosch, showbiz lawyers and accountants. Aaron Frosch was the muscle in the firm (and looked it) whereas Arnold seemed to do nothing except throw parties, to which would be invited everybody currently appearing on Broadway or visiting New York from London or Hollywood. The cast was, therefore, staggering and I have never since been in rooms so stiff with celebrity.

What did one say to Henry Fonda or Joan Fontaine? How do you start a conversation with Judy Holliday and not mention *Born Yesterday* (an error I fell into)? How be casual with Katharine Hepburn or do anything but gaze at Steve McQueen?

My best plan, I found, was to make a mental note of who was there so that I could write home that night, then go and get some food at the vast buffet and gracefully retire. But it often turned out that the nicest people were at the buffet, or at any rate people who were more interested in eating than talking and who thus presented less of a social peril. Charles Boyer, for example, who was appearing next door to us on 45th Street in Rattigan's *Man and Boy*. With Leslie Howard he had been a particular heart-throb of Mam's. Now, napkin tucked under his chin and in that all too imitable accent in which he'd said farewell to Ingrid Bergman in *Arch of Triumph*, he pointed out which of the salads came up to scratch. Actually Ingrid Bergman was there, too, somewhere.

Such ancient icons, stars who might now be in decline but who had shone in the cinema of my childhood, were to me far more glamorous than their current counterparts. Here was Maureen O'Sullivan whom I'd last seen as Tarzan's Jane in a skirt of palm leaves swinging through the jungly fronds in the arms of Johnny Weissmuller. Twenty years later, her star shone less brightly, though in reflected glory it would shortly rise again, for she was here with her daughter, a waif of extraordinary beauty wandering round the room as if somehow on offer; it was Mia Farrow, her mother therefore the mother-in-law to be of Frank Sinatra, and later still the tigerish adversary of Woody Allen.

Lauren Bacall, Gene Tierney, Laraine Day: here they all were in the un-cinematographic flesh, more worn perhaps than when we had first met in the ninepennies. But still cool, still sceptical (and still smoking, very often), though they were grandmothers now as they piled their plates at the buffet table. How say I had last seen them aged eight at the Picturedrome on Wortley Road, though I fear I sometimes tried – to be met with a patient, practised smile.

Arnold Weissberger was a keen photographer, at any rate of celebrities. Indeed, he later published a book of photographs of the famous people in his life. You might hope to get away from the party unobserved but Arnold would have spotted you and followed you into the bedroom where the coats were left. Following him would come his tiny mother, who seldom left Arnold's side. And there, sometimes with his mother, he would snap you looking slightly startled and with the mountain of coats in the background. Thus it is I have a photograph of myself, just having put on my coat, and beside me is Joan Collins, though this was before she was Joan Collins and so not someone worth writing home about.

There were parties, too, when Arnold came to London, generally with his long-time partner, Milton Goldman. They were held in the Savoy and were notorious for being graded according to reputation: the most famous or the eminently successful were invited on the A night, the less so on the B night and on the C night one could practically wander in from the street. I only once made the A night, shortly after *Forty Years On* had opened. The Burtons were there: it was not long after their marriage (or one of their marriages) and not seeing a chair handy Elizabeth Taylor, whom I had met in John Gielgud's dressing-room at the theatre, perched briefly on my knee.

This was for me such an atypical situation that I find myself wondering whether I am recalling it correctly: did she sit on my knee or did I sit on hers? But this cannot have been (how would I have dared?), though I'm sure her knee would have been more comfortable than mine.

Oddly, this was not the first time I had figured in the Burton story and in a curiously similar capacity. When we had been in New York playing *Beyond the Fringe* we had got to know Burton's first (or at any rate current) wife, Sybil. She was jolly, domestic, very Welsh and living in a vast apartment on the West Side. One Sunday in 1963 she phoned and asked me if I would go with her to a film premiere at the 59th Street cinema.

Whatever partner she had been planning to go with must have cried off. I doubt it was Burton himself: he and Sybil were long past picture-going by this time. It would probably have been somebody Welsh, as the evening had a strong Celtic flavour, the film being The Criminal with Stanley Baker. What I did not know, but presumably she did, was that this was the day Burton had chosen to announce his divorce from Sibyl. It followed that her companion had to be chosen with care, had not to be someone with whom Sybil could conceivably be thought of as conducting a liaison of her own.

Had I even the smallest liaison potential and certainly had I been something (or indeed anything) of a hunk my presence would have been noted by the columnists who were in the audience and the photographers who were outside. As it was, nobody even noticed me: Sybil might have been there by herself. Nor was there any going on to supper or the party afterwards. I slipped away, leaving Sybil to Stanley Baker and other expatriate Celts.

In retrospect I see these two brushes with the Burtons as having a certain symmetry. One wife hitting on me as a suitably flavourless companion for the evening, the other sitting on me as a knee that would raise no eyebrows, both made me a prop in the drama of lives far more interesting and celebrated than my own. I was, it should be said, an entirely willing prop, flattered to have had even such a small part to play in this legendary love story. Such brushes with the famous do have a name. That Elizabeth Taylor once sat on my knee is what in the Edwardian slang of the Baring family would have been called 'a Shelley plain' (after Browning's 'did you once see Shelley plain?'), an unlooked for and even incongruous contact with the great.

However that was not why the evening stuck in my memory, as I remember little of the film or of Sybil's mood or whether I even knew of the events in which I was playing a walk-on part. What made my heart beat faster was that while Sybil, the about to be ex-Mrs Burton, was sitting on my right, on my left was sitting Myrna Loy.

I had no notion as a child that going to the pictures was a kind of education, or that I was absorbing a twice-weekly lesson in morality. The first film I remember being thought of as 'improving' was Henry V which, during our brief sojourn in Guildford, was playing permanently at Studio I at the Marble Arch end of Oxford Street. I saw it, though, with my primary school at the local Odeon in Guildford, and that it was meant to be educational did not stop it being, for me, magical, particularly the transition from the confines and painted scenery of the Globe to the realities of the siege and battlefield in France. The reverse process had the same effect so that the final cut back to the Globe and the actors lining up for their call still gives me a thrill.

Seeing films one also saw – always saw – the newsreels, though only one remains in my memory. It would have been some time in 1945 and it was at the Playhouse, a cinema down Guildford High Street. Before the newsreel began there was an announcement that scenes in it were unsuitable for children, and that they should be taken out. None was; having already waited long enough in the queue nobody was prepared to give up their hard-won seat. It was, of course, the discovery of Belsen with the living corpses, the mass graves and the line-up of the sullen guards. There were cries of horror in the cinema, though my recollection is that Mam and Dad were much more upset than my brother and me. Still, Belsen was not a name one ever forgot and became a place of horror long before Auschwitz.

The moral instruction to be had at the cinema was seldom as shocking as this: just a slow absorption of assumptions not so much about life as about lives, all of them far removed from one's own. There were cowboys' lives, for instance, where the dilemmas could be quite complex and moralities might compete: small-town morality v. the morality of the gunfighter, with the latter more perilous and demanding of heroism, with High Noon perhaps its ultimate demonstration. There was the lesson of standing up to the bully, a tale told in lots of guises: in Westerns, obviously, but also in historical films – Fire over England, A Tale of Two Cities and The Young Mr Pitt all told the same story of gallant little England squaring up to the might of France or Spain, for which, of course, read Germany.

Then there were the unofficial heroes: dedicated doctors, single-minded schoolteachers, or saints convinced of their vision (I am thinking particularly of The Song of Bernadette, a film that had me utterly terrified). Always in such films it was the official wisdom v. the lone voice and one knew five minutes into the film what the hero or heroine (star anyway) was going to be up against. I suppose one of the reasons Casablanca or Citizen Kane stand out above the rest is that their morality was less straightforward. Empson never, I think, wrote about film but there are many the plot of which this describes:

The web of European civilisation seems to have been strung between the ideas of Christianity and those of a half-secret rival, centring perhaps (if you made it a system) round honour: one that stresses pride rather than humility, self-realisation rather than self-denial, caste rather than either the communion of saints or the individual soul.

It was a rivalry I was familiar with because it was always cropping up at the Picturedrome.

Banal though the general run of films was, I learned, as one learned in fairy stories, about good and evil and how to spot them: the good where one would expect only degradation and squalor, and the treachery and cowardice to be traced in the haunts of respectability. I learned about the occasional kindness of villains and the regular intransigence of saints, but the abiding lesson had to do with the perils of prominence. I came out into Wortley Road grateful that, unlike Charles Boyer, we were not called on to stand up against the Nazi oppressor or battle like Jennifer Jones against the small-mindedness of nuns or like Cornel Wilde cough blood over the piano keys in order to liberate our country from the foreign yoke. Films taught you to be happy that you were ordinary.

Ordinary but not respectable, because in films respectable generally meant cowardly and there were other perils besides. One character who was always cropping up seemed the embodiment of respectability and was often played by the same actor. Not a star (I have had to look up his name), he was called Thurston Hall. With his bright white hair and substantial frame he looked not unlike the local doctors in Upper Wortley, Dr Moneys and Dr Slaney, figures of some weight and even grandeur in the neighbourhood. Thurston Hall did play doctors from time to time but more often than not he was a businessman, highly thought of in the community, a person of unimpeachable morals who was ultimately revealed to be a crook. Kind to children, a president of orphanages, a donor of playing fields and a guarantor of symphony halls, he is prominent in every good cause. But the committee of charitable ladies who can always rely on him for a generous contribution would be surprised to learn that the money comes indirectly out of the pockets of their husbands, paid over to the many prostitutes of the city or in its poker dens and illicit drinking clubs, behind all of which is this impeccably mannered, immaculately suited villain.

That such a character in a film today would seem quite old-fashioned is the fault of the times. Villainy these days is more complicated and communities don't have pillars in quite the way they did. Two-faced respectability operates best in a setting of accepted values and that setting began to break up, so far as the cinema was concerned, sometime in the late 1950s, with one of its minor legacies for me a lifelong distrust of well-groomed, impressive middle-aged men. When I saw General Pinochet on one of his London jaunts I picked him out as a villain simply from the films I had seen in the 1940s.

To know that one is being taught a lesson or at any rate given a message leaves one free to reject it if only by dismissing plot or characters as clichés. But I had not realised how far the moral assumptions of film story-telling had sunk in, and how long they had stayed with me, until in 1974 I saw Louis Malle's film about the French Occupation, Lacombe Lucien. Lucien is a loutish, unappealing boy, recruited almost by accident into the French Fascist Milice. He falls in with and exploits a

Jewish family, becoming involved with – it would be wrong to say falling in love with – the daughter whom he helps to escape and with whom he lives. Then, as the Liberation draws near, he becomes himself a fugitive and is eventually almost casually shot.

The stock way to tell such a story would be to see the boy's experiences – witnessing torture and ill-treatment, falling for the Jewish girl – as a moral education in the same way, for example, that the Marlon Brando character is educated in On the Waterfront. That would be the convention, and one I'd so much taken for granted that I kept looking in the Malle film for signs of this instruction in the school of life beginning to happen. But it doesn't. Largely untouched by the dramas he has passed through Lucien is much the same at the end of the film as he is at the beginning, seemingly having learned nothing. To have quite unobtrusively resisted the tug of conventional tale-telling and the lure of resolution seemed to me honest in a way few films even attempt.

3 January 2002

The London Review of Books appears 24 times a year (twice a month). For further information about the magazine, or to subscribe, phone 020 7209 1141 or visit our website at www.lrb.co.uk.